D0138281

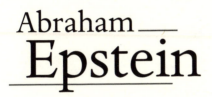

Abraham
Epstein

# Abraham Epstein

## The Forgotten Father of Social Security

PIERRE EPSTEIN

University of Missouri Press
Columbia and London

Library of Congress Cataloging-in-Publication Data

Epstein, Pierre.
    Abraham Epstein : the forgotten father of social security / Pierre Epstein.
        p.   cm.
    Summary: "Pierre Epstein takes readers behind the scenes of Roosevelt's New
Deal legislation to tell how his father, Abe Epstein, an immigrant Russian Jew and
author of "Insecurity: A Challenge to America," followed his vision of reform and
made significant contributions to the legislation that established social security in
America"—Provided by publisher.
    Includes bibliographical references and index.
    ISBN-13: 978-0-8262-1681-6 (hard cover : alk. paper)
    ISBN-10: 0-8262-1681-1 (hard cover : alk. paper)
1. Epstein, Abraham, 1892–1942.   2. Social security—United States.   I. Title.
    HD7125.E653   2006
    368.4'30092—dc22
    [B]

                                                                2006026995

♾ This paper meets the requirements of the
American National Standard for Permanence of Paper
for Printed Library Materials, Z39.48, 1984.

Designer: Jennifer  Cropp
Typesetter: The Composing Room of Michigan, Inc.
Printer and binder: Thomson-Shore, Inc.
Typefaces: Palatino and Dante

For Suzanne and Marc
Clara, Anya, and Jacob
Grandchildren and Great-Grandchildren of Abe

*May His Legacy Be An Inspiration*

# Contents

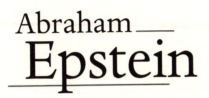

Abraham
Epstein

"Abraham Epstein . . . was a tireless social reformer of a type too seldom seen. His vision lives on in Social Security, the single most effective social program in our history."

—Daniel P. Moynihan, Senator from New York

"Abraham Epstein was one of the most extraordinary men I ever met. He was a rare combination of the Jewish scholar, the Madison Avenue publicist, the Broadway showman, the missionary social reformer, and the determined, persevering lobbyist."

—Wilbur Cohen, Secretary of Health, Education and Welfare

"If America were as disposed to build monuments to its social heroes as it is to its generals, every city would have an imposing statue of Abraham Epstein. He was a tiny man but a giant in ideas."

—A. H. Raskin, *New York Times*

"Abraham Epstein did more in my judgment to initiate social security than any other man of my generation."

—Paul Douglas, Senator from Illinois

"Blessed is he who considereth the poor."

—41st Psalm

1

My mother Henriette's new knee had been strapped to an electrical apparatus that was moving it up, down, and around with a regular rhythm, flexing it constantly to aid in her recovery. But her new knee didn't like it, and neither did she.

"Aieee!" she wailed in pain.

The odd device lay in bed with her. Dull metal and stained leather straps made it look like a piece of machinery that had seen too many years of service on too many knees, a medieval torture instrument resurrected from some dungeon deep in the bowels of the Hospital for Special Surgery.

A few days later, after her wires and tubes were removed, my mother began to ingest solid food. She was nauseated most of the day and for the first time I could remember did not finish everything on her plate. I began to have doubts. The doctors, both the surgeon and the arthritis specialist, assured me that her progress was admirable.

"After all she is ninety," the arthritis specialist informed me. "You have to expect some discomfort."

"How can you mutate the word 'agony' into 'discomfort'"? I wanted to growl, but I let it pass. His way of speech was just one of the marvels of a contemporary American idiom designed to avoid any emotional differences of opinion. But I let the doctors tell her in person, mostly to find a way to get myself removed of responsibility.

"You heard what Doctor Markenson said?" I asked her. "Yes?"

"Yes, I heard him . . ."

"What did he tell you?"

"I didn't hear all of it . . . he speaks too low . . . my knee hurts . . . aieee! . . . "

"He said you're doing just fine," I said slowly and emphatically.

"Yes, but I can't eat . . ."

"You will soon. It takes time." It wouldn't hurt her to lose a little weight.

"Aieee! . . . that machine! It's enough. Why don't they turn it off?"

"He said your progress was admirable," I found myself yelling. "Just what they expected. So you see . . . everything's OK!"

"Yes, all right . . . aieee! . . . that darn machine."

From time to time friends telephoned and asked when they should visit. I answered the calls and told my mother who it was. She pouted and shook her head like a little girl. "Later, later, when I am recovered," she grumbled.

The truth was she didn't have the force to entertain anyone, that force that lay at the root of the charm and talk that had kept her spry well into her ninetieth year. She didn't have it, lying in her hospital bed with her ever-rotating knee. In her present state she didn't want to be seen by others. She would only be seen with her hair done, wearing one of her gaudy print dresses, carrying the customary massive necklace around her throat, and looking, as she always did, like she was ready for a good time. Otherwise, they might see through her, and the whole house of cards would tumble.

No, she had decided that it was me and me alone who she would accept as her go-between with the world. She had thrown herself on my mercy. Now what? It was the start of a new intimacy. And where would it take us? It was only the first of two new knees.

---

My mother had summoned me from the other side of the continent, and I had taken the plane from Los Angeles to be with her on the night before the surgery. A taxi had then carried me through the misting, night-lit streets of Manhattan to the hospital. The city that I had moved away from not long before, that I had been part of from the age of six weeks, that I knew down to the last street sign, seemed indifferent to my return. All it would offer me in way of greeting was a wintry, dark, damp and cold gloom. But it was New York. It was my home. And when I went to bed in my mother's house, the peace and quiet of the surroundings became, without her hovering presence, a haven from the disjointed world of the hospital. In her cluttered home I was forced to put a small mattress on the floor for a place to sleep. But I didn't mind. When I awoke my eyes were flush with the ground, and I could look around at all that I had known since infancy. I was at the eye level of my childhood, when I played my made-up games on the geometric red and blue figures of the Persian carpet.

One morning when I awoke and my eyes fastened themselves on my intimate friend the carpet, my ears took in a transporting sound. The curtains were drawn, the room was dark . . . and there it was . . . could it be? . . . was it? It was a sound I would know anywhere—distinct and harsh, clear and comforting. It echoed in my brain. I had heard it in many places, but in places other than New York it was never what I wanted it to be. The sound always seized and lured me, rolling me into the past. It would draw me to the window to see if some miracle had taken place—and I was always disappointed.

I lay on my mattress, staring at the carpet, and listened, attentive and hopeful. It was a sliding, rasping, grating, edging sound, a noise without echo, without resonance, as if muffled. I got up carefully and meticulously absorbed each repeated rasp. Slowly I parted the curtains that hid the garden in the back of the house. The garden was bathed in white—a gentle casing of snow had fallen during the night and was still falling, covering everything. I turned from the garden and moved slowly to the front of the house. I opened the shutters and looked down at the thoroughfare. And there I saw what I was hoping for. A solitary man, bundled up with hat and scarf against the cold, held a shovel, a curved black shovel with a long handle, a New York shovel. And with it he was patiently scraping the snow off the sidewalk into the street.

Scraaaaaape! Scraaaaaape! The sound flew up into my smitten ears as I watched the man and his shovel move the snow that was doomed to turn from its glorious white to filthy gray and then black within a day or two. But at that moment it all looked radiant and pure, the man, the shovel, the snow. I returned to the window facing the garden and watched the snow fall quietly on every stone and tree. The faint sound of the shovel was all I could hear. Scraaaaaape! Scraaaaaape! It was snowing, and I was listening to a man with a shovel scraping the snow from the sidewalk into the street . . . and at that moment I was a boy again living with my mother and father in New York.

In 1941 I was seated in a large armchair by that same window overlooking the garden on the day Japan attacked Pearl Harbor and sent America stumbling into the Second World War. Curled up in comfort, I was listening to our grand "Pilot" radio, which when warmed up offered a mysterious green light that glowed throughout the room. My father was in his study with the door closed, and when he was there I had to be quiet. In the winter gloom I listened to the broadcast of the New York Giants football game with the volume turned down, while my eyes stared at the carpet and its markings, using them to chart the players and their moves as they rushed up and down the field. That carpet had the magic ability attributed to carpets to take me any place I wanted to go. But when the announcer broke in with the news that Pearl Harbor had been attacked, I tore myself away from my imaginary game and rushed to the door of my father's study.

"Dad, something happened on the radio!"

I was eleven, and my thoughts had already been consumed by the despairing news from the war in Europe: Poland conquered, France occupied by the Germans, England under attack, and I lived with those events at all hours, transfixed by the profound force they had on my mother and father, both of whom had been born in lands destined to be ravaged by the armies of fascism. In that room I had heard dozens of refugees tell vivid tales of their escapes from Europe to America, and, mute and unobtrusive, listened in on unending political discussions and countless horror stories about what the Nazis were doing to our beloved France. But there was one incident that had overwhelmed me beyond understanding. It was the day I saw my father burst into tears on the streets of Pittsfield, Massachusetts, as he let slide from his hands the newspaper whose headline announced the Hitler-Stalin pact of 1939. So when the news of the Japanese attack on December 7 came over the radio, I was bursting with the importance of it. Something monstrous had happened. I knew it would affect us all. I didn't know how, but I knew my father would. I rushed to the door of his study.

"Dad, there's been a bomb attack!"

Could I have done nothing? Could I have continued to listen to the exploits of my favorite football players with their short, throbbing names—Ward Cuff, Bruiser Kinard, Mel Hein—like any other New York City kid of the 1940s? No, because I believed I was special that day. When I knocked on my father's door, interrupting him, I was like the Greek messenger I had read about that year in school. I was Pheidippides returning from Marathon.

"Dad! Japan attacked us!" And I knocked loudly on his door.

My father burst from his study and headed straight for the green-glowing radio.

The snow continued to fall in the garden, the sound of the shovel was a faint rasp. Everywhere I looked I saw my father again, alive in those silent rooms. He was moving as he once had through that space, near the desk he had once used, by the books in the bookshelves, staring out from the posed photographs on the walls, a man to be reckoned with. His owl-shaped glasses. His short frame in his three-piece suit. His balding head.

I was desperate. I wanted him to be there with me again, to be able to turn and talk to him. Yet all I had were his written words.

"Dad, I'm going to read something you wrote. OK?" I said to what I knew was an empty room.

I turned to the bursting bookshelf in his old study, but most of what I was looking for was wedged behind boxes and books, invariably wrapped in suffocating plastic. My mother had decided that preservation was best achieved with plastic. This meant that every baggie that entered the house from the store was recycled for conservation, and that whenever I re-moved one book from the bookshelf to uncover another book I found my-self first staring at words like "D'Agostino" or "Big Apple." I knew that I must not leave a trace of my doings. I needed to replace everything just as I had found it. So I carefully folded the baggies and set them aside, to be used again. Anything not back in its proper jumble might bring protests from my hawk-eyed mother. I could even hear her questioning voice: "Who moved those papers?"

Nervously, with the imagined tap tap of her approaching cane and the fantasy of her looming presence, I managed to extract old copies of such magazines as the *Nation,* the *New Republic, Harper's,* and many issues of the *American Mercury.* There were many more I liberated from their plas-tic coffins, an array of yellowing but suddenly reanimated magazines, all with an article and a byline: By Abraham Epstein. In the *American Mer-cury,* for January 1929 there was one with a title I thought irresistible: "Is American Capital Intelligent?" Far from being geniuses, my father wrote, American capitalists did not know what they were doing most of the time. "We are rich because we have riches," he ended it. "And were we more truly intelligent, we might be happy in fact as well as in myth." Little bells of delight started ringing in my ears. How had he sensed that the great capitalist disaster of 1929 was lurking around the corner eight months lat-er? God, I thought, how that great American gadfly, the editor of the *Mer-cury,* H. L. Mencken, must have loved him.

The morning wore on and blended into afternoon, the snow continued, and I kept pulling works from the shelves. Finally, I faced a series of vol-umes, all with the same title. I had arrived at the many editions of my father's last and major work. I pulled the final 1968 edition from the shelf. It had a bright blue cover. Holding its nine hundred pages in my hands, I struggled with myself to avoid starting to read the book. My eyes returned to the title page: *Insecurity: A Challenge to America.* By Abraham Epstein. I flipped the pages again. I came back to the introduction. And then I dived deep into a place where I had not been for a long time.

> Ever since Adam and Eve were driven from the sheltered Garden of Eden insecurity has been the bane of mankind . . . it is the grim paradox of our present day society that with granaries bursting with food supplies, warehouses filled with shoes and clothing, and goods of every kind in overabundance, men, women and children go hungry and naked or depend on charity for their very existence. Fantastic and ridiculous as this would seem to a visitor from Mars, it is the stark reality today . . . the great insecurity of our day prevails despite our luxuriant plenty.

I looked away at the gently falling snow, and then down at the nine-hundred-page book cradled in my hands. The words I had been reading hit me like a message from the grave. They came from the heart of this long-dead man, my father, a fruit from his abiding harvest. And in the long-echoing aftermath of those words and of that time, I still bask in the glow of the green-lit shadows of that December night in 1941, and our special union, pressed next to one another, by that radio, by that window, by that garden, when we listened to the news of the coming war that would forever change our lives.

But it was not I, as Pheidippides the message bearer, who dropped dead but the man who received the message, my father, of a heart attack, some five months later.


2


New York was a deserted city over the long President's Day holiday when I brought my mother home from the hospital, against the grim advice of my former wife and my aunt, who told me I needed to rent an ambulance. While she was still in her hospital room, itching to get away from the bedpans, bad food, grimy windows, and the neighbor in the next bed who hadn't recovered from anesthesia and kept loudly repeating everyone's conversation, I softly told my mother what had been suggested.

"How much?"

"Two hundred and fifty."

"Too much." And she had shaken her head.

"To hell with them, we'll do it ourselves," I told myself. But when the nurse deserted us on the sidewalk I wasn't brimming with confidence. We were alone: my mother, tiny and withered in her wheelchair, clutching her little bag of belongings, and me behind her, numbed but determined to see the trip through. And then from nowhere a taxi appeared at the curb and the driver was Russian. It was a good omen, I thought. An image of comforting Russian nurses came to mind. Primo Levi, the writer and Auschwitz survivor, had written that after the liberation of the German extermination camps big Russian nurses had gently washed the prisoners with soap by hand. The Americans, when the same inmates had come back through their lines, had sent them into sterilized rooms where nozzles had sent out a fumigating gas. Primo Levi was whispering the story into my ear to buck me up.

"Iz your mother?" the driver asked me.

"Yes."

"Iz goot when children taking care . . . mother, father."

Right on cue. For a moment I knew that I could bring this looming odyssey to a calm conclusion.

But getting my mother into the taxi was more difficult than I had imagined. She needed to be lifted and slowly pushed on to the seat. Her knees would hardly bend, and so I moved her like a mannequin into an odd, upright position. She was strangely perched like a bird on a branch at the edge of the seat where it met the door. There was no room for me. I tried to budge her. Nothing doing. I got in on the other side.

As the taxi moved downtown I encouraged myself by exchanging banalities with the Russian. All the while my mother sat, unmoving and uncomfortable, almost a midget, her head barely reaching the window, pressed flatly against the side of the taxi. When we arrived at her door I extracted her shiny new walker from the trunk, unfolded its ugly utilitarian frame, and lifted her from the cab. As the walker sat on the sidewalk, waiting for me to encase my mother inside its forbidding metal, I thought it screamed out to all who passed by, "disease, decline, death." Slowly we inched our way through two doors and I stretched my body to its limits to hold both open at the same time. With her mouth open for air my mother tottered into the old, nineteenth-century brick house in Greenwich Village that had been her home for nearly all her years in Manhattan. I coaxed her nervously from behind as she painstakingly mounted the narrow, twisting stairs two flights to her door, grasping the railing with her hand and barely moving her knees at all. She appeared to raise them straight up from one step to another by some miracle. We moved in exhausting slow motion, and I felt like a character in an unknown Middle Ages morality play following behind a grotesque depiction of infirmity and old age, a vision of what awaited us all. But on we went, methodically from step to creaking step, until we reached her door and opened it. Triumph! Victory! And with no ambulance or anyone else to help us.

During the days that followed we retied the umbilical cord. But in reverse. I ran around. I got her up. I fed her. I walked her to the toilet. I answered the phone. I bought a toilet seat that allowed her to go to the bathroom without bending her knees. This involved searching for rulers, measuring spaces, and twisting myself out of shape to peer under the bowl looking for where to attach the seat. When I finally came back to the house, after carrying a huge box on the crosstown bus, I heaved a sigh of relief that it went on and fit as planned. Round and round I went, as if on a grimly turning carousel but without the merry music.

All the literature I had ever read passed through my mind as I searched for parallels to what I was going through. When I reached *The Brothers Karamazov* I thought Dostoyevsky might know what this was all about. I was the saintly Alyosha undergoing a forced act of penance, while the holy Father Zossima rose up before me intoning, "You have to do this, Pierre, you must give your mother what she needs, only then will you have peace!" And although my mother's body did not decompose and smell in front of my eyes the way Father Zossima's had done in the novel, still she trailed from time to time a strange odor of medical examinations and decay. I wiped the excrement that lingered on her body and on the floor, cursed as the toilet malfunctioned and overflowed with her newly deposited feces, and cleaned it all up, wondering if any of it would ever end. And as for Father Zossima, did he have any idea of what the hell he was talking about?

At times, after one of these episodes, as she was in the act of moving away from the humiliation, she abruptly turned and looked at me and for a moment appeared to cry in my presence. Without her false teeth in her mouth, her face would screw up like some ancient Chinese court mandarin, her head and shoulders rising and falling rhythmically, but there was no sound. Was she ashamed for herself? Sorry for me? What was she thinking?

I began to observe her more closely. When she concentrated, when walking or sitting, when reading or writing, she emitted little puffs of air, minuscule bursts of sound, like the little engine that could. We talked a great deal, which is what she liked the most. But I had heard it all and it was as always mostly about herself. Old information. Old stories. Old grudges.

At times she would lurch toward.me from the other end of the room to where I lay limp on the sagging couch, her new metal cane engaged in rhythmic tapping. Her moves were a sort of hobbling, an abrupt swaying motion as she approached. Her face was fixed in effort, her eyes focused on me, her jaw slightly parted, sending forth little puffs as she loomed into view in front of me. When almost on top of me, unbearably close, her mouth would break into a crazed grin, her eyes wrinkled, as if about to burst into insane laughter. She sensed that I thought she looked funny as she came nearer, looming like some ancient naval vessel on the high seas, and she tried to accommodate me and play along with the game. She wanted to show gratitude that I found some of what we were going through together comical. She was happy to be entertaining me. No doubt, she looked silly, like some herky-jerky wind-up doll with limited moves at its disposal. Then, when she finally stopped in front of me, what she said would often only heighten the absurd nature of our life together. All that effort and out would come, the slight remainder of her French accent still in play, "Do you want to watch Ted Ko-pelle tonight?"

When we had meals I felt my teeth start to grind in anger, an old reaction for which I hated myself. When eating she had always been as fastidious as a rabbit and as slow as a caterpillar, leaving the finished chicken bone on her empty plate as dry and bare of flesh as an anatomical drawing. The plate had no other food on it, only a dry tinge of color that showed it had not come fresh from the shelf. Eating was her principal pleasure. It had been so her whole life. But I had never been able to stand her painstaking thoroughness. Now, I spent long periods at the table with her, trapped, while she scraped everything off her plate.

In the middle of the night there were times when she did not make it to the toilet on time. This became visible in the morning when I could see a trail of slowly evaporating drips leading from her bed to the bathroom. As she had a habit of sleeping late I was careful to clean them up before she got up. She undoubtedly knew all about this but said nothing. I also said nothing.

I kept my eyes on her as she moved painstakingly across the floor from the garden to the street and back. I watched, forcing alertness, fearful that a fall could come about at any moment. My worst fear was broken bones, requiring a wheelchair and an even longer recovery, or perhaps never to see my mother rise on her feet again. What would I do then? My eyes and brain were exhausted. I had the eyes and reactions of a bird of prey, observing everything, always cautioning her, ready to grab her at a moment's notice. As she moved about she tried to show me how well she was doing. She sensed my exhaustion that life had turned into this painfully slow dance between the two of us and tried to prove to me that she was really making an effort.

"See how I am getting better," she said over and over.

I knew we were bound together in a sort of lunatic union but I yearned for smaller doses. I felt like a captive. I was doing my duty, but I was also tolerating a moment that could become, with the passage of time, intolerable. She held on to me with a hidden desperation before she would allow anyone else into her life. And I had, without a second thought, accepted her swarming need.

This exhausting routine seemed as if it would never end, until one day relief came in the persons of Marilyn, from the Visiting Nurse Service, Marie, the home worker, Claire, the physical therapist, and Valerie, the woman who stood by when I was finally able to get away. It was only with their presence that I could remain prostrate on the couch and watch them handle all of it with easy professionalism, my only task being to answer a question from time to time about where to find something in the clutter. I was over the worst of it, I thought; I would never have to do it again. But with the arrival of the outside world, I surprised myself by regretting the loss of our newfound bond. I knew something I had not known before: having to clean the shit from your mother's body, as she once had to clean it from yours, is to know how deep is the knot of motherhood, the bond of parent and child. It is a cord like no other.

I went back and forth across the United States a number of times, and once when asleep in my home in Los Angeles I awoke in the middle of the night not knowing where I was. The room was unfamiliar and I was scared. There was a presence in the bed beside me. Was it my mother, and if so what was she doing there and as silent as the tomb? My nakedness was mortifying. I jumped from the bed and tried to escape. There was a long moment at the window before I slowly pieced together where I was. I looked back at the bed. There was no one. Yet even now, I am uneasy and troubled by the phantom vision I experienced in the middle of the night.

---

Several months later my mother was able to get around, not with ease, still hobbling to and fro with her cane, but without the heavy pain that had tortured her knees for the past half dozen years.

One day, Marie, the little aide from Haiti, placed a gaudy necklace around my mother's neck, and said, "C'est joli. Whair you get eet?"

"My friend from India gave it to me . . . "

I saw my mother's old magic go to work. The words started to flow, the chat and charm opened up. Soon she was writing letters and making telephone calls. She labored and puffed her way back into her world of friends, dinners, and meetings. I had always thought of her extensive social activities as an act, remembering what she was like when I was a child. Then she had lived in her husband's shadow, and when he died suddenly the shock she underwent was not his loss so much as the people who abruptly disappeared from her circle. She was dropped and abandoned. She was not his equal and was made to know it. But as the years went by, and after a prolonged time of anger and bitterness, she somehow found a way to turn her frou-frou love of food, people, and fun into an asset. She lowered her sights a bit. She sought out and made friends of people she never would have paid attention to in the past. Gone were the writers, journalists, musicians, and social activists, to be replaced by retired store owners and teachers, people she had met on her travels. She stayed in touch with them and got them to stay in touch with her. She was determined not to be lonely, and she wasn't. She had outlived all those people who had dropped her when her husband had died. She'd showed them. Let them lie in their graves. She was having the last laugh.

"Your mother is such a fascinating person, Pierre," I had heard more than once. I would nod and say nothing. I knew it for the accommodation it was. I could see through her like the "visible man" or the "visible woman," those small dolls with see-through muscles and bones. But I was compelled to honor her savage battle to stay in the swim, an act she no longer recognized for what it was, a transformation of herself from the woman who felt at the center of the churning world of social activism in the 1930s to one of the charming survivor, dazzling all with her ability to stay above water.


3


With the help of Aunt Esther, my father's youngest sister, my mother started looking for a way to honor the fiftieth anniversary of her husband's death, which coincided closely with the one hundredth anniversary of his birth. She would resurrect the old fire and with one last burst of energy, in one way or another, she would find a way to keep the beacon lit. It was her husband she wanted to keep alive and herself as his partner in the bruising battles for reform in depression-era America. I was finally back in Los Angeles but she kept me abreast of all her activities. Typically, at one in the morning, New York time, I would hear a ring.

"Hello. This is Henriette."

The need to identify herself seemed important. It was clear she did not want to be misidentified with someone of lesser importance.

"Yes?"

"I received a letter from Senator Moynihan's office. They will definitely make a statement for your father's one hundredth birthday. But we cannot get any response from the *New York Times*. Do you know anyone?"

"I'm afraid not."

"When are you coming to New York?"

That, of course, was the important issue. We had agreed that in addition to all the work to honor my father we would also make a trip to his grave on the anniversary of his death. My mother wanted reassurance that I would not ignore the day and that I would take her there. On that score she need not have worried. Something in me had been uncovered on that snowy day in New York. I knew that no matter what, on the day he died fifty years earlier, I would stand before his grave. I would find a way to commune with the ghost of my father.

The campaign to bang the drum and remind the world that she had been married to a great man succeeded beyond her wildest hopes. Daniel Moynihan, the senator from New York, recalled her husband "as a tireless social reformer of a type too seldom seen, whose vision lives on in Social Security, the largest and single most effective social program in our history." Several other congressmen echoed those sentiments. A number of periodicals published brief articles, and the *New York Times* published a substantial letter which read in part, "Although poor in money, power and fame, he converted ideals into reality. His contributions have improved the lives of millions." The peak was reached when the Social Security Administration published an exchange of letters with her husband that told the story of how he had come up with the idea for those two words that have gone down in history, and that ripple always inside my mother's mind—*social security.*

She was jubilant. What she had known all along was now official history. To anyone who ever brought up the subject of social security she would inform them: "Those two little words were really like snowballs— little snowballs that grew into a big avalanche and it went down the mountainside. Those little words have brought hope, cheer, and happiness to millions of people in the United States and other countries . . . They became part of the great Atlantic charter between Roosevelt and Churchill . . . They meant freedom . . . Today very few people realize how these came about, and who was the man who started the term going."

The flame that she had kept alight through all those years of obscurity was still aglow. Now in her nineties—and grappling with two new knees—my mother had been present at the creation of *social security*, that monumental achievement, and the world had been told.

4

We journeyed to my father's grave site on Long Island accompanied by his last living sibling, my Aunt Esther, and another friend. It was my first visit in many years, and the cemetery looked like it was filled to overflowing. The headstones, like large marching icons, seemed to stretch away forever. What I remembered of my father's burial fifty years earlier bore little resemblance to what I was looking at now. Back then, near and around the dirt mound of his newly filled-in grave, there had been plenty of room. Now, it looked as if those Epsteins who had once lived (Abe, his mother, his brother Izzy) were packed in like sardines among the other Jews who had the right to be buried there because they had all come from the same town in Russia. The day was sunny and breezy. The strange Hebrew lettering cut into the stones was mysterious and funereal. My mother walked slowly and carefully, fearful of falling. My aunt and her friend kept up a constant babble, kvetching, as older people will do, about the road directions, about what a lousy job the cemetery had been doing on the upkeep of the graves, and about the strange taste of the spaghetti sauce at lunch. I needed an accepting patience as I threaded the three elderly women among the graves, with them wondering, I am sure, how soon they would be in there themselves. I was constantly occupied in answering irrelevant questions and making sure that the ancient female bodies did not fall and break into numerous pieces. I couldn't find the peace of mind to look squarely at the large piece of granite atop the remains of my father. I was looking to converse with a ghost but under the circumstances he was not available for comment. Fifty years earlier my father had died and been placed in this ground. And nothing I saw or tried to feel was about to change any of it. The facts were: He was dead. And my mother and I were not.

I settled for taking a number of photographs. One in particular now

Henriette staring at Abe's grave. Elmont, Long Island, New York, May 1992.

seems to haunt me. My mother is alone, frail and diminutive, planted in the ivy surrounding the many gravestones that tower over her, a solitary living person in a forest of graves. With vacant eyes she is staring at the engraved name of the man she had been married to so many years ago: Abraham Epstein. Her right hand has a firm grip on her cane, her left is gently touching the stone, her hair is a windswept halo of white. She seems yoked to that stone and that name. She, for one, may have found some communion on that trip.

# Part One

# The Socialist Johnny Appleseed

1

In 1973 the University of Wisconsin had asked Henriette to tape her memories of the struggle for social security and the story of Abe Epstein's life, and for several days she lived in glorious nostalgia for those exciting times. When she addressed the microphone she became the center of attention, in her mind the ultimate authority on the events she had witnessed and been part of. Her place in the sweep of the movement for social security was finally to be embedded in scholarly discourse. In all, she gave three different oral interviews for three different history projects, and was always ready to do a fourth if anyone happened to call. It was an easy way for her to write without the effort of putting pen to paper.

"My biography," she would call those oral histories. "My biography is tucked away over there." She would indicate a place on a bookshelf where it took a lucky streak to find anything among the overstuffed boxes and envelopes.

As she became more at ease in recording her memories, my mother determined that the world should hear her own story, not just the saga of her "humanitarian" husband. She made an attempt to explain her reasons for leaving the small towns of southern France, where she had grown up, to come to America in the roaring twenties. Unexpectedly, she once pulled the name of Gertrude Stein out of the air, like a newly blown-up balloon, and labeled herself a member of "The Lost Generation." At other times she said that it was fashionable for young girls in France to be sent to school in England. But she never explained what it was that made her think England or even America had what she might be looking for. Whatever the reason, in 1919, one year after the end of World War I, Henriette persuaded her parents to send her to a small school in England, at Woking in Surrey, so that she might learn English. She had a clear gift for it and went back to England in 1920 to take university-level courses at Leeds.

England was a revelation. She saw that the status of women was different than in France. English women had more advanced schooling and were able to have careers of their own. They had received the right to vote in 1918, something that the French Republic would not grant until 1946. There was as well a more developed sense of responsibility and fairness toward others, a type of behavior that did not exist among the anarchic and free-spirited citizens of her homeland. One story she loved to tell took place on her return to school. She had missed the train and neglected to warn the headmistress. "When I arrived she just lectured me about the sense of responsibility. Why didn't I send a telegram telling her I was going to be late? Because she stayed up all night and worried about me. I never thought anyone would feel that way. But there she was sitting up all night and worried about me, and I hadn't the decency to send a telegram. It was a good lesson to me."

The years in England turned Henriette into a committed Anglophile. She loved the countryside and its churches, its flowers and public gardens. And she loved her tea. Every night she made sure to brew her "cuppa" before going off to bed. The friends she made in those years remained friends for life. With the dogged knack that she carved into a fine art later on, she stayed in touch with them, through good times and bad. She wrote, she visited, made more friends, and maintained all of it throughout the dark days of World War II, including the "Blitz" and its grim aftermath when food was still rationed in England but not in defeated Germany.

After two years in England, with a new language under her belt, it was obvious that life with her family in a small French town no longer had much to offer. She told her parents she wanted to take courses at the University of Toulouse. It wasn't exactly the convent training her mother, Elisa Marie-Antoinette Fauré, had received or wanted for her daughter. But Henriette was an only child, she was headstrong, and she invariably got what she wanted. So she commuted to Toulouse from her parents' home in the Pyrenean town of Prades. And in Toulouse something unexpected took place.

She ran into a number of American women, the first foreign exchange students, inquiring types who could be seen freely wandering the narrow, twisting streets of the old "rose" city of Toulouse. The Americans were conspicuous inside the red brick walls of the Faculté des Lettres. One day Henriette heard English words echoing down one of the somber university corridors. A young American woman needed help. Henriette moved in and in perfect English came to the rescue. A friendship was born, Henriette began to meet other students from across the Atlantic, ideas were exchanged, and something in the sense of adventure that American females of the 1920s gave off lit a spark. All those free-spirited young women dazzled her. She invited several to visit her home in the Pyrenees. How could she resist the words addressed to her, echoing off the stones of ancient Toulouse: "Henriette, why don't you come to America?"

Those tempting words rolled around in Henriette's head, and she decided to make the leap. It was an exploit she came to believe made her part of an elite group of women who had dared to change themselves. She was one with Colette, Anaïs Nin, Djuna Barnes, and Gertrude Stein. Their names float in the air when one thinks of independent women in France in the 1920s, but I don't believe Henriette ever resembled any of them. I doubt she had even heard their names before leaving for America. She once sent me a book, *Women of the Left Bank*, in which the audacious lives of those liberated women were profiled. Several times she asked if I had read it and what I thought of it, but I always felt, from our talk, that it was the title that had really intrigued her. If she could identify with those women who broke convention, then her own motives for making a huge leap from one culture to another, a leap that was to last an entire lifetime, would make her part of a great moment in history.

Interpreting past history has a way of resolving the personal. After the First World War traditional ways of behavior began to disappear. There was nascent feminism, the vote for women, a desire for education, a less restricted life for the young, and more. Any young girl could feel new things happening around her. "Anything goes," they sang in America. Accordingly, Henriette eventually came to believe that she had been an early participant in one of the major movements of the twentieth century— the advance of women. I was never sure it was true—except once, in a box in New York, submerged faithfully beneath layers of blouses, I came upon clean, still crisp copies of the first French feminist journal, *La Voix des Femmes*, published during the 1920s, well before Henriette had landed on American shores. I asked her once to elaborate on all of this, to tell me why she came, what she felt, what decided her, but she abruptly dismissed the

Henriette in Atlantic City, 1924 or 1925.

entire subject. She told me firmly, "If I had stayed in France I would have had to become a schoolteacher, live in a boring town, and marry a man as boring as the town." In other words, another Madame Bovary.

In September 1924 Henriette Marie-Louise Castex arrived as a foreign exchange student on the campus of the University of Delaware. She thought that America would resemble England. It did not.

"It was ludicrous," she recalled. "Instead of greeting me with words of welcome, the dean sent me to one of the French teachers, who couldn't speak it very well. And the first thing she did was give me a copy of the rules and regulations. On top of that I found that the men and women went to different schools and were completely separated. They were not supposed to have anything in common whatsoever, I was informed by the dean, Miss Winifred Robinson." Just off the boat, and immediately she was battered by America's fine old Puritan culture. Nonetheless, the fun of 1920s American college life soon began to assert itself, as Henriette described in her first postcard from the United States to her parents in France. "I am sending you a photo of the house where I live," she wrote, marking a cross on the second floor of the classic red brick dormitory building, surrounded by the leafy trees of the traditional college campus. "Yesterday, I played tennis, and in the evening I went dancing. I had a very nice evening because my partner was a very good dancer and very interesting. Practically all the young girls were there . . . my first impression is a good one. There is more friendship between students and professors and it's a lot of fun."

But there were still a few surprises in store. One day, Dean Robinson casually informed her that the college was closing for the Thanksgiving holiday.

"You'll have to find a place to go."

Henriette had never heard about the American holiday of Thanksgiving, and she was incensed. But in an early display of a calling she would develop into a tactical art later on—the talent to rope people in to help her out—she promptly got in touch with some of the Americans she had known in Toulouse and went to Pennsylvania to visit them. Helen Fay and Augusta Galster were two of the students Henriette had befriended. They had met her family, spent time in her home, and may very well have been the ones who swayed her in the direction of America. Responding to Henriette's pleas, Helen told her to come for Thanksgiving, and Augusta offered her a visit to her home. And so Henriette journeyed deep, as she considered it, into the heart of the United States, ending up at Harrisburg, the state capital of Pennsylvania, where Augusta Galster worked.

"I have some friends who want to meet you. They are foreign like you," Augusta said on her arrival. "Emil Frankel is Viennese and his wife, Else, is German. They have planned a trip to the battlefield of Gettysburg and wondered if you might want to come along."

The car that was to make this holiday excursion belonged to another unknown with a foreign name. And when it was discovered that his car could only accommodate three people with any comfort it was decided that Henriette, being new to America, should be the one to take in this part of America's story, naturally accompanied by her friend Augusta. The Frankels gave up the trip but chivalrously decided to offer everyone dinner on their return.

"Well, he's not exactly my boyfriend," Augusta said to Henriette about the owner of the car on the morning of the outing. "But there are not so many men in this town, particularly in the Department of Welfare, where I work."

When they came down the stairs to leave there was a gentleman at the door dressed neatly in a three-piece suit. Short of stature, he had a large receding forehead, a left eye that seemed to wander, owl-shaped glasses, and a high-pitched, foreign-sounding voice. Henriette dismissed him as not particularly impressive.

The introductions were made, and the trio roared off to America's storied battlefield. Mr. Epstein—for that was the car owner's name—did not waste a minute. He immediately began asking Henriette all sorts of questions, including what she was doing and why she had come to America. Delighted with the attention, Henriette launched into the story of her experiences in England and France, and in particular she told the driver about the stodgy time she was having at Delaware. Mr. Epstein immediately went into a tirade about the state of Delaware being completely dominated by the Duponts. Henriette agreed 100 percent. The conversation continued animatedly in this manner, skipping from one thing to another. She talked, Mr. Epstein talked, and it just went on and on.

All of this, of course, took place while Mr. Epstein had his hands on the steering wheel of the car, maneuvering to and fro, attempting to show everyone the sights of the great battlefield of Gettysburg. A remarkable performance, and one in which that hallowed ground where Lincoln in person spoke his enduring message about the Republic, must have never received such scant attention. And what of Augusta Galster? She hadn't received much attention either. Had Mr. Epstein ever been really interested in her? Was her heart broken that afternoon among the graves of the Union and Confederate dead? Had Henriette, with her French guile, been too quick for her? "Poor Augusta Galster," Henriette once sighed. "I'm sorry but I was probably not very polite."

Even on arrival at the Frankels the getting-to-know-you chatter between Mr. Epstein and Miss Castex kept on flowing and continued through dinner. When the meal was over Mr. Epstein asked everyone over to his rooms so that the party could go on.

"Mrs. Frankel put a record on the Victrola and I don't know what got into my head, but I started dancing to the tune, and I danced and danced," Henriette recalled.

Ill at ease because the room was filled with a lot of intellectual talk about old-age pensions, welfare, and politics, of which she knew nothing, Henriette kept on dancing by herself in the middle of the floor. She skipped and twirled, as she always had in the small towns of southern France where people loved dancing in the public square. Soon she began to hear clapping. She turned to look and lo it was none other than Mr. Epstein, who seemed to be enjoying the whole performance. This surprised her, since she had thought him much too intellectual for such spirited high jinks. But he carried on clapping as she cavorted alone to some peppy tune. Out of breath, she finally sat down. And at that point Mr. Epstein came over and put a book in her lap.

He said: "This is my book."

Henriette was awed. "I didn't know people who had written books. The ones who did all lived in Paris. They didn't live in the south of France. We only had peasants. We were considered on a lower scale intellectually, so naturally I didn't know people who had written books. I was very, very impressed."

She had no idea what the book was about and its title, *Facing Old Age*, was a mystery to her. The author attempted a brief explanation but it didn't mean very much. She agreed instead to take it back to the University of Delaware and read it there. Who knows how far she got, but the words that Abraham Epstein had written had a great deal to do with the eventual Americanization of Henriette Castex, the girl from the small towns of southern France.

The Victrola that played the merry little tune that set Henriette a-dancing still stands in retired antique splendor in the fraying clutter of her Greenwich Village house. Along with the magical carpet and the green glowing radio, it is another of the objects I cherished as a child. Whenever I raise its lid, I am enchanted by the attentive little dog engraved inside the cover, his head cocked in wonder at the sounds coming from the long-armed speaker. And when I play one of the venerable His Master's Voice recordings of Feodor Chaliapin, Gallagher and Sheen, or the Two Little Wooden Shoes fox trot and listen to the scratchy sound, I find myself somehow in Harrisburg, Pennsylvania, during the Thanksgiving holidays of 1924, watching a young girl dance and a balding man clap, at a time when the glorious Victrola played Cupid and inspired Abe Epstein to say, "This is my book."

2

Whatever it is that remains of the man who had written that book, at present lying under the headstone of a Long Island cemetery, began life on April 20, 1892, in a Russian village named Lyuban. It lies north of the Pripyat marshes (an area every invader entering Russia has avoided) in a wooded, infertile land 150 kilometers directly south of Minsk, the capital of Belarus—formerly White Russia. In 1892 it was in the Pale of Settlement where the Jews were forced to live inside the empire of Alexander III, tsar of all Russia and a vicious anti-Semite. Coincidentally, exactly three years earlier, a man the world came to hate had also been born— Adolf Hitler. As the German dictator grew in power, Abe's friends always used to kid him about their shared birthday, but he never thought it was funny. If he had had any say in the matter, he once said, Hitler would never have made it out of the womb.

Not long after he turned eighteen in 1910, Abe Epstein left Russia and set off for the United States of America, one among the many in the great surge of emigration from eastern Europe. What he wanted above all was an education. Henriette eventually turned this fact into a mantra to be invoked time after time, as she sifted the meager facts of Abe's childhood down to several salient events. Over the passage of time they have grown in meaning and size until they became of almost mythological proportion.

In Lyuban, the Epstein family was poor. Leibel, the father, was a devoutly religious Jew, a kindly man but an impractical one who never had much success. Bela Raisel, the mother, ran a small bakery. They had six children, four boys and two girls, and Abraham was the eldest. He loved to read, but the books that absorbed him were not the religious ones his father had in mind. Abraham hadn't an ounce of interest in the Torah and its commentaries. It was the plight of the son—perhaps the classic plight of the modern Jewish son—who was infatuated with books that his unlearned and stubborn father did not want in his house. Young Abraham acquired several hundred books, which he bought with the small sums he earned by teaching children in the nearby villages. His little library featured Marx and Engels among other banned writers, and he loaned his books out to other boys in the community, an audacious act when the tsar's secret police were everywhere. One day a rumor circulated in Lyuban that the police had heard about the little lending library and in fact were poking around the village looking for it. Abe and a friend ran to

Abe, on right, as a student in Russia. Date unknown.

his house to save the books but when they got there they found that Leibel had already thrown them down the cellar stairs on the potato pile, where they sprawled, torn and wrecked. He was determined to end his son's rebellion. When Abraham saw what his father had done he began to weep, but he was cut off.

"No, no, no! I won't have my son arrested by the police!" his father proclaimed.

What happened afterward, what he may have thought, what he felt, Abe never said. But the relationship between father and son was never healed.

The second myth has to do with the departure for America. Leibel Epstein had traveled to America early in the century to find work in order to

Leibel Epstein, Abe's father.
Taken between 1910–1914.
Possibly taken in New York
before he returned to Russia.

send money back to his impoverished family. Abe wrote and asked if he could join him. His father flatly refused, so the young son went behind his father's back and appealed to a sympathetic uncle already established in Connecticut who sent him fifty dollars for the ship's ticket. Defiantly, Abraham immediately fled his native village for the Latvian port of Liebau. There during the early months of 1910 he waited with many others for a boat to take him to America. What happened next is a story that always thrilled Henriette.

While waiting in the offices of the shipping company to get his ticket, Abe found himself sitting on a bench next to a great hulking young fellow who was dressed in shabby, ill-fitting clothes too small for his large peasant frame. Abe looked up at the man's face and he could see tears streaming down.

"What's the matter?" Abe asked.

"They won't let me have a ticket," the big peasant said.

Bella Raisel Levovicz, Abe's
mother. Photograph taken
in 1940–1941.

"Why? You look like the perfect immigrant for America to me," Abe
said, thinking of his own weak body. "You're strong, you're big, what's
wrong?"

"A man said I have trachoma," the peasant replied between sobs. "I
don't know what it is. But they won't let me sail."

"It's a disease of the eyes," Abe said. "Just see a doctor, he'll treat you,
you'll be cured soon, and then you can sail."

"No," the man said, "I have no money for a doctor. I'll have to go back
to my village. I don't know what I'll do."

Abe looked at the big youth who seemed the picture of health. His face
had the look of total misery. Abe suddenly got up from the bench and pat-
ted the man on the shoulder.

"Come with me," he said. "I'll help you find a doctor who will help.
We'll find someone."

For the next two days Abe walked the cobbled streets of the port of
Liebau, trailed by the hulking peasant. He went from one doctor's office
to another and everywhere he was treated with cold indifference. One
doctor told him that so many immigrants had trachoma, it would be impossible to treat them all. The man should just try to sneak on board and
trust to luck when he reached America.

The big peasant grew more depressed, but Abe grew more determined.
He would not let the injustice of poverty prevent the man from reaching

his goal. He needed help. Abe would find it for him. He knew that somewhere there was a doctor who would be willing to help another human
being in trouble.

And Abe found one. Where or how he never said. But he found one who
would treat the young man until the trachoma disappeared. Before Abe
parted from the man he made sure the shipping company would give him
a ticket when the trachoma was gone.

"Now I don't know what happened to that big peasant after that," Henriette said when she told others the story, "but the little blond boy, so frail,
that was Abraham Epstein."

---

And that's it. That is all anyone knows of Abe Epstein's Russian childhood. Several biographies of him were written, but none were ever published, and they have little to say about those early days. The problem, of
course, was the subject himself. He said almost nothing about that time,
in public or private. It was obviously not a happy experience and he apparently preferred to forget it. And so these two stories that have been refined over the years, swollen in articles and interviews, emerged to codi-
fy Abe Epstein as a man who wanted an education and had a desire to
help the less fortunate.

It seems to happen frequently. A man does something important, a few
uplifting stories are told, and as the years pass only glowing myths remain
for eternity: Washington and the cherry tree, Lincoln splitting rails. But
Abe defying his father hints at another story, a forgotten and perhaps
more troubling one.

3

The tension between father and son may have found its way to the New
World. When the S.S. *Biuma* of the Russian Line thrust eighteen-year-old
Abe Epstein into the immigrant turmoil of New York City on July 18, 1910,
some have said his own father was still there but would not see him. Others said that his father, disillusioned with the profane nature of Jewish life
in America, had already gone back to shtetl life in Lyuban. There are con-
flicting versions of what happened, and no one living who can provide
the answers. But it's clear that when Abe came to America he never saw
his father again, either in America or in Russia. The break was final.

Alone in New York, young Abe Epstein did what most Jewish immigrants did: he struggled to find a job in the only industry open to a "green-horn," a garment factory. Eventually he was hired to lug bundles of cloth from the stockroom to the cutting table. It was tough manual work and paid the choice sum of three dollars for a week of fourteen-hour days. The owner looked over the young immigrant's scrawny frame, sneered, said he was hopeless—he would never move up to become a cutter. Better to forget the garment industry. So Abe moved on to a job delivering medi-cine and washing bottles in a drugstore, at four dollars a week. And when that fourteen-hour day was done he rushed from the Bronx downtown to Eron Preparatory School at 185 East Broadway, where he began his long-sought-after education on April 24, 1911, four days after his nineteenth birthday. There with a mob of other immigrants he studied English and arithmetic four nights a week. The room was so packed with clamorous students that they had to take notes on each other's shoulders. He rose at five o'clock in his room in a tenement at 27 Canal Street on the Lower East Side, studied English for an hour, at six took the elevated train to his job in the Bronx where he worked till nearly 8 p.m., and then rushed back downtown to his classes from 8:20 until 10:20 p.m. After a meager meal in a cafeteria he was finally in bed at midnight. Education was more impor-tant than work, so Abe asked the drugstore owner to let him off an hour early so that he could study a little more and maybe get a seat in class. This was such an odd request that his employer could only interpret it as a bid for a raise and offered him a dollar a week more. Instead Abe quit—and soon found out how hard it was to be out of a job in capitalist Amer-ica. For three months he failed to find work. He searched everywhere and found nothing. He had to survive on thirty cents a day from the small sum he had saved. Finally, one day after another fruitless job search, when he was walking home over the Brooklyn Bridge he stopped in the middle of the span and looked over the rail at the water swirling far below. Suddenly the total uselessness of his life in America overwhelmed him. He recalled the experience vividly and many years later described his feelings to a group of his students: "There I was, out of a job, but what was worse I felt that no one wanted me anywhere. There I was on the Brooklyn Bridge, coming back from a job hunt, watching people by the thousands going home from work. I was just an outsider looking in. There was no place for me. No one wanted my hands or my brains. What good was I? I stood at the railing and looked down at the water far below. Why didn't I just jump in?" That feeling of despair, of being useless, remained engraved within him for the rest of his life.

And yet unexpectedly he was rescued by another Epstein. Jacob Epstein was not a relative, but an old friend from his Russian days and sent Abe a letter inviting him to come to Pittsburgh to help teach Hebrew to the children of wealthy Jewish families. Abe borrowed four dollars for the train fare, and when he arrived he discovered Jacob was leaving. Abe could have all his students. He began to earn the princely sum of twenty dollars a month, and he was fed by the Jewish families where he taught. His passionate desire for education was obvious to everyone he met, but most of the families assumed he wanted to be a rabbi. They had no idea that for Abe teaching Hebrew was only a temporary halt on his path to getting an education. When he found time he would wander the city looking for opportunities. "I thought I had a real American style," he wrote in a letter. "There I was in a suit I had purchased when I landed, with pants so big there was room for me and two neighbors. What a picture." One day, clothed in that same king-size suit, he walked by a big white building with a large sports field next to it and a sign that said "The East Liberty Academy." Recklessly he pushed open the gate and entered the grounds. He did not notice that it was located directly opposite the massive grounds of the Andrew Mellon estate. He asked to see the headmaster and was told to go and see Doctor Armstrong, who when confronted with Abe courteously never made note of his suit but instead asked the youth in front of him what he wanted.

"I'd like to go to school here," Abe replied.

"Do you know, young man, that this is a private school and people pay to come here?" the educator informed him.

And then, like Charlie Chaplin in one of his two-reelers on immigrants, the slight, bedraggled Hebrew teacher shyly tilted his head and said: "I don't have the money to pay, Doctor Armstrong. What am I going to do?"

Armstrong said nothing, so Abe passionately spoke on at great length of his strong desire to get an education, something that had been denied him in Russia. Armstrong, in his starched white collar, did not recoil at the excitable young man's foreign sound nor his bizarre-looking suit. He nodded and said, "I see you have a lot of courage."

The word "chutzpah" might have been more appropriate.

No one knows what went through Armstrong's mind at that moment, but something must have impressed him because he said next, "As of now you are enrolled in the school. You pay me whatever you can. It doesn't matter."

The moment Abe had been waiting for had at last arrived. While continuing to teach Hebrew among the Jewish families where he boarded, he attended the East Liberty Academy for three years and in 1914 graduated

Abraham Epstein, graduation photograph, East Liberty
Academy, June 1914.

near the top of his class. His fellow classmates, with names such as Jones,
Young, and Crawford—whose main claim to fame was their batting av-
erages—voted him "most studious." They nicknamed him "Eppy" and
wrote in his yearbook, "He'll get to the top of the tree of knowledge and
probably be a Prof. in college." Eppy's educational achievements were
taken note of at the University of Pittsburgh, and the hardworking student was awarded a scholarship to begin his undergraduate studies. Doctor Armstrong quite obviously knew what he was doing, and Abe never
forgot it. It became one of his core beliefs that men like Doctor Armstrong
were the ones who made America a great country, men who were not
afraid to take a chance on a poor immigrant boy, who were open to all the
possibilities in another human being. It was a type of man he had never
found in Russia. "He taught me what real, true Americans are like, the
kind I admire!"

Henriette once tried to sum up Abe's struggles in Pittsburgh with a tidy
phrase, "Those rich Jewish mamas made sure that the poor intellectual

boy had enough to eat," and the quote was revealing. Although she eventually married a Jew, Henriette had a sneaking anti-Semitic streak. She had been brought up in the world of the French Catholic middle class, first communion and all, so it wasn't surprising. But when she said those words she had come to believe that her husband also shared her feelings. He always seemed to her totally indifferent to every aspect of his Jewish background. Teaching Hebrew was only a means to an end, for even as a young immigrant Abe avoided the clinging together of the newly arrived Jews who insisted on remaining special and apart.

In escaping from Russia, Abe had rescued himself from the horrors of a land he thought ignorant and backward and brutal. He thought that other immigrant Jews should feel the same. "If you wanted to come to America then you became an American," he once wrote. "Otherwise what's the point?" Not for him was nostalgia for the shtetl, that sort of feeling that, as Philip Roth puts it, makes people "worship at the shrine of the delicatessen and cherish *Fiddler on the Roof.*" For Abe to dwell on being one of the chosen people would have only been a waste of time.

Abe once told a story to a friend who wrote it up in an article in the *New York Day,* a newspaper published in both English and Yiddish. It was about the long list of faults Abe had "observed in Jewish clerical workers both in his own office and elsewhere." A "certain Miss Y, a Jewish stenographer, more competent and intelligent than her coworkers was far less industrious and reliable—moreover, an hour before quitting time, her relatives would troop through, with the result that she did hardly any work during that hour." The writer agreed with Abe's opinion and bemoaned the "noisy, vulgar and lazy jazz babies who try to get away with as little work as possible and then whine about anti-Jewish discrimination."

Abe believed that all new immigrants, including Jews, should take advantage of opportunities that were offered nowhere else in the world—they should become Americans and get an education. That is what mattered. And if this line of thought made any sense, then it was just possible for Henriette Castex, the Catholic from France, to look at her husband and think he was not really so Jewish.

---

At the University of Pittsburgh Abe's nascent radical ideas, taken from all the Marx and Engels he had read, were transformed and developed. He became one of the founders of the Socialist Study Club and its president. He organized meetings and conferences where major reform figures of the day, such as Florence Kelley and Harry Laidler, spoke before stu-

Pitt Socialist Study Club, 1916. A. Epstein, President, first row, second from right.

dents. During a violence-filled strike against Westinghouse, the Socialist Club tried to hold a meeting where the strike leaders could tell their side of the story, but the university banned it. Reporters found out, and the newspapers accused the university of suppressing free speech. So the newspapers offered several strikers a chance to tell their stories—free publicity, exactly what Abe had in mind. Another time the university refused to let Abe hold a meeting where a representative of Margaret Sanger would talk about birth control. Abe moved the meeting off-campus to a restaurant and was astounded when five hundred students showed up. The place was so crowded that Abe in his squeaky foreign accent had to introduce the speaker from the top of the kitchen range. But it didn't matter to him because he realized that people were paying attention. He had developed a following.

In June 1917 of his senior year, the economics department, where Abe was getting his B.S., undertook the study of a current Pittsburgh problem: the sordid living conditions of the growing Negro population. Walter May, the May department store magnate, sponsored the study, but when summer came all the students dropped out except Abe, who stayed on to

Graduation, University of Pittsburgh, 1917. Abe is on the right.

finish the work. He persisted in knocking on doors and asking questions up and down the streets of the Hill District where the Negro slums were. He survived on a stipend of fifty dollars a month from the generous Walter May. When the study was finished, it was published by the economics department, again paid for by the public-spirited Walter May. *The Negro Migrant in Pittsburgh* by Abraham Epstein appeared in December 1917—six years after he began to learn the English language. Abe had become an American author—and the squalor of Negro shantytown life had finally caught the attention of the public and the elite of Pittsburgh.

From his first days in New York, Abe had seen the ugly side of the country he had chosen as his salvation. And now he had gone into the streets and talked to another suffering people: the Negroes. What had he found? They were people who had no place to go because the rooms they lived in were rented in shifts. When one man got up, another man took over the bed. They were men who had been forced to leave their families while they struggled to find work as simple laborers. There was discrimination on the part of the unions that kept the new migrants, most of whom had been brought up north by labor agents, out of work. There were no parks. There were no welfare agencies. The only recreation was the street corner saloon. He used photographs to vividly illustrate the depravity of Negro living conditions: back-alley outhouses shared by a dozen families, abandoned boxcars used as homes, men standing around outside saloons. Abe became a known figure in the Negro shantytown where everyone called him "Doctor."

It is difficult to believe that the government could ignore the poor and destitute as totally as it did back then. But that was the real America behind the myth and arrogance of 1920s prosperity, and with his first published work Abraham Epstein began to grope his way onto the byways of reform. His bantam book, bound in black, was only seventy-four pages long. But the ripples that were spread from its little splash show his passions in their inceptive swell. Research was first, facts and figures taken from documents and interviews. He became a master at backing up everything he wrote, and the book's pages are freighted with tables and photographs. Following that was his developing philosophy that discrimination, unemployment, poverty, and all the social ills he was shocked to find in America were not just evil in themselves, but destructive of the very virtues that America bragged about.

It's not sufficient that we bring these people here, give them a bunk house or a basement to sleep in and a job in our mills for twelve hours ⟩a day. Once in our midst they become part of ourselves. Utmost attention is therefore essential to meet the maladjustments before they become acute; and we do not base this claim on sentimental grounds but upon the benefits of economic and social farsightedness. The fact cannot be overemphasized that the community ultimately pays the price for its stupidity.

As far as the blacks were concerned (he actually used that term a few times in his book),

Their migration is but the logical result of a long series of linked causes beginning with the landing of the first slave ship and extending to the present day. The slavery that was ended by the Emancipation Proclamation and the Fourteenth Amendment has been succeeded by less sinister but still significant social and economic problems, which are full of subtle menace for the welfare of America.

In this little opus the youthful Abe Epstein seems like a racehorse recklessly bursting from the gate, or like a medical student just out of school,
crying out that he wants to be among those who find the antidote. And
the solicitous department store magnate, Walter May, told the young
scholar to sell the book at fifty cents a copy—and keep the proceeds.

*The Negro Migrant* didn't change the misery of Negro life in Pittsburgh,
but it changed Abe Epstein's life. A member of the state legislature, James
Maurer, who was a committed Socialist and president of the Pennsylvania Federation of Labor, had succeeded in having a commission created
to look into the plight of the elderly poor. He took one look at *The Negro
Migrant in Pittsburgh* and called Abe's professor in the economics department of the University of Pittsburgh, Frank Tyson. Maurer listened to all
the good things Tyson had to say about his dedicated student, decided
Abe Epstein was just the man he wanted, and offered him his first real job
in America as secretary and research director of the newly created Pennsylvania Commission on Old Age Pensions.

Abe began to walk the path he would follow for the rest of his life. It
was 1918. He had just turned twenty-six.

4

The Pennsylvania Commission on Old Age Pensions had been approved by the legislature, despite Maurer's Socialist convictions, because
everyone liked him too much to turn him down. He was a strong, well-
built man with a booming voice, a bristling mustache, a comic streak, and
a glint in his blue eyes, and everyone called him Jim. His towering build
and lanky workingman's arms, his bowler hat clutched awkwardly in one
hand, anchor many a photograph. And he could tell stories by the hundreds. He had worked at every conceivable trade from day laborer to cir-
cus performer, and his Pennsylvania Dutch ancestry was a matter of great
pride; as he put it in his autobiography, his relatives "were real patriots, a
great majority of them being descended from men who had fought in the
Continental Army. In practically every household could be found some
relic of the Revolution, a sword, flintlock, or horse pistol." A committed
Socialist, he became that party's vice-presidential candidate in the elections of 1928 and 1932.

Abe met with Jim Maurer every day over the work of the commission,
and there seems to have been a meeting of the minds between the older
Socialist mentor and the young, impatient activist. Maurer was twenty-

Abe at work in his office of the Pennsylvania
Commission on Old Age Pensions, 1918.

eight years older and near the age of Abe's father in Russia, a man vanished from his life. It was a perfect fit, particularly for a son who had been
rejected and placed outside the pale of paternal sustenance.

Given two little rooms high up in the state capitol building at Harrisburg, Abe rolled up his sleeves and went to work with the same energy
he had used in researching *The Negro Migrant*. He prevailed on friends to
serve as volunteer workers, but the flu epidemic of 1918 forced a number
of them to drop out. Still, over the course of a year Abe interviewed 3,405
inmates of the state poorhouses, 2,300 in semi-private homes, 500 who
were receiving private charity, and 4,500 indigent aged who were still living in their shabby houses. He added detailed research on the twenty foreign countries that had some form of old-age benefits. His report to the
legislature contained a wealth of information, both anecdotal and statistical, showing how the laboring classes had little or nothing to support
themselves with in old age. The only public assistance of any kind was
that humiliating monstrosity known as the poorhouse. Abe's report—the
first of three he made in 1919, 1921, and 1925—was the first comprehen-

Pennsylvania Commission on Old Age Pensions, legislative
hearings, 1920. James Maurer, Abe's mentor, front row, first
on left. Abraham Epstein, front row, third from left.

sive case study of its kind ever made, so full of startling facts that its three
hundred pages were a shock to the lawmakers. They had not expected to
be confronted with the issue so soon and in such detail. Among the startling material Abe uncovered, in addition to all the statistics, were graph-
ic reports about the almost universal illiteracy of the poorhouse superin-
tendents: "Reports of state inspectors frequently contain such notes as
'superintendent can read and write a little'—'superintendent is very low
grade and his wife evidently a moron." Another told of how poorhouses
reeked: "Sections occupied by the inmates were so foul smelling that they
were almost unbearable . . . those who were unable to care for their physical needs . . . had to depend on other inmates for the most urgent wants
. . . there was virtually no medical supervision." No laws were passed—
such is the way with the democratic process as the ever-passionate Abe
was beginning to learn—but more study was called for. And to do this Jim

and Abe were authorized to go to Europe at the state government's expense to look at what was being done in other countries.

When the radical duo set off together, it was undoubtedly an odd spectacle. Jim, with his height and walrus mustache, towered over Abe, who was barely five feet and already balding. Still, their spirits were high when they arrived at the dock in New York, but as they were about to board the ship, customs officers barked at them to step aside. Forget about the trip, an inspector told them. "Hand over your passports," said another. "Sorry," the man in charge continued, "but 'Reds' are not allowed to leave the country!" It was 1920, the year of the "Palmer Raids," when the ambitious attorney general of the United States, A. Mitchell Palmer, known to the press as "The Fighting Quaker," began to arrest "Reds" and Socialists en masse across the United States, telling the country (like Joseph McCarthy thirty years later) that they were plotting to overthrow the government. The Bolshevik menace was out to get America, and the dynamic Abe and Jim were known to the government as noisy Socialists. When the story broke, the headline in large capitals in one New York newspaper read, "TWO REDS DRAGGED OFF S.S. LAPLAND." The reporter told his readers how the government had saved the public from those two "Reds" doing any further mischief on their travels.

Maurer got a big laugh out of the whole episode. "It's the usual journalistic exaggeration. We never even set foot on the gangplank!"

Nonetheless, he headed for Washington, where he confronted the attorney general in person. "Oh, no, no, that's not possible," Palmer soothed him. "It must be a mistake. I know you were on official business for the State of Pennsylvania." After a pause he continued. "But what's this speech you made criticizing President Wilson during the war? Were you a pacifist at that time?"

Maurer, who had a good command of the workingman's vernacular from his days as a machinist, restrained himself because Palmer promised to eventually get him a new passport. It was a cagey performance by the nation's first "Red Hunter," a role model for those who aspire to that august title. Abe's experience was even more bizarre. He was in no position to confront Palmer, so he tried to tell some other officials why he needed to go by showing them a contract he had to write a book on old-age pensions signed by none other than Alfred Knopf himself. "Nothing doing. You're not fooling anyone," the immigration official told him. "And besides, we know those signatures on that contract are nothing but messages in code!"

The story of the "Two Reds" eventually became a staple of Abe's hu-

Abe on board ship to
Bremerhaven, 1921.

morous repertoire, and, not at all daunted, he returned to Harrisburg and
went right back to work. Palmer's attempted intimidation just spurred
him to make sure that during the next few years the people of Pennsylvania would hear all about the plight of the aged. He also jumped into the
fray with a number of radical causes, including the famous steel strike of
1919. He interviewed the strikers and got their story into the newspapers.
That effort got him tagged once more as a part of the "red menace." But
Maurer was with him on everything he did, and to some he was soon
known as Maurer's alter ego.

Abe always revered Jim Maurer. What made Maurer special in his eyes
was his good old American know-how. Maurer could entertain people
with countless stories, could charm, cajole, and make speeches to rally the
troops, all in the service of the cause. He also knew how to get laws passed
and regulations changed. And that's what Abe learned from Maurer—
how to disarm all the governing bodies he would eventually face, how to
become the American he wanted to be, the kind of American who would

Abraham Epstein and Emil Frankel in Berlin, 1921, just
before Abe left for Russia. Emil was Abe's lifelong friend.
He was the first to use the word "security" when suggesting a name for Abe's new organization.

be listened to by other Americans to get laws passed and regulations
changed. As the late Senator Paul Douglas once wrote of Abe, "Tough
politicians in state legislatures and in Congress were always captivated
by him. He spoke their language and at the same time stirred their desire
to help people."

But with fathers and sons—as well as with imagined ones—relations
can become twisted and knotted. When the Pennsylvania Federation of
Labor resolved to start a series of classes in every Pennsylvania city—because, as Maurer reported to the unions, "the organized worker, in going
to school, declares: 'I shall no longer think at the command of big business,'" he called on Abe to join him in the project. Naturally, Abe threw

himself into the new work with more zeal and gusto than anyone else. On top of his job at the Commission on Old Age Pensions he was made general secretary (at no pay) of the Labor Education Committee, and like a rocket sent aloft he rushed around the state planning the classes. Labor unions in Allentown, Lancaster, Pottsville, Reading, as well as the metropolises of Pittsburgh and Philadelphia, saw this flying missionary and listened to his buttonholing.

But Abe's firebrand tactics didn't get things moving as fast as he would have liked. In 1920, workers and union leaders were often staid and cautious, not as radical as one might believe. They saw no reason why going to class after work to learn economic and political theories about capital and labor would make any difference in their lives. Still, Abe would not take no for an answer, and by the early part of 1921 he had managed to set up classes in ten Pennsylvania cities. A teacher was hired to tour the state and when he couldn't make it, Abe would speed to the location and teach for him. Always in a hurry to change the world, Abe began to see that the movement for workers' education had national possibilities, and he called for a meeting in New York. His dogged achievements received recognition and he was made secretary-treasurer and Maurer president of the Worker's Education Bureau. A first national conference was planned for later that year, and when it convened things suddenly turned sour for Abe. A number of people involved with the movement found his firebrand ways offensive. He was accused of being abrupt and dismissive, and he angered many people who did not like to be told what to do and how to do it. He was impatient with "dilly-dallying," as he called it. But to some he was just "a little dictator and know it all."

It was here that one sees for the first time a side to Abe's personality that frequently got in his way. He was never able to understand why the people he worked with didn't just agree with him. Doing things his way was just common sense. After all, he had studied the subject more than they had and knew more about it than they did. In most cases that was true, but he could never admit that his attitude might be arrogant. When the conference convened, he got the first big shock of his life in his beloved new land. He was voted out and a safe choice was chosen to replace him, a man who never did much to elevate the Worker's Education Bureau into a major force in the labor movement.

The punch that really sent him reeling, however, came from a very unexpected person. As the éminence grise of the bureau, Jim Maurer could have stopped the moves against Abe and put over any candidate he wanted. But he never said one word in support. He just let Abe sink to the floor, undefended. When the vote was over and Abe was cut loose something in him just snapped, like a limb breaking from a tree without warning. All he could see was how exhaustively he had given himself to the work and now nobody cared about it or him or his ideas. It was an ugly wound. He abruptly quit his job at the Commission on Old Age Pensions and fled from Harrisburg.

Maurer never said a word to him—at least publicly. But well after the calamity, in a possible act of contrition, he reported to the Pennsylvania Federation of Labor "that whatever the future success of this work in this state, we will always be deeply grateful for the foundation he has laid." But it was all too little and too late. Abe was gone from Harrisburg, living instead on a farm where he tried working as a simple laborer. He told those who asked what he was up to that he was going to spend the rest of his days as a farmer. His friends were puzzled. The cartoonish image of this short, frail man carrying slops to the pigs could only have evoked strained smiles from most of them. They all knew that all he cared about was books and meetings and political action.

Abe Epstein's first complete defeat in America came at the hands of a man he loved, who had picked him out of the throng, who had lifted him up and then without warning dropped him. The scars must have run pretty deep because he kept the story to himself for a long time. And never once did he blame Jim nor hold him accountable. Many years later when Henriette became aware of what had happened, she was indignant. "After all," she fumed, "you could say he was Maurer's political son!"

5

Of course, Abe's life as a farm laborer wasn't going to last very long. Something inside had been stirring and foaming. On April 2, 1920, he made an unusual entry in his mostly empty pocket diary: "Happy day. Received first letter from home in 3 years." He noted his reply the very next day, his first letter to his family in nearly two years. His last entry for 1920 was, "Determined to go to Russia in the Spring," and true to his word he left for his homeland on July 21, 1921, full of optimism, because Alfred A. Knopf had agreed to publish his first book on old-age security. The manuscript had been put together by Abe from all the research he had done for the Pennsylvania Commission on Old Age Pensions and closely followed his report to the legislature.

That his oppressive feeling of defeat had been cast off is clearly visible in an extensive group of photographs of the trip back to Russia. In dozens of pictures Abe can be seen posing against the ship's rail or lounging in a deck chair as he crossed the Atlantic. With his cap at a rakish angle and a big smile on his face, he is encircled by a flock of women. There are more photographs from Berlin, where he toured the city, watched the parades, visited the monuments, and swilled beer in an open air "garten." Again he is in the midst of friends and beaming women prettily peering out from behind parkland trees or smiling coyly from café tables, beguiling in their frilly 1920s dresses and little cloche hats. Even the future head of the U.S. Communist Party, William Z. Foster, who was passing through Berlin at that time, couldn't spoil the fun. Foster had just come out of Russia, looking emaciated and sick, and when introduced to Abe, he warned him not to go back to his homeland. Too dangerous, he said. But as always with Abe, "no" was not acceptable. He found a way to slip across the border into Russia, which was not easy in those days, and traveled on to Moscow.

The psychological change in Abe from depression to lightheartedness grew out of a range of ideas tumbling around in his head. The land of his birth would welcome him, he thought, and with his new American know-how he would be able to help the great revolutionary cause. He also decided he would report on all that he saw and experienced. He had even given the book a tentative title: "The New State." Moscow brought him down to earth. He found he could accomplish very little. Hunger and scarcity were everywhere, and he had to stand in long lines just to get food and wood to warm his landlady's apartment. When he came back with the wood it had to be brought up instantly lest it be stolen. And when his landlady went out for food he had to stay in the apartment for fear that intruders would quickly ransack it. After great effort—it took days to get an appointment—he waited for five hours outside the walls and passed through seven sets of sentries before he was finally permitted to enter the sanctum of the Kremlin to interview one of the secretaries of the Communist Party. He asked if he could see the minutes of the party meetings.

"What minutes?" was the irate reply. "We don't have time for minutes when we are building the Revolution!"

Another time he managed to get into a courtroom and observe the new Communist judicial system at work. The newly appointed judge was a notorious man named John Kotek who had returned from Kansas City and his job as a meat packer to work for the struggling Revolution. He had been put in charge, without any judicial training, of one of the new revolutionary courts. For several days Abe watched Judge Kotek at work inside a decaying building filled with soldiers carrying sinister guns. The

Lyuban, Russia, 1922. Abe and his family. On back is written: "In front of our house. Abe Epstein, Bella Raisel Epstein, Gertrude, Sam, and Esther." Note the rough wood sides of the typical Russian house.

courtroom had little light, the floors were wet from the snow, and the paint was peeling off the walls. The judge's method was simple and fast. One young girl was crying loudly. She had a job making out permits and had saved some money from her work. Abe was not sure what she was accused of, but the judge yelled at her.

"How much did you save during this period?"

"I have nothing, absolutely nothing," she bawled.

"Where have you been since you were arrested?"

"In jail."

"Sit down!" Kotek pronounced.

And then two guards dragged her back to jail.

A man accompanied by his wife and two children was similarly taken away when Kotek asked him, "What party do you belong to?"

The man, who didn't know any better, answered, "I belong to no party." He disappeared just as quickly.

People were scared, Abe realized. They said nothing to defend themselves. They knew they had no chance.

Lyuban, 1922. Abe with his sister
Gertrude and another relative.

One young woman was accused of spending money to buy face powder. Kotek was indignant.

"How could you do that when people are starving?" Kotek asked.

The woman's meek reply was, "Well, a woman must keep her nose powdered."

With no prosecutor, defense lawyer, or even a witness, Kotek sentenced everyone to jail as quickly as he could, no matter what the charges. Later Abe went and interviewed the meat packer turned judge, who was living in a shabby rooming house. Kotek told Abe he was twenty-seven and had gone to the United States in 1913. He had worked on a farm, in a foundry, and finally in Kansas City as a meat packer. When the Revolution took place the Communist Party called him back to Russia, and since the Moscow Soviet needed judges who believed in the Revolution he was made a judge and given a courtroom.

"Russia is the land of the free and the land of the workers," Kotek told Abe.

"Well, if that is so," Abe asked, "how do you think Russian courts compare with those in the United States?"

"Our courts?" replied Kotek deliberately. "Our proletarian courts are run by the workers and peasants. They are fundamentally different. The advantage of our courts is that no lawyer is here, there are no fees for lawyers. Everybody's given a fair trial, and every defendant is his own attorney."

"Well," Abe asked, "Do you give out sentences of death? Do you feel anything? Does your conscience bother you?"

Kotek admitted, "The work is difficult. But a Communist cannot tremble. The Communist acts on his conviction, what he believes is good for the Revolution, and when he does that he fears no one." Abe tried to describe Kotek and the frenzied zeal of his courtroom in an article he wrote on the new Russian justice called "Inside the Red Court." But he seemed at a loss. His final assessment was: "Revolutions are the creators of careers and the mothers of strange children." The article had no takers.

Everywhere he went he took in scenes of monstrous brutality, hunger, and thievery, though later on he found something to laugh at. He was standing with a horde of people waiting for a glimpse of the great Trotsky, one of the founders of the "New State." The charismatic revolutionary leader never seemed to arrive, and Abe, fed up, decided to leave. He put his hand in his pocket only to find his wallet had vanished. His ironic comment: "A comrade with a lot less reverence for the moneyless, communitarian ideals of Russian communism had picked my pocket."

Abe's proposed book, "The New State," was never written.

---

Abe had not seen his family in more than ten years, but going to their home in Lyuban was not a simple undertaking. The trains from Moscow were few and followed no timetable. In time he found one that was going to Minsk and struggled with a crowd of people to get on board. After a harrowing two days living in a cattle car, where those without food stole from those who had it, he finally arrived in Lyuban. Nowhere did he ever say or write down what he felt when he was reunited with his destitute family, but the photographs he took seem to tell the story—only images of poverty and desolation, in contrast to the fun days of shipboard life. On unpaved, rutted, filthy streets, relatives and friends wrapped in ragged clothes, eyes pained from the glare of the feeble sunshine, stand stiffly posed against the traditional rough-hewn log buildings of the Russian village. Others, all bent over and covered up, walk down muddy paths. Not a smile can be seen, for the brutality of Russian revolutionary life was just as widespread in this little backwater as it had been on the streets of the capital. There had been two pogroms in the last two years and people had been killed. One death had been particularly grisly. Bandits in the area were determined to wipe out the Jews, and to prevent this a detachment of the Red Army had been sent to protect the village. An officer had even been stationed in the Epstein home. But when the "banditen" swarmed into the village the soldiers could do little to stop them. They ransacked the town and rounded up most of the Jews in one of the synagogues. They were about to set fire to the wooden building when someone ran to get the Russian Orthodox priest. When the priest saw what was about to take place, he pleaded with the bandits to stop. What he said somehow staved off the looming fire; the bandits left the synagogue alone and took flight back to the forests, leaving Lyuban looted and littered with bodies. Abe's youngest sister, Esther, who was six, had been sent to hide in a barn loft with a friend when the attack started. As she lay silently beneath the hay, through the cracks in the floor she watched the bandits underneath hunting for Jews. When she eventually came down into the street she was terrified by the sight of three bloody corpses, one a woman whose long blonde hair, she recalled, seemed to flow out into the earth. At home the Russian officer had been shot dead, his brains spattered against the walls of the main room. Of her Russian childhood, Esther has only two memories she can bring herself to talk about. One is the bloody sights of that murderous pogrom. The other is the sweet smell of the lilac bushes when they bloomed on the raw wooden fence surrounding the house of the Russian Orthodox priest.

Later, in America, Abe told only a few stories of what he had seen. One was about the local village idiot—known in Russian tradition as "God's Fool"—a beggar who went from door to door. The local commissar shot him as Abe watched; Abe was told that "He was of no use to the Revolution." What caused Abe even more anguish was the look of his former schoolmates and friends. They were wrinkled and bearded and stooped like very old men, and unrecognizable. In a few letters to friends, and in several articles that never made it into print, he told of the rude awakening he had experienced. It dawned on Abraham Epstein that the great revolutionary party he had wanted to be part of was over and done with.

Reconciliation with his own father was no longer possible. After an earlier pogrom Leibel Epstein had suffered a heart attack and was dead well before his son arrived in Lyuban to see him. Abraham was now the eldest, and even if he had little feeling for Jewish family life it was clear he had an obligation to take care of his mother and brothers and sisters. It was his turn to take over as head of the household and demonstrate at last the rightness of his choice when he had defied his father and fled Russia. Between father and eldest son—who had once lived together in the old traditions of Jewish shtetl life, with its kosher food, religious schools, separatism, mud, dust, and poverty—it was now over with forever. Whatever Abe felt or thought about it all is unclear; there is not a word, not a note, not a trace. "When something was unpleasant he had a tendency to forget it, to sweep it under the rug, and not talk about it too much," is how Henriette would explain it. "You had to prod him a good deal and that's what happened with Russia."

Instead, he took action. He got his family out as fast as possible. He returned to the ordeal of Moscow and, maneuvering his way through the maze of Russian bureaucracy, succeeded in getting the necessary papers by bribing several commissars. With his mother, one brother, and two sisters he made it to Riga, Latvia, on May 18, 1922. From there, with exit permits, transit visas, and immigration papers, Abe and his family traveled through Poland to Berlin, arranged for another brother who was waiting there to follow them, and moved on to Hamburg, where Abe gave them a preview of their new life. He fed them in good restaurants, bought everyone new clothes, and took them sightseeing. He took pictures in a park of everyone looking smart and a bit startled in their new finery, a way of exorcising the wretched images he had captured of them earlier in Lyuban. On May 31 they sailed for New York in second class (the Epstein family, he was determined, would not arrive in their new home as poor immigrants the way he had) and disembarked on June 10. The trek out of Russia was over. The Epstein family, every one of them, was safe from the horrors of the "New State." Of that classic exodus, Abe's youngest sister, Esther, is the only one still living, and all she remembers is that "somewhere in Germany, I don't know where, maybe it was Hamburg, Abe bought me my very first ice cream cone. Oh, I will never forget that wonderful taste!"

---

In years to come Abe would sum up the saga of his Russian return with a classic story that always brought laughs.

One of the Russian revolutionary comrades was standing in Red Square, shading his eyes and looking into the distance, in the stereotypical pose of the American Indian watching the horizon. The comrade was there day after day, always in the same position, always looking into the distance. Finally, Abe went over to him one day and said, "What are you doing, Tovarich?"

The man replied, "I am watching for the approach of Communism."

(This was always the first laugh.)

"But I saw you do this last week and the week before."

"I work for the government. And we work three shifts. There has been a depression," the man answered.

"How much do they pay you?"

"Two hundred rubles."

"I'll tell you what," Abe told him. "Come to the United States of America and we will pay you two hundred dollars! All you will have to do is to stand on Wall Street and when people ask you what you are doing just tell them that you are watching for the approach of prosperity. What do you say?"

The tovarich paused for a long time and thought. Then slowly and painfully, he finally replied, "No thank you"—another pause—"but, you see, this is a permanent job!"

When Abe told this story during the depression of the 1930s, the punch line would always get a huge guffaw. But it was beneath this kind of joke that Abe buried his true feelings about Russia. He told everyone that it was true that the land of the commissars was no longer the land of the tsars, but other than that not much had changed. It was the same vicious malevolence everywhere. Russian communism was a failure. The only hope for the future was democracy, the American way, which despite all its shortcomings, the slowness, the graft, the ineptitude, was the only true path to reform. As one of his biographers described it, "Epstein felt the Soviet revolution failed to materially improve the lot of the common man and change through orderly democratic procedure was preferable to revolutionary upheavals in society."

The return to Russia demolished all of Abe's "New State" ideals and changed his thinking permanently. His disillusionment came more than thirty years before it did for other committed Marxist-Leninists in the 1950s. A few other Socialist believers, such as Bertrand Russell, had also had their eyes opened when they visited Russia in the 1920s. For Russell, the regime was "unspeakably horrible." But not many had shared his revulsion like Abe had. "Lenin fostered a double truth," Abe wrote, "just like Hitler and Mussolini. He took the law of Christ and said, *Thou shalt not kill the PROLETARIAT.* But he turned his back on massacres of the bourgeoisie. With Stalin's oriental taste for blood added to an established custom of brutality that has coarsened the fibre of the nation, Russia is doomed through her own excesses." It was a very prophetic statement.

The pain and horrors of Russian communism took their toll in personal ways as well. The experience of the return to Lyuban may have exorcised some of the demons of Abe's hideous shtetl childhood, but it's not clear it relieved him of any guilt connected with his escape to America. What went through his mind when he first hit Lyuban's muddy streets and saw what he had abandoned eleven years earlier—his impoverished family and his now-dead father? But on these emotional subjects there is not a word anywhere from Abe. In the opaque curtain that circles this man who kept his personal feelings to himself there are a few feeble cracks, but what is visible inside those tiny pinholes is very cloudy indeed. And about his Russian childhood—nothing.

Perhaps, after eleven years in New York, Pittsburgh, and Harrisburg, Abe Epstein was no longer much of a Russian Jew but rather more of an American than he knew. He had become an American citizen on April 5, 1917. He foresaw the brutal ruin of his Russian homeland before many another disillusioned idealist. The uncovering of Stalin's Gulag years later would have been no surprise. When Abe returned to America with his mother and brothers and sisters, he knew it was time to forget the horrors of Russia. It was time to bury the past and its beliefs forever and get on with it in America.

6

"The days of our years are three score years and ten—and if by reason of strength they be four score years, yet is their strength labour and sorrow—for it is soon cut off and we fly away." Taken from the 90th Psalm, those words appear on the introductory page of Abraham Epstein's first book, *Facing Old Age.*

When he set off for his Russian homeland in 1921, Abe Epstein was just one more fervent Socialist rattling around the edges of the American labor movement. But safely back in America from that shattering odyssey, he was amazed to discover he was now an authority on old-age pensions. While he was away Knopf had published *Facing Old Age,* the very book he had tried to research in Europe when the immigration clerks told him they knew he was a "Red" and his contract was nothing more than a se-cret in code. The book's powerful message came from the statistics he had prepared for the Pennsylvania Commission, at the time the most up-to-date information on the plight of the elderly worker with no pension and no retirement savings. It opened with a chapter called "After Sixty—What?" and was filled with facts, figures, statistical tables, biblical refer-ences, and a survey of what other countries had done—viewed as well from a long historical perspective. The book was interspersed with little stories about the plight of the aged that lifted the bare facts off the page, such as the one about an army mule named Rodney. It seemed that Rod-ney had served bravely in battle during the Spanish-American War, was never sick for a day, and after twenty years in the army was retired to pas-ture at government expense, a sort of equine old-age pension. A postal clerk, recently let go after fifty years of service with not a cent of retire-ment from the Postal Service, noticed the story in the newspaper and wrote to his employers "that it would have been better if I had been born a horse than a human being. I have been a wheel horse for the govern-ment for fifty years and cannot get a pension. All I can say is lucky old Rodney!" It was the sort of anecdote Abe carved into a fine weapon in his later writing. The book concluded with a reprint of the law Abe had draft-ed and sent to the Pennsylvania legislature for passage. Expanding on the ideas that had made *The Negro Migrant* so relevant to the people of Pitts-burgh, Abe made it clear that government was obligated to do something for those that modern industrial society had left impoverished. The Unit-ed States had done absolutely nothing and was at the bottom of the list, alongside China and India.

*Facing Old Age* brought Abe unexpected attention, and he received nu-merous offers to do graduate work with scholarships at Harvard, Min-nesota, and Clark. But he was unable by temperament to sit behind a desk doing research while watching the world reform itself without his help. So when the Fraternal Order of Eagles, taking note of Abe's sudden prominence, asked him to take over their efforts to lobby for old-age pen-sions, he grabbed the job.

In the 1920s, America's zoological spectrum of lodges—the Elks, the Moose, the Lions, the Eagles—were looking for causes. They were im-portant organizations in American provincial life, with a longstanding tradition of public service, and were not happy with the way their mid-western brand of boosterism was satirized by writers such as Sinclair Lewis and H. L. Mencken. They wanted America to know of all the good work they did. The Moose had taken up the cause of orphans. The Fraternal Order of Eagles thought the other end of the spectrum would do the trick for them—old-age pensions. Founded in Seattle, the Eagles had branches all over the United States and Canada but were headquartered in the Midwest in South Bend, Indiana. What made them ridiculous to many was the way they went about their work. Local branches were called Aeries, and there were many of them. Every summer a huge convention was held and these were called Grand Aeries. During the Grand Aerie of 1921, Frank Hering, a "Past Grand Worthy President," pushed for the Eagles to get involved in a campaign for state old-age pension laws. The Grand Aerie seemed pleased with this idea, and in September 1922 Abe Epstein was hired to get the work under way. Finally, he was getting a chance to put his ideas into practice.

Accordingly, the entire Epstein clan—mother, brothers, and sisters—settled down on a leafy street in South Bend. If it is possible to imagine a place more provincial than Harrisburg in those years, it would have to be South Bend, home of Notre Dame and its fabulous football team. Take a load of poor, uneducated Russian Jews, just off the boat, uproot them from the ravages of the "New State," settle them down in a peaceful midwestern town—and what you have is a recipe for confusion at best, disaster at worst.

In the first place, Abe's mother had never wanted to come to America. Lyuban was her home, the place where her husband was buried, a place where she had always lived. Also, she could not understand why her son was so relentless in wanting to convert all of her children into instant Americans by sending them immediately to school and supervising their studies. Two of them were happy to go along with this hurried assimilation, but his mother and the oldest girl, a teenage beauty who immediately attracted many boyfriends, were not so eager. They fought back. Clashes sprang up over such irritants as cooking kosher food.

"Be like an American and cook like one," Abe scolded his mother. "Make salads."

In Russia she had run her own household and needed no one to tell her how to do it. In South Bend she spent most of her time alone, in a community where no one spoke Yiddish. She was unable to pick up English with the ease of a teenager, but her son was adamant that she make an effort. She resisted, and this infuriated him. Screaming fights, filled with vigorous and lively curses in English and Yiddish, sailed through the house. Abe was a juggernaut with his family—everything had to be done his way. His obsessive longing to wipe out his Russian nightmare at the speed of light is the only possible excuse. But his bitterness about life in

Russia and his longing to give his family an instant education—it haunted him—meant very little to his mother. To her it looked like he was just
trying to replace her deceased husband, and she would have none of it.

In the midst of this growing upheaval some good things came about.
One brother—named Berul in Hebrew, Beryl in Russian, rendered as
Berek on his travel papers, renamed Boris in America, and finally triumphantly Americanized (by himself) into Bernard—entered Notre Dame
as an undergraduate. The others were getting some serious schooling for
the first time, and Abe kept up his own education. From the good fathers
of that Catholic school he took courses in English and public speaking,
and when the students were asked to stand up in prayer, Abe—in belief
that he was part of the great American melting pot—resolutely stood up
with them. But beyond that, nothing much worked for the Epstein family in their new American home.

For one, the Eagles job soon turned into a complete fiasco. Frank Hering, Abe's boss, had been a football and baseball star at Notre Dame, and
among his achievements before his involvement with the Eagles was his
creation and promotion of Mother's Day—which Woodrow Wilson proclaimed in 1912 as the second Sunday in May. In the view of Hering, and
thus of the Eagles, "Fraternity was basically built upon the home," and in
the name of that institution it was time to stop sending "our unfortunate
aged citizens to pauper institutions, humiliated, humbled and degraded."
Beyond that, though, he knew very little about old-age pensions. Still, Abe
and Frank Hering managed to work together until sometime in April
1923. Hering had praised Abe to others for the work he was doing and
had been told by none other than John Andrews of the American Association for Labor Legislation that Abe was the best assistant he could ever
have, and that "his reports were the best produced in America." But Hering was no Jim Maurer, who had let Abe run his own show. Rather, as the
former president of the Eagles, Hering was looking for a lot of publicity
to make them look good, and he also wanted plenty of it for himself as the
guiding genius. Typical of the problems between the two men was that
Abe wanted to go to hearings and propose legislation. Hering wanted him
to churn out a lot of press releases. In addition, when Abe set up appointments for Hering to meet and influence lawmakers, he refused to go,
afraid that Abe might be stealing his thunder. Abe was furious and felt
that Hering was afraid of his influence. So he went behind Hering's back
and had meetings with lawmakers himself. When Hering discovered
Abe's independent behavior he ordered him to confine himself to research
and sent him clerical work to handle. When lawmakers then wrote to Abe

personally, Hering was irate and insisted that all communication be addressed only to him. He even fired a stenographer in Indianapolis who was communicating with lawmakers on Abe's behalf. What really infuriated Abe was that the Eagles supported inadequate laws, but Hering pointedly refused him any say over policy. In Abe's view the Eagles' willingness to sponsor almost any law as long as it contained the words "old-age pension" would only ruin the old-age pension movement. Explaining his philosophy, Hering told the Eagles that "the pensioner would have to be an exceedingly good citizen, with a history of habitual industriousness, habitual loyalty to family obligations, and freedom from all crimes involving more than four months imprisonment." All this was ridiculous to Abe, who hated such indignities. He pointedly criticized the Eagles for not objecting to the humiliating poorhouse laws—Hering was just confusing his personal morality with economic deprivation, and doing more harm than good. In a year Abe's job was at a dead end, and on July 1, 1923, Hering fired Abe. Insulting letters were hurled back and forth between the two men. Hering accused Abe of egotism and inordinate personal ambition. Abe retaliated by telling his friends that Hering was pygmy-minded and a main-streeter (referring to the title of the Sinclair Lewis book), in addition to being a moron.

Unfortunately, the dispute badly damaged Abe's reputation among reformers. The received opinion was that he was difficult and uncooperative. As always, whenever there was a crisis he reached out to his friends for support. But not all of them saw it his way. "I know your assets and liabilities," one wrote, "and your boss had a great measure of justice in his complaints . . . how foolish to write letters [about Hering] on office stationery with office stenographers . . . I hate to feel that these characteristics will stand in your way." Another tried to get him a new job with Brookwood Labor College but admitted that those she approached "seem to feel just as Hering felt.—that you just can't cooperate—that you have an enlarged impression of your own importance."

The difficulty he had in restraining himself was an emotional problem that dogged Abe for the rest of his life, and with Hering the end result was that each man formed a bitter hatred for the other. Hering remained part of the pension movement for many years, leading the Eagles in backing mostly bad legislation, taking credit whenever he could but for the most part remaining a marginal figure. For many in the movement he was more hindrance than help. Some years later he was convicted of swindling money from the Eagles. He had concocted a scheme on membership turnover by which he and an associate split three dollars of the five-dollar membership fee. When Abe was working for Hering, more was going on than he realized.

---

Abe was soon back in Harrisburg at his old job, which Maurer had kept open for him. The family packed up and went back with him, with the exception of Bernard, because Abe insisted he finish at Notre Dame. And then the fire and rocks spewed out of the simmering family volcano. With his anger and frustration over the Eagles job as backdrop and the discord with his mother mounting, Abe turned violent one day and slapped his oldest sister for defying his wishes over her schooling. He followed this up with a series of raging threats to all the others. The incident remained vivid to everyone for years. His mother, however, knew how to stand her ground and dealt with the matter very simply. On a day when Abe was absent on a trip she gathered her brood, packed her belongings, and left for New York to stay with relatives. Abe came back to an empty house and was shattered. He pleaded with friends to come and see him, and they became channels for his outbursts of unhappiness. "I have been in worse than a state of hell the last ten days," he wrote to one. "The last few years seem to have conspired against me and I feel almost overwhelmed and unable to resist much longer. The long and short of it is that my mother picked herself up last Saturday and went away with the children without even telling me where she was going or say goodbye. I have not had a line from them since. Of course it is not possible for you to surmise what this thing can mean to one who has given up everything for their sake. I am utterly crushed and I confess I dread the future as I have never dreaded it before." He felt used. He had sacrificed for his family. He was doing everything he could for them. Why must they resist? It was only ignorance and stupidity on their part. That he might be acting from other motives, that he might be trying to show them he was a better father than their own, never occurred to him. Their father, it was clear, had come to America, hated it, and failed. Abe had stayed and succeeded. How could they not see that? And now America was open for them as well—no more pogroms, no more starvation, no more fear, only opportunity. A lawyer friend of the family in New York held a different view. "Your mother tells me," he wrote, "that your late father never in his life found fault with her cooking, that he was always kind and gentle, that he never lifted his hand to administer even the mildest chastisement to any child."

For Abe the best medicine was always work, and he plunged into it. Work, hard work, burying himself in it, the fifteen-hour days that became his trademark, was apparently the only way to relieve the anguish of his damaged pride. With his mother he never found a way out of the conflict. A truce came about eventually, but they saw little of each other for many years. Unyielding, he never let up in his efforts to educate his brothers and sisters and turn them into Americans. Two of them took his advice: Bernard got his degree at Notre Dame and Esther graduated from Wellesley. Abe footed the bill for both of them. The other two, Gertrude and Sam, went into the delicatessen business, never lost their thick accents, and became as American as anyone can possibly become in that line of work. The score between Abe and his mother, who never mastered English and knew only Yiddish, was two to two as far as her children were concerned—a standoff.

Despite the frenzied turmoil of his newly acquired family responsibilities and the frustration with Hering and the Eagles, Abraham Epstein was certain of where he wanted to go. Regardless of every obstacle in his path, including the many he placed there himself, he knew what he must do in the brief time we have to live: he must fight—something he was always eager to do—for the welfare of the aged, the infirm, the unemployed, and his family.

None of this can explain the single-minded passion that propelled him. All I am able to do is uncover the silhouette of a man hidden behind the parable of the frail, hungry, immigrant youth, who as Philip Roth writes, is "the Jew set free, an animal so ravished and agitated by his inexhaustible new hunger that he rears up suddenly and bites his tail."

And then Henriette Marie-Louise Castex danced into his life.


7


When Cupid withdrew his shaft and left Henriette with a three-hundred-page book in her lap called *Facing Old Age,* what followed was not sweetly colored like the amours of a Fragonard painting. Rather, the picture might resemble the aftermath of a tornado. The twister has approached from a distance, dancing and twirling around the people it ensnares, then carries them off in a parable of the *Wizard of Oz.*

Shortly after the incident of the dance and the book, Henriette was surprised—she said—to receive a letter from Abe Epstein inviting her to lunch in Philadelphia. She went, and once again they talked and talked— about the postwar problems in Europe, and how awful the Women's College was—and soon little notes began to fly back and forth between Harrisburg and Newark, Delaware. On small sheets Henriette wrote sparely to "Mr. Epstein"—as if she wanted to leave no evidence—about meeting places and train times, and soon the agreed-upon trysting place became the halfway point between them, Philadelphia, the City of Brotherly Love. But Henriette was uneasy and insisted to Mr. Epstein that she not be kept waiting for one moment at the train station. His replies to her anxieties have not survived the natural scattering of objects, but he made a few excited entries in his little pocket diary: "Letter from Henriette. Happy anticipation."

---

Visions of early romance have stirred my imagination. I can see Henriette in her shapely fur-collar coat, searching nervously throughout the cavernous hall of the Philadelphia train station for a sign of Abe Epstein. And then suddenly there he is, rushing toward her, his boxy, sturdy winter coat flying, his shoes echoing through the vast space. To try and find the truth of this story I have pulled letters from envelopes, checked diary entries, looked at pictures, panting for some bit of revelation, that moment of intimacy that would tell me what happened next, but the words and photographs have refused to elaborate. Still, when Henriette was in her eighties and we were seated uncomfortably close on the ancient sagging couch, I once brashly asked her what she had felt when she first started seeing Abe, but she looked away and immediately began to talk about something else.

"You must remember," she told me, "that at that time I had played a lot of tennis in the south of France. I played with the heir to the throne of Annam, Bao Dai, who was going to be the emperor under French rule in Indochina. He had cousins and various relatives where we lived. And I became friends with all of them."

When I recovered from the astonishing change of subject I realized that the diversion was meant to remind me of who was the real star in the story I was looking for. It was not Abe Epstein, but an attractive and untested Henriette, fresh with an English education, tennis racquet in hand, a young lady much in demand in the circles that surrounded a Vietnamese emperor in waiting. For someone who had lived until then, apart from her English sojourn, a life in keeping with the rhythms of rural France, it was a thrilling time. She was socializing with people who were involved with government, with politics, with culture, people who were "interesting," as she put it. She would soon come to contrast all of it with Delaware and its College for Women, which had turned out to be just the opposite.

"Lights shall be extinguished at ten p.m. Fridays and Saturdays at 10:30 p.m." read the rules. Overnight absences had to be requested and approved in writing, chaperons were required at evening parties "where men are present," and it was Dupont this and Dupont that and mustn't we thank the Duponts. She had applied to go to Vassar or Bryn Mawr, but was told she was going to Delaware, a place that no one in France had ever heard of. She was stuck—literally—behind the walls of the Women's College.

But then Abe Epstein came bursting upon her with his car that could only hold three people. He was definitely "interesting." Far more "interesting" than the Women's College. He could hold her attention. He had written a book. And best of all, he listened to her. Her head began to spin. Who on earth would want to remain at the Women's College of the University of Delaware under the watchful eye of Dean Winifred Robinson when the outside world had so much more to offer?

The Philadelphia rendezvous picked up in frequency. Abe took her to the theater and a salvaged pile of programs points to *Cyrano de Bergerac*, starring the great Walter Hampden—taking her to a French classic in English was a nimble choice. His pocket diary began to fill up with references to her: how happy she made him, how eagerly he wanted to see her, how he loved her hair. They went to more plays in New York. They took off for Atlantic City together, where they strolled the boardwalk and watched the sunsets. Photographs were taken—Henriette in stylish short-bobbed hair, frilly flapper dress, posed as if ready to prance on the beach, Abe in hat and solid winter coat, with the faint trace of a smile. She wrote her parents about him, said it was a "hint," and scolded her mother for not getting a shawl to her on time because she wanted to wear it on Saturday in "Philadelphie."

"Everything you send is late because you write the address badly. It's Newark, the W's are badly written," she wrote in irritation. Her mother composed the address in capitals and the postal clerks became confused. Was the letter for New York or Newark?

She began addressing Abe as "Dear," then "Darling Boy," then "Baby," and finally "Baby Boy." It was very "twenties," and Henriette was catching on. Abe's diary started filling up with phrases such as, "How wonderful the world can appear when there's love and returned love." Indeed love was merrily awhirl—when without warning Dean Winifred Robinson called young Mademoiselle Castex into her office and told her bluntly that the college did not approve of girls meeting boys unchaperoned. Henriette was stunned and then irate.

Abe and Henriette in Atlantic City, 1924 or 1925.

"I don't know what's in the back of their heads at the college, but it's medieval—like a convent in the Middle Ages!" she bristled to Abe Epstein. "I can't believe it's America at all."

But that was only the beginning. Into this idyll the cold wind of "Society," as in an Edith Wharton novel, started whipping up a storm. She had been seen by two other girls in Atlantic City—with a man! Dean Robinson wanted to know what was going on. The college authorities were angry. If she kept up that sort of behavior she would be sent back, they told her. Henriette began to panic. She felt the walls closing in. She hated the Women's College and their "old maid stupidity," but her reputation was at stake. A whirlwind was in the making. A man named Champenois, in charge of the French exchange students, informed her that she had violated the terms of her scholarship. She had a non-quota visa to be in the United States, conditioned on her moral behavior as a student. If she carried on like this she would be tossed out of the country in disgrace. The stern Miss Robinson wanted to know who the man was. An old friend of the family, Henriette stammered and lied. How long could that story hold up? Mrs. Virginia Newcomb, who lived on Park Avenue in New York and was a grand lady of influence when it came to French exchange students, refused to even consider seeing Henriette, and instead cast doubts on her worthiness as a scholarship holder. Hysterically, Henriette pleaded with "Baby Boy" to help her out. She asked him whether all he had written was just "words, words, words." She was being treated like a tramp, she wailed. They would send her back to France, to the boring life of a small town, her reputation as a woman, a woman entering the adventure of life, forever damaged.

"Baby Boy" was unfazed and like a true knight errant rode to the rescue. From what he had been through, Henriette's torments must have seemed like nothing more than a pin prick on the arm. Special Delivery letters (a now-vanished breed) flew back and forth between Harrisburg, Newark, and New York. The name of Abe Epstein surfaced and the dreaded Champenois telegrammed that it was imperative she come to his office with Epstein "if you wish to avoid trouble." Epstein calmly replied by letter that they would be there and he would clarify everything. And as quickly as the menacing storm arose, it also swiftly rumbled away.

---

Marriage, coupled with the coming of Spring, had chased the threatening clouds away. Never one for subtlety, Henriette gushed to Abe in gratitude, "if winter comes can spring be far behind. Don't you think it applies to you and me?" Expulsion from the United States was no longer a threat. The dreaded Champenois was no longer a menace. Henriette Marie-Louise Castex would become Mrs. Abraham Epstein and could stay in the United States as long as she wished. Even the august Dean Robinson was mollified and wanted nothing better than to offer a going-away party. Her fellow students were thrilled. She had gotten herself a man in no time, something that Henriette had no idea they all desired so ardently. The air around her was suddenly transformed and bubbled with excitement. The marriage would be in Philadelphia at the end of February. Could they go to New York first for three or four days, buy some things, hear a concert or two, and most importantly see his family, Henriette asked? She was happy, back in the center of things, feeling admired for what she had accomplished. Augusta Galster must come. Would it fit into her schedule? Tell her to write, Henriette insisted. On and on she babbled, sounding very relieved and much loved. The twister had been blown off course and Henriette's effusion about the coming Spring sent her thoughts leaping overseas to her parents' magnificent garden in the mountain town of Prades. She wrote Abe that in that paradise "there is a little tree which blossoms by the end of January and the flowers are red, all red, almost like flame. When I awake in the morning I see, from my bedroom window, the little tree, so fine, so brave, which manages to look pretty and sweet in spite of the cold north wind which nips the tender little flowers! I always admired that tree. It is very courageous."

Henriette's literary framework came from the world of the British Romantic poets with their love of flowers and nature, which she had dutifully absorbed during her English school days. But a closer look at the above text provides an eye-opening insight. In the last sentence the word "He" is blacked out and changed to "It," so that a sentence that once read "He is very courageous" becomes "It is very courageous." The tree, with its valiant little flowers, is now not a man but gender neutral, and since French has no neutral, only masculine and feminine genders, the person who is so pretty and sweet, so brave in the face of the wintry blasts of Champenois, Robinson, Newcomb, and company can only be Henriette. But digging deeper, who was the person responsible for fending off that "cold north wind"? Who took the icy blasts and blew them right back in the face of the enemy? Why, none other than "Baby Boy" Epstein, who had little fear of the prim world ruled by such capitalists as the Duponts and their minions. Opposition brought out the best in him. When he knew what he wanted he set out to get it, and when the Women's College wanted to be paid for the entire year although Miss Castex was no longer in attendance, "Baby Boy" shrugged it off. He let the authorities stew in their own juices for a year, then with little fanfare dropped a check in the mail, remarking to a friend, "In the old days they used to buy their brides. I suppose that's what the University of Delaware wants."

Throughout her life Henriette rarely acknowledged the contributions of others in solving her life's tribulations. She would trumpet her victories over the forces that were aligned against her. She never admitted the presence of someone else's aid. But she would have been wise at this time to see that it was her future husband, the militant Abe Epstein, who had bailed her out of a situation fraught with risk. His nature, his single-mindedness, his ability at handling officialdom, were sides of him that she never entirely appreciated. In her mind she was always her own hero.

---

The garden in Prades and the world of its flowers had a lot more to say. "That little tree seemed to get angry every time I plucked one of its branches, simply wouldn't let me do it and every time I was sure to come back with little drops of blood on my fingers. The irises were always willing to keep me company . . . and talk to me . . . and the beautiful mimosa trees must be all in flowers now, like waves of gold, but of a refined, pale, airy and dainty gold . . . the trees belong to me and if I cut a little branch, the bigger branches will die. Trees are like people, didn't you know that? They have their own personalities, characters, whims, just like you and me—perhaps they think. If that were true, I wonder what my favorite trees and plants would think of my little boy."

Henriette loved gardens and trees all her life, but that they were also a language for the expression of her subconscious feelings came as a jolt. Plainly, their delicacy and fragility are her delicacy and fragility—their whims are her whims. And lurking beneath her canny parable was the question of whether her "favorite trees and plants" would approve of "Baby Boy." A gentle warning is contained in the ability of the trees and flowers to think, and sadly, those warnings from the world of plants came to life, years later, in words of rage.

---

Henriette was never very interested in talking about her romantic past. "I'm not the type of person who falls in love with people and can completely obliterate her own character and completely submerge herself into someone else's personality . . . but I was not surprised when he asked me to marry him. Of course I was not happy at Delaware and meeting a man like Abe was a great relief from all that monotony. I thought that life with Abe would be a challenge and would have many interesting moments," is how she once told the story of her marriage. But this emphatic declaration was offered after many years had gone by. The wonder of new love had been forgotten. She was safely enthroned where she wanted to be, at the center of the story.

The truth, I believe, lies elsewhere—in the fluttering endearments she coined, the kisses she sent, in her loving to bite his neck, in her coquettish reproach to him for tearing her dress and messing up her hair, and all the other words she wrote and passions she felt at that time. She had once experienced those feelings but in later years would never discuss them. But they come back to life for me in Abe's scrawled words of joy—"the joyous heart . . . Hurrah for love and life!" Henriette enchanted him. Her flirtatious ways, her skipping and dancing, her French background, and the fact that he was to be finally married, like all his friends, made Abe happy perhaps for the first time in his life. Those feelings overwhelmed him and led to his union with Henriette on March 17, 1925, in Philadelphia, four months after they had met, and six months after she had arrived in America. It was simply love—between two very unlikely people: a poor

Russian Jew with a reformer's flame, and a French Catholic daughter of the bourgeoisie looking for something new. The ceremony took place in the rectory of a Catholic Church, St. John the Evangelist, because Henriette wanted no trouble from her parents on that front. A dispensation was secured from the diocese in Washington by telephone. Abe the fixer had friends in high places and knew how to get things done fast.

He did not forget to enter the moment in his little pocket diary: *"The Greatest Day!"*

8

As soon as the ceremony was over the newlyweds caught the train back to Harrisburg, and the very next morning the groom went off to work leaving the bride to face an irate landlady demanding more rent for another person in the house. No one had informed her that her bachelor tenant was returning with a wife. When the new husband arrived home expecting to be greeted lovingly by his bride on the second day of marriage, he received an outburst instead.

"This isn't the kind of life I expect to have in this country. I didn't leave Delaware for this sort of thing."

"Well, you can come and work in the office with me, but you won't be paid for your work."

"Why?"

"Well, in the first place, you don't have experience in the kind of work I'm doing . . ."

"Well, that can be acquired. That's not very difficult."

"I know you can do it very quickly. But there is another drawback . . . in the state of Pennsylvania husband and wife cannot work in the same office, and I might have a lot of trouble . . ."

"Oh . . . in that case I will work for nothing. I would rather do some work because that's what I came to America for. I didn't come to be idle. I didn't come to become a good wife and mother and be engrossed in the care of a house, in cooking, cleaning and all. I might as well have stayed in France for that."

"Yes . . . of course," was the muttered reply.

The next morning husband and wife went to the office together, causing quite a stir. The young ladies who worked in the Department of Welfare at the state capitol, who were not all that young, were not too happy to see one of the single men go off and get married. Abe was not the world's sexiest man. He was short, balding even then, tended to a paunch, and always wore glasses. But he had been eligible, one of the few, and he seemed to be going places. And now he had gone off and married "some little French girl," confirming everyone's suspicions in the backwater town of Harrisburg of what French girls were really like. Henriette managed, nonetheless, to find a place for herself in the office. She knew her English. She knew it better than some of the native-born she worked with. She set about correcting one of the reports.

"What are you doing?" Abe asked.

"How can people understand English like this?" Henriette retorted. "Look at the sentences. Why do people write such clumsy language that no one can understand? I know English and this isn't right."

And she went to work, all the time looking over her shoulder at the reactions of the "Harrisburg maidens," as she called them. She knew the office workers gossiped behind her back, murmuring to each other that Mr. Epstein had made the mistake of his life in marrying "that stupid French girl," and how he would live to regret it.

One of Henriette's trusty beliefs was that when someone thought they had her pinned down she was capable of turning the tables on them and winning all by herself. Many years later she received a letter from one of the "Harrisburg maidens" who had been eying Abe Epstein, and was told that no one else could have done what she had done. Henriette chortled in vindication. "The stupid French girl" had triumphed at last. In Henriette's mind people always lived to regret their misguided opinion of her.

Then a forgotten imperative began to seep into the enchantment of newlywed life, demanding that Henriette do more than ask someone else to bail her out. Her parents wanted her back in France. They wanted to know who her husband was. They wanted to meet him. They had been warned about the dangers their headstrong daughter would face in America. Before Henriette had sailed for America an old friend of the family had predicted that she would run off with "un homme des Amériques" and would never come back to France. Now what they feared had happened, and they were bewildered. She sailed back to somehow explain this startling turn of events in May 1925, leaving her new husband behind, the prey of those jealous "Harrisburg maidens." It was agreed, nonetheless, that he would tear himself away sometime that summer and sail to France to meet the folks.

Party life on the S.S. *America* kept her anxieties at bay temporarily, but when the week at sea was over and the ship moved slowly past the breakwater and into the harbor at Cherbourg, her parents, Jean-Marie and Elisa

Castex, sailed out from the dock on the ship's tender so that they might be the first French on board. Henriette quickly seized the initiative and before her parents could ask one question escorted them to her cabin where they could view the many flowers and candies bestowed on her by Abe as a parting gift. They were impressed, and saw that her husband, whoever he was, at least knew how to pamper their daughter. Then it was on to Paris, where Henriette returned to her old way of life with surprising ease. Her parents shopped for her, bought her clothes and china, and spoiled their wayward child. She went to the theater, saw Pavlova, the great Russian ballerina, and a dance piece by the risqué Loïe Fuller, famous for appearing near to naked in flowing diaphanous skirts. Her devout and Catholic mother refused to accompany her—for her the city of Paris was a cesspool of immorality and the theater its cardinal sin. It troubled Henriette. She wrote Eppie that she couldn't imagine any "modern American girl promenading in Paris and not accomplishing what she intended." And then one morning after breakfast in their grand hotel on the boulevard Haussman, near the Opera, her mother stunned Henriette with a confidential talk on the subject of love and marriage. "Maman said something horrible this morning . . . that men were charming the first months of their marriage . . . then love never lasted long and faded with the years of mutual life. All men do the same and there is no exception in this world." These shocking words led to an outpouring of love toward her beloved Eppie. "Last night I actually cried in bed and in the morning I awoke with 'little Eppie' on my lips." She had been too hard on him, she confessed. "I have an evil conscience. I have been playing with your beautiful love like a naughty kitten pulling and scratching the threads of a splendid embroidery. The idea that you will not always love me and stand by my side is entirely unbearable."

Abe's reply to the panicky Henriette was to assure her that "Maman" was wrong about men, and even if it was true he was the exception. He tried to cheer her with the tale of a dream he had on the sleeper returning from Denver, where he had given a speech. "The gorgeous dream I had last night has impressed itself indelibly on my mind. I can still see the picture of our walking arm in arm over the gardens of our new villa which we had just built over the sea. As we were walking I picked the most beautiful flowers for you which you carried in your arm and in your marvelous hair. Something you said smilingly pleased me so much and gave me such a thrill that I started hugging and kissing you with all my energies. The Pullman pillow must have given way to my powerful squeezing and I awoke. Now I submit for me to dream such a dream is a mighty indica-

Abe and Henriette in the
Pyrenees, 1925. On the back
is written in Henriette's hand:
"Eppie and Baby near a
shepherd's hut. La Bouil-
louse." La Bouillouse is a
lake in the Pyrenees.

tion of the power and purity of my love and can be nothing but a good
omen." "Baby Boy" had taken Henriette's language of flowers and made
it speak for himself and his feelings.

Eppie, as everyone now called Abe, hit the shores of France at the end
of June. Henriette had warned him to kiss everyone on both cheeks, keep
his pocket handkerchief well folded, and let no one know that he had traveled in second class. And it was imperative he show everyone in France
how much he loved his "baby girl." Well coached, Eppie performed all
the appropriate courtesies demanded of an American who had shocked
everyone by marrying the daughter of a well-established provincial bourgeois family. The meeting with Père et Mère Castex went well, despite the
fact that Abe spoke almost no French and they spoke no English. Everyone seems to have had a good time together in spite of the language bar-

Prades, France. 1925. Abe and Henriette in the garden of her parent's house.

rier, judging by the photographs of rambles in the Pyrenees where everyone posed with flair by streams and mountain huts, their canes at the
ready. The newlyweds were also captured in stylish '20s garb, white pants
and blue blazer for Abe, flowing flapper dress for Henriette, linked arm
in arm in the garden of the house at Prades, surrounded by the lush plants
and flowers that grew there in abundance and that had inspired so much
ardent prose.

It was all perfect—except for an aspect of Henriette's skittish nature
that was triggered by life back in France. In the rush of infatuation with
Eppie, she had forgotten that France was her childhood home and the
south and its mountains were the places she loved most in the world. It
was in those picturesque surroundings that she had lived a pampered and
comfortable existence for her first twenty-five years. Suddenly, it dawned
on her that life with Abe would not be so cozy. It would be in America,
probably Harrisburg, one of the dullest towns in the not particularly exciting state of Pennsylvania. Her attraction to Abe was more of a romantic fantasy than she knew. His ability to write books and organize, the respect he received from his colleagues, his energy, all that had been more
of a glamorous attraction than a reason to change her way of life. In France

she had lived the good life—good food, good wine, good clothes, and maids. In Harrisburg it would be life in an apartment, in a world full of polemics and anxiety, and an uncertain place in the hard-working Eppie's world.

During the course of the "get to meet the folks" summer, Abe and Henriette began to look down into the chasm that separated them, a hollow they had skipped over when they fell in love. Eppie returned to Harrisburg in late August and Henriette lingered on, enjoying the luxuries of life with her family, but she was soon sending a steady stream of letters flowing on the great ships back to the United States, a torrent of gripes.

"The idea of staying in Harrisburg is unbearable . . . Your recklessness renders every plan of mine impossible and I will ask for a complete account of everything and every bill so that I can see what the matter is with you, and if things do not meet with my approval you will indeed have a terrible time . . . My family is not at all pleased with you and they have hinted several times that I should not stay in America, indeed a great many people have mentioned that America was doing me a lot of harm since I was completely changed . . . For your sake I now have a collection of dresses for the office with collars and long sleeves according to the 'modesty pattern' you like . . . "

His letters were too short, she complained. He was busy, she knew, but didn't he owe her more than a few words if his love for her was so great? She wanted more work in the office and wanted to be paid. "I must be very frank with you," she wrote, "and confess that the prospect of another winter in Harrisburg is far from being pleasant. Happiness is like a very delicate plant," she stated, employing her floral metaphor for the hundredth time. "It has to be cultured, it has to be nursed, and taken care of." In America, she was now fully aware, she would never be the princess she had been in France.

Abe did his best to reason with her. "Why are you so keen about worrying yourself tired on account of all sorts of imaginary ills?" he wrote after she had seen a doctor about unsettling pains in her stomach—certainly an expression of her resistance to returning to Harrisburg. "You worry yourself to exhaustion for fear of not getting paid for your work whereas I have already gotten a check for you." Then he said what was really on his mind. "Must one always run away with her emotions instead of facing at least a few of the actual facts? And above all why draw final conclusions about the future? Where there's love there's no place for prejudices and superstitions . . . I look at the office, the apartment, Harrisburg, our entire struggle, as merely passing moments on the road towards a perfect love and an all embracing happiness." But with Henriette it was best to keep a sharp eye, and he ended his letter: "Of course, dearest heart, this is no lecture and I do not want you to take it as such. I have really not missed dreaming of you sweetheart a single night for almost two weeks."

Abe's words had the expected soothing effect, for although she could not abide the thought of Harrisburg, Henriette looked forward to being once more in the arms of her "baby boy." The doctor had "looked everywhere and discovered nothing wrong with little tummy." His advice was open air and exercise and "since my troubles are of a nervous origin, not to get homesick!" She celebrated the good news by rushing back into the mountains, climbing and picking mushrooms. "Such a fine day in the woods. Baby was running wild, kicking like a horse and jumping and shouting." She was bringing back a lot of lovely objects from "fair France," including a big fat French cookbook. "Now Mr. Cook," she twittered, "please get ready!"

Of course, there were a number of special needs that needed to be met. As a non-American she would be waiting in line longer than the natives when she disembarked. Could Eppie get on the tender, as her parents had done in Cherbourg, and board the ship before anyone else? Perhaps he could finesse her through immigration ahead of the other passengers? He was also warned about the U.S. customs—all that she was bringing back must get in without a hitch. But despite her demands she looked forward to the reunion, and signed her last letter, "Yours eternally, who loves you more than ever. Baby Girl."

What this impassioned pair truly needed was something that they had missed in the rush to matrimony. "2 or 3 days of honeymoon will be more than necessary, will be essential, because I am hungry, no starved for your sweet, charming presence and one day will not be enough to devour you with kisses. You better do as much work as you can before I come and leave 2 or 3 days for the meeting." She returned to New York on October 5 to what was, one hopes, two or three days of glorious bliss. But time has passed and with it even the tiniest whiff of what happened on those autumn days.

## An Affair with the Atlantic

June 1992. *Long and lonely, the curved bulk of the Queen Elizabeth 2 looms at rest over the empty piers and gray waters of Manhattan's Hudson River. Painted a stark black and white, she sports a touch of red on her smoke stacks, like an ancient lady off to a ball with a bright scarf at her neck to remind her of gaiety long past. The roofed dock is long and hollow, like a stadium the fans have emptied when the game is over. The men taking the passports and tickets, and the sailors in their naval whites standing idly, are distant spots in the emptiness. The steel sky and grim water offer a view barren of ships. The great harbor and river of New York seem to have lost all purpose. A small number of elderly people move resolutely through this shed of echoes toward the gangplank, nearing a youthful crew posed in lounging boredom against the dock's barriers, while a desultory ship's band twangs out the notes of "Annie Laurie." I gaze on these aged, slow-moving, silent few.*

*My mother is among them.*

---

*Henriette first crossed the Atlantic Ocean in September 1924, to come to the United States as an exchange student. Not many months later she recrossed it back to her native France on the S.S. America to explain to her astonished mother and father how during that brief time away from them she had met and married an American. Deferring any thought of the inevitable confrontation over her marriage to a politically radical Russian Jew, she made sure to have a high old time on board. In a shipboard letter she twittered away to her husband of three months: "I did dance with 3 or 4 men, uninteresting ones compared to my sweet little boy . . . till I did hit a nice boy from Arkansas . . . as to my love story he remarked: 'your husband must be a clever boy to get nice things as soon as he sees them.' This, dear boy, is all the flirting I have done. Another boy also tried to learn French from me . . ."*

In another letter she wrote, *"Monday evening—Grand Bal Masqué said a big sign and of course I didn't want to be entirely left out of the fun! My position as a respectable married woman forbade me anything too daring as was the habit in my younger days. Masquerades were a delight to me, and I successfully appeared as a tawny-face Gypsy or a flighty Spanish dancer with a comb as big as a plate . . . and a fan to give boys an opportunity to pick it up when it fell on the floor. The happy era came to an end when my dear boy stepped into the dance. So I remembered his Socialistic theories and how sacred labour is to him and therefore dressed as a . . . maid—yes dear I was a maid: my black velvet, a little white apron with lace and a delightfully charming cap formed all my apparel—with rouge naturally. People said I looked 'cute.'"*

It was then that my mother began her love affair with the Atlantic.

───────────

That frisky crossing was the start of a way of life on the high seas that became for Henriette forever part of who she was. She loved the crossings, she loved the ocean, she loved the food, and she loved the ships. For her, life on the great transatlantic liners became a world within a world, an ocean home in passing, a city suspended somewhere between her two worlds of France and the United States, between her family and Abe. She met people, she talked, she danced, she had "fun." It was a society where all that mattered was that one be entertaining and be entertained, a life in limbo, where she was free to create and imagine herself in any role of her choosing, and where there was no one who could tell her what to do. The ships of the French Line, with their studied elegance and renowned cuisine, welcomed her on their crossings during the 1920s and 1930s. The Champlain, the Paris, the Lafayette, the Ile de France, there seemed to be a never-ending line of ships moving east and west on the Atlantic waves. Her own mother once wrote in amazement, when waiting for Henriette at Cherbourg, "4 ships came in today. The Majestic, The Leviathan, The America, and one more. There were also four departures . . . quel mouvement."

It was the Second World War that lowered the curtain on the world of the transatlantic liner—as it did on many other things. The Champlain struck a mine and sank. The Paris burned. The Lafayette sank in port. The Normandie burned and capsized in New York harbor. One by one the great ships of the French Line vanished from the Atlantic, including, after the war, the Ile de France, the Flandre, and the Liberté, all sold or confined to the scrap heap. A last stab at maintaining the elegance of the French Line's Atlantic crossing was a ship named simply France. But she failed to turn a profit and was sold, and a way of life fad-

*ed to near oblivion. Now there was one ship remaining, the Cunard Line's QE 2, but she was only a pale version of the French Line's greyhounds of the 1930s, a humdrum stainless vessel making fewer trips every year—and she wasn't even French.*

*Nonetheless, like the custodian of a vanished religion, Henriette brushed all that aside and remained loyal to her world in limbo. Twice a year she boarded the QE 2 to make the trip from New York to France and back.*

---

*Henriette has asked that a wheelchair be provided for her before boarding the ship and after a short moment it is brought by a bearded Scots purser, his voice a rolling burr of words. She is not the only one to be so shuttled. Like bodies on a conveyer belt, many like her, rolling along in their stainless rigs, are moved mechanically into the belly of the ship. The feeble strain of music coming from the small ship's band tries vainly to ignore this pitiful scene and evoke instead the grand, fun-loving ocean departures of the past. But compared to the packed sailings of years ago only a small number of people disappear behind the steel plates of the Cunard Line's finest.*

*Those graceful vessels of the past were palaces on the water that resonated with the glamor and gaiety of ocean travel: the champagne drunk at departure, the chanted cries of "All Ashore!" the fond, hugging farewells, the ringing of bells, the sound of whistles, the dockside crowds waving and cheering as the massive steel sides of the ship slowly separated from the land, the basso blare of the ship's horn, the colored streamers unfurled and flying through air, dying in the lengthening expanse of water between ship and dock, and the ship itself, grand and majestic as it made its stately turn to face down the Hudson waterway, diminishing gradually, its fluttering flags barely visible as it moved past New York's Statue of Liberty. Now the sensual and bacchanalian tone of those vintage departures has been transformed and turned in on itself. From a spectacle where those who floated away blew kisses to those who remained behind rooted to the land, the scene is now one of a vanishing village of the near dead, its residents barely able to raise their arms in a wave. The passengers are graying and feeble, the sailors young and languid. As they board their Queen of the Seas, everyone seems to be playing some mock-up game of the good times gone by.*

*The band switches tunes, injecting pep into the moment with a slow-paced version of "Volaré."*

*Henriette insists, as always, on having her picture taken by the ship's photographer with me at her side. I am suddenly on edge.*

*"Mother, we already have this picture, many times over. Do you really want another one?"*

Henriette's last voyage by ship to France, June 1992.
Accompanied by the author and his son.

There is already a file of QE 2 photographs at home that run to more than twenty-five. We're always caught in the same stilted pose, a lifesaver with the ship's name beside us, like some shot taken at a carnival that will be viewed many years later with puzzlement.

She ignores me. "Oh, but it will be a lot of fun! I will send you a copy," she tells me as she offers the photographer her most alert smile, one that seems to characterize almost every photo ever taken of her.

I lean over her diminutive frame in the wheelchair, waiting for the photographer to get it over with. I look down on her white scattered hair, her colorful print dress covered with an aging car coat, her knees wrapped in her ever-present leg warmers as insurance against the cold. She wants this memento desperately, and bravely she struggles to make it festive. It is as if by repeating this moment year after year we trace a line down into a richer and more radiant time, that of the enchanted past.

"How much fun can this really be when everyone is so old and feeble?" I think.

*But the words remain unspoken. I sense instead that I am looking on the end of a world in limbo that began for Henriette with her arrival in America in 1924.*

*When the photo opportunity is over, the next aging passengers are lined up to have the same popping flash done to them, and I scrupulously watch my mother as she is slowly wheeled away by the burly Scotsman. My eyes never leave her. But she has already forgotten my presence. They have started to talk, and he bends over and tries to make her more comfortable by adjusting the small bag that hangs from the wheelchair. She rolls away and disappears momentarily behind a barrier, then reappears for an instant, managing a few final waves accompanied by one of her patented forced grins that are meant to remind me of what a good time she is looking forward to, before vanishing for good up the covered gangplank. That grin, that moment, will become a stop-frame in my mind.*

*I slowly move away, down the emptiness of the pier. I feel my face involuntarily tighten. My eyes are constricted. I suppress tears. All I can see before me is the past—like the arc of one of those colored streamers flying and dying between ship and shore—and its unforgiving sadness. I am moving away from an event, one I have seen too many times and that has now become the final act in a shadow play. I turn to one side looking for another living person. There is no one. I am walking in a graveyard. There is only the cavernous dock, the hollow, the echo. And into that void my tears just keep on coming.*

9

Henriette somehow survived another grim winter in Harrisburg, but as soon as June 1926 came she made a quick exit back to France. From the pier in New York, Abe watched her leave. He was not happy about it, but Henriette was not in a loving mood, and her first letter set the tone for the rest of the summer separation. "I tried to find you at the extreme end of the dock. You were interested in everything else and didn't concentrate on Baby."

Abe tried his best to calm her. "You think I didn't go to the end of the pier. I was there . . . Boris and Izzy (his brothers) lifted me on their shoulders and I saw you and shouted but you didn't hear me."

She hadn't seen or heard, and once back in France both the frolic and malaise of the previous summer started spinning like an old recording. She compared their great love to the unhappiness of others—her mother and father—gloried in the food, flowers, and wines of France, pleaded with him to find work in Europe—she would never be happy unless he did—and had her customary check-up for the problems of "little tummy." Her watchful mother even wrote "Cher Eppie" to reassure him after the X-rays that "tous les organes étaient bien à leur place"—all of Henriette's insides were in their proper positions.

But underneath the testy chatter, Henriette was being sucked, bit by bit, into Abe's prolific activities. "Don't forget to keep me informed of everything . . . don't let anybody take advantage of what you are doing . . . and work hard!" was how she stayed involved at long distance. She even tried to copy Abe's assertive writing by carving her own niche and labored over the draft of an article she wanted to send to a French feminist journal. "The other day I met with my French friend who is opposed to Women's Suffrage," she began, and then after a page and a half she sent it to Abe. "Please give your opinion of my little article." This stab at asserting her female rights was proceeded by a long tirade. "I think Daddy is not quite pleased with you for the bad care you have taken of his little girl . . . If you persist in your ridiculous ways . . . I shall have to break our association and rely on somebody else to provide for my future."

Her rambling letters were contradictory, hardly the correct pose of a determined feminist; perhaps they only reflected the protests of a young married woman who was spoiled when back home and not ready to accept a relationship with a man who had done nothing but work all his life. Henriette was in the throes of a fluttering, blundering, unknowing struggle to find a balance between her two competing selves—one who enjoyed the pampering comforts of her French life, and one who lived in America, trying to adjust to the busy world of the enterprising Abe.

When Henriette returned in September, dreading yet another winter in Harrisburg, she found Abe feverishly occupied in working on an idea for the future of old-age security. At that time a law on pensions had actually been passed by the Pennsylvania legislature and signed by Governor Gifford Pinchot on May 23, 1923. It had called for a stipend of a dollar a day for anyone over seventy who had lived for fifteen years in Pennsylvania and had less than a dollar a day in income. There were some odd conditions as well—for example, that the pensioner must not be a tramp or a beggar. But there was a hitch: the legislature had appropriated only twenty-five thousand dollars for the next two-year fiscal period for administrative costs only. Yet despite this limited budget, Abe had been working hard to create the office that would actually hand out the money when the law was fully funded, and was seeking out prospective pensioners as well. The dream of his youthful altruism was being fulfilled, when with almost no warning—before a single dollar could ever leave the state treasury, be transferred to Abe's new office, and handed over to a poor old man or woman—everything suddenly fell apart. The law had been challenged in the courts by an irate business community on the grounds that it was an improper delegation of legislative power, discriminatory in its age limits and qualifications, violated the Fourteenth Amendment, and, to top it all off, appropriated public money for private purposes. This last charge was unearthed based on an old Civil War statute that said the state was not permitted to give money to individuals. On August 4, 1925, the law was ruled unconstitutional in the Dauphin County Court. It was immediately appealed by the State of Pennsylvania, but on February 2, 1925, the state supreme court settled the pension battle once and for all and ruled it unconstitutional as well. A dollar a day was just too much for them to stomach. The humanitarian edifice that Abe and his allies had labored to erect in Pennsylvania crashed to the ground, never to rise from the dust. Five years would be needed to bypass the court with a constitutional amendment, a process far too arduous for the impatient Abe. When his rage had cooled and his disappointment died, he mocked the judges' preposterous reasoning. "Under the clause Pennsylvania is not allowed to make contributions to hospitals or to pay pensions to mothers or even judges—but the state does. Indeed, the judges took very great pains in pointing out that there was a very clear distinction between the judge's pensions and our form of pensions. The judges' form of pensions, they said, was not a pension at all, but was merely 'compensation for hazardous public service.'"

But after that satirical blast, and despite his anger, Abe did not descend into a funk. Instead, his antennae were up and quivering, and he went on a very capricious escapade. A man he did not know had written from Cincinnati, asking for help with his plan to pay old-age pensions throughout the country. "Here, you buy these stamps and I'll see to it that you get a pension," is how the man convincingly put it.

Abe decided he wanted to meet this man and he took the night train to Cincinnati, spent the day there, and returned to Harrisburg that evening with a collection of the little stamps. They featured pictures of nice old men and nice old ladies, sold for a nickel or a dime, and when gathered in a little book over the years, like Green Stamps, could eventually be redeemed for a pension, or so the man said.

Abe was troubled. "This man is a nut. He wants to collect dimes and nickels from old people by selling little stamps and he's promising a pension now!" he told Henriette.

The man in Cincinnati was more than likely a con man, with a Ponzi scheme to make himself rich. But something from the encounter resonated within Abe. The little stamps would be sold across the country, and the image of a national scheme propelled Abe to come to terms with something he had avoided ever since his experience with the Workers Education Bureau had ended in his nervous collapse. It was time for him to get out of Pennsylvania and present his ideas on the American stage. That is what he had been working on. And what Henriette had no way of knowing was that her real adventure in America with Abe was about to begin.

10

On a cold, gray winter day in 1927, on the banks of the Susquehanna River as it rolled past Harrisburg, Abe was off on a walk pondering his future moves. With his head bowed in thought, he watched the dark water flowing by, and when he looked up he saw his devoted friend and matchmaker, Emil Frankel, another immigrant Jew, coming toward him. Emil thought Abe looked depressed and asked what was wrong.

"I've been working for five years to create pensions for old people, Emil," Abe said. "We finally persuade the legislature to pass a law—and the state supreme court overturns it. I've got to get out of Harrisburg."

"Where will you go?"

"New York, to continue the work. Forget Pennsylvania. It's hopeless." Abe looked determined. "It's time for a group that will do nothing but work to create old-age pensions."

Frankel nodded. He had known Abe since their first days in America together. The man who stood before him, bundled up against the winter cold in hat, scarf, and long bulky coat, still spoke with a heavy immigrant accent. His already balding head seemed too big for his slight body, his eyes were weak, and he always wore the same round-rimmed glasses, giving him an intense owlish look. His major handicap in Frankel's mind was that he was too prone to let any rejection turn rapidly to anger. Frankel knew how impatient Abe was and how many obstacles were in his path. He was not optimistic for his friend.

"Are you sure you want to give up the Pennsylvania job?"

"I have a meeting in New York next week with supporters who are behind my idea," Abe replied. "But I need a name. What do you think of 'The American Old Age Pension League?'"

Frankel shook his head. He told Abe he did not think the word "pension" was a good one. "That word . . . now-a-days," Emil shrugged. "Most people think it means you're getting something for nothing."

Abe frowned. He knew exactly what Frankel was talking about. Pensions meant you were lazy. If you had not saved for your old age it was your own fault.

"You should forget the word 'pension.'"

Abe was at a loss. "What word would you suggest?"

Frankel, suddenly enthusiastic, said one word: "Security."

Abe looked straight at his old friend and exclaimed, "That's it!"

Several weeks later, on February 27, 1927, twenty prominent union and religious leaders met with Abraham Epstein at the Civic Club in New York and founded the American Association for Old Age Security. Abe was named executive secretary. He was not yet thirty-five. The word "security" joined with another Abe added six years later would resonate into an idea that would change American life: social security.

Wearing the armor of that dynamic new name, Abe marched out of Harrisburg in search of people who could assist the fledgling group. There wasn't much choice. The Fraternal Order of Eagles was still poking its head into old-age pensions, but with its chief, the publicity-seeking Frank Hering, still in place, asking for help from the Eagles would be a fruitless undertaking. The only other group working in the field was the American Association for Labor Legislation, established in 1906. They had struggled mightily in those days to stop the excesses of big business. During the Progressive Era, with the strong backing of President Theodore Roosevelt, there had been a period of reform. New laws on wages and working conditions had been passed, and the first environmental regulations created. The AALL had pushed hard for laws to cover workmen's compensation, unemployment, and health insurance as well, but the votes in Congress and the state legislatures were not there, and during the reactionary 1920s, with Harding, Coolidge, and Hoover in office, the group was lying low. John Andrews, who had been in charge of the AALL from the beginning, was considered a major force in the world of American social reform. Abe had given talks at his conventions, so Andrews was a natural choice for help.

Andrews was very tall, with the patrician airs of his old American roots, and very much the archetype of the virtuous do-gooder. He towered over the diminutive Abe, and when Henriette had first met him and been introduced as Abe's wife, she found him pompous and overbearing. It seemed to her that he thought neither of them understood the United

The delegation to Albany, including members of the American
Association for Old Age Security, 1930. Abraham Epstein, first row,
on left.

States, not being "real Americans." "I am happy to see you and your new
wife," he had said to Abe, and when shaking hands added firmly, "You
look so much better." Then, with his eyes trained on Henriette, he added,
"No doubt you must be cooking him very good French food."

But Henriette would not allow the put-down, and shot right back, "I
don't know how to cook!" There was no way she would let Andrews tag
her as some flighty French girl who could only cook, clean, and be a du-
tiful little wife. Henriette was actually telling the truth—she had never
been more than a passing presence in her mother's kitchen.

But now in this second meeting Abe needed Andrews's help and was
not about to let Henriette's pique get in his way. He told Henriette to but-
ton her lip this time. But right away she could tell that Andrews was still
a snob and hostile to Abe's ideas. He told Abe he saw no need for another organization in the field of pensions. "We're doing the job," he said.
This was not true. Andrews and his organization hadn't pushed for anything on old-age pensions for a number of years and scarcely mentioned
them anywhere in their literature. Abe pleaded with Andrews to help his

new association in any way he could, by making a financial commitment or serving on the board. He pointed out that he had already secured the backing of a number of important people, including two of the biggest leaders of American reform, Jane Addams of Hull House and Florence Kelley of the National Consumers League. It was essential that another group devoted solely to old-age pensions come into existence. But Andrews would not budge.

When they returned to the hotel, Abe was discouraged and at a loss as to why Andrews had turned him down.

"Isn't there such a thing as jealousy?" Henriette inquired.

"Well, I don't know, isn't that something women do? . . . "

"Haven't you heard of singers and actors? For instance. It may be the same thing in the professional fields."

Henriette was not far off, because the real reason behind Andrews's refusal to help was his fear of Abe's focused and outspoken energy. Abe and his allies might take sudden, bold steps that he didn't approve of and couldn't control—moves that might lead to the AALL being supplanted in a field of reform that Andrews considered to be his and his alone—and he was alarmed. Andrews felt that his ancient lineage in the American reform movement, dating to the days of Teddy Roosevelt, qualified him to be the natural leader of the troops—Abe's new group was just a Johnny-come-lately. And they would both be competing for the same money. Abe was bewildered. There were new ideas in the air and Andrews was certainly aware of them. It was time to join up with the new reformers, and there was little time to waste, because there were more and more charlatans responding to the needs of the aged by coming up with dangerous pie-in-the-sky schemes, such as that of the man Abe had visited in Cincinnati.

What really divided the two men were the ideas that make a Socialist different from a Progressive. Andrews believed that social insurance—laws covering pensions, unemployment, and health—should not be forced on anyone, but be written with the help of the employer and be optional with the states, even with the counties. Abe, who at the time was one of the few to have done original field research on the plight of the destitute and elderly, was convinced that a patchwork plan would never cure the problem. Government needed to take over the entire matter. The aged poor had waited far too long.

But Andrews wouldn't agree to help, and Abe decided he would just have to move ahead on his own, whatever the cost, and not wait for an agreement with AALL. Then, when Andrews realized Abe was enrolling members and raising money for his own group, he feared his AALL might lose influence over the campaign for old-age pensions. He tried to undermine Abe by using his long-standing connections and influence to intimidate him. Letters unearthed from the Andrews archives in the 1970s show clearly how he had tried to contain the threat. He informed his many supporters, including charitable foundations, of the menace of the new group: "If Epstein's movement . . . becomes a really effective national organization it will divert from our Association a certain amount of interest . . . and financial support," he wrote. He made an alliance with Abe's old nemesis, Frank Hering and the Eagles, to push for AALL's voluntary version of pensions. And he quietly raised a six-thousand-dollar fund to do it, a large amount in those days. Years later, when Henriette was shown that secret trove of letters demonstrating what Andrews had done to sink the fledgling American Association for Old Age Security, she was furious: "I'd like to know what he did with all that money, that six thousand dollars!"

She had not liked the man in 1927 and now, more than half a century later, she knew she had been absolutely right.

The struggle with Andrews turned into a terrible feud. For Abe it was a battle he could not avoid. He was never afraid of a fight, and his hot-tempered nature made it difficult to find a compromise. A number of peace negotiations were held to find a way to bring the two associations together, namely through the efforts of Paul Douglas, at that time an important University of Chicago economist. But Andrews was adamant and would not receive Abe in his office unless he agreed to certain conditions, and Abe, just as stubborn, refused to meet Andrews there except as total equals. Even Mrs. Andrews herself became an issue, for when Henriette tried to say hello to her at a meeting, she was snubbed, an act that was not forgotten. Attempts to bring about compromise, with Paul Douglas still the middleman, continued for several months. Andrews eventually said he would accept Abe's group into the AALL but only as another department, and under his orders. Abe said he would join up with Andrews, but only with complete autonomy. No one would oversee him. He knew how he wanted to create old-age pensions and did not want a boss with a restraining hand. He had been through all that with Frank Hering and the Eagles. The attempt at compromise failed, and Abe never became part of the AALL.

In 1927 Abe was determined to push his way onto a bigger stage than the state government of Pennsylvania, come what may. But the rift with John Andrews and his AALL was a source of disruption between two potential allies that led to great turmoil in the fight for old-age pensions. The disagreements were never resolved, and although Abe and Andrews continued to communicate and occasionally came together to support certain legislation, they often fought publicly and while trying to raise money from the same sources would frequently belittle the other's policies. Abe even stole a number of prominent supporters from the AALL, such as Paul Douglas and I. M. Rubinow, causing Andrews to resent Abe even more. The clash was inevitable. Both men were ideological opposites, and the energy they used fighting each other took a terrible personal toll on both of them.

But when Abe moved out on his own, Henriette was thrilled by the coming challenge and told her scrappy husband, "You're just as good as Andrews is. Just go on doing your work. And we'll see who the winner is in the end." In the end it was Abe.

## 11

Henriette kept a little diary of her trip with Abe across the United States in 1927. Her first words were concise.

"July 22 Friday leave Harrisburg for better or worse."

In her later years she wanted to revisit the places she'd seen then. She would call me in California and ask when she could visit.

"Whenever you want."

"I want to see California again."

"I'm afraid you won't recognize it."

"That trip was so much fun. Your father was so determined to get people going . . ."

When I visited Henriette back in New York, we would be seated side by side on the venerable couch, overlooking my old childhood friend the Persian carpet, and I would prod her to tell me more about that epic journey. But she could remember very little. What she had completely forgotten was that she had once written it all down on a little notepad, most likely purchased at the five and ten.

The little notepad had been placed inside an envelope long ago with the customary lettering on it: "Important. Please Keep." Then at some point it was entombed in a nearly impenetrable back room in her home, the source, it seems, like Proust's madeleine, of all memory. There it lay, undisturbed and unremembered, until a time when boxes and bureaus were uncovered and opened, and I moved deeper into an earlier civilization, coming upon the little pad as if it were an ancient cuneiform tablet.

I was not sure what I held in my hands, but as I leafed through its 3×5 pages, I suddenly felt like a gold miner making a strike. I had stumbled on the tale of the little French girl who finally got to see America—before the mall had been invented, where roads were unpaved, where little was known of what took place beyond the county line, and where each state had its own distinct character. She saw the wonders of Yellowstone Park and the Grand Canyon and roamed on bumpy one-lane gravel roads through places where no modern interstate dares to wander. She marveled at cowboys whooping it up at a rodeo, and was awed when she came upon her first Native American. "What a thrill to see my first Indian on horseback," she gushed. The lavish flowers of her French garden must have seemed very tame indeed.

The diary is divided into two parts. First are the daily expenses ($1.50 for a night in a cabin in Montana—35 cents for ice cream). The second part provides the drama, where in short bursts of information Henriette recorded the day-by-day events. For example: "Nice cottage, good bed, oil lamp—Roads worse, very narrow, rain soaked . . . made of 'gumbo'— impassable—No eggs, so breakfast of mountain trout—Steep climbs, sharp curves, road full of holes . . . very dangerous—Enter the Bad Lands, sandy rocks with curious shapes." Those short bursts of description became the opening chords of Henriette's new and excellent American adventure, the little Rubicon she crossed that set the stage for her ultimate commitment to America over France. What I had also stumbled on was the passion of Abe Epstein, his own boss—finally.

———————

The American Association for Old Age Security had been set up, a board selected, and in a daring move that left John Andrews literally standing by the wayside, Abe decided to hit the road like a traveling salesman. He would tour the land and broadcast the news: old-age pensions were on the way! Where and how he got the idea no one knows, but Henriette was thrilled: "At last I am going to see America!" Little did she know that Abe had desperate need of her as a file clerk to maintain and organize all the papers necessary for his seeding of America. What he wanted was not just an informational tour, but the creation of committees everywhere that would funnel themselves directly into his new association and be fed by it as well. He fired off letters and set up meetings and speeches everywhere he could. It appears he knew his American history, for what he wanted to put in place was a sort of "Committees of Correspondence." If it had worked to create the American Revolution, it could do the same

Abe standing by "Madame Nash." Harrisburg, 1927. Henriette is visible inside.

for the cause of the aged in America. So on that summer day in 1927, when Abe and Henriette climbed into their new car—lovingly christened "Madame Nash" by Henriette—and headed toward Buffalo and the great falls of the Niagara, the back of the car was "loaded with all kinds of pamphlets, literature, letterheads, and what have you . . . to awaken America." And at last, it was farewell to the boring, dead-end city of Harrisburg.

The first big stop was Chicago, and they arrived in the middle of rush hour. Henriette was amazed at the sight of thousands of people enjoying summer on the beaches of Lake Michigan, and Abe was reunited with his brother, Boris. The next eight days were frenzied, rushing from Chicago to Milwaukee to Minneapolis. Abe consulted with Jane Addams of Hull House, made speeches, organized committees, gave newspaper interviews, and raised money. The pièce de résistance was a ten-minute talk on radio station WCFR, a first for Abe.

The round of visits in civilized America ended in Portage, Wisconsin, where they had lunch with Zona Gale, the winner of the Pulitzer in 1921 for the Broadway play she adapted from her best seller, "Miss Lulu Bett." With Sinclair Lewis, Sherwood Anderson, and other writers of provincial America, she was outspoken in her scrutiny of family and marriage in the world of small-town America. A longtime friend of Jane Addams, she was a supporter of numerous Progressive Party causes.

"For once, here was a beautiful home," Henriette cooed. "She was a very charming lady and was talking the sort of language I could understand." Abe apparently talked her language as well, for he signed her up, and for many years her name was featured on the letterhead of the association. She told him that she would write a little story to publicize the plight of the aged poor, and indeed "Lights Out" is about an aged farm couple separated for the first time in their lives when, their savings spent, they are moved into the poorhouse where they cannot even wave goodnight to each other from their separate male and female dormitories as the matron informs them, "All lights are out at nine o'clock sharp!" For Henriette that simple, sentimental tale—repeatedly used by Abe in his publicity—became a way to identify with the work her husband was doing, and a way to eventually involve herself with the American Association for Old Age Security.

Then the real adventure began—"Madame Nash" rolled into the wilds of South Dakota. "Cross the Missouri and enter the West," was Henriette's laconic description. "Poor looking farms, some of them miserable shanties, villages far apart. Pick up rough looking cowboy. Roads still slippery and dangerous. Wautega is in the Indian Reservation. Meet some of the town's characters, the cattle buyer—big rattlesnake. Eat pone meal," is a typical breathless entry. And that was only South Dakota. The next state, Montana, almost put an end to the entire adventure. It started off well enough with one of Abe's explosive capers. The county commissioners were holding a meeting, and Abe barged in, demanding to be heard. A feeble state law on old-age pensions had been passed in Montana, but it was optional for each county and this particular county hadn't budged. Abe harangued the locals on their responsibilities. The stunned commissioners, who had probably never seen an obstreperous Russian Jew before, nodded wisely and agreed that something had to be done. Henriette's contribution was to follow up the blitz with a spirited distribution of literature from the trunk of the car.

For the first time Henriette saw the man she had married go into action. She never got over it. "He seemed to have a sort of charisma. Now you couldn't say anything about good looks . . . he was short . . . he had a high pitched voice . . . but it's strange, very strange to me, the minute he got into a room people paid attention. He seemed to convert everybody as he went along."

A story typical of that legendary trip I have named "Abe and the Cowboys." It is set in a tiny no-name town in the dusty plains of South Dakota, with no paved streets or sidewalks. There, as Abe walked along he came across a number of retired old cowboys with no savings and little to live on. He started talking to them, and they listened. Soon their notions of rugged individualism seemed to fade as they became enthusiastic converts to old-age pensions. Whenever I think of this nearly eighty-year-old story, mythical in size, my thoughts roll back into the past, to a place that I can only imagine, but where I see myself peering through a half-opened door. I am watching a short, balding thirty-five-year-old man in a three-piece suit with owl-shaped glasses perched aggressively on his nose, giving a rousing lecture to a gathering of boot-hobbled, lanky old cowhands leaning against a couple of fence posts. I hear his high-pitched voice, words rushing from his mouth, fervent and rational, something like:

In this country almost two million aged persons are dependent, having no means to provide the barest necessities. The poorhouses are often terrible places, including young and old, feebleminded and epileptics, prostitutes and deserted babies, drunkards, and forced to mingle with these, the worn-out toilers. It would be much cheaper for the state to maintain an old age pension system than to keep up the poorhouses . . . China, India and the United States are the only populous states in the world that have no governmental provision of some sort for their dependent aged.

I could hear those cowboys shouting "Whoopee!"

But it was shortly after the successful conversion of the cowboys that Abe's little propaganda machine almost went off the rails. The gravel roads of Montana, soggy with rain, heavy with "gumbo," a word Henriette loved to repeat in her diary, did them in five miles west of Billings. Abe was barreling along, in a rush as always, when the Nash hit some loose gravel, skidded, and flipped over into a ditch. As Henriette crawled from the car, bruised, in shock, her dress torn, Abe, upside down and hanging out the door, called out, "What about the papers in the back? Are they all right?"

In Billings it was news. "Car Flops in Gravel: Injuries are Slight," the *Billings Gazette* reported. But help arrived quickly. They returned to Billings and holed up at the Hotel Lincoln for twenty-four hours. Total damage: Doctor—three dollars—medicine—fifty cents—car—$17.50. And those papers? They survived, and were sorted out and ready for the next rally. Henriette, however, was not. Enough flummoxing about on the wild roads of the West, she chided her husband. "You should have a little vacation . . . and rest your throat from so much speaking . . . And I should have a little rest too from folding leaflets and all those routine chores." It was time to stop the crusade and see some of the beauties of America. And Yellowstone Park was just over the next rise.

Her pleas led to their spending five lovely days wandering the Rockies, seeing the geysers, the lakes and falls, all noted on the little notepad: "Leave Yellowstone through beautiful forests, flowers, streams and high mountains." Henriette was giddy at the sights, reminded of her beloved Pyrenees. Then, "Madame Nash" went on a straight bumpy ride through the wilds of Idaho and Washington all the way to the Pacific Ocean, where the crusade started up again. In a frantic sequence of maneuvers, meetings, and speeches, they dashed down the coast stopping at all the big cities—Seattle, Tacoma, Portland, Salem, Sacramento, San Francisco, San Jose, Bakersfield, Los Angeles, San Diego, and Los Angeles once again.

The pot of gold at the Pacific end of the United States, the spirit of the Forty-Niner, had drawn multitudes to Washington, Oregon, and California. But by the end of the 1920s the pot was cracked and the mine empty. Like the cowboys in South Dakota, people on the West Coast were trying to adjust to the collapse of America's most insistent illusion: prosperity for all. A great tide of migration had brought large numbers of the elderly to the golden land. The numbers of those over sixty-five was twice the national average. California was fertile ground for the seeds Abe was planting.

As they moved down the coast from meeting to meeting, Abe and Henriette became aware that they were traveling in another country, one far different from the sophisticated East. Audiences were friendly and gatherings easy to organize. People listened intently and rarely bothered Abe with the sort of idiotic, lawyerly question that could rouse him to a wrath. It was clear that on the West Coast "people were acutely facing the problem," Henriette wrote. Abe's rallies often had the intensity of a preacher working the crowd in a revival tent. The man in charge would introduce Abe Epstein as a sort of wonder worker, "a marvelous expert who knows all about it," at times even as part messiah. "You have to talk as if it's God's will. God wants to do this for you," was an idea that had been proposed to Abe by a man named Mills, who traveled part of the way with them, helping to set up the meetings. An old Socialist of the down-home California variety, he had traveled the world, and he made an unforgettable impression on Henriette. Even as she forgot most of the trip, she could still visualize Mr. Mills, his vivid white hair and beard that made her think he was another George Bernard Shaw. Like Shaw he was a vegetarian, living on vegetables and olive oil. His folksy understanding for the downtrodden who came to the meetings was a great help and by following Mills' advice Abe found that people were moved whenever he made references to God's will. In most cities it was either the Central Labor Council or even the legislature who were the first to hear Abe give a talk. But with the "just plain folks" crowd the missionary fervor of his pleas for help for the aged went over big. At times Abe and Henriette were received as "representatives of Christ himself, by spreading the message of helping the poor and the old." Henriette was fascinated. "People talked about God often, there were even signs on the highway about him." Abe had adapted quickly to his audience of Westerners, and what he said about the need for pensions for the old found a response deep inside them, most of whom were at the end of the line as well as at the end of the continent. For its growing number of aged, California was a far cry from its advertised glories.

After ten barnstorming days, Abe pointed "Madame Nash" back east and by the light of the moon they crossed the Mojave Desert to avoid the August heat. The night was eerie, and Henriette pleaded with Abe to drive more slowly so that she could make out the strange shadows of the Joshua trees. It had been an amazingly successful trip. Many committees had been set up and money was raised, and perhaps because of it Abe delivered on a promise he had made to see the Grand Canyon. Another detour, another rained-on gravel road, but this time the car stayed upright, and the next morning when they awoke, the beauty of America's greatest natural wonder was at the doorstep of the little cabin where they had slept.

"I had never seen anything like it . . . so I gazed and gazed. Abe himself was impressed—struck by the beauty of nature. I don't think in his life he had ever had a chance to enjoy beautiful things . . . his background in Russia, the hardships of America, I felt it was wonderful he could have a good time."

The old-age security show continued east, passing through the marvels of the Petrified Forest and the primitive mud village of Quemado in New Mexico. In a little town named Magdalena they stumbled on an end-of-the-roundup rodeo, where they were kept awake all night by the rowdy cowboys' endless shouts of "Yippee! Yippee!" On they moved, as in a movie montage, through Texas, Kansas, St. Louis, Chicago, Louisville, and Pittsburgh. Everywhere Abe held more meetings, made more converts, and created more committees. Finally, the circle was closed. They pulled into Harrisburg, lingered briefly, and on the last day of September 1927 crossed the Hudson and entered the streets of New York. The pilgrimage was over—and when the final results were in Abe had addressed thirty-five different groups in nineteen cities, and held conferences and meetings in another thirteen cities. His total audience had exceeded eight thousand, and he reached many more through newspaper coverage, and who knows how many from his one speech on the radio in Chicago. "Madame Nash's" contribution, with her numerous breakdowns and tire punctures, was to log almost ten thousand miles on her odometer without collapsing altogether on America's rugged roads. There was never any tally of how many pieces of literature Henriette had put into the hands of those who were eager to find out about the American Association for Old Age Security.

Henriette had never been happier. The trip, even as her memory faded, assumed mythopoetical proportions. When Abe yelled at her in such places as San Francisco as they crossed the Bay Bridge, "Get in back and fold the literature," and Henriette squawked in reply, "But I want to see the sights!" and Abe responded, "Never mind the sights. We have a meeting—don't forget!" even then she always looked back on the trip with a romantic glow in her face. She had discovered her own America. And she fully embraced the apostolic nature of her experience when she told an interviewer: "It was like the trees planted by good old Johnny Appleseed. And I can never see apple trees in bloom without thinking of that little trip. Abe was just throwing those seeds away all over the country . . . and they sprouted, which is just what will happen with seeds, they always sprout somehow."

# Part Two

## The Blooming

1

In New York it was now the Jazz Age, the day of the flapper; of Prohibition with its hidden speakeasies where people drank lustily and without guilt; of the movie palace and thrilling newspaper headlines about the latest gangland murder—of flagpole sitters, Wall Street tycoons, dance crazes, and newfangled consumer goods like the gramophone, the telephone, the radio, and the Ford Model A. The reform movement of the early twentieth century—which had forced Congress to end child labor, regulate food and drugs, promote the rights of unions, allow women to vote, and create antitrust measures to curb the robber barons of American business—had now been silenced by a prevailing spirit of aggressive materialism. Calvin Coolidge, who called business "one of the greatest contributing forces to the advancement of the race," reigned in the White House, and Herbert Hoover, who would preside over the debacle that would close out the 1920s, was only a remote presence as secretary of commerce. But above all there was, in the words of T. H. Watkins, author of *The Great Depression*, "the Lorelei of possibility," the obsessive vision of limitless prosperity, a cornucopia of wealth that could be plucked from almost any tree in the great United States.

But when Abe, Henriette, and their belongings rolled into boom-time Manhattan on the last day of September 1927, only one consideration seemed to run through Abraham Epstein's preoccupied mind: a mere six states had passed a law on old-age pensions, and in only two did any real dollars go out to 1,255 "needy, worn out toilers," as Abe described them. Those two states were Montana and Wisconsin, and even there it was up to the counties to carry out the law if they so wished. He also knew that the average American worked nearly fifty hours a week for a salary of less than twenty-six dollars, and would never have a shot at being part of the great party of the roaring twenties. In fact, in the words of the historian, David Kennedy, "Retirement was an elusive fantasy for the average American worker, whose days of toil extended virtually to the end of the life cycle."

Determined to move fast, Abe set up shop in a one-room office at 104 Fifth Avenue. His mailing list consisted of four hundred newly enlisted dues payers and a bank balance of twenty-five hundred dollars, almost all of which had come from his savings. Yet by the end of his first year in New York, the American Association for Old Age Security wrote and submitted old-age pension laws in twenty-seven states and sent out a four-page monthly, *Old Age Security Herald*, filled with facts, figures, and charts about laws and legislation. Abe's most brilliant move, though, was an alliance he put together and named the New York Permanent Conference on Old Age Security. It met once a month, and all groups interested in passing a pension law sent a representative: Catholic Charities, Jewish Social Services, United Neighborhood Houses, Greenwich House, the Association to Improve Conditions for the Poor, International Ladies Garment Worker's Union, and many others. It eventually numbered more than two hundred organizations and became a powerful lobby for Abe's legislative moves.

On April 10, 1928, at the Roosevelt Hotel in New York this intense little man with the heavy Jewish accent passionately addressed the first conference of his new association: "Now as to the question, 'Why only old age pensions?' I think everyone in this hall would stand with you and say, 'Well, if we can have everything let us have everything.' I think none is limiting himself to old age pensions . . . We are emphasizing old age pensions because old age pensions—and that is the strange but true history of every European country—are always the first step in social insurance . . . in the United States old age insurance will come ahead of health insurance and unemployment insurance." Abe's gaze was set far into the future, at something that he would eventually name "social security."

But the business community of the time, rolling along in cocksure optimism, was defiant. They had no intention of letting social reformers pass pension laws that would cost them money. When a New York state assemblyman named Frank Miller tried to introduce the first pension bill in 1927, he told delegates at the association's first conference, "They threw papers and boards at me . . . in a tumult and uproar . . . when the roll-call was taken I received only 13 votes out of a membership of 150!" "Pensions," declared the conservative political opposition, would "undermine the time honored tradition of American individualism and self-reliance . . . weakening the moral fiber of the individual by giving him something for nothing." It would also be "unconstitutional, un-American and socialistic . . . people would shirk personal responsibility . . . squander their savings so as to be eligible for an old age pension." "Those Republicans," Henriette could not resist smirking, "they said pensions were against religion and morality, against motherhood and apple pie . . . and also corn on the cob!"

Creating old-age pensions in the prosperous 1920s seemed an almost hopeless proposition. Then from an unlikely out-of-the-way source a faint chirp of support was heard. A somewhat conservative Democrat running for governor spoke up. "It just tears my heart out to see these old men and women in the County Poorhouse," State Senator Franklin Delano Roosevelt said in a speech. He promised to call for an "immediate study towards passage of a proper and adequate old age pension law." Those apparently heartfelt words were like the forewarning blast of a herald's trumpet announcing the official push for old-age pensions in New York and also the start of the fragile relationship between Abe Epstein, the now forgotten reformer, and Franklin Roosevelt, the much-beloved future president of the United States.

Roosevelt's motive in coming out for old-age pensions in his gubernatorial campaign was no doubt to capture votes. But there was as yet no groundswell for pensions anywhere in New York. Some have seen his position as a sure sign of his uncanny ability to listen to the people around him and smell out an idea for its political value well before it would become an issue in the election. Whether talk of pensions made a difference is hard to say, but while Herbert Hoover was winning the presidency in 1928, Roosevelt squeaked into office as governor of New York. In fact, at midnight on election day, when the first newspapers came out, Roosevelt, prefiguring Harry Truman in 1948, was declared the loser to Albert Ottinger, the conservative Republican. In those days election results came in slowly; ballots were counted by hand, and it had been the tradition in certain conservative upstate counties to delay the results as long as possible to see which way the vote was going and then take action. Roosevelt made note of this, and told reporters, "the Republicans are up to their old tricks of delaying the vote and stealing as many of them as they can from us." Phone calls were made to upstate sheriffs, but the ultimate threat came from the Democratic Party boss of the Bronx, the tough Ed Flynn. At two o'clock in the morning he told the newspapers he had one hundred lawyers ready to take the train upstate that morning to uncover fraud and "to prevent any further frauds." The threat worked. Soon the votes from upstate poured in, and Roosevelt edged ahead. He had made it into one of the foremost elective offices in the nation by the narrowest of margins, winning by a little more than 25,000 votes out of a total of 4,234,000.

It was hardly a mandate, and if it hadn't been for the likes of an old-fashioned politician such as Ed Flynn, Roosevelt might never have been heard from again. But Roosevelt had made it—his stand on pensions an incalculable part of the equation—and Abe promptly made his move. He asked the banker Charles Burlingham, a member of the board of the association, to set up a meeting. Despite his deep socialist convictions, Abe always knew how he needed to operate in a capitalist society. He always had businessmen and clergymen on his board, and at one point even prevailed on Alfred DuPont to become a vice-president—sweet revenge indeed on the powers that controlled the state of Delaware and its college for women. On December 14, 1928, five weeks after the election, Abraham Epstein strolled into the governor-elect's New York office.

There are no official notes from the meeting with FDR. Abe took along several associates: the president of the association, Francis T. McConnell (a Protestant bishop), the banker Burlingham, and the prominent Reform rabbi Stephen Wise. Abe was cleverly showing FDR the range of support he had. He let the others do most of the talking. Wise, with his massive head, piercing eyes, and Roman nose, was a particularly impressive figure, in contrast to the fervent, diminutive Abe. Wise was also a dramatic orator with a thundering bass voice, and Abe wisely let the eloquent rabbi explain why the time was ripe for old-age pensions. FDR was fascinated by Wise's flamboyant personality and told the four men he would do what he could. True to his word, in his inaugural address as governor, he spoke up for a system to prevent "old age want," and it was not to be the dole, nor the voluntary system sponsored by John Andrews's American Association for Labor Legislation, but a program to help the poor and aged based on contributory social insurance, just what Abe was promoting in his proliferating writing. The legislature was still controlled by the Republicans, who had no wish to further the career of the new Democratic governor—but Roosevelt's instincts as a political animal were craftier than those of his opponents. "Judging by the number of letters I am receiving, there is more widespread popular interest in the subject of old age security against want than most people in public life had realized," he told the newspapers. The Republican majority, suddenly hearing the patter of many feet behind them, quickly set up a committee to study pensions.

As legislation became a possibility, the American Association for Old Age Security stepped up its public activities, mailing out literature and holding meetings and conferences in twenty-one New York cities. Abe published nine magazine articles and gave an interview that was reprinted in sixty newspapers. Supporting committees were created throughout the state, and in February 1929, Abe had a second hopeful meeting with Roosevelt. The governor listened politely and reportedly said, "Let's try for a good law."

The biggest fusillade in Abe's drive for pensions was the publication of his new book, *The Challenge of the Aged*. He felt the need to place a new book before the public to take advantage of all the publicity the association was generating, and he didn't want to wait. So with the support of the Vanguard Press and its "Joint Publication Offer to organizations engaged in education and propaganda in the social sciences," the book came out in October 1928 as a joint publication of Vanguard Press and the American Association for Old Age Security. Of course, Abe, through the association, had to put up some of the money, but the book got attention. "Mr. Epstein's book is no harangue," wrote the reviewer for the *New York Times*. "He does not accuse—he explains . . . It is a challenge distinct and powerful." The idea of a challenge, as in a duel, became in time a key word in Abe's political writing.

The book was a revised and expanded version of *Facing Old Age*, with an introduction by the great settlement house reformer Jane Addams. It included a vast survey of everything related to old-age security in the United States and the world. There were statistical tables throughout, providing information on a state-by-state basis of what had been proposed, what had been done, and what it might cost to create adequate pensions. But the tone of the book was more belligerent than that of the earlier one. Abe attacked the "Pollyanna economists" who praised America as the land of the chosen people, "a happy place full of bathtubs and Fords." He contrasted that blithe phrase with the ruthlessness of the modern American juggernaut for most aged wage earners who are "left to tread the narrow path of old age dependency which ultimately winds over the hill to the Poorhouse." The image of the poorhouse was becoming an essential metaphor in his writing.

Having met with Roosevelt on at least two occasions, Abe had some sense of the man he needed to influence, and knew he had to do as much as he could to get the future president's attention and infiltrate his thinking. The first edition had been dedicated to three of his old deceased allies, Bishop Ethelbert Talbot, the first president of the association, William

Kent, and Royal Robbins, "pioneers in a righteous cause." But he made a switch for the second edition because FDR was now the governor-elect, and he took advantage of that piece of good news to write a dedication "To Franklin Delano Roosevelt, Governor and Herbert H. Lehman, Lieutenant-Governor, who by their intellectual leadership and passion for social justice have succeeded in awakening America to a realistic appreciation of old age want," and sent them both a copy. He also included, in an afterword to the second edition, flattering words about the governor: "No single man has contributed so much to this aroused public sentiment on pensions as Franklin Delano Roosevelt. By his burning and challenging appeals . . . Mr. Roosevelt has brought the issue to the front pages of our newspapers." It was a nice try, but later, when Roosevelt historian Kenneth Davis took a close look at the matter, he saw that "Roosevelt may have been influenced by Rubinow—the theorist of social insurance—and Epstein, or by their ideas, while yet governor of New York . . . but not by his reading of their books (almost certainly he never read them)."

The bruising pain of the struggle for social security in the United States might have been very different if Franklin Delano Roosevelt, while lying in bed in the governor's mansion, reading the newspapers, as he always did, had one morning instead picked up his copy of *The Challenge of the Aged*—and read it.

2

The move to New York exceeded all of Abe's expectations. The American Association for Old Age Security was so busy that it doubled in size to two rooms at 22 East Seventeenth Street, around the corner from Union Square, the center of radical politics in New York where the left wing massed for labor rallies, May Day parades, and other tumultuous demonstrations. Abe was away on the road for weeks at a time in states such as New Jersey, Ohio, and Iowa, starting campaigns, proposing laws, and creating more liaison committees. Henriette began to see that she too had a place in the movement for old-age pensions. But her view of the struggle was always a literary one. What she saw was the nineteenth-century world described by Dickens and Zola. From that distant perch she could feel emotional about the cause and know why old-age pensions were worth fighting for. The poorhouse, with its degrading, repulsive, uncaring treatment of the old, appalled her. But she had never come near one in real life. Instead she took in the horror of the story from Abe and what he had seen and told her about his visits when he researched them for the Pennsylvania Commission on Old Age Pensions.

---

The American poorhouse was an out-of-date institution, modeled after the ancient English poor laws brought to the colonies by the first settlers. In most states they had remained in effect and unchanged for nearly three hundred years, and the statutes were almost identical in language with the English Poor Law of 1601, written during the reign of the first Queen Elizabeth. Every state but New Mexico had poorhouses, and most of them were operated by the individual counties. In England the poorhouses—sometimes called workhouses—had already been closed down and replaced by a system of old-age pensions funded by employee, employer, and the government, but in the United States in 1927 poorhouses were widespread, and the only form of public assistance, other than charity, for the indigent aged.

The poorhouse was a catch-all institution and frequently the sole place of refuge for a mixed group of both young and old victims of misfortune. Sheltered together were the feeble-minded, epileptics, cripples, imbeciles, prostitutes, and abandoned children, as well as former criminals, alcoholics, the diseased, the maimed, and worn-out workers. It was often sarcastically referred to as the home for "the veterans of dissipation and the veterans of labor." The housing was typically a dormitory with no individual rooms, so that privacy was impossible. Married couples were generally separated, and the inmates were regimented as in a prison. Private possessions, except for clothes, were not allowed. "Rusted tin dishes, heavy cracked enamelware, and bare table tops set the tone for these institutions," reported the study commissioned by the New York legislature in 1930. And in most cases the proprietor of the county poorhouse was a political appointee, the job given to him as part of the local spoils system. An even earlier study had found that most poorhouse directors disliked the inmates and had little education. A number were even illiterate.

Roosevelt himself came to have strong feelings against poorhouses, and when running for president in 1932 told of an incident that had deeply affected him. At Hyde Park, his ancestral home on the Hudson River, he had farm neighbors, three brothers and a sister, all in their eighties. "The best of our citizens," he called them, but when he returned one spring he found that one of the brothers had fallen down and frozen to death in the snow. The town authorities had then taken the other brothers and placed them in the county poorhouse, and had taken their sister to the insane asylum, although she was not insane—just old. "That sold me on the idea of try-ing to keep homes intact for old people," Roosevelt said. Even the secre-tary of labor under Coolidge, James J. Davis, had denounced the poor-houses: "Our present poorhouse system is a disgrace and a fraud. It works not for good but for evil."

In *The Challenge of the Aged,* Abe had devoted one entire chapter, "What Price 'Over the Hill to the Poorhouse?'" to describing the appalling con-ditions and the waste of money inherent in the poorhouse system. Even those in the city of New York itself were a disgrace. The dependent aged, the criminally insane, and the sickly poor were all nicely isolated in a group of grim brick buildings on Welfare Island—the now rebuilt, re-named, and firmly middle-class Roosevelt Island—in the East River. Once known as Blackwell's Island, it had been the spot, starting in colonial times, where New York stuck its diseased and destitute out of sight. A re-port by the New York City commissioner of accounts used by Abe in the May 1934 issue of his newsletter revealed the criminal neglect and brutal treatment of the inmates of the Home for Dependents on Welfare Island. The elderly were found tied to chairs with bedsheets. One woman with broken ribs was left in a chair for three days before a doctor was sum-moned. There was a notorious "ulcer clinic" run by a former ship's cook. "He showed the investigators the penknife with which he scraped ulcers, cut wounds, to treat the most varied assortments of diseases," the report said. The photographs were so revolting that the newspapers wouldn't print them. Petty thievery of money and food by the attendants was com-mon. The higher-ups frequently had the inmate's insurance policies trans-ferred to them. "The inmates—over 2000 of them in the greatest and rich-est city in America—were beaten, insulted and constantly reminded that it was their fate to be buried in Potter's Field. There was not even a resi-dent physician in charge of the Welfare Home." One day Henriette de-cided that she needed to see it all for herself and accompanied Abe on one of his trips to Welfare Island, and was horrified that people were living in such degrading, prisonlike conditions in the middle of glamorous New York. She came home with a headache and it took her three days to re-cover from her nausea at the smell and filth she had witnessed.

---

One day Abe had a visitor to his tiny office. Harry Elias was a friend in public relations who offered Abe free advice on publicity.

"You know, Abe," Elias told him, "you could use the evils of the poor-house as a means of getting the association more on the map."

The Missouri poorhouse food line. Photo used by
the American Association for Social Security.

Abe looked dubious. "How?" he replied.

"You have a marvelous story here," he said, "why don't you use some pictures?" Henriette's ears pricked up.

"It costs money," Abe cut him off.

"Oh, no it doesn't," Harry went on. "Print pictures of dear old ladies and dear old gentlemen, looking very sweet and nice and unhappy. I'm sure you'll get a much better response. I'll help you to set it up."

Henriette was enthusiastic. With Harry Elias as her guide, she began to sift through the 100 Neediest Cases in the *New York Times* and the *Evening Post* for stories and photographs. All of them seemed to point to the frightful world of the poorhouse. Abe remained ill at ease with the idea, but he was desperate for money and finally decided to let her work on the human-interest side of the crusade.

"Lights Out," the story Zona Gale had written especially for Abe and the association after he met her in Wisconsin during the 1927 trip across America, was the inspiration for the new campaign. Brochures with depressing photographs of old people on their way to the poorhouse went out as fund-raisers. In one, the forlorn and wrinkled faces of eight old men and women floated across the top of the page like a chorus line of misery. In another a bedraggled man and woman said good-bye to each other as they were parted on the poorhouse steps. "Over the Hill—To the Poorhouse—Separated" was the caption. In another version of the same idea, an old lady and old gentleman waved to each other from separate poorhouse dorms. "Well, I'll put my geranium by the window so that you'll know I am here," she called to her sweet-looking husband. In contrast there was a photo of a neat, elderly couple, "At Home—with their loved ones—Pensioned." Other mailings highlighted "The Missouri Poorhouse Line," a wintry scene of old people in shabby, torn clothes waiting outside in freezing weather for a meal. "Home Sweet Home in . . . poor house" showed two elderly women, backs to the camera, seated on beds in a bare attic, slumped in despair. A frequently used picture, meant to shock, showed an elderly bearded man staring out from behind bars, his eyes blank and lost. The caption reads, "Well mentally when sent to poorhouse a year ago—now insane." The text of these fund-raising brochures was simple, offering only a few facts and figures ($40 a month to support an old person in a poorhouse, only $22.35 to support him on a pension). There were quotes from Alfred Dupont ("not charity but justice") and from FDR ("No greater tragedy exists than the aged worn-out worker who can only look forward to a dismal poorhouse").

But when each new set of proofs appeared in the office, Abe grabbed them, looked them over, and exploded. "This is terrible!" he stormed. "It's wrong and undignified. You offend people with such photographs." The work should be factual and informative, he explained. People should know why pensions were better. They were cheaper and more humane, kept families together, and thereby benefited all of society. And that should be enough. Abe rarely let his deepest feelings speak for him openly. All he would say was that it was wrong to expose people in publicity. It stole their self-respect and was humiliating. A man and woman had rights to personal dignity no matter what their economic status. It was important to treat the poor man as you would the rich. He once explained in a letter that his humanitarian impulses had been born during the brief time he had studied at a yeshiva in Slutsk before leaving Russia. There were deep ethical underpinnings to his brash social activism and intense sympathy for the poor. Its source was the Old Testament. The story of Adam and Eve opens his major book, *Insecurity,* and the first words of *Facing Old Age* are from the ninetieth Psalm. But all that heartbreaking human interest was something Henriette could relate to, and over time the sad pictures and stories that went out in mailings helped to increase

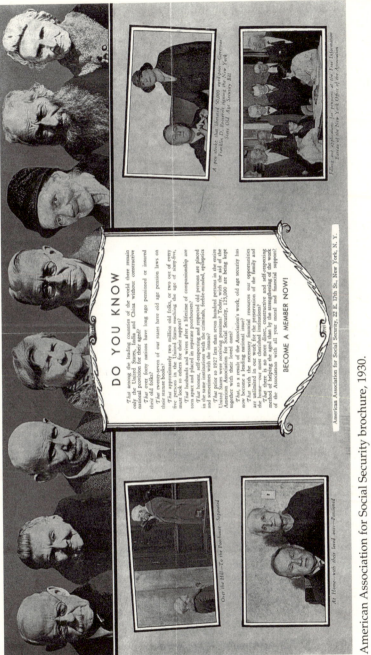

American Association for Social Security brochure, 1930.

contributions and members. Harry Elias was right. Using photographs worked.

"The great humanitarian" was the ponderous, mocking label Henriette often used to describe Abe when she was irritated that he never appreciated all her hard work. She groused once about a list of names she had collected by going through the phone book. "It was a very tedious job for me, to have to use my eyes on the telephone book—but it was a tremendous help financially . . . I don't know whether he appreciated it at the time. He may have thought it was rather silly on my part." The fear of looking frivolous was always there, that she would be ignored by Abe, and that she would always be tagged by others as "that silly French girl."

Abe did little to boost her confidence. She was never paid for her work, and only many years later received a twenty-five-dollar-a-week pittance. During those early years, Abe himself was never paid more than fifty dollars weekly, and in the summer he worked for free because most people of influence in those days were away on vacation and the office was not busy. He never allowed her name to appear on the letterhead, and it hurt her, but she could never get him to explain why. After all, she told him, John Andrews had done it for his wife, Irene. Abe did offer her recognition in *The Challenge of the Aged* by writing, "I am indebted to my wife Henriette Castex whose reflections and many hours of toil are inextricably embedded in this volume." That was in 1928. But Abe was a driven man, and it was the last time he could ever find a way to praise her in writing.

Still, Henriette was now a recruit in the campaign for pensions and not just a clerk handing out brochures in some dusty, unheard-of western town. She was as far from being a "cute French cook" as she could be. "When I left France I left because I felt I had no future, and was bored with the good life," she once said. "Now, for the first time, I felt I was doing something . . . although it was hard, and I knew I would never get thanks for it." She spent her days in the little office at 22 East Seventeenth Street, licking envelopes and stamping letters, checking the newspapers for items of interest, helping wherever she could, being a pest to her husband. Then one day he turned to her and said, "You had better get used to calling on the telephone because there's a lot of work for you to do."

What Abe had in mind was a show of force in Albany on the day the legislature would hold hearings on a possible old-age pension law. "Abe had the idea of a crowd marching on Albany! We decided to have a special train. We had the delegates bring little American flags with them . . . and we embarked, flags and all, to Albany. Oh, it was a lot of fun on that

The March on Albany, 1930. Henriette, in the back wearing a cloche hat, barely visible, behind the man on the left holding a placard.

train. I don't think Abe sat down for a minute, going from one group to another, talking. He was absolutely overwhelmed with joy!"

The march on Albany took place on March 11, 1930, and was the high point of the three-year effort to create pensions in New York. The joy and excitement of that day remained forever fixed deep in Henriette's memory. She treasured her photographs of that great display of force setting off for Albany, the crowd on the sidewalk in their winter hats and coats, smiling eagerly as they waved their American flags, while others held aloft large signs advertising their mission: "Old Age Pension Hearing—New York—Albany." She was fiercely proud of those pictures. On more than one occasion she supplied them for books and articles written about that period, and she told anyone who ever asked about her early life in New York how brilliant Abe had been in that campaign.

"Before every meeting of the Permanent Conference on Old Age Security, he would call the *Times*, the *Herald*, and the other New York newspapers and tell them to send a reporter and they nearly always did. He really had the Madison Avenue technique . . . it came to him naturally . . . newspapermen loved him and helped him. Abe Raskin of the *New York*

*Times,* who became famous later as their great labor reporter, even volunteered to write our press releases. The tide went the other way—toward
security instead of against it. Abe had been able to unite all the advocates
of old age pensions . . . he was on the right track, and I told him, 'Tell John
Andrews to go to hell! We've got him licked!'"

---

"I do want to go on that train," she told Abe as the day of the march approached.

"Oh, you're going to be an awful nuisance," Abe retorted.

"No, I will not." Henriette stood her ground. "This is your first great
success. So as I had to do the telephoning and get people lined up . . ."

She got her way. She paid her fare, like the rest of the crowd, and boarded the train at Grand Central. And then one day, not long ago, as I looked
over those pictures with the aid of a magnifying glass, I suddenly saw
something I had never seen before: It was Henriette! Unmistakably! She
was off to one side, on the edge of the photograph, stylish and cute in her
fur-collared coat and little cloche hat, eying the growing excitement, timid
but wanting to participate. I fancied her coming to life, grabbing a flag,
flaunting it wildly, hoping the photographer would spot her. She had been
there, she had been part of it, no one was going to stand in the way of her
being on that train, least of all the galvanized Abe—but at that moment,
when the train departed, she never acknowledged she was four and one-
half months pregnant, and that Abe might have possibly been thinking of
her health and their coming only child.

Then, when the troops arrived at the train station in Albany and
marched up the hill to the Capitol, she couldn't contain herself. She turned
to the radical crusader marching beside her, her husband, and cried out
as loud as she could: "Not over the hill to the Poorhouse! But up the hill
to the Capitol!"

Later she recalled, "But he never heard me. His mind was elsewhere."

The great march on Albany—the euphoria and joy of it—could not conceal all the dissension fermenting below. Abe had converted a key Republican legislator to the cause and through him a number of other conservatives. But the law the Republicans were willing to vote for paid a
pension of only a dollar a day to anyone over the age of seventy, and it
had many restrictions. In fact it was just a small, state-funded pension and
contained not a word about a true contributory plan for old-age insurance. What Abe was pushing with such a loud banging of drums was far
from fulfilling the goals of the social insurance forces. Many did not like

the proposed pension law and felt that true social insurance principles should not be abandoned for a quick fix. Abe was stuck and needed to make a choice—whether to hold out for something better, hoping that the Republican majority would not vote it down, or go along with a pitiful law he was sure could be passed. There was fierce infighting between the old-age groups—pensions or insurance—foreshadowing the ferocious battles to come over the enactment of FDR's Social Security Act in 1935.

The difficulty for the true believers was that pensions were only a stop-gap solution, an urgent and a necessary one of course, an obligation on the part of state government to help those who after a lifetime of work deserved more than charity or the poorhouse. With qualifications relating to age, wealth, and residency, pensions were to be paid out of the state's general fund. Old-age insurance, on the other hand, was part of a much larger idea based on the theories of social insurance. A retiree's old-age benefit would be funded by a system of insurance contributed to by employees, employers, and sometimes even the government. When a person qualified, the fund would pay out a monthly stipend. In the case of old-age benefits it was simply based on age. It was meant to insure against the tribulations of old age by preparing for the future in a group way. It did not resemble a pension in any way because the lawmakers did not have to vote to fund it.

The difference between old-age pensions and old-age insurance is significant, and for many years the latter was considered too radical for an America clinging to ideals of self-reliance, rugged individualism, and take-care-of-yourself maxims. Pensions, on the other hand, might be looked on as neither socialistic nor permanent, but as an act of Christian duty to those less able to endure life's trials. Nonetheless, conservatives—who did not believe in any form of state help—always referred to them disdainfully as "The Dole!" But when the Great Depression of the 1930s swept through the land and affected rich and poor alike, conservatives were forced to admit that Christian values could do little to save the old from the disaster of an industrial economy in free fall. Pity, charity, and the poorhouse could not prevent the suffering that modern laissez-faire economics can bring to human beings.

Abe had one story in particular he loved to tell to his rapt audiences. A soldier severely wounded in the First World War was lying in the hospital. An officer came and asked how he had been shot. "Well sir," the soldier replied, "when we went out of them trenches and over the top we wuz tol' to avoid them bullets by zigging and zagging. I guess that bullet caught me when I was zagging instead of zigging." That was Abe's metaphor for what happened to the aged worker under capitalism.

Abe had struggled for years to create old-age pensions in Pennsylvania. When he went to France to "meet the folks" in 1925, along with being newly married, climbing the Pyrenees, and enjoying the French way of life, he had also spent time looking at European systems of social insurance then in effect in England, France, and Germany. He became convinced that those government-supported compulsory plans were the wave of the future. The split with John Andrews, his American Association for Labor Legislation, and the six-thousand-dollar propaganda fund was above all about those European systems as opposed to an American plan that would be strictly voluntary. As Roy Lubove makes clear in his book on the history of social security, "Andrews was critical of the shift from old-age pensions to insurance which Epstein and Rubinow were beginning to urge. The AALL had adopted a pension policy in 1922 and Andrews remained firm in its support." With Abe's old employer, the Fraternal Order of Eagles, the split was even more dramatic. They had no idea of what social insurance was, and while they were still urging the passage of pension laws, their leader, the shallow Frank Hering, insisted, "the pensioner would have to be an exceeding good citizen." These disputes and the name-calling fights they brought on began to raise havoc during the campaign for social security in depression-era America.

In 1930, the people campaigning for old-age security were unknown to most Americans. Even congressmen and state legislators understood little about what the reformers believed in—a comprehensive social security system that would embrace not only old-age insurance but also include unemployment, medical, disability, and widow's and survivor's insurance. It was a program the reformers passionately believed was better for America by a mile than just helping people haphazardly when it was too late.

---

Abe was always an impatient man. After three years of hard work in New York he was not about to endure the pain of another defeat as he had in Pennsylvania. He had too much invested in the New York campaign to come away with nothing. He knew the old-age pension bill before the New York legislature was pitiful, but he thought it was the only one that "had a chance in hell" of winding up on FDR's desk for him to sign. He decided to throw the full weight of the association behind it. He paraded his view that it was important to have a law passed. He tried to point out its positive aspects. It abandoned forever the county option, the bastion of poorhouse politics and abuse. Instead, the law was statewide and would be supervised from Albany. And most important it was the first time an aged person with no resources could receive help without being forced to go to an institution like the poorhouse. The law did not embrace basic social insurance principles, but it was a start. Once passed, the pension advocates could work to improve it. Miracles were not about to happen overnight.

But this line of reasoning didn't work with a lot of people. Many thought it was wrong to compromise, that it would be better to hold out for perfect legislation, for a real insurance plan—particularly since Roosevelt had said he wanted one. A number of Abe's fellow experts were surprised at his energetic support for the Republican proposal and angry at him for going it alone. But Abe felt certain the Republicans he had talked to would never go for real old-age insurance, and he was determined to get a law passed. No one else's opinion mattered. He was fed up with waiting around for results. Secretly he had a scheme in mind, and wrote to one of his intimates, "If we can persuade the public that this is an Old Age Pension law it will be considered and administered as such. Should we take the position that this is nothing but poor relief it would remain as poor relief. And we would have no argument with which to go to other states. The example of New York will be tremendously helpful in our campaigns all through the country." He wanted a win, a tactical propaganda victory, whatever the cost, for the American Association for Old Age Security, one that could be blasted out across the land by his increasingly loud and energetic trumpet. And that is what happened three weeks later, on March 31, 1930. The New York state legislature passed the first old-age pension law in the nation that had any teeth, however dull they might be. It had been a long journey from the day when poor old Assemblyman Miller had been forced to duck papers and boards in those hallowed chambers.

Shortly after the Albany victory, Henriette sailed for France, determined to give birth in her homeland. Her mother was overjoyed to oversee the arrival of "un héritier," but true to her old-country ways scolded her daughter for not having the baby at home. She felt Henriette was giving herself airs in insisting on a modern clinic. But fancy clinic it was, and, in spite of all that was going on in New York, Abe made it to Toulouse for

Witnesses at Old Age Pension hearing, Trenton, New Jersey,
undated. Abraham Epstein, second row, second from right.

the great event on July 27. He behaved correctly, kept his handkerchief
folded—as Henriette always insisted—greeted everyone with kisses on
both cheeks, and promptly sailed back to his Union Square aerie where he
had rented yet a third room for his office. He was readying an information bureau for the new old-age pension law when it went into effect on
September 1. At last he was going to do what he had always ached to do—
see to it personally that those who deserved pensions were going to get
them. A near mob of the elderly showed up at his door—fourteen thousand in the first year alone. In a photograph taken to publicize the free information bureau, Abe is seated at his desk, looking official in his habitual three-piece suit and owl-shaped glasses, a no-nonsense look on his face
as his pen is poised to attack a sheet of paper. He is surrounded by seven
aged citizens, courteously clutching pension applications, gazing expec-
tantly, as they wait for help. "Old men and women will be furnished with

whatever legal advice may be necessary about the new measure without charge," it had been announced in the press. The photograph is stilted and quite plainly posed. But it appeared in a number of newspapers and succeeded in publicizing the existence of the association and its mission. To look on Abe is to see a man of thirty-eight, deeply engrossed and determined to sign the form that would guarantee a pension to all the "worn out toilers" gathered around him. It was the peak of Abe's career in New York, and more than a moment of pure elation.

---

While the aged poor crowded around Abe, seeking his counsel, Henriette rested in France, complaining of the overabundance of milk that was staining her lovely dresses. But even as she smiled happily in photographs clutching her new baby, she couldn't resist a little jab at the father of her child and his self-renouncing ways. She felt that since the "great humanitarian" had given a number of newspaper interviews when he stepped off the ship on his return to New York, he should say something about his new son. "Such fine publicity," she wrote, "just like a great man! Why not get your son's picture in the Sunday *Times*, under the heading: son of the great humanitarian arrives in New York. At the tender age of two months he is interested in his father's work . . . and perhaps one day he will even surpass you."

But when Henriette returned and saw what Abe had been doing she was awestruck. "He wanted people to know their rights and what to do. Some of them were quite old—some of them were not very literate—some of them were a little senile and brought in by their children. Some of them came with no money, and Abe would put subway fare in their pockets." For Abe and Henriette, 1930 closed out as a time of great promise—success in New York, a newborn son—but elsewhere in the United States the Great Depression was taking hold and slowly infecting every aspect of life in the once-prosperous land.

There is a photograph of the great moment when FDR signed the Old Age Pension Law and gave out the pens in Albany on April 10, 1930. It shows a very tired FDR, shadows under his eyes, sunk in an oversize chair, handing away the first pen, and crowded in by a mass of bright-eyed pension advocates. Tucked away in this throng, somewhere behind the governor's left shoulder, barely visible because of his height, is a stark-eyed Abraham Epstein. His eyes are focused straight into the camera in seeming shock, very much alone among the brazen publicity seekers. FDR wasn't being fooled, he knew. The governor did not think much of the bill

New York Governor Franklin D. Roosevelt signing Old Age Pension bill, Albany, March 1930. Abe, barely visible, staring into the camera, behind the left shoulder of the man shaking FDR's hand. Henriette commented: "You could see he had been pushed aside."

and had reportedly said in an aside that it was "scarcely better than the dole."

---

I have often stared at that photograph, the picture of an era that now seems positively prehistoric. Henriette's only comment on that photograph had always been, "You could see he had been pushed aside," with a grim tone in her voice. But I have always seen something deeper and more alarming. Abe's eyes seem frantic, near to hallucination, and when I gaze at those eyes, I hear his high-pitched voice whispering to me: "Does anyone care that I am here?" His look is pleading, mixed with an edge of fear, as if he fully knew what fate had in store, what was in the back of FDR's mind. Will he pay for his fervor for a law that FDR had grumbled about to one of his aides, "Is this the lemon they are handing me?"

But I look deeper and I see something even more excruciating: ascending pain, a scream about to pass Abe's lips at any moment, an eerie re-

The Free Information Bureau of the American Association for Old Age Security, New York, September 1930. Prospective pensioners requesting help from Abe.

semblance to the man in the Edvard Munch painting at the precise moment before he opened his mouth in a wailing howl.

### 3

Whatever dread Abe may have felt standing behind FDR at the signing ceremony, it quickly passed when he went on the road to broadcast New York's great achievement. He was always catching trains, rushing from New Jersey to Ohio to Illinois to Nebraska, striding to podiums to lecture, cornering legislators, speaking at hearings, and trying as hard as he could to put pressure on reluctant politicians, encouraging them to do the same as New York had done. He was a whirlwind of promotion, often putting in sixteen- to eighteen-hour days, and one of his associates asked him how he found time to eat or sleep. Friends warned him that he was burning himself out, but Abe paid no attention. What mattered, he reported to the members of the association, was that "the movement is spreading like wildfire and we are making wonderful progress."

Abe's system of work was autocratic and centralized. He hired state representatives, but their main role was to prepare the way for his energetic descents into hearings and meetings. At the time, such single-minded but exhausting energy was an effective way of getting the message out. The mass media of today did not exist. Newspapers carried the news. Those in power could be reached easily by mail or talked to in person. And good field workers were readily available. In the dark days of the depression people needed jobs and were grateful for whatever pittance the association could pay them. Abe, with his high-intensity passion, had little trouble infecting them with the justice of the cause. But they were to make no decisions on policy; all was to be controlled from the New York office, which, of course, meant by Abe and no one else. "The little dictator and know it all," as he had been called in Pennsylvania, would be damned if he was going to let anyone tell him how he should do the work. "Too many cooks spoil the broth!" was a cliché he loved to quote.

Still, some came up with inspired ideas of their own for passing old-age pension laws. The representative for Missouri, for example, a state known for the worst poorhouses in the nation, put up signs along the roads with the slogan, "Vote Yes on Amendment #1—Keep Out of The Poorhouse!" It worked. Missouri passed an old-age pension law in November 1932. The many men and women who did the field work for Abe became intensely loyal to him personally and to what he stood for. They frequently came to the house in New York for dinner, and for years after Abe had died many of them wrote and came to see Henriette. They were family.

---

Abe was not alone on the front lines. At least three others were prominent in the early efforts to create social security in the United States. I. M. Rubinow, the first man to draw attention to America's need for a true system of social insurance, was, like Abe, a Russian Jew who had emigrated to the United States in 1893 at the age of eighteen. He went to Columbia, became a medical doctor, and worked in settlement houses among the poor. Over time he became a skilled statistician and director of important philanthropies. For many years he was part of the American Association for Labor Legislation directed by John Andrews, but he began to see that Andrews's voluntarist ideas would do nothing to change the problem of old-age poverty. In 1913 he published a seminal book called *Social Insurance,* which for many years was the most influential piece of writing on the topic. He became close friends with Abe when Abe worked in Harrisburg, and when the fight for old-age pensions in New York began to take shape he moved into Abe's orbit and offered his expertise to the campaign.

Rubinow was at heart a scholar and scientist, and in person he was eloquent and dignified. He was twenty years older than Abe, near the age of Abe's father, and he had been part of the movement for social insurance for a long time. He was someone Abe always looked to for advice and counsel. He, in turn, was drawn to Abe's energy and passion, and served on his board and spoke at his conferences. He supported Abe's high-powered campaigns on all fronts, but there was a moment—when the battles got heated—that he chose to remain on the sidelines. He was by nature not a combative man, and perhaps that is why he was often referred to as the "theoretician of social insurance." Abe pleaded with him on many occasions to become more involved in the work of the association, but he would always back away. He had a family to support, he told Abe, and felt he could not work for little or no wages.

Paul Douglas, another of the early activists, was a rising star in economics at the University of Chicago in the 1920s and author of an important book in 1925 called *Wages and the Family*. Like Rubinow, he had been part of John Andrews's AALL, but when Abe's group came on the scene he realized that it was more assertive and would get more accomplished, particularly in pushing laws based on contributory social insurance. Douglas made a great impression on FDR when he was summoned to Albany to run a major conference on unemployment. His grasp of the subject allowed FDR to preside over the meeting in remarkably impressive fashion, it was said. FDR respected Douglas and relied on him for advice, but this did not prevent Douglas from having a relationship with Roosevelt that was as tangled as Abe's. Eventually Douglas became an influential senator from Illinois and a potential presidential candidate. Paul Douglas worked with Abe all over the country, participated in the national conferences, and understood Abe fully for what he was: a man on a mission. He never forgot Abe and his achievements, and wrote a glowing introduction to the 1968 reprint of Abe's major book, *Insecurity*.

Finally, there was Frances Perkins, the first woman to become a member of a president's cabinet. She had first known FDR when he was a young lawyer in New York and had dismissed him as just another conservative son of the Establishment. Her involvement with progressive causes led to her being appointed by New York's Governor Al Smith as a member of the Industrial Board. When Roosevelt was elected, he moved her up to the post of industrial commissioner, where she was in charge of labor issues, and from there she exposed FDR to many of the new ideas and programs for social reform then stirring in the United States. She was a strong ally to Abe and the association, but when FDR won the presidency and made history by appointing her secretary of labor, she became an unpredictable and unavailable figure to many in the movement for social security. She got along well with FDR and had his confidence, but she was shy and retiring, and struggled with difficult family problems in New York while serving in Washington. She was never an activist and invariably was wary of the energetic opinions of experts. She had her own ideas about how social security should be carried out and was influential in creating the Social Security Act of 1935, but she may have also been following the lead of her boss, whom Kenneth Davis described as having "an inclination toward deviousness, or at least against forthrightness, whenever dealing with anyone whom he regarded as a rival for power or a threat." And for Perkins, this eventually meant Abe.

---

In 1931, when unemployment was soaring—although the exact numbers were a mystery as the U.S. government in those days had no reliable means of getting statistics—FDR, whose presidential ambitions were now obvious, made a bold and unexpected move. He gave a carefully planned speech before the New York legislature on August 28. Seated behind the dais, where his canes and steel leg braces could be carefully hidden, he went on record before the lawmakers and the nation in favor of government intervention on a massive scale. He spoke up for a "definite obligation to care for those who through accident or old age are permanently incapacitated but also for men and women incapable of supporting themselves or their families because of circumstances." The state is the "creature of the people . . . for their mutual protection and well being," he said. "Government is but the machinery through which such mutual aid and protection are achieved." These were unprecedented ideas for a politician pursuing the presidency, and amazingly close to the sort of government help people like Abe had believed in.

FDR's speech made a big hit with those in the social security movement. No more self-reliance—state intervention instead. Abe, Rubinow, Douglas, and all the true backers of social insurance felt that with a politician like FDR on their side, victory might not be far off. In 1929, for example, when Abe had given a speech, the audience rarely numbered more than thirty or forty. But by the early 1930s he was drawing crowds of two or three hundred, and sometimes as many as five hundred. And whereas in 1927 there had been only 1,255 old-age pensioners in all of America, by

1935 the states themselves were paying pensions to over 231,000 aged retirees. The association's monthly, *Old Age Security Herald,* carried cheering
headlines: "Pension Wave Sweeps Nation," "Half of Union in Pension
Column," "Social Insurance Becomes a Leading Campaign Issue." The
seeds sown by Abe were sprouting all across the land.

One example was Ohio. An old-age pension bill had passed both
houses of the legislature and awaited the governor's signature. But before
it reached his desk politicians on the joint conference committee rose up
and threw out the bill in its entirety. Abe, along with his Ohio allies,
worked to create a referendum on the issue and collected 130,000 signatures to get the old-age pension law on the ballot. Like the rocket he was,
Abe spent weeks crisscrossing the state, speaking wherever he could,
pushing the referendum, but as voting neared he sensed the public had
little interest. Discouraged, on election day he left on the overnight train
for Chicago to meet Paul Douglas and discuss the next move.

"As the train drew into the station the rain was pouring down in solid
sheets and as Abe stepped down to the platform, his face was just as
gloomy," Douglas recalled. "'Paul,' he croaked, 'I have never had more
than twenty people at any meeting. There is absolutely no interest in old
age pensions. We've been ingloriously licked.' 'Before you decide on that
look at this story in the Morning Tribune.' There it was on the first page,
'Old Age Pensions Carry 3 to 1 in Ohio!' People had quietly made up their
minds, they didn't need to go to Abe's meetings. They had decided inde-
pendently . . . that they wanted old age pensions."

For Douglas it was a transcendent moment. "We knew then that we
would ultimately win. It was no longer a question of whether but when
and how." Such was the bubbling optimism of the social security movement even as the Great Depression was making Americans more pes-
simistic.

4

The depression in America, with its bread lines, apple sellers, evicted
families crowding the sidewalks, unemployed mobs at factory gates, and
Wall Street tycoons jumping out of windows, may look to many like a sad
but colorful time from quickly turned pages of photographs in a history
book. What cannot be pictured as effortlessly, however, is the real America, a land in rebellious agitation, menaced by violence and crawling with
reformers and messiahs of the most unsavory kind. Panaceas were bel-

lowed from pulpits, left-wing groups screamed for attention, and hare-brained proposals to cure unemployment were being offered by desperate politicians. Every American had his or her own wild solution to unbeliev-able misery. Old-age pension clubs were sprouting up everywhere, though most were just scams run by charlatans, like the man Abe had met in Cincinnati who told him that if people would buy his little tickets for a nickel or a dime he would guarantee everyone a pension. And raucous ag-itation came from both sides of the political aisle. On the right it came from demagogues such as Father Coughlin with his anti-Semitic tirades and the proto-fascist governor of Louisiana, Huey Long, with his "Share Our Wealth" plan and its slogan of "Every Man a King." On the left there was the eccentric old-age pension leader Francis Townsend with his millions of followers, as well as the Communist Party with its growing influence over many of the reform groups. The time was rife with strikes, mass demon-strations, and angry marches. Everywhere the police were clubbing the un-ruly public. Violence seemed ready to engulf America. "There probably had never been so many eruptions of public unrest in such a short period of time over so wide a spectrum of geography and population in the na-tion's history . . . between the winter of 1930 and the winter of 1933, each incident seeming to grow bigger and more menacing than its predecessor," historian T. H. Watkins recalled in his book *The Great Depression*. It was a frightening reminder to Abe of the abuse and suffering of his Russian youth and of the dangers in view if the Communists gained a substantial measure of power. Fascism was on the rise, with Hitler and Mussolini al-ready entrenched in Germany and Italy. Could America disintegrate as well? It was a real possibility. Sinclair Lewis would soon issue such a warn-ing in his 1935 novel *It Can't Happen Here*, and he would not be alone in fearing for the future of America's democracy.

But for the American Association for Old Age Security, times were good. Membership was up, conferences were well attended, the monthly newsletter had more subscribers, and its leader, Abraham Epstein, was of-ten in the news, no longer a lonely Don Quixote but a respected veteran of the legislative wars. The campaign for old-age insurance was expand-ing all over the country, and when FDR won the presidency and the Dem-ocrats came back into office, Abe was convinced the moment had finally arrived to move real social security ideas out into the open. "Why only old age pensions" he had asked in 1928, "why not have everything?" American society could be transformed, capitalism might even be saved, Abe believed, by an all-inclusive system of social insurance.

Abe's new book, *Insecurity: A Challenge to America*, was published in

1933 by Harrison Smith and Robert Haas, and in it he pulled together all his ideas about how to save his cherished adopted country from its present crisis. Beginning with his first work, *Report of the Pennsylvania Commission on Old Age Pensions*, (1919), then *Facing Old Age*, (1921), *The Challenge of the Aged* (1928), and finally *Insecurity*, the titles of his books tell how much his thinking had been broadened and deepened. Technical concepts embodied in descriptive phrases such as "social insurance" were transformed into much larger societal issues with the emotional overlay of a word such as "insecurity."

But in his heart Abe had only one message. Take action *now* for the old, the unemployed, the sick, the disabled, and all widows and orphans. And stop waiting around. All of Abe's zeal in his books, articles, and speeches was meant only to move lawmakers into action. He hammered away with research, charts, statistics, polemics, sarcasm—when speaking to the uninformed in his squeaky foreign accent as well as in his writing—that it was in America's self-interest to create a just and fair society. From one book to another Abe's writing became more comprehensive, the chapters became more current, and the statistics became more up to date. But his ideas remained resolute: social security could save the American people from disaster and turmoil, and bring to life the myth of happiness claimed for them by the Declaration of Independence.

What *Insecurity* proposed that was distinctive in the early 1930s was a vast new way to look at what we now disparagingly label "the safety net." Roy Lubove and a number of other historians have pointed out that more than any other reformer of that era, Abraham Epstein believed that "social security was a means to economic redistribution. He urged the need for the government's financial participation to achieve this redistributive purpose. Otherwise the burden of cost would fall most heavily on those least able to afford it." Abe wanted to pass down some of the wealth at the top to those at the bottom via social security, thereby narrowing the income gap and keeping American society free of economic difficulty. That was what social security was meant to do. It was the way to social preservation of American values and away from social disintegration. The seeds for that idea had germinated in his first little book, *The Negro Migrant in Pittsburgh*, in 1919, when he had warned that all the city's citizens would suffer unless something was done to help the new, unfortunate Negroes in their midst.

Drawing on his friendship with Frances Perkins, Roosevelt's new secretary of labor, Abe asked her to write an introduction to *Insecurity*. It was reminiscent of an earlier move when he had dedicated *The Challenge of the*

*Aged* to FDR, but this time the results were more satisfying. "Material distress and deterioration of human values," she wrote, "grow at a greater pace than the preventive measures we take. Most European countries have nation-wide unemployment insurance, medical care provisions and other forms of social insurance . . . in America reality calls for action. Social insurance is one step further toward insuring against uncertainties and more *equal distribution of wealth."* Abe was elated. Perkins was publicly supporting his theories and goals. With her on his side, and through her the new president, he was convinced he would have a role to play in the New Deal's plans for social security.

---

To celebrate the publication of *Insecurity*, a large party was held at the home of a wealthy association supporter named Warren J. Vinton. It was an elegant private home on the east side of Manhattan, and the party swarmed with guests on its several floors. A number of newspaper reporters and critics had been invited to generate publicity, as at a fashionable gallery opening. The food and drinks were plentiful, and Henriette was bedazzled by all the attention Abe was receiving from the guests. Except for several right-wing newspapers, the book reviews were all favorable. The *New York Times* gave it a full page: "Mr. Epstein knows what he believes with clear-cut finality . . . that arouses one's admiration for its completeness . . . a great and comprehensive body of knowledge . . . that is notable for its almost world-wide sweep and its richness of detail." But when confronted with the author's fervor, the critic was ill at ease. "He has written an interesting, timely and valuable book, which would, perhaps have been more persuasive if he had seen fit to restrain his ardors of conviction." Abe the scholar was admired, but his militant beliefs—that side of him which made him seem like a one-man revolutionary juggernaut—were not to everyone's taste.

*Insecurity* went through three editions (1933, 1936, 1938) and grew from six hundred to nearly nine hundred pages. It was one of three books published in the 1930s that helped turn the tide in favor of social security. The other two were by Paul Douglas and Isaac Rubinow, so that by 1933 the three musketeers of social security were attacking in unison.

# The New Element

*I slowly climbed the stairs. Their creaking sighs announced my arrival.*
*"Ah, there you are at last," Henriette called out. "I have something to show you."*

*I entered and found her unable to rise easily from the fraying couch and its sagging springs. She made a motion for me to sit next to her, an act that I knew would make me uncomfortable. A plastic baggie lay at her side. She held out a photograph. I took it and saw a picture of the house at 389 Bleecker Street in September 1929. It was a rear view that showed a small enclosed backyard and two clothes lines full of wash stretching between crumbling wooden fences. A neighboring house could also be seen with two sheds in the back, clearly outhouses.*

*In 1929 Henriette and Abe had been living on 185th Street and Riverside Drive for two years and commuting back and forth by subway to the office on lower Fifth Avenue. She was tired, and Abe was exhausted. As she later told an interviewer, "Apartment house living was not for me. I had always lived in lovely, big, spacious old houses in the south of France. The last one had a 1789 date engraved over the doorway."*

*A group of intellectuals in Abe's circle had come together to make a community of houses for themselves and their children in the heart of the old twisted streets and run-down houses of New York's Greenwich Village. "Cooperation" was one of the buzzwords for the progressive-minded of the era, and the group, which included the teacher and poet Mark Van Doren, the civil libertarian Roger Baldwin, the philanthropist Evelyn Preston, the journalist Max Lerner, as well as several artists, had wanted to create a little oasis for themselves, hidden away from the clamor of the big city and the new high rises sprouting up everywhere. Fourteen houses were put together as a joined community and named Bleecker Gardens, because most of the houses fronted on Bleecker Street between West*

*Eleventh and Perry Streets. Henriette bought one of the last houses left despite the advice of almost everyone she knew, including Abe, who had always lived in apartments and had no interest in being a capitalist owner of property. For Henriette there had also been another motive. "With Abe you had to tie him down . . . so that he would not give all his money away. He was going to invest his civil service money from Pennsylvania with the association. I stopped that. Buying the house in Greenwich Village, at least he would be tied down with mortgage payments." Henriette and the reluctant Abe acquired their first and only home in September 1929, shortly before the stock market collapsed. Less than a year later I was born and became a part of the life of that house.*

*Greenwich Village at that time was a crumbling area of old single-family homes. Most of the residents were Italian immigrants who crammed the houses with children and filled the streets with vegetable pushcarts and strolling musicians, making the streets look and sound more like Sicily than New York. Nearer the Hudson River the dilapidated buildings were filled with immigrant Irish who worked on the docks as stevedores. The houses of the newly joined community were mostly from the mid–nineteenth century, and the one at 389 Bleecker Street had been built in 1852, but all of them were in a state of deterioration and none had electricity or hot water. Many still had outhouses, and all were stuffed with "roomers." The intellectuals' novel plan had intrigued a real-estate editor at the* New York Times *who wrote, "In a very forceful manner they are returning to the privacy and comfort of one's own distinctive dwelling as contrasted with the huge human habitations each of which is tenanted by more than a score of families." In a year's time the houses were repaired, the outhouses disposed of, the fences taken down, and from the once-separate backyards a common garden was created, with flower beds, trees, a fountain, and a wading pool, "furnishing the little tots of the community," the* Times *reporter added, "with means of healthful exercise amid perfectly safe conditions." But despite the privies being turned into flower beds, a few dissenting voices had been raised against the invading intellectuals. The owner of an old "notions" shop on the ground floor of one of the houses had put up a sign: "Sorry we have to move—the new element is moving in!"*

*That "new element," in most cases, has long since departed this world. The Van Doren house was inherited by son Charles Van Doren (of television's $64,000* Dollar Question *notoriety) who soon sold it when newspapermen found out where he lived. When Roger Baldwin died, his heirs chose to rent rather than live in Bleecker Gardens. And the children of the various artists—none of whom became well known—chose to sell rather than stay after their parents died. Everywhere, new owners now live in the houses that were rebuilt in 1929. Except for*

*Henriette, who had hung on tenaciously to 389 Bleecker Street, remaining on the grounds like a character in a Chekhov play, almost an artifact, a reminder of New York's socially conscious past. All that was in her home in the 1930s was still there now, as in a long-forgotten and uncared for provincial museum—timeless, frozen, and possessing an air of faded gentility, if not downright decay. The photograph of 389 Bleecker Street that Henriette had uncovered had nothing to do with nostalgia. She was communicating the value of property. When visitors marveled at her foresight in owning a house in now stylish Greenwich Village, she would show them the picture of the backyard, the clothes lines, and outhouses of 1929, and would gloat without hesitation, "Everyone thought I was crazy! But now they all envy me."*

*Sitting next to Henriette feels like being poised on the edge of an extinct volcano. For from 1930 to 1942 the house at 389 Bleecker Street had been filled with people, food, drink, and passion, a gathering place for reformers in 1930s America, a salon Henriette created where activists of all stripes gathered to plot the advancement of social security. There is little that remains to recall that glowing era, except the shredded and sagging sofa, the baby grand piano (now unplayed, out of tune, and covered with letters and papers,) the unsteady claw-footed desk (where Abe worked and wrote), and the books and papers on the overstuffed shelves, now carefully wrapped in plastic baggies. What also survives are the scratched and repaired tables and chairs where people ate, drank, and argued, and behind the cranky cupboard doors lie the china, silver, and glassware used by those who struggled for reform in the United States so long ago. The past is still present, and the current radio, for instance, sits exactly where its green-glowing predecessor sat, on the same shaky table by the window overlooking the cherry tree in the garden. The tree itself, planted when the "new element" arrived in 1929, now towers over much of the greenery, shutting the garden out—but every spring it still flowers majestically, laying a magical carpet of pink over the varicolored stones that were laid to cover the rubbish and outhouses of previous generations. 389 Bleecker still retains a touch of unexpected glory.*

5

One day when I was ten and standing in Abe's study, I gazed up at the volumes of books on his crowded shelves.

"Why are there so many books up there?" I asked.

"You know, Pierre," he answered calmly, "the pen is mightier than the sword!"

Bleecker Gardens. The
author with Abe
and Henriette, 1934.

I had no idea of what he was talking about. I could not imagine how a
flimsy ink pen could outlast a mighty flashing sword.

"Try it on Joe Louis," I thought. But I said nothing.

Instead I looked up at Abe, waiting for an explanation. I remember how
he looked at that time: a little man, with thin arms and a large belly, and
one eye that often drifted away from center behind the owl-shaped glasses he always wore. He was always smoking, and his balding head seemed
much too large for his slight frame. Only now, when I look back, do I understand what the little man who looked down at me was trying to explain: "Look at me. I am a weakling. So if I am going to ride out like a
mounted knight and battle injustice, then my only blade will have to be
this pen."

Abe had always spent a lot of time learning to write English and studying public speaking. He took courses and studied wherever he could—
Pittsburgh, Harrisburg, South Bend, New York. And eventually his almost
illegible scrawl was transcribed by devoted secretaries into typewritten

manuscripts that turned into good prose in books and articles, rip-roaring out into the world of political reform. "Epstein . . . contributed more to the old age pension movement than any single individual," wrote Roy Lubove in his book on social security. Similarly, Kenneth Davis pointed out, "More than any other man he was responsible for the fact that when the New Era collapsed and the New Deal began, social insurance was again a live idea in America." Indeed, Abe's pen had made social security a hot subject when Roosevelt took over.

He had no interest in writing for the ages, or in being remembered. What he wrote was meant to resound like a military anthem, or like a banner to be carried into battle. He wanted his books and articles to be like a Bible for the social security missionaries, just as that book had been for the early Christians or the Old Testament had been for the Jews. In fact Abe carried a certain religious fervor into all that he did. That is why he met with such success on the 1927 tour across America, why he had no trouble when asked to speak of God's will. Those retired, worn-out old cowboys in a small town in Montana had been converted to old-age pensions by him in the way a preacher would have tried to save their souls.

The religious sense of mission seemed to lie under almost everything Abe wrote. *Insecurity,* his most comprehensive statement on social security as the savior of depression-shrouded America, opens with clear reference to the Bible and what it meant to him:

Ever since Adam and Eve were driven from the sheltered Garden of Eden, insecurity has been the bane of mankind. The struggle of human progress has been a battle for security. From the very beginning of group life this has been the principal aim of civilization . . . A vital test of the progress of a society is the degree of security it affords its members. It was, indeed, to provide security to life, liberty, and the pursuit of happiness that the United States was founded in 1776.

The challenge confronting us in the twentieth century is that of economic insecurity, which weighs down our lives, subverts our liberty, and frustrates our pursuit of happiness . . . Economic insecurity, as we know it at present, did not exist in earlier societies. It is our present complex civilization which, while conquering nature, time and space, has made men the slaves of their jobs . . .

Those words are ones that any American would be happy to read, even a fundamentalist Christian, for Abe was fully aware that religious pieties lie at the core of American political life and he invoked them before proceeding on to more radical thoughts. But in order for his message to work, he made a subtle transformation in the conventional meaning of the Garden of Eden—instead of a land from which we had been ejected by our knowledge of good and evil, he changed it into a "sheltered" Garden. Adroitly, he recast the home of man from a God-given paradise that can never be regained into a place where God saw to it that the first man and woman were protected and secure. This to Abe meant they were *not insecure*. It is a sly and almost imperceptible change in emphasis, which he then coupled with the patriotic catchwords of the American republic, "life, liberty, and the pursuit of happiness." Who in America would want to argue with the Garden of Eden, and life, liberty, and the pursuit of happiness? But a sly twist had been put into those shibboleths, creating a tiny curtain hole that changed their meaning and through which Abe was able to pour the main thrust of his entire argument: No civilization will ever be great, nor will it come upon paradise, unless it provides "security" to its people.

With the phrase "frustrating our pursuit of happiness," he enlarged the hole. The power of the word "frustrate" emphasizes how much the pursuit of happiness can be thwarted by the absence of security. In the nine hundred pages of his book Abe exposed the criminal who would seek to destroy our cherished way of life. The name of the brute was "insecurity."

Not long before he died in 1942, Abe said in his final speech: "The mechanism of social security can not only help to mitigate, but can do much to avert economic crisis, for the underlying basis for social security is not a newfangled theory of governmental pampering of the individual, but part and parcel of the deeply-rooted, primitive desire for social preservation." That last phrase—"primitive desire for social preservation"—illustrates how his thoughts were linked to ancient articles of belief. More than economics underlie the words Abraham Epstein chose as his battle cry— social security.

Abe's success at converting people to the religion of social security was due to what Henriette called "charisma." She claimed she could see it when he walked into a room and people turned to look at his tiny, energetic presence. She stretched it a bit when she said he had the same effect on people as the glamorous John Kennedy. But she meant it, and it was certainly the reason why so many people came to the house in New York to eat, drink, and listen to what Abe had to say. For me, one moment is unforgettable: the day Japan attacked Pearl Harbor on the afternoon of December 7, 1941, and I had rushed in to bring Abe the news. Later, when night descended on New York, 389 Bleecker Street was filled with people who wanted to be with Abe at the moment when everyone knew that the terror of war was now going to envelop America: the hulking, mustachi-oed Romanian refugee writer, Konrad Bercovici; the sly intellectual French-man, Georges Deutsch, who in an act of patriotism for his occupied home-land changed his name to Boinet and went to Washington to work for the Office of War Information; the courtly, always immaculately dressed Vir-ginian, Harry Elias, who ran the publicity for the association; and the Rus-sian refugee musician, Igor Bouryanine, who had already escaped two to-talitarian regimes, the Russian and German ones, and had no interest in being caught for good. They rang the bell, came up the stairs with their wives and friends, ate the food that Henriette served, and seemed to hud-dle together for comfort, their many different accents coloring the dark-ness of that night like a map of the suffering world. They wanted to be to-gether, and they wanted to be with Abe. They all listened when he spoke and seemed to derive comfort from his words. That short, dynamic man seemed to many to radiate something special.

Abe's ultimate volume became Henriette's personal Bible. Despite the difficulties she had with Abe as a husband, she never wavered in her ad-miration for his magnum opus. The book had been so successful that Ran-dom House had taken over publishing it for the revised editions in 1936 and 1938. In the 1950s when they let it go out of print and wanted to scrap the plates, she protested and had them trucked down to 389 Bleecker Street and lowered into the basement, where they lay dormant, waiting to rise like the Phoenix and enlighten America once more. From time to time people asked to quote from *Insecurity* or even to use sections as an exam-ple of good declarative writing. But even as late as 1979 she was still try-ing to get Abe's message across as she talked with one of her uninformed oral biographers. Social security, she explained, was "Number 1, purely for humanitarian reasons. Number 2, it was one of the measures to avert economic crisis, to keep the country on an even keel, to prevent unem-ployment. Third, he had seen the Nazis at work in Germany, and knew that people who are insecure will turn to violent solutions, and he point-ed out Italy, Germany, and of course, the biggest of them all, Russia." But she never felt that any of her interviewers fully grasped the great ideas the book contained, and in one particular case she just quit trying. Testi-ly, she told the interviewer, "Oh . . . It would take me until next year per-haps to explain all this."

Henriette never got over falling for a man who had written a book, and she would not permit *Insecurity* to disappear into the void. She undertook her curatorial duties like a missionary teacher in an illiterate land. She kept up a never-ending correspondence suggesting people quote it, use it for source material, and give full and ample credit to the author. In the 1960s and '70s it was still used as a text in universities, and when a reprint suddenly became possible in 1968, Henriette rejoiced in her brilliance in not listening to others. Paul Douglas, then a senator, honored her request and wrote a loving introduction to the new edition. Henriette had triumphed. Abe's great book was alive. Even now it is still in use as a basic text in the social sciences. The silly French girl had done it again. In spite of everyone. Including the long-dead Abe.

6

In June 1933, Abe made a big move. His creation, the American Association for Old Age Security, went out of existence—and immediately rose again as the American Association for Social Security, a name that seemed to many of his supporters to come out of nowhere. The monthly bulletin became simply *Social Security*, and the first issue informed readers that the transformation was done to awaken America to the need for not only old-age security but also unemployment, medical, disability, and widows and survivors insurance—the entire range of social security. Abe had decided it was time to rush from his self-imposed corner in old-age pensions. With his fists cocked, he was aiming for a knockout blow against the forces of reaction. But his opponents in the ring of public debate were ferocious battlers. Not only that, but in 1933 the words "social security" would undoubtedly make most people shudder at how much they resembled that dreaded word, "Socialism!"

One month after the change of name, Abe boldly jumped into the frenzied controversy surrounding unemployment by running a conference to draft a model bill that would reflect his and I. M. Rubinow's ideas. It was heavily publicized and became the lead article in the fall issue of *Social Security*. It was a pure social insurance concept. When a worker was unemployed, he would be able to receive benefits from a central fund to which the worker and employer had contributed, regardless of where or for whom the employee had worked. "Abraham Epstein, a fluent and powerful writer in the social security field, not only favored [these] funds . . . but could see no escape from governmental participation on the British model," Arthur Schlesinger explained. Paul Douglas and other experts agreed with him.

When Abe decided to speak out on unemployment, no one could say how many millions were out of work. The government did not know how to collect the statistics. But the unemployed could be seen everywhere, like a menacing army loitering on the streets of every city and town. By then the politics and fury of the struggle to save the country from the anger of the jobless had moved leftward. People spoke openly about overturning the capitalist system and declared it was time for a revolution. Elected officials, such as the governor of Minnesota, Floyd Olson, declared that the government should nationalize key industries. The American system was in crisis and the social insurance reformers found themselves caught in the middle. They were vilified by both the Left and the Right. The Republican conservatives accused them of being part of the Communist plot to take over America, and the Communists assailed the social security movement as a capitalist sop to keep the masses under control. Abe was a target of the Communists in particular because of his outspoken hatred for Soviet Russia. They "openly despised virtually all other groups on the left and attacked them with a ferocity that was reciprocated," the Whittaker Chambers biographer Sam Tannenhaus has noted, "and for many years Socialists would bitterly remember being branded 'social fascists' by Communists in the early 1930's." Communist Party activists convinced a number of members of the American Association for Social Security to resign in protest because its plans weren't radical enough. One philanthropist, who had been introduced to Abe by Norman Thomas, the head of the Socialist Party, would contribute a thousand dollars at a time, an enormous sum in the 1930s. She suddenly withdrew her support, incited by "fellow travelers," nonmembers of the Communist Party who followed the party's instructions. Defections like hers created a big hole in the budget, which, along with personal attacks on Abe, added to the tensions facing the new association.

Despite the change of name and emphasis, membership stopped growing. Supporters were confused, and Henriette herself was baffled. She always started her day by opening the mail, hunting for checks, renewals, and new members. But with the new name the checks began to disappear—sometimes only one a day. Henriette hoped that Abe would be out of the office when the mail came. She tried to hide the results, but Abe always asked about how much money the mail had brought in. She had to tell him, and she could see his grim look as he went to his desk. The change in the association's mission had been abrupt, and she found the new work difficult. "I had to redraft all the little folders . . . now they had to stress the idea of unemployment, with breadlines and poor people being out of work. They just didn't help us much." Promoting unemployment and medical insurance did not look as affecting in the brochures as that of the plight of a sweet, aged couple on their way to life in a poorhouse.

When Abe startled everyone with the change of name of his association, there was a sort of hushed silence. People were puzzled, and then asked questions. Who was going to do all the work? Where would the money for expansion come from? It was too sudden. Abe was accused of being uppity by injecting himself into the unemployment insurance debate. The new association had no business getting involved, despite the fact that the nation was consumed by the problem, and that possibly as many as fifteen million Americans were out of work, on relief, or selling apples. Most public figures looked on unemployment insurance as an outlandish foreign plot. Thomas Eliot, the lawyer who drafted the Social Security Act, colorfully described the mind-set. "Oh, yes, I. M. Rubinow, Abraham Epstein, and Paul H. Douglas had written books about it, but who read those books? I remember a scene in a play I attended in the early thirties—some characters entered the stage carrying placards reading, 'We want Unemployment Insurance,' and this got a big laugh from the audience . . . It was always referred to as the 'dole.'" People did not want another voice in the halls of Congress or anywhere else challenging their thinking, particularly the hot-headed words of a man like Abe. Concerned friends told him it was more than one man could handle.

The grand scheme for social security in America, with its major publication, *Insecurity*, did not run from the gate like the winning horse it was supposed to be. Publicly, Abe was not worried. He just plowed ahead, refusing to wait for others. With his own ideas and proposals for laws he went on the attack. His major comrades in arms, such as Rubinow and Douglas, stuck by him. But others were angry at his go-it-alone tactics and began to criticize him, including the long left-by-the-wayside John Andrews. Still, despite his driven, self-centered methods, Abe never had trouble finding followers. One historian, noting how Abe was the most vocal and colorful of all the reformers, believed his flamboyance, combined with his quotability and knack with reporters, made it easy for him to attract the attention of politicians. His statements in the press always made news, and when he testified before lawmakers he was praised by both Republicans and Democrats. Arthur Capper of Kansas, a major power in the Senate, told reporters, "I would accept his judgment above all others in the social security field." Also, Walter George, the conservative Southern senator, publicly maintained that "if more of his ideas had been written into law we would have a better social security system in the United States." Abe was convinced his grand ideas were breaking through, despite the enmity that began to surround him. But some of his closest friends felt that the enormous energies pushing those ideas might be nearing their limits.

---

In 1934 there was a bitter battle to have an unemployment insurance plan adopted in New York modeled on the ideas that Abe, Rubinow, Paul Douglas, and others were supporting, in essence a pooled fund for all unemployed workers. It was known by then as the "Ohio Plan" because it was making headway in that state. The main opposition to it came from a venerable idea that was called the "American Plan." It was a name carefully calculated to let the public know that the plan was not a subversive foreign idea like Britain's government-funded system, but a native-born plan, or as Paul Douglas put it, "they hoped to head off demagogic criticism that it was un-American." Unfortunately it had almost nothing to do with helping the unemployed. It sought instead to "stabilize" employment—every individual business or group of allied businesses had to create its own fund to insure its own employees from unemployment. The more employees you placed on unemployment, then the more money you would have to keep in your unemployment fund. This stratagem was meant to encourage companies to fire fewer people because companies with the most unemployment had to pay the highest rates. This scheme not only had the advantage of being a home-grown idea but was already in existence in the state of Wisconsin, where it had become law in 1932. When enacted it no longer needed its patriotic cachet and became known simply as the "Wisconsin Plan." It was a plan originated by Professor John R. Commons at the University of Wisconsin in 1921, so it had a long history. It was thought of as a way to avoid social insurance ideas and preserve the American entrepreneurial spirit. As Commons's students marched out from the University of Wisconsin to take their place in the American reform movement, they popularized his ideas. And one student in particular, John Andrews, with his American Association for Labor Legislation, was a very effective propagandist. But oddly, despite its official status, the Wisconsin Plan never really got very far in Wisconsin—it never helped anyone who was out of work. The legislature postponed its financing until July 1933 because business interests complained, in 1934 they had not yet started to collect the premiums, and by 1935 when FDR had already begun work on his own unemployment plan—which was based for the most part on the Wisconsin Plan—it still had not paid out a cent.

From those hectic combative times there are many slogans that still ring faintly. In addition to the Wisconsin Plan and the Ohio Plan (favored by Abe, Rubinow, and Douglas) there were the "Townsend Plan," the "Ham and Eggs Movement," "Share Our Wealth," and the "Lundeen" bill in Congress. As a child I knew which ones to be for and which ones to be against, but I didn't have the faintest clue about what they meant back then. And now those phrases have all faded into oblivion like the dust storms of the 1930s that wiped away a part of America's landscape.

There is one set of words, though, that still resonates: "Merit Rating"— a catchword from the 1930s. No one I know today has ever heard of it— but those two words stuck in my throat when I was a child. We—the Epsteins—were solidly against it. I heard those two words vilified so frequently around the dinner table, or with guests in the living room, that I imagined them to be some vile animal ready to sneak into the house at any moment and poison everyone named Epstein. I encouraged every use of the term so that I could loudly demonstrate my disapproval. "Merit Rating—Ugh!" I would shout with scorn. Henriette had told Abe how good I was at making noises like all the animals when back in France— the cat, the dog, the sheep—but that I was at my best when imitating the singing of the priest. With those blossoming thespian talents, dressed in my pajamas, I started marching around the living room at bed time, spitting out the hated phrase with brio. Waving my arms in the air like a union member on strike, I would chant "Down With Merit Rating!" Abe loved it and collapsed with laughter. I kept it up as often as possible and added another protest to my repertoire: "I'm on strike against bed!" which seemed to offer more possibilities. Like a good militant I would exclaim those words as well, and Abe, trying to order me to bed, would again be helpless with laughter. After long weary hours in his office, sprawled on the couch, in shirt and loosened tie, his vest open, the evening newspapers scattered around him, he would be forced into a good time in spite of what might have happened during the day. If I could make Abe laugh, then I was part of the action. He could count on me too.

What was the despised "Merit Rating"? Or, as it was sometimes called, "Experience Rating." It was a term used to describe how an employer had to keep more money in his reserve fund if more people had been fired. The fewer people he had on unemployment, the smaller his reserve. A business could save money by not firing anyone. That was the despised "Merit Rating." It was as simple as that.

Abe fought a high-powered campaign in New York against John Andrews and his supporters. He was determined to destroy the entire concept behind the Wisconsin Plan, and he imprudently denounced John Andrews personally on a number of occasions. Abe was caustic in his analysis of the Wisconsin Plan. In a snide article called "Faith Cures for Unemployment," he wrote: "To penalize individual employers who have the most unemployment . . . was simply to penalize the weakest. I cannot see that much stabilization can be achieved through such a method." At that time Abe still had some control over his anger. But later, when his pen was overflowing with vitriol, he slammed the Wisconsin Plan as "the most stupid undertaking that has ever been suggested . . . a fantasy." For years there was no doubt in my mind that the people of Wisconsin were beneath contempt. The drive to pass the Ohio Plan in New York included another special train to Albany filled with sign-waving supporters. Henriette was blasé about how she had become adept in organizing those attention-getting outings, but in her own opinion entertainment had done the trick. In the middle of the angry legislative battle she came up with the idea of a cocktail party, and invited everyone remotely involved in the campaign down to 389 Bleecker Street.

"Of course I didn't invite John Andrews," Henriette recalled. "But right here, in this very room from where I'm talking, there were almost a hundred people—they went practically all over the house. We did serve them cocktails, so it made them very cheerful . . . and very agreeable to our idea."

At the party, Abe roamed everywhere and harangued everyone he could on the merits of the Ohio Plan. The biggest catch was George Meany, who at that time was president of the American Federation of Labor in New York. The labor unions had been mostly noncommittal, afraid that any government plan would hurt their independence. But Meany came around and offered the AFL's support. Whether it came from too many cocktails or Abe's buttonholing, getting organized labor on his side created a powerful future ally. Union support made the difference when the Ohio Plan easily passed the New York legislature on April 16, 1934. Abe was jubilant and reported that Andrews "was routed and received no support from any organization." In fact, Andrews and only one other man had spoken in favor of the Wisconsin Plan. Abe had triumphed, and for Henriette the Bleecker Street purchase as a social and political vortex was fulfilling its mission, proving to her once again how smart she had been. Still, the Wisconsin Plan would always haunt Abe, particularly when it was turned into Wagner-Lewis—named for its two congressional sponsors—and almost became law in 1933.

After his New York victory, Abe was exhausted. His schedule was crammed with meetings and travel, and he never seemed to get enough rest. Besides, the battle in New York had been costly. The association was spending more money than it was taking in and membership was still dropping. Supporters were also upset with Abe for his blunt speech and the ruthless way he had attacked John Andrews. Though she never liked Andrews, Henriette was uneasy with the personal animosity between the two men. "Although they were followers of the same cause . . . they could never stop clawing at each other. I sometimes think they were like two tigers devouring each other."

The battle for social security was nearing its emotional peak.

7

When Franklin Delano Roosevelt rode down Pennsylvania Avenue under gray skies in an open car to his inauguration on March 4, 1933, Herbert Hoover sat beside him in stony silence. As FDR doffed his top hat to the cheering crowds, Hoover stared straight ahead. The night before he had tried to get the new president to act jointly with him on the failing banks and the flight of gold from the treasury, but his request had been rebuffed. It would be a clean break. Hoover's slogan, "The New Era," was banished to the judgment of history. The New Deal boys were coming to town, just itching to clean up the Republican mess. Furious at Roosevelt's snub, Hoover refused to reply to the new president's attempt at conversation as they rode the mile from the White House to the Capitol. He knew then that the catastrophe engulfing America would be blamed on him.

Action on old-age security and unemployment were said to be high on the New Deal agenda. But in fact a congressional bill on old-age pensions had been in the hopper since 1927, awaiting passage. Abe, along with Paul Douglas and Isaac Rubinow, had made numerous trips to the nation's capital to push for a pension bill written by the association. Eventually Senator Clarence Dill of Washington and Representative William Connery of Massachusetts would sponsor it in every session. It was a modest bill that proposed spending ten billion dollars per year as grants-in-aid to those states that had passed effective old-age pension laws. It was a beginning, a way of encouraging individual states to pass pension laws with a federal money guarantee, but it failed to pass year after year. Hoover, if he'd ever given it a thought, might have given the Dill-Connery bill a little push, but as the nation staggered deeper into economic depression he remained in dreamland, repeating the moribund phrase, "Prosperity is just around the corner."

The ever-tenacious Abe tried one more time during Hoover's last year in office. On January 12, 1932, he hosted a large gathering at the elite Cosmos Club in Washington. Six senators and twelve representatives were present, and twenty others sent letters of regret. The speeches and reports were a rousing success, and the next day Abe dashed off a note to Senator Dill about how he was "still under the spell of the meeting we had last night . . . we all went away with a definite feeling that this is our year." But despite the rallying of the troops, the bill did not get past the Rules Committee and died in Congress once again. Herbert Hoover, without showing the slightest interest, had given away his chance to go down in history as the father of social security.

Social security was ignored for most of Roosevelt's first year in office, and the delay made it the prey of every crazy scheme imaginable. Sponsors of wacky ideas came out in the open, caterwauling for attention. In California, the novelist Upton Sinclair led a group called EPIC (End Poverty In California) that called for a federal old-age pension of fifty dollars a month. As the economy got worse, the figure soon rose to four hundred. Huey Long had his "Share Our Wealth" clubs, and there was another crowd with the quaint name "Ham and Eggs" that wanted "$30 every Thursday." Eventually "Ham and Eggs" collapsed in scandal—some of its leaders went to prison—proof of the many con games behind the plans to help the elderly.

The one proposal that came closest to success was the well-publicized "Townsend Plan." It called for two hundred dollars a month from the government to everyone over age sixty-five as long as they spent it in the same month. At the peak of its influence in 1935, the Townsend Plan clubs had 3.5 million members, a formidable lobby, and several members of Congress whose election was due to the clubs' support. By 1934 the government was being pounded from all sides. There were more than two dozen mostly preposterous pension bills rolling around under the Capitol Dome, and there was increasing left-wing pressure for social welfare legislation less rationally conceived than any proposed by Abe, Douglas, and Rubinow. Roosevelt, in the eyes of many, could have calmed the tempest by asserting leadership and having Dill-Connery passed along with Wagner-Lewis, a stop-gap companion measure on unemployment. But he was noncommittal, and the agitation grew more confrontational.

Finally, in early 1934 the president decided he had to do something about social security, but let it be known that all ideas on the subject would have to pass through his secretary of labor, Frances Perkins, before they got to him. When the news came out, Abe hurried down to Washington to see her. He had many other allies in and out of Congress, but the one he knew to be the most influential was Perkins, the first woman to become a major figure in American government. She had always supported his work in New York and had written the introduction to his most recent book, and he thought of her as a friend. In her office Abe pleaded with her to publicly support Dill-Connery, which was the only sensible old-age security measure before Congress. The impoverished elderly were in desperate need of help before the quacks took over and wrecked everything, he told her.

She reassured Abe when she told him, "I am definitely in favor of the legislation." Abe went away with optimism in his heart and told everyone the bill was going to pass this time. Dill also talked with Perkins on three occasions and was confident she would persuade FDR to encourage Congress to enact Dill-Connery. Abe thought another grand evening at the Cosmos Club full of senators and congressmen might nudge things along, and this time he gathered together more than thirty of them, Democrats and Republicans alike. The event was well reported in the newspapers, but despite the publicity it had no effect on Roosevelt, who had mysteriously clammed up on social security. As the congressional session was winding down, Abe made a final plea to Perkins that perhaps, unwisely, contained a veiled threat:

> The Dill-Connery Bill has reached its most critical state. We have carefully canvassed and are convinced that it not only meets with the approval of the American public but also the overwhelming approval of Congress. There is every desire of Congress to enact this bill into law . . . but they hate to do so before receiving a word of encouragement from President Roosevelt . . . they believe that silence on the part of the President means he does not approve of it . . . With the best interests of the Administration at heart we are anxious to avoid a situation which could be interpreted as anti-administration. I assure you, that it would be most painful and regrettable for us to be compelled to state that this humane and enlightened legislation, so widely accepted everywhere, was not favored by the Administration. I know how devotedly you have worked for this cause . . . we would be remiss in our duty and devotion to you, however, if we had not again appealed to you to intercede with the President at this most critical moment.

But beneath the surface Abe sensed trickery, for there were rumors floating around that Roosevelt had ideas of his own on the matter. "The President's attitude is more than an enigma. It approaches a form I do not want to characterize in a letter," was how Abe felt about the looming deviousness.

For more than a year FDR had stalled on social security, and to this day historians cannot settle on the reason. Biographer Theron Schlabach suspected "that rather than merely approve congressional measures, he wished to win political support by proposing his own program." Kenneth Davis thought that "by ostentatiously taking over, he could receive maximum popular credit . . . or that Roosevelt was at heart opposed . . . and so paid it only lip service . . . others accepted at face value the official explanation that the complex problems required more study." Arthur Schlesinger, Jr., suggested a political twist: "It was clear that if the Administration did not take action its hand would be forced . . . FDR wanted a program that would have maximum political effect." The columnist Walter Lippmann was caustic: "Roosevelt belongs to the new postwar school of politicians who do not believe in stating their views unless and until there is no avoiding it." This reason may be as good as any, since FDR's positions on most issues were enigmatic until the last moment.

When pressed, Roosevelt had said he favored Dill-Connery, but he never made a move to have Congress pass it. Nonetheless, in 1933 Dill-Connery got out of committee and passed in the House of Representatives, which was major progress, but Schlabach felt that "had Roosevelt encouraged it, it might have passed in the Senate" as well. Instead, counting on his extraordinary popularity, the president caught the nation and all the social security groups by surprise when he sent a now famous message to Congress on June 8, 1934. "I place the security of the men, women and children of America first," he said, and suggested "some safeguards against misfortunes which cannot be wholly eliminated in this man-made world." He then appointed a major new committee, composed of members of his cabinet, to come up with a program he could approve—but the report did not have to be on his desk until the last day of 1934, which meant the "safeguards" would have to wait for at least another six months, or for two years after his inauguration.

The year 1934 had started full of promise for Abe. He was appointed an American representative on the social insurance committee of the International Labor Office in Geneva, and when the news reached Henriette's family in Toulouse, her mother paraded the story loudly to all her friends and wrote Henriette, "What an honor it is for us to have such a son in our family." Abe had happily responded by sending a new American-made radio to his father-in-law, telling him he was intending to spend part of the summer of 1934 on vacation in France. But Roosevelt's announcement put an end to the dreams of summer frolic. For Abe it was like a violent wind had suddenly come up and knocked him off his feet. He felt betrayed by those he thought he could count upon, particularly Frances Perkins, who had told him she would support Dill-Connery. He was incensed at what he felt was her deception. It was the first sign of where he stood with the New Deal. The strain between Abe and Henriette also became more eruptive. She felt unwanted and unappreciated but seemed resigned to her misery, telling him, "I occupy so little room in your life."

What had in fact been going on surfaced years later in a letter that Louis Leotta—who had been writing a Ph.D. dissertation on Abe and the movement for social security—elicited from Perkins. Dill-Connery and Wagner-Lewis were a "trial run only," she wrote, for Roosevelt to gauge how much support existed for social security. FDR's endorsement of both bills had been pure ruse, and Perkins had just followed her boss's lead.

Everything Abe and his allies had tried to accomplish in Washington for the last seven years had been pushed aside. Abe now understood that he was almost nonexistent to the New Deal, akin to his image buried behind FDR in the photo of the Albany signing ceremony. Discouraged, he wrote one of his friends, "I am far from certain they will invite us for any discussion as to their plans. I doubt whether even the old age pension study will be entrusted to me. Of course if they called those who understand the problem . . . but all their history shows that they never consult the right people . . . I am frankly fearful." He shared his disappointment with Senator Dill and told him Roosevelt's message "would not only delay any achievement in Congress but would also prevent any real progress in the State legislatures in 1935 when over forty of them will meet." Perkins herself felt the same way. Thomas Eliot recalled that she "was eager to have the bill enacted so that the states in 1935 could take advantage" of the federal money. For the first time in his career Abe had been left out of anything to do with social security. There were hard times ahead, he warned his coworkers, but if anyone thought he would just fade away, they were wrong. If the New Deal's social security program was "unintelligent, the better policy would be to fight it from the start rather than try to go along."

8

In June 1934 the French Line's *Le Champlain* prepared to sail gracefully out to sea past the great towers lining New York harbor, and Abe, Henriette, and I were on board heading for a summer in France. But when the "All Ashore" sounded, Abe quickly vanished, darting down the gangplank and out of sight before anyone could notice. Happily occupied with all the friends, gifts, and champagne that filled the stateroom in the fashion of the 1930s boozy bon voyage party, I was unaware that Abe's disappearance was prearranged. He had decided to stay behind, like an alert watchdog, determined to find out what the New Deal was up to on social security, and I hadn't been told for fear that a screaming and uncontrollable child carrying on for days beforehand would have made life even more tense than it already was. But Henriette bore the brunt of the deceit, because as the ship sailed into the Atlantic I screamed furiously, over and over: "Why did Daddy go away? Why did Daddy go away?"

As the last piece of American soil faded from view my tantrum subsided, and I was sent off to the children's playroom while Henriette went to the majestic main salon and took a seat at one of the elegant inlaid writing tables by the windows overlooking the endless gray ocean. "I am utterly depressed," she wrote. "I can't tell you how worried I am about you. Please let's forget all the harsh words. I didn't mean to say them, neither did you I know."

Two years before, in 1932, when Henriette had gone back to France to show off her infant son, burglars had come in via the back garden and robbed 389 Bleecker Street. Precious jewelry and antiques had been stolen, and when informed of the theft, Henriette had been irate that no one would tell her exactly what had happened. She reproached Abe about how little he cared for all she had done to a make a home; her fury lingered for years, and she always pointed the finger at him as the reason for the theft. He was irresponsible because he had left the house in the care of another of his indifferent-to-private-property Socialist friends, and the result was that everything was gone and wrecked. "I do not know whether I shall be going back to such a jackass as you are—you have your old age pensions and do not need either Pierre or myself," she had berated him from the sanctuary of her parents' home in Toulouse. But the truth was that she loved her new American life and had no desire to abdicate her role in Abe's world of notables and activists to live in France with a small child in tow. "I hope you are not going to send the appeal to our members before I come back," she instructed him. "Someone has to sort out the mess." But the robbery, his absences, and his obsession with Washington politics were unnerving her. It was the start of the splitting apart of the Russian Jew and the French girl.

On arrival in Toulouse in 1934, I revived my fury, and Henriette made sure Abe got the point: "Daddy went to the meeting—daddy always goes to the meeting—daddy isn't nice to go to meetings," she quoted me, and then commented, "He considers it no less than a desertion." She continued the scolding: "In the world of admiring old maids where you love to be, there is at least one person who is not an old maid and wants to tell you a few things for your own good . . . when you confine your fighting to the enemies of old age pensions, instead of the whole world, you will be happier . . . nobody can occupy your position and act like a petty, stupid, narrow-minded friendless person." She accused him of being jealous of the fun she had with friends when he was away on the road. She also rebuked him with phrases such as "your tactics of always ignoring me, of dealing with me as a superior being to an inferior being," then paradoxically ended with words of praise: "I am glad the papers admit that Roosevelt was inspired by your book. We are very proud of it and happy."

From three thousand miles away, Abe paid little attention. Perhaps he was relieved she wasn't still in New York looking over his shoulder. Although he wrote to Toulouse faithfully twice a week, the letters are lost, and none of her replies indicate that he reacted harshly to her complaints. The summer ran on and I eventually calmed down, but Henriette did not. The New Deal's new attention to social security would help Abe morally but not financially, she told him. Possibly it would sell more copies of his book, but the writing was too technical and "most people will give it up at the start." When he wrote he was going off to Pennsylvania for a few days to help his old friend Jim Maurer with his biography, she was indignant. She accused him of doing things for Maurer that he would not do for his family. Trying to calm the tempest, Abe sent an article about him in a Jewish paper that had mentioned her, but she scornfully replied that he had probably given them the information reluctantly, and what was so extraordinary anyway, the Jews were always trying to claim credit for his brightness.

---

Abe did not go to France in 1934. Instead, he went fishing. Trolling quietly in a rowboat with his fishing line strung out behind him had a calming effect. Alone or with a friend, moving slowly through the water in the middle of a forested pond made him feel he was away from all his problems. And during the quiet of August, when official Washington was on vacation, he managed to get up into the wilds of Canada for some fishing. With two friends he drove two hundred miles north of Montreal, seventy-five miles away from the end of the railroad line, another thirty-five miles beyond the last village, and there in a little clearing on a wilderness lake the men camped and ate the trout and muskelunge they had caught. When Abe returned to New York, relaxed and calm, and bragged to Henriette that on the first day he caught three good-sized trout and cooked them, she complimented him but then cracked that she was astonished that his magnanimous soul had not given those poor fish back their freedom. When he sent her a picture of himself on a horse, she told him it was the first time she had ever seen him do any exercise. He should also take up tennis, she added. But that brief escape to the wilderness was all Abe could manage to keep calm while waiting anxiously for news from Washington. Earlier in the summer he had read disquieting items in the press. Then the first blow came when Frances Perkins was named chairman of the group that would recommend an economic security plan for the president. In view of their deteriorating relations, Abe did not feel he would have much influence with her. But the next appointment really disheartened him. The executive director, the man who would do all the hard work, was Edwin Witte, someone Abe had known for a long time; in fact Witte had served as a member of the advisory council of Abe's American Association for Social Security. But although he had expressed some belief in Abe's theories of income redistribution, he was always a strong proponent of the despised Wisconsin Plan on unemployment. Abe wouldn't have much influence there either. Finally, Witte's assistant director was to be Arthur Altmeyer, who was already working for Perkins as assistant secretary of labor. Altmeyer was also from Wisconsin and had been appointed to administer the Wisconsin Plan when and if it went into effect in that state. Abe was looking at three fast strikes against him. Last, the committee had been given a title with distinct political overtones: the Committee on Economic Security, a name that was a clear reminder to everyone who had ever identified themselves with the terms "social insurance" or "social security," including Abe, that Roosevelt was the boss. Fishing for a week in Canada did not suffice to calm Abe's tormented mind.

He was able to ignore Henriette's continuing broadsides for most of the summer because he was busy drafting a major article intended to head off possible bad moves by FDR's new committee, an article he hoped would also make him prominent again in the eyes of the New Deal administration. Henriette encouraged him, for she was always proud to see her husband's name in print. But when he sent her a copy and told her where the article would appear, she put up a squawk. *Harper's*, a sophisticated monthly, had been her choice, but instead Abe sold it to the *American Mercury*. It was a misguided selection, she said. The English was faulty, and why did he use the word "capitalism" so much? Didn't he know it would brand him right away as a Socialist? "Social Security—Fiction or Fact?" was published as the lead piece in the October 1934 issue. Abe worked hard to turn it into a considered and measured plea for FDR's new committee to follow sound social insurance principles. He even sent the galleys of the article to Edwin Witte, hoping to open a discourse with an acquaintance who was suddenly a very influential person. Abe believed that what the Roosevelt administration was promising on social security was so new to the public that it needed to be described in plain words. Still, he could not resist his usual mocking tone. "Lulled into the belief that the New Deal had more than fulfilled its promises, the American public was surprised to learn that something strangely new was still in the offing . . . As with Couéism, the New Era, and Technology, the unpretentious subject of social insurance is presented as an instrumentality of wonder-working and utopian powers."

But the main thrust of the article was an outline of what social insurance could and could not do, particularly that it could not solve all the problems inherent in the American system of capitalism. And he warned that any prospective federal program, unless written carefully, would have trouble getting by the Supreme Court, which regarded states' rights as primary. If the Supreme Court opposed it, prospects for social insurance would be destroyed for years to come. Social security must be comprehensive, he went on, and along with old-age and unemployment insurance, it had to include coverage for disability, medical care, and support for widows and survivors. Otherwise, a large number of the destitute would be left out of any national plan. But any plan, he emphasized, must include government help for those who needed it immediately: pensions for the aged and relief for the unemployed. He anticipated how difficult the fight would be. "Employers rarely oppose legislation on purely economic grounds but on public and moral ones. The slightest reform endangers the very foundation of the Republic . . . this sentimental blah is immediately taken up by the press and sometimes even by the courts." But he ended the article on a hopeful note with a forthright plea to FDR. "The opportunity to accomplish something of fundamental significance is before President Roosevelt. And it is an ancient truth that it is wisest to lay the foundation solidly and slowly so that the structure built upon it will not totter before every stress and strain."

It was Abe at his most heartfelt.

---

As Henriette prepared to return to New York, the caustic tone of her letters died down. She sent Abe a million kisses and signed her last letter, "Baby." For a moment it looked as if the old days were back. But Henriette was wary of Abe's volatile moods and assured him before she landed that he was not to worry if he had a meeting and couldn't greet them at the pier because she and Pierre could take care of themselves. When she returned to Bleecker Street, Abe was instead feeling optimistic and delighted to see her. Edwin Witte had made a special trip to New York to talk to him, and told him that his recommendations on social security would be of great importance to the committee's work.

All the same, the mystery of who might receive an admittance ticket to the staff that would write FDR's economic security plan dragged on, and while waiting for the names, Abe, Rubinow, and Douglas amused themselves by writing glowing reviews of each other's new books in the *Nation*, the *New Republic*, and other journals. "It looks like a triumvirate, doesn't it," Rubinow chuckled, "and if FDR had the good sense to let us prepare a program for him ..." But then rumors began to circulate, including a bizarre one that said Roosevelt had told publisher Oswald Garrison Villard that he was going to rely on Abe's close friend I. M. Rubinow to draw up the economic security program. Another was even more baffling. A friend wrote Abe, "Did you notice in *The New Leader* that the correspondent from Washington had it on good authority that the President's security message was considerably influenced by your book? The fact that Miss Perkins has written a preface is considerably emphasized." If the story was true, he told Abe, then he might be doing a considerable injustice to the president and Perkins by getting so angry at them. But there is no evidence that any of it was true. It is more likely that the stories were leaks calculated to throw adversaries off course by appealing to their vanity with rumors that they would be principal players in Roosevelt's efforts to create social security, while in fact leaving them out in the cold. That is certainly what happened when Edwin Witte told Abe he would seek his advice and then never did.

When the list of people who would be appointed to draw up the economic security plan was announced, Abe's lingering optimism was quickly deflated. Neither Abe, Isaac Rubinow, nor Paul Douglas had been asked to serve in any capacity, directly or indirectly. In fact, none of their allies were called upon. In a confidential meeting with Perkins, Roosevelt had told her he wanted only people who would follow his line of thought, and no one who had a previously well-known opinion. FDR's line of thought was never very clear, but basically it was cautious. Witte admitted in his 1962 memoir that he was never really sure what the president had in mind. But Perkins and Witte did as FDR wanted, and those appointed to the committee reflected Roosevelt's conservative bent. One critic of the committee pointed out, however, that if it was Roosevelt's policy to appoint no one with a previous well-known opinion, then why include Witte and Altmeyer? Both men were known proponents of the Wisconsin Plan on unemployment. In addition, an adviser who had been in on the meetings said later that it seemed absurd to exclude anyone who had a previously known view on social security, because where would the ideas come from? But the president was determined to stamp his name on a plan that expressed his thinking, and his secretive behavior was to become characteristic of the committee's work.

Abe had no knowledge of what was happening in the closed meetings in Washington. All he could see was that Frances Perkins was the problem. She asked him on one occasion to come to Washington and talk with her and to bring his own list of people he thought should do the work. He took the train to the capital and met with Perkins in her office. She thanked him for taking the time to help, and he told her that he had been careful to include people from all points of view on his list. She was pleased and assured him she would look it over carefully. After saying good-bye he was upbeat, but in the anteroom he saw a friend and asked him to look at the list of names he had suggested. The friend was astounded and said, "Why, the entire committee's already been selected!" Abe left Washington enraged, and when he told Henriette what had happened, she raged as well. Perkins's deceitful behavior obsessed Henriette for years. She never forgot the humiliation Abe had suffered from her devious treatment, and she made sure that all her oral biographers heard the entire list of Perkins's slights.

But some insight into why Abe in particular was shunted aside came to light in a letter that a top Roosevelt aide, Tommy "the Cork" Corcoran, wrote to Felix Frankfurter, then a Roosevelt adviser. "The Cork" was particularly worried that Perkins might appoint some of "the Epstein crowd who will be thoroughly and impracticably wild." But Abe had no knowledge of what was going on behind the scenes. And in the face of secretive

and frustrating treatment, his bewilderment at being continually excluded from what had been his life's work mutated rapidly to venom.

9

Abe's feud with Frances Perkins had a certain inevitable thrust, like the
plot of a Greek play. For a long time she was friendly. She had written the
introduction to *Insecurity*. On old-age security she agreed on the need for
Dill-Connery. And on unemployment she also had serious reservations
about the Wisconsin Plan. Abe thought he had her ear. He was so confident, in fact, that in October 1933—long before Roosevelt spoke out in favor of social security—he had proposed that the Department of Labor
hold a general conference on the topic of social insurance. She agreed, and
Abe had been asked to prepare a list of those to invite. Determined to
make it look fair, he had included every group and individual advocating
the Wisconsin Plan as well as those in favor of the Ohio Plan. But the Labor Department had delayed and postponed, constantly changing the
dates and terms of the proposed conference. Then, while Abe was still ne-
gotiating with them, Perkins set up a conference on unemployment insurance and Abe was not invited. It was mystifying because earlier she
had asked him personally to help get the unemployment bill known as
Wagner-Lewis passed and she knew that some of his revisions had been
accepted by the bill's proponents. But Abe didn't know of his exclusion
until several reporters called to tell him—and shortly the Department of
Labor was peppered with telegrams called Night Letters from Abe's
friends and allies about his being left out. Soon he was asked to participate but was told that his being omitted had been because Perkins had not
wanted to include any private organizations. Several of Abe's newspaper
friends didn't buy it—the account was false, they said. It was just plain
oversight, was the final excuse. But the bungling apologies left a sour
taste.

Later, in February 1934, Perkins sponsored a two-day conference on labor legislation, and again Abe found out indirectly that he was not on the
list of attendees. Rubinow had been left off as well, and he was very hurt
by the slight. But this time Abe decided to make a public protest and he
called on several journalist friends to mention it. It was the same excuse
as before, they were told, no private organizations had been invited, only
personal friends of the secretary. Again reporters didn't buy it, dug a lit-

tle deeper, and Louis Stark, the prominent *New York Times* columnist, wired Abe that "personal friends" meant John Andrews and the Wisconsin Plan people and no one else. Once more, telegrams and Night Letters flew down to Washington, including one from Stark himself. Someone in the Department of Labor felt the pressure, because Paul Douglas was asked to call Abe from Washington to tell him that Madam Secretary—as Perkins liked to be called—wanted him there. Henriette was sitting at her desk at the time and overheard the entire conversation.

"Abe was in the office in New York, fuming . . . knowing perfectly well what was happening. Douglas called at three o'clock in the afternoon. 'I'm calling from Washington in the name of the Secretary.'

"Abe answered, 'Go to hell!'

"'There's been an oversight, she wants you there.'

"Abe didn't believe it.

"'But come anyway in good spirits and take the floor.'"

So Abe went to Washington for the second day of the meeting, and when he entered the room people stopped what they were doing, astonished by his unexpected presence. One of the conferees had been giving a speech in favor of the hated "Merit-Rating," and as soon as the speaker was finished Abe rose from his seat and asked to be heard. Unable to conceal his fury, he let his opinions of "Merit Rating" be known, giving exactly the sort of hot-tempered opinion that Frances Perkins had not wanted to mar a quiet and low-profile conference.

Abe's feelings of rejection brought out the worst in him. Against the advice of friends he refused to let the matter fade away. He sent a four-page memorandum to all those who had lobbied Perkins on his behalf, including the newspapers. He detailed the entire history of his relations with the Labor Department, of how he had been stymied when trying to set up the conference on social insurance, and how he had found out through private sources "that the exclusion order had come directly from the Secretary of Labor." Paul Douglas received a copy and tried to smooth things over. "I understand the feeling you have," he wrote, "but it would seem to me a mistake to carry the matter as a personal feud." He hoped to pacify Abe by telling him that John Andrews had made an ass of himself at the conference and prejudiced everyone against him. Still, nothing could change the facts. Abe Epstein was a force to be reckoned with, and Frances Perkins did not want him around. But Abe would not go away and he would not be diplomatic about it. It was an undoubted error to attack Perkins, but patronizing her would have meant compromise, and Abe was incapable of compromise.

Should Abe have heeded the warning signs from Perkins? Was he rubbing her the wrong way by making her feel he was trying to steer policy? Was he gaining a reputation with the New Dealers for being too hard to handle? What did Tommy the Cork really mean when he wrote, "the Epstein crowd who will be thoroughly and impractically wild?" Was there someone out there muttering under his breath, "Here comes that pushy Russian Jew again?"

Abe found it hard to accept that in Washington he did not have the same access to the corridors of power that he had in New York. In New York he could deploy his troops and coalitions, as he had with the Permanent Conference on Social Security and the American Federation of Labor, and easily vanquish any opposition, including Andrews and the Wisconsinites. To Abe that was proof that aggressive tactics worked. But some of his friends did not agree. They suggested looking for compromise, listening to others, and heeding the feelings of those who resented his strident militancy. Rubinow told him that for "people like Miss Perkins . . . mightn't there be something in the attitude you displayed that might admit of a correction?" But Abe ignored him. He was fierce in his beliefs: "I do not see that it is up to us when we are winning rapidly, to take the initiative in regard to compromise . . . our New York tactics have proved 100 per cent correct, even though this may seem a conceited assertion." With Perkins there was nothing personal, he told several friends, although in a telling remark he added, "I do not expect many people to believe this . . . so it really makes no difference." Abe never really cared about what other people thought. What he could not stand was their incompetence and ignorance, and more and more he began to insult those who opposed him, labeling them as just plain stupid. "It was the adjectives he used, sometimes ruthlessly," Henriette observed. "He had no use for people who disagreed with him." If you weren't one hundred percent with Abe, then you were one hundred percent against him and ripe for verbal annihilation—something he was good at.

When Abe was spending so much time studying English he also succeeded in mastering the art of sarcasm, honing his verbal sword into a pesky dagger. His articles frequently had scornful titles such as "That Stabilization Nonsense," "Is American Capital Intelligent?" "Killing Old Age Security With Kindness," "Is It a New Deal?" "Economy or Greed—Which Is It?" And vivid sentences stood out: "The panacea industry has never known such good times," "The social insurance rabbit is not pulled out of a hat by a code of cabalistic hocus pocus," "Producing hokum is today the only really prosperous industry in America." He scoffed at any organization or individual that clashed with him. When social work groups spoke out against social insurance because they believed financial dependency was a psychological problem, he mocked their rhetoric: "They speak with the polished tongue of the financier through expert press agents and high pressure publicity . . . their only crusades are community chest drives which they conduct with the zip-zip of a successful team's cheerleader." One of the wittiest descriptions in his catalog of derision appeared in H. L. Mencken's *American Mercury*. In 1931 Hoover had tried to show his concern for the aged by sending a commission to Europe to study old-age insurance—only it was made up exclusively of executives from the Metropolitan Life Insurance Company. Abe snidely remarked that Hoover's move was "tantamount to having Al Capone and a commission of bootleggers report on the workings of Prohibition." (No wonder Mencken loved Abe's writing.) Some of his other scathing characterizations were guaranteed to offend almost anyone. Of politicians who refused to see that anything was wrong with American capitalism he observed, "during the prosperous days we developed a New Economic Theory of Optimism . . . based primarily on the ancient doctrine of a Chosen People, to which the Jews have laid claim unsuccessfully for over three thousand years. The Almighty, in His infinite wisdom, had placed a protecting hand over the United States . . . no possible evil could befall us . . . the country was immune from the social and economic ills that plagued the unregenerate nations . . . a few doses of pap would suffice to allay every sort of economic fever in America." Abe's writing was aggressive, subversive, and it also pissed people off.

The problem, of course, was that people in the public eye did not like being ridiculed so openly. And sooner or later Abe's intemperate words were bound to reach someone who would be angry enough to retaliate. Many of his comrades in arms were dismayed by his mounting and unbridled sarcasm. For the most part they were resigned to the fact that policies were not unfolding the way they wanted and were willing to look for compromise. But Abe had no intention of doing so, and when the New Deal, Frances Perkins, and the Wisconsin group of experts denied him access to the deliberations of the Committee on Economic Security, his stabbing pen lashed out at all of them. His frustration mounted into a foaming fury and flowed into all the other areas of his life.

A flashing series of disjointed, excruciating images reminds me that I was one of his victims. A baseball once flew from my hand, accidentally hit a tree, and tumbled down on him while he was outdoors seated on a lawn chair, writing. He rose and whirled on me in fury, his high squeaky voice screaming.

"I don't want to see that bat, ball, and glove ever again. I'll throw them out!"

All I could do was slink into the shadows behind the house and hope he wouldn't notice or follow me.

On a hot summer afternoon he said he was fed up with my feeble attempts to learn to ride my bike.

"Why are you so backward?" he burst out.

I was terrified, but he would not relent, and under his hot-tempered gaze I struggled and crashed time and again, trying to make one turn around the yard. My knees were blue with bruises and red with scrapes when I finally made one wobbling circle without a fall, and only then did he turn away and leave me in peace.

On another day he forced me to take swimming lessons with the lifeguard from the camp across the road. I pleaded with him that the lake was infested with leeches.

He erupted with startling rage. "In Norway the fishermen just throw their children into the ocean and that's how they learn to swim," he said. "How would you like that?"

I also watched in frightened silence, unseen in the shadows of the house, the roaring verbal assaults that rose up without warning between Abe and Henriette.

---

Abe's most difficult year was 1934, a year of great personal torment, and it scarred him for life. Everything that he believed in and had worked so hard to create was being rejected in Washington, and he began to resemble the two-headed Janus, not knowing which way to turn. On the one hand the official stance of his American Association for Social Security was positive and optimistic. Cheering headlines in the newsletter such as "Nation Stirred by Insecurity as Election Approaches" and "President Demands Social Security for Entire Nation" announced the good news in a way designed to hold on to old members and find new ones. But the truth was that membership and revenue were declining. People thought the struggle was over because Roosevelt had promised to create social secu-

The author, struggling to ride a bike. West Stockbridge, Massachusetts, 1940.

rity. And Abe himself was in agony. Almost completely shut out by the New Deal administration from the work of FDR's committee, he sat on the sidelines, grasping at rumor and suspicion. When he did find out what was going on it only made him more furious. In what Paul Douglas described sarcastically as "that bewildering cluster of sub-committees created by Perkins and Witte"—there was a technical board, an advisory board, sections and subsections to study every aspect of social security—there was total turmoil. Behind closed doors almost all the appointed staff had rejected the Wisconsin Plan on unemployment and its ugly brother, "Merit Rating." But nonetheless it was being forced on them by Perkins and Witte. Madam Secretary had said publicly that the "states should solve these different problems . . . according to their own particular genius," a direct contradiction of her earlier opinion on the need for a nationwide plan. As Kenneth Davis pointed out, all the staff knew "that a national plan was favored by Rubinow, Epstein, Douglas and virtually every other theorist of social insurance, none of whom (this was remarked upon at the time) was called in for direct formal consultation."

For a time after his rest in the Canadian woods in the summer of 1934, where he was "completely cut off from civilization" as he put it, Abe felt revitalized. But it was short-lived. When he got back to town the rumors and maneuvers of the new political season pounced on him vindictively. The association was teetering on the brink of financial disaster—unpaid bills had been piling up—and in August it had not been able to pay salaries. Abe was trying to raise money, schedule a major conference on health insurance, write an article for the *New Republic* for an ongoing series on social security, and also respond to a request for a meeting from Barbara Armstrong, the head of the old-age security section of the Committee on Economic Security. She was the only possible ally he had among all the staff. Her section was smaller, not under public scrutiny like the unemployment section, and all the members knew Abe and wanted his advice. But on any other issue it was a struggle for him to be heard, and the more he tried to gain admittance to other aspects of the committee's work, the more he was rejected. He saw doctors more frequently, and the one he had known since his Pittsburgh days told him to work fewer hours to avoid a "greater burning up of the candle." More and more he was becoming a victim of overwork, stress, and, most important of all, impotent rage.

10

The wear and tear on Abe's frail, high-strung body took its toll, and in October 1934 he collapsed. He was unable to work or sleep. He had difficulty getting up from the couch in his office. He lay there for long periods, unable to go to his desk or make a phone call. His doctor had warned him he was overweight, smoked too much, did not exercise, took little rest, and had chronic high blood pressure. Now he insisted Abe had to leave his office and get some peace and quiet. "Nervous breakdown" were the words spoken in hushed tones. But the true source of Abe's emotional malaise was not hard to find. It was his barely concealed fury at what was going on without him behind closed doors in the Committee on Economic Security. Abe believed there was still someplace where he had a chance to be consulted, if not appointed, by those doing the work. He could not believe that with all he had accomplished since his start in America as a poor immigrant—the books he had written, the testimony he had given, the respect he had earned—he could be dismissed so completely. Reluctantly, he followed his doctor's advice and alone took the train down to Atlantic City for a week of rest, just as the gray days of winter were coming on. He holed up at the Chalfonte-Haddon Hotel on the boardwalk, and in the gloomy atmosphere of a seaside resort in autumn was told to read, take walks, and above all do no work.

His secretary, Belle Frendel, a remarkable woman devoted to Abe and his work from the very first days in the office on East Seventeenth Street, tried to keep everyone away from him. To those who tried to get in touch she replied, "He is beginning to feel a bit better. To break down seems easy in comparison to building up." Still, no one could stop Abe completely. The politics of social security were never far from his thoughts, and he wrote an associate from his ocean-view hotel, "What you say in reference to the Washington situation expresses everything I have been feeling, and that alone is enough to give one a nervous breakdown. I feel angry and tempted to call up *The New Republic* or *The Nation* and ask them to do a dirty editorial."

After his week of forced rest, which had meant writing and telephoning as much as walking peacefully on the boardwalk, Abe returned to New York. He reassured his old friend Isaac Rubinow "that he had learned his lesson and would abide by his doctor's orders." But like an injured athlete fearful of losing his place in the starting lineup, Abe would not be stopped from reentering the game and was already planning his moves. "I believe we should try to cooperate as much as we possibly can, even though we are invited only through the back door," he told Rubinow. Rubinow did not agree and pleaded to Belle Frendel, "I hope you will see to it that he doesn't get back to his desk too soon. There is a limit to what one can accomplish even if one has the amazing energy of Epstein." But Rubinow himself, "living in the sticks," as he called it, was also feeling the strain. He had gone to Washington, where no one would meet with him, and he was bitter. He told Abe that if anyone on FDR's committee wanted to consult him they knew where to find him, but he would not run around town "peddling social insurance." Abe was more tenacious. When Barbara Armstrong said she would come to New York to get his advice as soon as he was recovered, Abe immediately set a date. Henriette encouraged the reluctant Rubinow to participate in the meeting with Armstrong: "I agree with you that the experts have been deliberately ignored, but I believe they ought to push their way in nevertheless . . . but of course it is not up to me to decide the policies of two very wise gentlemen."

Then events took another bewildering turn, as if the Furies themselves were determined to unleash more havoc. The administration called a grand conference to make a report to the nation about all the good work being done by the Committee on Economic Security. The country knew little of what was going on; most of the work was in secret, and a head of steam was building up from many public groups clamoring for results. As Abe described it, "The Townsendites were mewing and cat-calling and everything all over the back fences of Congress." An offer to attend the first public presentation was to be extended to anyone who had ever been interested in social security, but once again the invitations were slow in coming, and it looked to Abe and Paul Douglas that another conspiracy to keep them away was in the works. (Witte later offered the excuse that the Blue Room of the White House, where Roosevelt wanted to speak, could only hold 150 people, so it would be difficult to choose who should hear FDR in person.) But Rubinow was beside himself. The newspapers, he noted, had said, "Experts in many fields of Social Security will be invited." If he and Abe were to be excluded once again then he was determined to have nothing more to do with the Committee on Economic Security, including Barbara Armstrong. "I would be a laughingstock among my friends," he wrote. Abe said he understood but pointed out he could not refuse so easily since he represented a major organization. He thought Rubinow might be soothed with a joke, and quoted his secretary, Belle: "She said it is really complimentary to all three of us to not be invited . . . since the nuts are paramount." But Rubinow didn't think it was funny, and wrote back, "the whole thing has left a very nasty taste in my mouth."

Eventually the three musketeers of social security received their invitations, pressure being applied by a number of people, including the ever-supportive Louis Stark of the *New York Times*. Abe Epstein, Isaac Rubinow, and Paul Douglas journeyed down to Washington for the New Deal's grand conference on November 14, 1934. When the social security troops were gathered in the ballroom of the Mayflower Hotel they were addressed by Harry Hopkins, the relief administrator and a member of the cabinet committee that steered the Committee on Economic Security. He roused them to "enthusiastic heights" (one newspaper reported) when he said, "I cannot see why we should wait until Kingdom Come to give security to the workers of America. I am convinced that now is the hour to act. And by a bold stroke we'll get it." Abe couldn't contain himself, leaned over to his neighbor, Paul Douglas, and murmured, "it all seems very theatrical to me." He was right, because the real motive behind the gathering was in fact no more than a media event aimed at putting the New Deal in a good light. Edwin Witte begrudgingly admitted it years later: "They had been asked to come for no purpose except publicity and felt slighted because they deemed themselves specialists who were not really consulted."

Three hours later the 150 chosen experts were shifted over to the Blue Room of the White House to hear the president in person. The room was extremely crowded and all the invitees were forced to find a place to stand, while Roosevelt himself remained seated at his desk, as he frequently did at such gatherings. When everyone had squeezed in, the president began to read a speech that had been written for him by Witte and approved by Perkins, and it was in those august surroundings that Roosevelt almost completely squashed the great law on social security with which he is now credited. Unemployment insurance, he asserted, should emphasize employment stabilization (the "Wisconsin Plan"), be run by the states, and, using the customary conservative cliché, added that it should not become "the dole." As Arthur Schlesinger, Jr., observed, "the staff seemed to be steering clear of unemployment insurance experts, like Epstein, Paul Douglas, I. M. Rubinow . . . known for their advocacy of the national system." He also rejected any form of health insurance as an "unfair burden upon the medical profession"—the American Medical Association, everyone was aware, had already applied heavy pressure. But then FDR shocked all the delegates when he proclaimed, "I do not know if this is the time for any federal legislation on old age security."

Reactions were immediate and furious. "It's the kiss of death!" Barbara Armstrong is alleged to have shouted out, seeing all her hard work on old-age security going down the drain. The press had a field day, attacking Roosevelt for abandoning the aged. The *New York Times* was scathing, and Louis Stark persuaded a number of other journalists to write articles in protest. The administration was stunned. Roosevelt, Perkins, and Witte were caught off guard by all the negative publicity the president's words had provoked. Perkins was hastily sent out the next day to tell the press that nothing was changed, the president had been misunderstood and wanted a "broad comprehensive program." Abe could not believe his luck: "Miss Perkins and Witte burned their fingers beautifully with the President's speech on the 14th . . . In addition Madam Secretary antagonized the newspapermen on the 15th." Witte sent off a letter to all the invitees who had stood in the Blue Room, explaining that FDR had only meant to say he "had not decided precisely what sort of program he would present on old age security." Abe did not believe it for a moment and, with sly sarcasm, told Witte he was delighted "to learn that the newspaper interpretation of the President's speech was incorrect." But as Witte admitted, "the Conference had been badly handled, and its net effects harmful, rather than beneficial."

The administration's incompetence offered the association's bulletin a great break. On one page, in parallel columns, it made comparisons between Roosevelt's June 8 message and his November 14 speech—the contradictions were obvious. Arthur Krock of the *New York Times* made use of the bulletin's clever comparisons, calling FDR's speech "the elements of a first-class political enigma. The title of this might be, 'The Mystery of the President's Speech or Does the English Language Mean Anything?'" The social security reformers were elated. Roosevelt's conservative posture was a flop, and for many it was hard to fathom what had been in his mind and those of his associates. On June 8 he had told the nation he would come up with a complete plan for old-age security, unemployment, and medical care. And then on November 14 he offered the American people a near empty bottle. The creation of social security was being played out against what historian Kenneth Davis called the "cautious conservatism of Franklin Roosevelt."

The disastrous conference had also worked to Abe's and Rubinow's advantage in other ways. While the storm was breaking in the press, Abe and Rubinow had remained in Washington to meet with Barbara Armstrong and the members of the old-age security section to see what help they could offer. "They have indeed been desperate," Abe commented, because he knew that if Perkins and FDR were ever going to be persuaded to offer proposals on old-age security, two highly complicated matters had to be resolved: the manner in which old-age benefits should be calculated and the financing of the benefits. Abe and Rubinow felt that benefits should be at a flat rate, the same for all. A flat rate would serve as an aid to income redistribution. Everyone would receive the same money, whether rich or poor. But the old-age security section was not eager to go along with a flat rate for fear that Frances Perkins would shoot it down. She had said on one occasion that "a man who works hard and earns high wages deserves more on retirement than one who has not." Years later she changed her mind, and acknowledged that a flat rate might have been a better idea. But in 1934 it was not to be. And it still isn't.

Even more difficult to resolve was the financing. Abe and Rubinow believed it should be a pay-as-you-go system, with any emerging deficit to be made up by the federal government. The basis of this idea was again income redistribution, since the well-to-do paid more taxes and therefore more of their money would support old-age security. But the president, it was obvious from his last speech, would not be easy to convince. The compromise that was reached took the form of some pay-as-you-go—a payroll tax—and some government financing.

"Neither Epstein nor Rubinow could approve this compromise on grounds of logic or justice," Kenneth Davis explained. "And Epstein even found it impossible to accept, as Rubinow was inclined to do, on grounds of pure expediency." Payroll taxes would start at one-half of 1 percent for both employer and employee. But for Abe such a tax was unfair to the workers. The employer could pass on his share of the tax to the consumer in the form of higher prices. His employees could do no such thing. Many agreed with his thinking, including eventually Frances Perkins, but FDR wanted a plan that looked like private insurance, and that is what the committee had to deliver. For Abe, however, income redistribution was one of the key goals of social security. If the government did not put in money then the poor would always be subsidizing their own retirement out of their own pockets. Abe believed that any worker contribution to social security should be for psychological purposes, not financial—then the employee would feel he had a stake in the system. "The proposed programs actually relieve the wealthy from their traditional obligation under the ancient poor laws," he wrote. "Epstein's argument was powerful," Kenneth Davis points out, "was indeed unanswerable on its own terms." It was based on the benefits of income redistribution in a capitalist society, and that was not where American businessmen wanted to watch their money disappear.

For a brief moment it seemed that both Abe Epstein and Isaac Rubinow would be able to make an important contribution to some part of the New Deal social security proposals. After all the neglect, Rubinow was suddenly asked to come to Washington because Witte was anxious to consult with him. "Madam Secretary does not feel quite as sure of herself as she did before," he told Abe. But, ultimately, after the two men went home from the offices of the old-age section they were never called in again. It was as close as they ever got to truly influencing the shape and form of Franklin Roosevelt's proposals in 1935 to create a social security system for the United States.

11

On the same day that Abe was standing in the White House crowd listening to FDR's personal interpretation of social security—November 14, 1934—Henriette's father, Jean-Marie Castex, came down the gangplank of the French Line's *Le Champlain* and stepped onto the streets of New York for the first time. He was a portly little man who seemed very French to those who met him, with his sporty mustache, hat set at a rakish angle, and ever-present hand-rolled cigarette dangling from his lips. He had just retired from a lifetime of work as a civil engineer in the French National Railroads, mostly in rural parts of southern France. He longed to see America where his daughter lived, and though he knew almost no English, it didn't matter to him. Henriette's mother, Elisa, had refused to make the trip, in spite of one of Abe's infrequent letters inviting her. She had never left France, had no desire to do so, and was wary of "le mal de mer," that the ship might sink, and other unnamed disasters—but insisted firmly that she must be written to regularly with every detail of the visit. Her father had no such qualms about ocean travel, and no sooner had he set foot on the pier than he was dazzled by the wonders of New York. During his three months in America he was given the royal tour—the Metropolitan Museum, the Natural History Museum, Central Park, the Empire State Building, Broadway plays, the Cloisters—to remind him of his life in Prades where the Cloisters came from—and knowing of his love for the railroads, to Grand Central Station, Pennsylvania Station, and by train to Washington, D.C., and Boston. Henriette even had his portrait sketched by an artist friend in Greenwich Village. But fun was not the only reason for Jean-Marie Castex's presence in New York. The anger and tension between Abe and Henriette had reached all the way to Toulouse, and the news of Abe's breakdown had stunned her parents. "Is Eppie completely cured?" Elisa asked several times. And indeed Abe's outbursts of rage were more frequent and more irrational.

"I cannot get a moment's rest in my own house," Henriette complained to him. "I cannot stand it any longer. I want to avoid an unpleasant scene, which will come soon."

My memory of that scene is very vivid. One day, hearing shouts I could not make out, I came up the stairs and peered silently from a distant corner of the dining room, hidden behind the door frame. From there I watched Henriette suddenly plunge to the floor, pounding and screaming, a full-blown tantrum in front of Abe and her father. I can still see her dark flowing dress and flailing hands slapping at the floor boards, but I cannot remember a word of what she was screaming. All I have is a frozen image of Henriette throbbing and thrashing in uncontrolled rage, like the suspended fury of a mounted horseman in a Delacroix painting of a wild cavalry charge. Henriette's fit may have been a replay of childhood petulance because her father was there. Or it may have been fully justified because of the way Abe was treating her. What is certain is that a crisis of enormous dimension raged between Jew and French Girl.

Henriette's father struggled to see both sides. He knew there was something wrong with Abe. He also knew of Henriette's willful temperament. He tried to be a calming presence, but he understood little about Abe's political battles and what was making him so emotional. Abe was rarely at home, preoccupied totally with affairs in Washington. So when Henriette's father sailed back to France three months later he had not been able to improve things. From Paris, even before traveling home to Toulouse, he still felt the need to try and help. He wrote and thanked Abe for all that was done for him in New York and for all the wonderful things he had seen. But he was disturbed by "the little incidents between you and Henriette which will appear insignificant later on when the state of your health is better." He begged Eppie to take care of himself and "whenever you have the chance get some rest. The state of your health leaves much to be desired for at least the last 2 or 3 three years." He suggested a way that would help, by "having marvelous distractions with little Pierre. Do as I do, have fun with him, it will do you enormous good and will distract you from your occupations." But none of what was written remained private since Henriette translated all the letters.

Emotions calmed down for a bit after Jean-Marie's return to France, but it was not long before Henriette began to complain again. She was angry because her father had not fixed things the way she had asked him to. Her parents, in turn, insisted she be patient and remain calm, but this did not appease her. Abe's assistant was turning him against her, she told them. There was a woman who edited the monthly publication, Adele Bloom, who spent more time in the office and was better paid than Henriette. She and her brother were probably Communists, she had heard, scheming to take over the association if Abe were to collapse altogether. She'd even heard a rumor that Abe was having an affair with her. She felt helpless to thwart what she thought was a conspiracy to drive her out of Abe's life. Her father could not believe this was true. Even her mother was dubious. "Why would she do such a thing? To replace you?"

Henriette's father decided he had to do something. He wrote to one of Abe's closest friends, a lawyer named Walter Frank who had been involved from the start with Abe and the association and who was well aware of Abe's precarious mental state. "Mr. Epstein himself admits that he is not well and that he is losing control of his actions. He has not been well for at least 4½ years for when his son was born he said so himself at my home following a very painful scene." He laid the blame for Abe's behavior on all the hard work he had done to succeed in America, his studies, and the back-breaking work of running the association. It was more than he could handle, he told Mr. Frank. If things did not improve, he would come back to New York and stay until matters were decided, one way or another. He sent a copy to Henriette, carefully done in his own hand, at the end of which he warned her, "In no case abandon Eppie. You will tell M. Frank that it is your duty and that I recommend it." Abandonment seems to have worried him the most. He knew that Henriette was not up to the task of taking care of a man in Abe's unstable state, but he felt it was her duty to try.

More anguished words continued to flow back and forth across the ocean, and one day Henriette's staunchly Catholic mother took a decisive step. "If you can not take all the misery any longer you have only to ask for a divorce—in spite of the pain it would cause us we would not blame you." But those words never became part of the letter, at least officially. Henriette's father read them over, took a pen, and ran a line through them. He then printed neatly above his wife's words: "Never abandon Eppie, never ask for a divorce. You will be criticized by all your friends." Both suggestions were clearly visible on the page.

Everyone was at cross purposes.

---

When Abe returned to New York after his intense Washington ordeal, suddenly without warning an exhausting feeling of paralysis enveloped him and he was unable to get out of bed. He tried going to his office several times, but when he finally made it he was too tired to do anything. He lay on his couch, staring into space. It was another nervous breakdown, and he was sent away this time for a longer rest to a hotel at Hot Springs, Virginia, where it was warm and where he would be much farther away from the office. For Abe, nothing was working. The Committee on Economic Security's report to President Roosevelt would be written without his participation, and on top of that an important financial backer had criticized his work and stopped sending money. The American Association for Social Security was in such financial trouble that it was in danger of closing down. All Abe could see was failure.

Henriette was confused and miserable. She began to think that more than the overwork of fifteen-hour days was the cause of Abe's continuing breakdowns. "I'm trying to figure out whether it was the foreign personality," she blurted out once when going over the episodes of Abe's collapses. Then she corrected her thoughts and said "his own personality."

She was searching for an explanation that might help her, clear up what was happening to Abe. Perhaps it had something to do with Jews and anti-Semitism, but she was afraid to speak openly about it. She could not understand where all the boiling turmoil was coming from. What was wrong with Abe? Was it the pressure of events, or something else? Abe's old friend I. M. Rubinow may have been the one who understood it best when he wrote, "There is a limit to what one can accomplish even if one has the amazing energy of Epstein."

12

In the spring of 1935, when Abe was slowly recovering in the calming air of Hot Springs, he received a letter from Frances Perkins. "I should like to have a talk with you in the near future . . . call my Secretary when you are in town again," she wrote. Abe was still feeling drained when he was allowed to leave Hot Springs, but he stopped in Washington and called on Perkins. He wondered what had brought about his sudden change of status with her. Perkins gave him a warm greeting as soon as he walked into her office and asked how he was. "Much better," Abe replied. Then Perkins looked straight at him and said, "Congratulate me, Epstein. I have good news."

"I don't know what it's all about, but anyway I congratulate you," Abe answered.

"I've just sold the president the bill."

Abe was puzzled. His hopes had initially been raised by Perkins's summons and he thought she might be ready to listen to his advice. But now her words made absolutely no sense. Everyone knew the president was a hard customer; still the committee had been working on a bill at his orders—why would he have to be sold a bill? Soon, however, it became evident to Abe that Perkins was no longer as self-assured as she had been earlier. The Committee on Economic Security's report was ready to go before Congress and would be open to public scrutiny for the first time. Her reputation was at stake, and she knew the report would be a tough sell. She was looking for help. She knew Abe had many friends in Congress, and by appealing to his earlier belief that he had some place in the government's plans she might be able to win his support. Still, she said nothing to indicate he had regained any real influence. In spite of her friendly welcome, Abe was not sure where he stood. She was still Perkins as far as he was concerned, and totally noncommittal. What had changed—and

Abe was not fully aware of its extent—was that the battle for the president's bill had become political and not economic. Perkins was in need of help.

When the Economic Security report arrived on FDR's desk, it contained the problematic compromise on old-age insurance funding and an unemployment proposal that left it up to the states to create their own laws. Roosevelt had added thoughts of his own on how he much preferred the "Wisconsin Plan" approach. This had infuriated many of the staff members and section heads who had worked hard to come up with something different. Any attempt to offer health insurance had been thrown out.

According to Thomas Eliot, the lawyer who wrote the report, "the original bill was certainly not well drafted. It was indeed a hodgepodge—not of unrelated subjects, but of drafts prepared by various people, drafts that I either accepted in toto . . . or edited far too hastily . . . Inevitably, too, it reflected a heedless failure to resolve many small but significant policy issues that had been discussed little or not at all by the president's committee." The hodgepodge had been written in great haste in order to get it before Congress before the session ended.

To add to all the in-fighting, at the last minute, the secretary of the treasury, Henry Morgenthau, had stunned the committee by removing his signature from the final report. As Thomas Eliot explained,

When he . . . saw a copy of the press release . . . he demanded a special meeting of the *Committee,* at which he announced he was withdrawing his signature: to say this was an insurance system, he thundered, and then thirty years hence have the federal Treasury subsidize it out of general revenues was a fraud on the taxpayer. Wallace rolled his eyes and looked at the ceiling, Harry Hopkins and Mr. Holtzoff stared open mouthed. Miss Perkins, her voice rising, said "But Henry! But Henry!" Morgenthau interrupted her by slamming his hand down on the table, "This is Henry Morgenthau, Jr., speaking and these are his opinions!" Late the same day word came from the White House . . . that the bill would have to be changed; the taxes for old age insurance would have to be increased, so that ultimately the reserve fund would be six times greater than the *Committee* had contemplated and no "government contribution" would be necessary, ever.

In addition, Morgenthau insisted on dropping benefits for farm workers, migrants, and domestic workers—among those who needed it the most—because of the cost. And he insisted no old-age pensions should be paid until 1942, seven years hence, so that a reserve fund could be built up without any government help. Roosevelt happily agreed and summoned Frances Perkins to tell her that the report's scheme for financing the retirement plan was the "same old dole under a new name." When Morgenthau's interference became known to the committee's staff, they were even more furious at what they now felt was an act of betrayal by both Perkins and Morgenthau. In defense of Perkins, she may have thought that Roosevelt was starting to backtrack over the entire idea of social security because of criticism from some of his powerful conservative friends. She may have really meant it when she told Abe she had "sold" FDR the bill, because any idea of transfer of moneys from the rich to the poor through government contributions was, in the president's view, unfair to the rich who had worked so hard to get it, and his banking friend, Morgenthau, had provided him with a way out of the dilemma.

But as Eliot points out, it was a confusing document, and it hurt Roosevelt politically. When the president held a press conference to tell the newspapers how much he liked the bill, he fell into a trap. He did not approve of government financing, he said with confidence, and none was proposed.

"Not so," a reporter blurted out, "on page 33 the government is to make contributions in 1956."

FDR was furious. He had been counting on others to fill him in on the details, and it was obvious he did not know exactly what the bill contained. Rubinow felt the mess should be blamed on Perkins, and wrote Abe. "The President may be excused . . . as it is something of a technical problem, but Madam Secretary has no excuse as she wants to pose as an expert . . . she has many experts to advise her instead of which she preferred to entrust the most important measure before the American people to a nit-wit like Mr. Witte, whose name certainly belies him."

---

Still, in the spring of 1935 the Economic Security Act began to slowly roll through the committees of the Senate and House. It was there that Abe thought he might have one last chance to change things for the better. His many congressional friends would listen to him. He would be able to speak out, and his words would be heard and reported. But a number of circumstances worked against him. For one, the bill was assigned to the wrong committees—Finance in the Senate, Ways and Means in the House. They were tax committees, not labor or welfare ones, and were chaired by very conservative southerners. Among their numerous objections was the fact that they did not like to pass laws that would benefit poor Negroes in the South.

When Abe went to Washington to testify, he agreed to serve as a government witness to help Edwin Witte, the director of the Committee on Economic Security. Though Witte was wary of what Abe might say, the committee needed help wherever it could find it. Abe also pursued the separate idea of having Perkins and Senator Wagner call a conference of "experts" to offer amendments. He had an important interview in the Scripps-Howard newspapers on that proposal and told Henriette to tell everyone in New York he was making headway. What he had to say on social security was still news. But Wagner wouldn't budge. "He is not a fighter," Abe reported. "He is ready to make a deal . . . I frankly believe he does not know what the bill really contains. Of course, when you explain it to him he sees with us . . ." Trying another tactic, Abe drew up a list of amendments himself and persuaded Senator Hugo Black to sponsor them in the Finance Committee. They were voted down, and Abe began to lose heart: "I am frankly convinced that almost everything we do is futile . . . it is impossible to bring a clear understanding of the issues involved." Rubinow was as frustrated as Abe. No one in Congress had gotten in touch with him about testifying, but Abe told him he was not the only one. "All of us have volunteered and almost forced ourselves to be heard."

Abe busied himself as well with preparations for the association's annual conference at the end of April 1935, keeping a wary eye on the progress of the economic security bill. Despite his anxieties, he was determined that the meeting would be a showcase event, a comprehensive gathering to cover all aspects of social security, including the neglected medical part—publicity that might influence the Congress to improve the bill. Rubinow had agreed to chair the general session and to present a paper on the "whole conception of a unified system of social insurance"— but he never made it to New York. He had become seriously ill and was not allowed to travel. Still, there was cheerful news, he told Abe. The B'nai B'rith, where Rubinow was the executive director, had decided to move its headquarters from Cincinnati to Washington, D.C., and the move would bring him closer to Abe. Together, they would be able to check up on all parts of the social insurance movement, "which, as you and I know only too well, is just beginning."

The May issue of *Social Security* gave a full and enthusiastic report of the annual conference. Everything sounded positive, and more people than ever had attended. The June-July issue followed with Abe's personal analysis of the proposed economic security bill. It was long and not written with Abe's customary clarity, as if his anger made him unable to cope with the entire issue. He tried explaining what was confusing—the act tried to do too much and had been put together too rapidly. He went through all the bill's proposals, and told his readers, "there was an insistence that the bill be jammed through . . . a real dilemma to the earnest members of Congress genuinely interested in bringing about social security. They could not physically find the time to master the details." (Many reports had been prepared but no one in Congress had asked for a copy, and Witte himself felt that few of the members of the Committee on Economic Security had read them either.) Abe concluded that "this most unique opportunity ever offered any nation" had been "inexcusably fumbled . . . shrouded in mystery. Months of valuable educational work were lost." Still, he was hopeful. "The main principle of old age security upon which the Association was founded will in a few years definitely come to fruition, provided it can be kept out of politics . . . the nation has definitely committed itself." Then at the bottom of page 2 there was an ominous note. A little box informed readers that "stringency of funds" would not allow for an August issue and the next one would not appear until October. For more than two months no words would be sent out to rally the troops. It was getting harder and harder for Abe to see a path for himself through all the pressure, financial as well as emotional.

Because of his frenzied work pace, Abe was rarely in New York, and there were fewer complaints about him in Henriette's letters to her parents. Her father thought his plan might be working. Indeed, although his English was nonexistent and Abe hardly knew a word of French, there was a subterranean level of understanding between the two men, particularly over Henriette's willful nature. But Henriette's mother did not agree. Her feelings veered to the melodramatic. "As for me," she wrote, "tell him I will behave like a lioness whose child is being harmed." She undertook methods of cure for Abe's illness rooted in French rural superstitions. "I have been busy and went to see certain people capable of giving me help. I am doing everything I can to save him . . . I have been promised success." But Henriette was not comforted by her mother's mysterious references to magic spells. Her father should have stayed longer, she protested. She wanted real help, and the only place she felt she could get it was from her parents.

Then as the social security battle in Congress began in earnest and Abe was rushing back and forth to Washington, Henriette suddenly skipped town. In the month of April she sailed off to the Caribbean, leaving everyone behind. She removed herself to her favorite world, the land of shipboard limbo. Her mother was stupefied. "You don't say where? Are you taking Pierre?" No, she hadn't. The ever-mercurial Henriette had decided that what she wanted for herself was "all the fun in the world basking in the Caribbean sunshine." From Jamaica she wrote, "The crowd is fine and the rum is delicious." A dozen black-and-white photographs, with her smiling coyly in the middle of happy shipmates, chronicle her fun at sea. Henriette's way out of the stress was to get herself invited to a party. The growing strain was leading husband and wife to go off in separate directions.

---

What is it that fueled Abraham Epstein's explosive and often irrational behavior? It was said by many at the time that it was due to his bitter disappointment at being excluded by the New Deal from its social security plans. Still, what inner demon was he fighting to make him so angry and exhausted? Like others who have probed this parental mystery, I am still searching for the heart of the man who helped to give birth to me, who is part of me as I am part of him.

## Sinclair Lewis, Dickens, and Me

*Between Abe and Henriette there was from the beginning an inner rift. And it was made crystal clear by their tastes in literature. When Henriette sailed back to France shortly after their marriage in 1925, to while away the time on the eight-day ocean voyage Abe gave her a copy of Sinclair Lewis's* Main Street. *However-er, the world of Gopher Prairie was not an easy read for Henriette. It bore no re-semblance to the English writers she understood and loved: Wordsworth, Keats, Shelley, and all the books of Robert Louis Stevenson. They were the authors she had studied during her two years as a student in England, and they had been her gateway from French into English. She had been taught to appreciate the beauty and style of what they wrote. The social message was of lesser importance. With Abe it was the reverse. His favorites were the new American realists, such as Sher-wood Anderson and Sinclair Lewis. He understood and approved their stinging criticisms of American bourgeois life. But the true hero in his pantheon of writ-ers was the formidable Charles Dickens, and the twenty-volume set of his books that Abe acquired during his early Pennsylvania days still sits in serried splen-dor on the bookshelves at 389 Bleecker. Wrapped in the omnipresent plastic, with which Henriette preserved all that she cherished, those red and black covers are an intimidating presence. One day for no obvious reason, my eyes looked up at the first volume,* David Copperfield. *And I suddenly plunged into a fire-hot memory of a day when I was ten and Abe told me it was time for me to read that great book.*

*He took it from the shelf, handed it to me, and left the room. I dutifully strug-gled through the first forty pages, but when I realized Dickens was in no way as much fun as reading my favorite comic books, Superman and Batman, I gave up rapidly. I also wondered why there was no* David Copperfield *on the Classics Illustrated comics list of which I was a devotee and on the merits of which I once harangued Abe with absolutely no success. The best I could do to hide my failure*

166

*was to stall and avoid him when I thought he might bring up* David Copper-
field. *But he wasn't a man to be easily fooled, and one day as I entered the living
room he looked up at that row of red and black volumes and said:*
"*So, where are you in* David Copperfield?"
"*Me? I don't know.*"
"*Have you been reading it?*"
"*It's hard.*"
"*Are you reading it?*"
"*I couldn't . . . why can't I get it in Classics comics, like* Three Musketeers?
*They've got pictures," I burst out.*
    *And then from out of nowhere there came an eruption of rage, a roaring anger
directed at me, just like the explosions I endured when Abe was in a fury about
my learning to swim and my trying to ride a bike. I was terrified and backed away
from him to a far corner—and there the moment ends, like a black curtain falling,
sealing all memory. He bore in on me with furious impatience, and I recoiled.*
    *The* David Copperfield *incident is a fleeting one that I slide over in discom-
fort, but its ultimate effect was that I never finished the novel. Like a child who
has thrown up his rice pudding and never wants to touch it again, I was afraid I
would never be able to stomach Dickens. I would choke on the odd language and
winding descriptive passages.*
    *And then only recently, with Abe and Henriette dead, I became aware once
more of that shelf of red and black books, and the first one that I focused on, of
course, was* David Copperfield. *My eyes lingered for a moment, then suddenly I remembered Abe's rage and immediately looked elsewhere at another title:*
Bleak House. *Hesitantly, I reached up and took it down from its perch and
opened it. What I first saw was the name "Abraham Epstein" written inside the
cover. I began to read it carefully, a few pages at a time, hoping that I would not
react and shut the cover quickly. But I continued and slowly began to engross myself in the details and colors of the opening chapter with its magnificent description of the mire and fog of London. Soon I was rapturously living in that damp,
dirty city of "trickery, evasion, procrastination, spoliation, botheration," existing
with those extraordinary characters, that wonderful language, those long descriptive passages, all the wonderful adventure of* Bleak House. *I knew then,
with a relieved inner sigh, that I had finally done it, and I was in the presence of
a master. Now when I look at that shelf of books, I am no longer ill at ease, but
sense myself standing in the presence of an invisible man in a three-piece suit and
owl-shaped glasses, a father trying to educate his rambunctious son, whom he
once described in a letter to his brother as "a typical New York roughneck." I feel
his ache to pull that balky son somehow into his way of thought before he was no
longer around to serve as a teacher. If there was ever a time when I would want
Abe's ghost to come and visit in the middle of the night, it would be to tell him,*

*"I have now conquered* Bleak House *with abandon and I await* David Copperfield *without fear."*

---

*Why was Dickens so important to Abe? Why was he so insistent I read Dickens? Simply this: what Dickens described as the grimy oppression of nineteenth-century England, Abe had seen for real in his childhood as a Jew under the tsars and in his early immigrant struggles in New York and Pittsburgh. He had seen it when he researched his early book,* The Negro Migrant, *in the slums where the blacks lived. As director of the Pennsylvania Commission on Old Age Pensions, visiting the many poorhouses in the state, he had seen it in the despair of the aged residents. But there was something else in Dickens that captured Abe's imagination. The great writer was a man with a social conscience, who cared deeply about the fate of his fellow man, his individual fellow man. He came from a civilization in direct contrast to the overheated one of the Russians, Germans, and Jews where Abe had grown up. Dickens had been brought up in an Anglo-Saxon society, under the rule of law, a culture far removed from the gloomy, unruly, totalitarian world of Abe's Russian brethren. Dickens's England was a land where it was possible that justice and consideration might eventually prevail over brutality and exploitation.*

*But neither Dickens's England nor Abe's Russia nor Sinclair Lewis's America was the land of comfortable middle-class France where Henriette had spent her childhood. She was an innocent when it came to poverty, exploitation, and American boosterism, and her family and friends were wary of anything that smacked vaguely of socialism. As she sailed eastward to France in 1925 and gazed down from the bow of the ship slicing the waves, she could not find a way to finish* Main Street. *"He thinks as you do and all your friends do," she wrote. "This is interesting to me but he is a little too cynical and he only sees the worst side of human nature . . . the book makes me lose faith in life and your love. The author ought to be a little less of a skeptic." During the summer of her return to France, before Abe journeyed there for the first time to meet his new, decidedly bourgeois in-laws, Henriette began to see the nature of the rift that separated her from her husband. It was a gap neither had noticed when they fell in love. It grew into a hard-edged chink between them.*

*And as the years went by the chink widened.*

## 13

How would I ever come to know Abe's inner man? Going to the archives seemed the only approach. But words from the writer Mary Gordon surfaced in my head: "All of us in the archives are acknowledging the insufficiency of memory . . . the loss of living speech . . . can facts make up for this?" I was sincerely hoping they might. So, on a steamy summer day I sat down in the air-conditioned seclusion of the basement of the School for Industrial and Labor Relations at Cornell University and there, with the files of the American Association for Social Security spread before me, I began to read letter after letter, article after article, report after report, the entire story of Abe's work from 1927 until his death in 1942. But what I read was all businesslike, the daily doings of the association, and as the days dragged on not a single piece of paper turned up that might give me a hint about the emotional insides of Abraham Epstein.

People may have been reluctant to talk about such matters in those days. Perhaps they did not understand them. Those who worked with Abe rarely said a word about what some historians later alluded to as his colorful but difficult personality, and no one mentioned his nervous breakdowns. All I had been able to trace was a pattern of high achievement followed by frustration, anger, depression, withdrawal, and rebound. It was visible in his creation of the Worker's Education Bureau in the 1920s and his later rejection by it, his subsequent retreat down to the farm, and the rebound and trip to Russia. Then there was also the high achievement of his first book, *Facing Old Age*, succeeded by his frustration with Frank Hering and the Eagles, anger with his mother over the education of his siblings, followed by dejection and withdrawal, and again a rebound when he met Henriette, fell in love, and was married. There were undoubtedly more such episodes lurking out there. But it all seemed like stereotypical psychoanalytical thinking.

The librarian at Cornell was a middle-age man with a mass of graying, reddish hair who always wore a sweater. He must have been an acute student of his researchers, for he could obviously see my dejection as I copied endless pages from the files. My sighs and fatigue were more pronounced as the days wore on, and one day, shuffling quietly about the room with masses of folders in his hands, the librarian stopped in front of me.

"You know, if you're not finding what you want, you might try I. M. Rubinow's file. We have all his papers here as well."

"Oh?" I answered, then added, "He was a good friend of my father."

"Yes, I know. Rubinow's daughter gave us all his material. She told me that he died a very depressed man. He could not overcome the disappointment he felt at the failure of the social security law in 1935."

"Just like my father," I exclaimed, and looked at the librarian in a new light. Here was another man who knew something of the pain of those times.

The librarian nodded, as if he knew the whole story, and soon brought me the first of the boxes devoted to the papers of Isaac Max Rubinow. I knew almost nothing about him except for his stature as a scholar and the enormous respect Abe had for him. But as I began to read the letters between Abe and Rubinow I felt something magical taking place. I had uncovered a hidden tablet inscribed with a banquet of words between two immigrant Russian Jews, whose friendship had grown deeper and more intimate over their years of common struggle. Their intellectual intimacy had continued after death, their papers lying near to one another, deep in the earth of upstate New York.

---

When Abe was still an obscure public official in Harrisburg he was surprised to receive a letter from Rubinow asking for a copy of his book, *The Negro Migrant in Pittsburgh*. In 1924 Rubinow was the preeminent authority in Abe's field of study, and the author of the most significant book on the subject, *Social Insurance*, published in 1913. Abe was thrilled. He had been hoping for years to work with Rubinow and wrote back the same day to say he had no more copies, but if Rubinow needed any help in any other matter he should please call on him. Later that year at a conference in Philadelphia, Abe saw Rubinow enter the room. He rushed over, introduced himself, and quickly handed the astonished Rubinow a copy of the legal briefs he was using to overturn the Pennsylvania Supreme Court's rejection of the recent old-age pension law. Rubinow, intrigued by Abe's brash behavior, took the briefs away and then sent Abe a wry letter: "I have enjoyed your own contribution, both from a scientific character and the spicy way in which you put your argument—something not altogether usual in legal documents."

The role of witty mentor was one that Rubinow delighted in, and in Abe he thought he'd suddenly found a willing student, one who might help to carry out his ideas on social insurance. Rubinow was fifty and Abe was just past thirty, and though ideological soul mates and Russian immigrants, they had come of age under very different circumstances. Rubinow was the son of a privileged family. His father was a well-to-do merchant who had been granted the right to live in Moscow, one of the few Jewish families permitted to live outside the Pale of Settlement. There, Rubinow had been able to attend an elite German gymnasium, but when the anti-Semitic Alexander III came to power and the Jews were kicked out of the cities, the Rubinows left for America in 1893, not as poor immigrants but as a well-to-do middle-class family. Isaac Rubinow was able to continue his studies at Columbia University and eventually received an M.D. degree. He had an education most immigrant Russian Jews could only dream of.

Abe, on the other hand, had not come from middle-class ease but from a rudimentary world of hard labor and poverty, where bellowing, brawling, and fighting for survival were part of everyday life. He was an Ostjuden—an eastern European Jew—a name given them by the German Jews who had sponsored their emigration, viewing them as illiterate riffraff who gave respectable Jews a bad name. But that was the culture where Abe had been brought up, a society of oppression inside Russia, where if you wanted something you had to fight for it. And what Abe had always fought for was an education. He came to America to get it.

The friendship with Rubinow bloomed. Soon both men saw something in the other that could be useful. Abe asked Rubinow to look over his writings, hoping for insights from the most recognized scholar in his field. Rubinow was delighted, and quickly told Abe he thought he was a born journalist. But his advice also included an area of criticism that rested on their sharp differences in personality, a problem that was to last for the length of their relationship. Rubinow was cautious and methodical. He approached social insurance scientifically through actuarial statistics. Abe, by contrast, was an agitator, speaking from table tops when still a student at Pittsburgh. He wanted results and he wanted them fast, and he was not afraid to challenge anyone in authority. Rubinow suggested he try to tone down his inflammatory rhetoric.

A typical exchange came about when Abe published an article denouncing the passive stand of labor on old-age pensions. Rubinow warned Abe he was asking for trouble from the very men whose support he needed. Of course, it was just a line of caution from an older man, he acknowledged, but did Abe really want to take such a risk? The student jumped at the chance to test himself against his teacher, and Abe jauntily replied that all the labor leaders with whom he had spoken had told him the issue was worth raising—he carefully left out any mention of whether they had agreed with him. Rubinow persisted. Abe should calm his temper when he spoke in public, and make an effort at listening to the opinions of others. The rebuke caught Abe off guard, and like an errant son, he sheepishly admitted the criticism was valid. "Somehow I lose control every time I talk about the opposition."

When Abe labored over his second book, *The Challenge of the Aged*, Rubinow became his toughest critic, accusing him of overstatement, faulty English, and too many overemphatic adjectives: "You never speak of the aged except as this 'decrepit' or some such picturesque term." Typical of what annoyed Rubinow was Abe's description of a poorhouse. "Tens of thousands of old men and women spent their Christmas in antiquated, degrading soulless poorhouses, brutally separated from their life-long mates, fast sinking under an agony of despair and inhumanity. Throughout the country, aged misery slept fitfully in doorways, shivered and starved in cold rooms. The doom of neglect sped them to a welcome grave." Rubinow warned Abe that "A book is not a speech . . . and a calm argument will carry you further. Remember the Russian proverb, 'what is written with the pen cannot be destroyed with an ax.'" (I still hear the echo of Rubinow's advice whenever I recall Abe's words to me, "You know, Pierre, the pen is mightier than the sword.")

The scholarly Rubinow was drawn to Abe's energy and will to get things done, something he had not seen since the first campaigns for social insurance during the Teddy Roosevelt era. As one historian put it, Abe "had revived an American social insurance movement that had become virtually moribund." In fact, Rubinow was so rejuvenated by Abe's passion that he dropped his association with John Andrews's American Association for Labor Legislation and joined Abe's fledgling American Association for Old Age Security as a vice-president. He was even tempted to accompany the new Johnny Appleseed on his 1927 cross-country trip to sew the seeds of social security in America, and insisted Abe send regular reports on his progress. Against his normal caution, Rubinow was becoming infected by Abe's single-minded vitality. But he couldn't resist warning Abe that he had to be careful. "Don't give John Andrews a chance to say you are an impossible man to cooperate with . . . after all the cause of old age pensions is bigger than you or I or Andrews."

Rubinow believed he had the seniority to be a calming influence, but his uppity student could never be counted upon to do what he was told. When Abe published an article entitled "The Soullessness of Present Day Social Work" in the June 1928 issue of *Current History*, Rubinow was aghast. Abe had accused social workers of trying to defeat old-age pensions. Where once they had pushed for better welfare laws, now all they cared about was the mental state of the person who was unable to provide for himself and his family. Where once they had been revolutionary idealists like the great Jane Addams in Chicago, now they behaved like technicians, no better than doctors who only want to cure headaches and stomach pains. Rubinow, who was then a social worker—running the Jewish Welfare Agency in Philadelphia—insisted that Abe's article was a gross exaggeration and a serious error because wherever he went he would need the help of social workers. When the article appeared Abe was in France, intending to relax with Henriette and put the finishing touches on *The Challenge of the Aged*, but he seemed to relish the chance to go head to head with his mentor. He sent off five dense pages of rebuttal, covering everything he couldn't stand about social workers—for the last eight years they had stood in his way wherever he tried to pass a law, they were against old-age pensions because the social work movement no longer had any interest in fundamental economic change, only personal adjustment. "The movement is based entirely and essentially upon the voluntary contributions of the super-rich for the benefit of the poor . . . and what the poor need is dignity not counseling." He pushed the needle in a bit deeper and told Rubinow, "In no industrial country in the world is a man of your genius so confined in his sphere of achievement as you are in social work."

Rubinow's reply to Abe's "somewhat violent letter . . . and your analysis of the decline of my revolutionary enthusiasm," was that if Abe had any knowledge of psychology he might be more skeptical of revolutionary zeal. "Self-restraint is often very much more difficult than self-expression," he chided. But Abe would have none of it. Modern psychology was not the answer. "Regardless of Freud, Watson and a host of others, economic factors still play a leading role." The needs of the poor can be met "much more by fundamental social and economic changes than by 'personal adjustment.'" Abe tried his best to remain analytical with Rubinow, but with others he could rarely hold his temper.

At a conference in Wisconsin, Henriette had watched Abe humiliate an innocent female social worker at breakfast. When the friendly morning talk had turned to the subject of pensions, the young woman, unaware that she was sitting next to a seething activist, mildly piped up, "Oh, you know, the social workers were not much in favor of that law for old age pensions." Abe had turned on her in fury, and in his high, squeaking voice railed that she was uninformed, stupid, and didn't know what she was talking about. Henriette was mortified. And when Abe would not stop his fulminations she stood up.

As loud as she could she told him, "It's time to go to the next meeting!"

Abe stopped, and as Henriette dragged him away from the stunned breakfast crowd, she pleaded, "She doesn't know any better . . . why do you have to argue with people about it?"

But Abe's brain would churn in fury over such people and their ignorance. And it was this kind of encounter that made him want to write scathing articles like the one on social workers in *Current History*. With Rubinow he tried to rationalize his explosive behavior. "I know that I have a terrible reputation as one who will not and cannot work with anyone else. I have frequently wondered at the origin of that reputation. My record is at least 90 percent contrary . . . ," and he went on, as if by sheer rush of words he might convince Rubinow. "I have had only three stenographers in the eleven years since leaving college . . . this is an example that Dr. John Andrews could not possibly show. You will find a new set of girls every time you go into his office." Rubinow eventually grew tired of receiving endless tirades, but Abe was relentless. "I believe in fighting for the things I believe in . . . that may jar some of our hypercritical Anglo Saxons. There may be plenty of compensations in being harmless and wearing an afternoon-tea smile . . . but unfortunately it will not bring any results. You may not agree with me but I am absolutely convinced that if it had not been for the *Current History* article last summer, the New York social workers would have definitely come out against the old age pension bill . . . I have had too many inklings of absolute proof of this assertion." Rubinow finally gave up, but with a warning. "Your name should really not be Abraham but David. You have a tremendous lot of courage. Best of luck to you. You have made some very interesting but very powerful enemies." But Abe would not let it rest. "I am only doing this because I do so much value your faith in me."

It was a revealing phrase, like a little boy to his father, and it was only with Rubinow that Abe adopted this adolescent tone. But despite the occasional apologies from Abe, Rubinow's fatherly advice never really worked. Abe would always come out swinging when he did not like what someone said, and "the enemies" Rubinow spoke of kept increasing. Abe refused to admit he was to blame for their existence, and he even believed he could prove to Rubinow that his methods were sound. "You well know how I treasure your advice and counsel. I am not, however, as rash as you think me to be. If I were, I would not have been able to hold together nearly two score committees throughout the country, each embodying from 40 to 300 different organizations . . . the work of the Association presents some evidence that I am not so tactless. Our only difference, perhaps, lies in the fact that I believe there is a time when fighting is better than taking things calmly. I am absolutely convinced that there can be no progress in the United States without hurting the enemies of progress. Militancy, to my mind, is the most essential thing in American legislation. Without it there is no hope of achievement."

In Abe's view strong tactics worked, because change in a conservative country such as America could only be brought about by picking a fight and brawling with your opponent until he was down for the count. Just like life in the world of the Ostjuden. But Rubinow grew tired of scolding and replied to Abe's tirade on militancy with resignation. "I have no intentions of preaching any sermons to you. Frankly, everyone goes along according to his own temperament and best judgment . . . my method is usually one of give and take. Perhaps few people can work as hard as you do."

Rubinow, to his credit, never gave up on the Abe project. He knew Abe looked up to him and he always believed he could eventually restrain his fiery student. And at one moment it looked like it might work. In March 1932 he suggested Abe call a national conference of all the different state unemployment insurance commissions: the Wisconsin Plan and the Ohio Plan were angrily fighting it out in several states. Rubinow proposed they all sit down and have a meeting "where this matter could be fought out, or at least thought out." Abe liked the idea—he obviously cherished the prospect of delivering a knockout blow to the Wisconsin idiots—but it was not the right time. When his and Rubinow's books had been published and the Ohio Commission had given its report, then the propaganda would be in place, he replied. Then he would be ready. Otherwise he would only be "accused of trying to undermine the 'good work' done by John Andrews" and others. When Abe felt confident, he was a smooth and clever operator. It was when he lost control over issues that he also lost his ability to act diplomatically. He was a fluctuating mixture of assurance and anger.

Another revealing exchange illustrated how their differences in temperament had spread to other areas. When the Jews in Germany were coming under savage attack from Hitler's thugs in 1933, Rubinow, who was then secretary of the national B'nai B'rith, had called for American Jews to remain calm, hoping not to antagonize the Nazis into more anti-Semitic violence. But on the issue of the Nazis, Abe was outspoken. Jewish groups should call for demonstrations and marches; Jews needed to retain self-respect by fighting back. Rubinow was irked. "I can understand your feelings . . . maybe there is the inevitable difference of age . . . but no amount of marching and militant protest would help the Jews in Germany who had begged by letter and phone not to jeopardize their lives for the sake of self-expression." Still, Abe could not resist confrontation. He told Rubinow that he had not always been so cautious, and praised him for an article in the *Nation*. "It recalled your earlier days . . . wonderful to see you in a fighting mood." It was the sort of jab that always seemed to get on Rubinow's nerves.

Despite the turmoil of their lives and work, there were times when both men seemed in step. They egged each other on in a delightful pas de deux when both had books that were about to be published. *Insecurity* appeared first in late 1933, followed by Rubinow's *The Quest for Security* in 1934. Each man asked the other to read and criticize his manuscript, but Rubinow, with characteristic formality, did not want to pore over *Insecurity* too deeply for fear of being influenced by Abe. Nothing of that sort bothered Abe. He heaped nothing but praise on Rubinow: "Beautifully done and so mellowed with philosophical ripeness that it is a joy to read." But even as he praised *The Quest for Security*, he was aware that his battle with the New Deal was nearing a peak, and what he really wanted was Rubinow working by his side. "I am hoping that the day will come soon when you will be able to take a much more active interest in our work." Rubinow's wistful reply cast doubt on the possibility: "Some day you and I may be able to work together in a real earnest way in furthering of this cause."

When FDR's economic security bill was before Congress in 1935, the frustration felt by Abe and Rubinow led to their first ideological clashes. In a desperate attempt in the Senate, Abe persuaded Hugo Black to sponsor his amendments, and in his correspondence with the senator he used a rather acid quote from Rubinow. When Rubinow heard about it he was indignant at having his words exposed before a major public figure without his consent, and he questioned Abe's motives. An even more serious split came about over pensions as opposed to insurance. Abe had always believed in government pensions—it was the government's duty to help the poor, no strings attached. Rubinow did not like them. Only a contributory insurance plan would guarantee that old-age security would not depend on the whims of lawmakers. Morgenthau's meddling over the financing also contributed to the split. Abe felt that if Morgenthau's payroll tax went as high as 10 or 12 percent, then the consequences of that much money being taken out of people's wages would lead to economic recession. "The blame shall fall upon us . . . as nuts and impossibilists," Abe warned. All that Abe liked in the Social Security Act of 1935 was the old-age pension plan. But on this Rubinow drew the line. Abe's pet plan was no more than "gratuitous" money. "I know what your personal contribution has been . . . and your enthusiasm for pensions . . . But I cannot consider such a system . . . as anything more than a relief measure." They differed on how the poor should be treated, and how their dignity should be preserved. And the anguish of being cast aside during the writing of the social security bill of 1935 made the differences between them more acid.

Theirs was a relationship of bristling intimacy, filled with missed opportunities. But what they wrote, what they said, the way they expressed

hemselves, the deep feeling they had for each other, and their shared be-
iefs in a better America rose up from under the earth of Ithaca and lived
again through words on paper that lay all around me. The Ithaca archive
et me inside a hidden part of Abe. What I saw, like a mountain peak vis-
ble above the clouds, was how Abe could never resist challenging the
man who seemed to be almost a father to him. Abe was at times reverent,
playful, defensive, and militant. But much of what he wrote to Rubinow,
it was clear, was a way of acting out the never-resolved antagonism with
his real father. What Abe could never do was tell that dead man of his success in America. It was no longer possible to prove the value of his revolutionary vision to the old-fashioned religious Jew who had given him
life, yet had refused to let him leave Russia to get an education. Over the
years Rubinow was transformed by Abe into an older authority figure for
a rebellious son still entangled emotionally with a long-dead yet still fet-
tering father. Abe was the eternal rebel, against his father, against Russia,
against the New Deal, against complacency, against "wearing an afternoon tea smile." But when times change, when issues evolve, when others take over, tightly wound men such as Abe always seem to suffer.

14

On the stand at last, his glasses perched on his nose, his hands stabbing
the air, Abe read from his prepared statement before the House Ways and
Means Committee. He praised the Economic Security Bill as "the most
outstanding and courageous program that had ever been attempted in the
history of the world." He was fulfilling his agreement with Edwin Witte
to appear as a witness favorable to the government. But as soon as he finished his prepared text he turned into the wolf in sheep's clothing that Edwin Witte had been afraid of. Abe began a scathing criticism of the Wisconsin Plan unemployment provisions. Witte should have realized that
Abe could not be controlled. In fact he never truly understood the depth
of Abe's hatred for the Wisconsin Plan. In the opinion of Theron Schlabach, Witte's sympathetic biographer: "The Committee had ignored two
of his [Abe's] emphatic precepts: the utter depravity of the Wisconsin plan
for unemployment and the need to subsidize social insurance from the
general treasury in order to redistribute wealth."

Abe had pulled every string he could to be called as a witness before
the House Ways and Means Committee. It had not been easy. To Rubinow
he confided, "the Administration has definitely instructed the House
Committee to pay no attention to any of us and to rush through the hear-

ings as soon as possible." Finally, when he was summoned it was mostly because he had made the deal with Witte to be a favorable witness. Still, the chairman would allow him only five minutes, and Abe had to hold his tongue while his friends on the committee asked for more time. Eventually he was allowed an hour and twenty minutes. The difficulty from the very beginning, in Abe's view, had been that no one in the nation's capital had any idea of what was in FDR's proposed Economic Security Bill. Nor did they know whether to be for it or against it. Abe's Washington supporters told him they had never seen such confusion among the members of Congress. One House member complained he had never seen such "gross ignorance" of any bill ever. Even a senator as important to the New Deal as Robert Wagner had his secretary call Abe to ask him if he knew where the president himself stood on the bill. Was he pro or con? Several sections of the bill had to be rewritten by congressional aides for the wording to make any sense. The old-age insurance provisions—the bedrock of what we now think of as social security—were almost sent back to the committee by a group of angry House Republicans. In the Senate most of the Republicans voted to eliminate the old-age provisions. Hastings of Delaware fumed that the bill would "end the progress of a great country and bring its people to the level of the average European." On and on it went, the turmoil growing worse, and Abe had been at his wit's end. He did not know how he could bring any sense to the proceedings. He could not believe that the administration had willfully created a quagmire out of such an unprecedented opportunity. The mess in Washington was also hurting the association. Financially, it was the worst year they had ever faced—more than twenty-four hundred people had failed to renew their subscriptions to the monthly bulletin because they were convinced FDR had solved old-age security and unemployment forever. Publicly, Abe expressed confidence that his fiscal problems would clear up in the coming year, but he was bitter at his nemesis: "Most people believe that Fanny Perkins is giving us a complete program on a silver platter . . . but we will have to pay the price for Fanny's follies. The only thing to do is let nature take its course," he grouched—an odd expression coming from the peppery Abe. Perhaps it was just another one of those American clichés he found slipping from his lips when he felt bewildered.

In the Senate Abe did better and stayed on the stand before the Finance Committee for three days. He ridiculed the Wisconsin Plan as being as bad as the Townsend Plan. "Everybody seems to have abdicated thinking," he told the senators. From all accounts Abe gave a remarkable performance before the Senate Finance Committee because a number of senators sent im flattering letters. But most of them had been his allies all along. Pushing as hard as he could, Abe gathered twenty-four experts on unemployment, including Paul Douglas and Eveline Burns, and had them testify before Congress as representatives of the American Association for Social Security. All of them condemned the Wisconsin Plan and advocated some form of governmental subsidy on unemployment.

None of Abe's testimony, articles, newspaper interviews, and conferences made a bit of difference. When the bill finally passed both houses of Congress, even Rubinow, who always tried to be optimistic, was scathing: "This is the kind of mouse that the big mountain has given birth to . . . professional cartoonists could utilize the occasion to advantage and Mickey Mouse might very well be the symbol of the Presidential Security Program."

Roosevelt signed the social security bill on August 4, 1935, in a formal White House ceremony where he was encircled by a few smiling members of the Senate and House, all happy to take credit for the bill's passage. Frances Perkins, wearing her ever-present three-cornered hat, occupied the place of honor and stood directly behind the white-suited FDR, her face devoid of expression. The president, his pen poised, his head cocked to one side, a pleased grin on his face, could not conceal his feeling of triumph. It was a far happier look than when he had signed the New York Old Age Pension Law five years earlier. Then, engulfed by the dense, almost unruly crowd of passionate pension advocates, he had looked very ill at ease, as if he did not really approve of what had taken place. Now in 1935 the ceremony was calm and dignified, as befitted a great White House moment.

Neither Paul Douglas, Isaac Rubinow, nor Abe Epstein was present to receive pens. Historians have been quick to note that they had been pointedly excluded. In fact, none of the social reformers who had worked so hard for more than ten years to promote the cause of social security were asked to the signing—except for one, Abe's onetime boss, that discarded relic from the Fraternal Order of Eagles, Frank Hering. Roosevelt had pardoned him from his prison sentence—for the crime of swindling those very same Eagles—so that he could be present and receive a pen. The Eagles were an influential group, old-age pensions had been their pet project, they voted in great numbers, and the presidential election of 1936 was not far off. Hering's presence seemed fitting, because as one of the president's most respected chroniclers, William Leuchtenberg, described

the law, it was "an astonishingly inept and conservative piece of legislation."

---

Despite the torment he endured, for Abe it was only round one—he
would keep on fighting, he would find a way to win. He would unsheath
his pen as sword. Well before the White House signing ceremony, he started to bang the warning drums. But as he moved into the ranks of the New
Deal's opponents, some part of him began to unravel. "From now on our
fight will be in the open and it will be a bitter one. I am definitely planning to start a bitter campaign attacking the unemployment and old-age
contributory features of the Social Security bill," he announced to Rubinow. But in this time of anguish only his oldest and deepest friends would
stand by him. He was more and more a bundle of ragged nerves, looking
much older than his forty-three years.

Rubinow was alert to Abe's bitter tack and tried to steer him away from
it. "Social insurance is not a gift from heaven. We were all a little naive
that 1935 marked a social revolution . . . progress remains a slow and tedious process. Being some twenty years younger than myself you should
have more patience than I have." But patience is what Abe never had. The
annual conference and the dinner that accompanied it in 1935 kept his
mind focused, but it was obvious to many, including Henriette's mother
in far-off Toulouse, that Abe was in bad shape. After gazing at a photo of
the dinner, she wrote Henriette that "Eppie seems more and more depressed, his mind seems empty of thought—it hurts to see him in such a
state, we have little hope that he will get better."

Problems first began to surface with the publication in the June–July issue of *Social Security* of Abe's long piece criticizing the new law. The association's board of directors had looked it over and asked Abe to take out
his "undignified statements," which he did reluctantly. People near to
Abe, including Rubinow—who had found the article too spiteful—tried
to stop him from antagonizing too many people. The board was beginning to divide between those who supported Abe's attacks and those who
wanted him to tone down his writing. The crisis was such that in the summer of 1935 the vacation in France was abandoned for the first time. Instead, Henriette and I were sent for the summer to a little stone cottage by
a gurgling brook on the grounds of Brookwood Labor College in Katonah,
New York, where Abe had taught from time to time. Abe shuttled back
and forth between there and the office, eventually giving rise to anxious
letters from Toulouse. "Tell us all that is going on, and why he stays by

The author's fifth birthday party, where he threw a tantrum.
Brookwood, 1935. Abe's mother is in the rear.

himself . . . Remember that he is sick and that he has the right to patience
. . . don't agitate him unnecessarily." Henriette made efforts to avoid Abe's
moods, but she secretly wrote to Rubinow, asking him to be more involved
with the work of the association. "My husband needs very much your experience and advice—and a good deal of trouble would be avoided."

I also began to contribute to the turmoil, throwing my own tantrums,
scowling in photographs at aunts, uncles, and cousins who had come to
celebrate my fifth birthday. I screamed that I wanted to be left alone to
play with my new toys. Ordered to pose with all the guests, I stood in the
middle of the group in little satin shorts and slicked-back hair, a sour expression on my face. My Russian grandmother—a woman who never
seemed comfortable in any photograph when her militant son was in the
vicinity—was scowling as well.

Abe's summer away from the family was spent in the office on East Sev-
enteenth Street where he worked late into the night on articles for the
*Nation*, the *Crisis*, the *Annals of the American Academy of Political and Social
Science*, and *Harper's*. He warned Rubinow, "Frankly, the more I think and

write about the Social Security Act the madder I get at its stupidities and complete imbecility." Abe was moving fast, and Rubinow was impressed. "You are Johnny-on-the-spot," he told him. "I had offered my services to Harper's and they told me they had somebody else . . . I guessed it was you." But Abe could always find a way to irritate Rubinow: "I have deliberately abstained from criticizing it [the Social Security Act] publicly because I am convinced the present act will fail." Rubinow, who was a close reader of text long before that phrase ever became fashionable, saw where Abe might be heading. "What exactly do you mean when you say 'the present act will fail.' There should be a demand for improvement . . . but that does not mean that the act . . . will fail." He was afraid that Abe would suggest publicly that the entire act should be thrown out by the Supreme Court—exactly what had happened to Abe's plans for old-age pensions in Pennsylvania in 1927.

Abe's pen finally drew blood when his Harper's article, "Our Social Insecurity Act," appeared in December 1935. He had written two earlier pieces attacking the act, but the Harper's article got the attention he was looking for. Parts of it were widely reprinted in major urban dailies in New York, Chicago, Baltimore, San Francisco, and Cleveland, as well as in a number of smaller newspapers. It began with a facetious description of the great signing ceremony in the White House:

> Surrounded by flood lights, news-reel cameras, and a squad of reporters and administration dignitaries, the Chief Executive gave his approval to a piece of legislation which almost defies analysis and which few understand. There was applause for the bill . . . but who knew what was in the bill or what it really meant? . . . Secretary Perkins had said that it was "one of the most forward-looking pieces of legislation in the interest of wage earners"; but the bill was signed without the presence of a single representative of labor. It took a score of pens to sign the document . . . some were presented to Southern politicians who, in times past, had been opposed to all labor legislation . . . it was all high thought and fine ceremony and total befuddlement.

With a sarcastic flourish he went on.

> Even after enactment of a bill that is a perfect labyrinth of constitutional and administrative puzzles, the newspapers, with tiresome reiteration, have hailed it as "the beginning of a new era," "humanity's greatest boon," and as "the translation of the cross of Christ—the life of the world."

He then launched into a crisp history of social security in Europe, pointing out that most of what the administration was trying to do had already been going on for nearly fifty years in the Old World: "Mr. Roosevelt might have drawn on these actual European experiences," he wrote. Instead, the New Deal administration's ignorance of social insurance was colossal. Neither business nor labor had ever expressed much interest in the subject, and the universities had ignored it. So when the cabinet committee was created, headed by Frances Perkins and "euphoniously designated The Committee on Economic Security," no one had any idea of what aspects of social insurance should be included in a bill. He retold the story of the committee's bitter deliberations and FDR's embarrassing blunder on November 14 when he said it wasn't the right time for old-age security. He made sure to include Arthur Krock's snide analysis of the president's words, "Does the English Language Mean Anything?" He blamed Perkins for the entire mess: "Two weeks before the bill was presented to Congress Miss Perkins did not know what plan for unemployment insurance the President would favor." The House committee was so annoyed that it "ordered its own draftsmen to rewrite the bill and humble Miss Perkins by making the administrative board entirely independent" of the Labor Department. Finally, when Congress failed to vote any money to run the new Social Security Board, the New Deal blamed it on Huey Long's "miniature filibuster." Roosevelt could have kept Congress in session to get the money, Abe wrote, but he didn't in order "to out-hooey Huey." The bill was a mish-mash and "a typical New Deal product."

As expected, he approved of the federal subsidy for state old-age pensions but tore into Morgenthau's creation, the reserve fund for future old-age insurance. In this he made sure that his favorite image would be part of the debate: that of the rich who "ever since the Elizabethan Poor Law three centuries ago have shared in the maintenance of the aged poor" and would now no longer have to ante up a cent. He blamed Perkins for the fifty-one unemployment insurance schemes that differed in every state and territory instead of one national plan because of her refusal to accept the recommendations of both the committee staff and the advisory council. The article was sprinkled with a salvo of wicked barbs: "The enactment of this slovenly program . . . its bungling nature . . . inherent and unnecessary blunders . . . economic and social fallacies . . . the dangers which lurk behind this scheme doom it from birth . . . palpable nonsense or worse for Miss Perkins to arouse great hopes that this Act will give protection to the working masses."

After eleven pages he finished, like a pitcher throwing as hard as he could in the last inning of a game he was losing: "It is a confession of complete ignorance of the principles of social insurance for liberals to argue that with all its faults the Act 'makes a beginning.' A beginning toward what?" He growled that it was more likely an ending, perhaps even a "death blow to the entire movement for many years . . . The 'New Deal' Social Security program is not only inherently menacing," he wrote, wrapping it up with another fastball, "it may actually stifle the growing movement for social insurance . . . by shattering the hopes of a distressed people." It would never "meet the Gargantuan problems of insecurity."

It was typical of Abe that he was at his most newsworthy when he could bombard the opposition with caustic words from his solitary foxhole. But now he was out in the open, a sitting duck for anyone who could not stand him and his opinions. Many who read the piece thought Abe was now joining the Republican opposition to social security, and this puzzled them. Both Rubinow and Douglas cautioned him about his constant negative attacks. But Abe was thrilled, enjoying his newfound notoriety. In January of 1936 he pridefully wrote to Rubinow, "When I go to Washington I get better hearings now than I have been able to get in the past two years." The people who didn't like Roosevelt were now beginning to appreciate Abe for his pungent denunciations.

---

Abe may not have won the fight for genuine social security in 1935, but he came away with an underlying philosophical victory. Several members of the House Ways and Means Committee did not like "The Economic Security Bill" as a title. They also wanted to assert their independence. Originally there was to be a Social Insurance Board to administer the bill, but some of it was to be administered by the Department of Labor. The committee decided to take it away from Perkins and the Labor Department and put it under an independent board with a new name. There was a free-for-all discussion, both Edwin Witte and Thomas Eliot recalled. Ideas went back and forth. And finally Roy Woodruff, a Republican from Michigan, spoke up. He knew Abe, had spoken at several of the association's conferences, and was one of the few lawmakers who believed in Abe's concept of social security. "Call it the Social Security Board," he suggested. There was silence for a moment, almost no discussion; then the committee voted to adopt the name and sent the bill to the full House of Representatives as "The Social Security Act"—the words that Abe had first brought before the public and that Franklin Delano Roosevelt had wanted to avoid.

Abe never understood the victory he had achieved. For no new names could change one basic fact. Roosevelt had grumbled when signing the first old-age pension law in New York, "Is this the Lemon they are handing me?" Now, five years later, he had signed another "lemon." Only this time it was a "lemon" of his own creation. And it left a very sour taste in Abe Epstein's mouth.

## 15

In attacking the Social Security Act, Abe derived a perverse pleasure in the reactions he aroused. Among the first to feel Abe's sting had been Frances Perkins. She was a reticent politician who avoided the limelight. Photographers never seemed to get past her official bland look and her ever-present three-cornered hat. But when she unexpectedly ran into Abe in New York it was more than she could take. On the dais as the guest speaker at the annual meeting of the National Consumer's League on December 10, 1935, she saw that Abe and Henriette were in the audience. At one point when Abe got up and left the room to make a phone call, Perkins noticed and stopped her speech. Something buried inside her took over and she launched into a defense of the Social Security Act, attacking those who were against it, including, "Abraham Epstein, who has made an inexcusable and unjustifiable attack on the act . . . it's too bad he wasn't elected president of the United States so that he could have modified the bill." She was about to go on when Abe suddenly reappeared in the back of the hall. She paused, looked down at her text, and quickly returned to her written speech. But it was too late. By then several New York reporters had cornered Abe, and, hoping for a good quote, asked with relish, "Well, Abe, did you hear Perkins just now? What do you think of what she said about you?" Abe smiled and said nothing. Henriette, who had remained at the table feeling very ill at ease, turned to see where Abe might be. He was at the back of the room, calmly leaning against the doorway with an ironical smile on his face, appearing to enjoy every bit of the secretary of labor's invective.

The next day the incident was major news in both the *Times* and the *Herald Tribune*. Perkins' words about Abe were quoted, and the headline in the *Tribune* read, "Secretary of Labor attacks Epstein; uses language like a fishwife." The incident gathered Abe a good deal of favorable publicity; it isn't everyday that one is attacked by a member of the cabinet. Henriette also reveled in the drama, and Abe's joy at the sympathy he received, by casting herself in a central role. In her version when Abe was out of the room and Perkins went into her outburst, "she had been staring at me, as hard as she could . . . and I couldn't move."

But others did not find such events so amusing, including as always Rubinow and Douglas. They had warned Abe that the more he continued to antagonize important New Deal politicians, the more he would lose any influence with them. Rubinow in particular was becoming more distressed. He accused Abe of helping the enemy and quoted a letter he had received about Abe's influential article, "Our Social Insecurity Act." "It is being cited . . . by groups who are opposed to unemployment insurance as evidence that the Federal Law will not work." Abe was not impressed—he was determined on a course of action, egged on in part by his newfound celebrity. It was a sudden turnaround for a man who had been shunned by the highest government officials. Now, everything Abe said hit the papers, and he was deluged with requests to speak around the country. Indeed, many public officials were realizing that the Social Security Act was not what had been promised.

Abe's cavalier and pugnacious behavior finally made Rubinow quite angry. He rebuked Abe on the only part of the act he supported: pensions for the elderly. "Do you mean to compare them with, and prefer it to, the system of insurance which guarantees to the insured wage worker an income at the age of 65?" But he reached the boiling point over Abe's publicly stated wish to see the entire act tossed out by the courts so that a better law could be written from scratch. Something enormous had been accomplished, Rubinow felt, and what was needed was the desire to improve the law, not an attempt to scuttle it.

"We have worked for years together but on that platform you and I cannot stand. With the best of feelings for you personally . . . if that attitude should be announced publicly as the attitude of the American Association for Social Security, I will be unable to retain my connection with it." Rubinow, without telling Abe, warned the association's board that "Abe has gone entirely too emotional on this whole business . . . Points of view are becoming so divergent that some of us may not find it possible to continue cooperation." It was the start of an ideological and personal rupture, deepened by the basic difference in temperament between the two men.

If Abe had not been fooled by the attention he was getting, he might have been able to avoid confrontation with the man who meant so much to him. But he could not resist challenging his older mentor, even when Rubinow sympathized with him on how badly he had been treated by the New Deal administration. He begged Abe to not let his emotions get the best of him—anger was blinding him on basic economic principles. But battling with Rubinow seemed to strengthen Abe. He wrote long, defensive letters of reply to pleas for restraint—but there was no mention of the hidden cause of Abe's vitriol: his rage at being rejected. His underlying emotional pain and Rubinow's physical pain stained all the twists and turns of their correspondence. Their letters only discussed ideas and political positions. But the fact was that Rubinow was slowly dying and had less than a year to live, while Abe was physically and emotionally worn out, yet refused to let up.

In April 1935, after his two nervous breakdowns, Abe went back to Pittsburgh to see his old doctor, an eccentric character named H. A. Shaw. The test results were forwarded to New York, accompanied by Shaw's personal letter of tortured, metaphorical prose. Abe was "living at greater pace than economical consideration would indicate," and this meant, Shaw wrote, "that you wore your kidneys, your blood vessels, your heart muscle, your blood generating organs with greater intensity . . . the remaining amount must be dispensed more economically." Shaw then became even more inscrutable: "You are undoubtedly familiar with a certain engineering maxim which states that if impact against a bridge or any other structure is constant, wear and tear is speedier than when impact is intermittent . . . therefore if you have to shock and jar your physical structure do it in such a fashion that periods of activity would be followed by remission. Quoting an Egyptian wizard, whose name escapes me, the best and greatest progress is made by 'rowing your boat and letting go,' etc. etc." Finally, after two pages of convoluted rhetoric, Shaw managed to offer some practical advice. "Vacation does not mean work away from the office . . . summer ought to be spent . . . out of doors, largely on one's back." But Abe paid no attention and refused to take any time off. Instead, he spent the summer and fall of 1935 at full throttle, writing article after article. No one could really understand what was driving Abe into such a self-destructive frenzy.

Henriette became more worried and furtively wrote to Rubinow, asking him to talk to Abe to try to slow him down. For although Abe paid scant attention to anyone's advice, she was sure he would listen to Rubinow. She did not know how badly the relationship had deteriorated. "Your letter is really heartbreaking," Rubinow replied. "Whether I could do anything by a personal interview must remain a question." He told her that he had secretly urged the association's board to tell Abe to take a long rest, but they had not acted. He would be willing to come to New York for a talk to try and straighten things out, but his own doctor had forced him to return home from a meeting and he had been hospitalized for ten days. "Abe's is a medical problem," he told Henriette. "He hasn't been well since his breakdown . . . if you can induce him to undergo a thorough medical examination . . . I mean a really thorough medical examination, which might require his going to a hospital for a few days." He suggested a doctor on East Sixty-fourth Street. "All of us are concerned about social security and about the Association but in addition you and I are concerned about Abe and at this particular moment that should be our first concern." But Henriette could not bring herself to confront Abe with Rubinow's advice. She was afraid of his reaction and put the letter aside. Sixty years later it appeared from under the scattered papers of a cluttered back room at 389 Bleecker Street. Never seen by Abe. Never acted upon.

Despite his failing health, Rubinow finally made it to New York in January 1936 for a meeting with Abe to work out their philosophical differences. On a Friday night they sat down together at 389 Bleecker Street for a long talk. Henriette left them alone. What was said by those two sickly social security warriors is not known. But it ended unpleasantly. Rubinow returned home and immediately wrote to Abe, asking him "not to inject yourself emotionally to such an intense degree . . . you and I should have been able to discuss . . . without getting excited and somewhat irritated at each other." But Abe refused compromise and wrote back, "I frankly cannot see much in giving aid and comfort to the enemy. I presume throughout civilization critics of existing situations were attacked on this ground. The only alternative to this is either that of going along or silence . . ."

Rubinow finally became angry and accused Abe of meddling with his efforts to get an improved unemployment insurance bill through the Ohio legislature. He also resigned as a vice president of the association. Abe denied he had done anything of the sort, only that when in Akron he had given a speech pointing out some defects of the Social Security Act. He did not see what he was doing to a relationship with a man that he had cherished since 1924 and coldly cut the cord: "but since you insist I shall submit your resignation to the board."

It was a concluding and very painful split. Rubinow went back to the hospital and eventually got a letter off to Abe. "Apparently it is useless for me to try and convince you that there is some flaw in your reasoning

... I tried to do it the last time I was in New York and wasn't particularly successful. Postponing an opportunity for a discussion ... I must insist that you withhold from interfering with our initiatives and plans in the state of Ohio."

Those harsh words are the final ones that passed between Abe and his mentor. Their ardent, personal, and long-standing ideological intimacy was washed away by anger and illness. Abe sent one final note expressing his concern over Rubinow's illness, but his mentor was back in the hospital and too weak to reply in person. His secretary did it for him: "he appreciates your best wishes." I. M. Rubinow was transferred to Montefiore Hospital in New York later that summer and died there on September 1, 1936. The last words he had written to Abe were to stay out of Ohio.

---

Later that summer in London, where Abe had gone to do research, an English associate called him at his hotel and told him Rubinow had died. Abe was dumbfounded; he had never realized how sick Rubinow had been. The enormity of the loss was devastating, and he tried to come back for the funeral. But it was too late. All he could do to express his grief was to write to Rubinow's widow, Ida, that her husband's death was "a true national calamity." She thanked him and said that amongst the many letters she had received, "I liked yours the best for it shows not only great admiration ... but also great love. We knew for months that he did not have the slightest chance of recovery." But on one important matter she agreed with Abe and not her late husband, and that was on Abe's feelings toward the Roosevelt administration. At a memorial meeting held in Cincinnati, Paul Douglas had quoted FDR, who had reportedly said that he regarded Rubinow "as the greatest single authority on national social security." The *New York Times*'s obituary of Rubinow also related a story of how Roosevelt had allegedly sent him a copy of Rubinow's own book, *The Quest for Security,* with an inscription by the president: this "reversal of the usual process was explained in view of the great interest I have had in reading your book." But Ida Rubinow was not taken in. "If the President thought so," she wrote Abe, "why didn't he call Dr. Rubinow to meetings then?"

Abe never lost touch with Ida Rubinow. It was as if through her he could still be nurtured by his vanished mentor. In 1938, in the final edition of *Insecurity,* Abe changed the dedication "To the memory of Dr. I. M. Rubinow, cherished friend and profound teacher." He sent Ida a copy with a special inscription. She was deeply touched by the gesture. In New

FDR, triumphant, signing the Social Security Act, August 15, 1935. Frances Perkins has a blank expression among the smiling senators and congressmen. No one connected to the social security movement is present.

York, Abe helped organize a memorial service and gave one of the eulogies: "In his death America has lost one of its best equipped social thinkers . . . the writer has lost his staunchest colleague and most valued teacher and friend. The fight for social insurance in America without 'I. M.' at one's side seems an almost impossible and fruitless task."

But Isaac Max Rubinow was no longer at his side, and Abe confessed to Ida Rubinow that he could not believe he would be unable to "get back to him for spiritual guidance and fatherly help." Abe knew what he had lost: his guide, and the father figure he was always searching for.

# Part Three

## Abe's Bitter Harvest

1

Two months after Rubinow's death, America went to the polls. The economy was still in a slump. There was massive unemployment, violent labor riots in Detroit and elsewhere, rejection by the Supreme Court of most of the New Deal programs, starvation in the drought-stricken South, Communist agitation, and serious dissension among the Democrats because most Southern politicians hated Franklin Roosevelt. A betting man would not have blithely put his money on the president getting a second term.

The one bright spot in all of this turbulence was the Social Security Act of August 1935. Roosevelt was triumphant and had handed out a profusion of pens to a bevy of grinning politicians in a grand White House ceremony. Things were finally going to change—FDR was delivering on his promise of a real New Deal for the unemployed and the aged who had been waiting for help for so long. The president was going to ride that "major turning point of American history"—in the words of biographer Kenneth Davis—to victory in 1936.

It was all phony and a lot of nonsense in Abe's view. He had lampooned the religious fervor for the act in his *Harper's* article as "humanity's greatest boon . . . the translation of the cross of Christ." But that was mild compared with the anger and sarcasm fermenting inside of him. Roosevelt's vainglorious statements on social security would only make matters worse, and the people who had created the act had only deceived the public. All Abe's frustration and resentment was channeled into one more try at reform. Down to Washington he went once again. Pressure on Congress from the administration had subsided, and all of a sudden a lot more doors were open to him. He lined up appointments with senators and congressmen—with national elections looming, the lawmakers were interested and available. They were extremely confused about the law and had no idea what position to take in the coming campaign. Abe did his valiant best to explain why the law would be a catastrophic failure and why they must support immediate reform. First of all, the payroll tax would be ruinous: take-home pay would be smaller, it would be seven years before any benefits would be paid out, and a gigantic reserve—to reach forty-seven billion dollars—would just sit in the treasury doing nothing except to siphon money from the economy. Purchasing power would decline and economic recovery would stop. The unemployment provisions were even worse. Run on a state and territorial basis, they were a maddening miscellany of fifty-one plans, no two alike, and with no carryover from one jurisdiction to another. Worse yet, most legislatures had yet to vote them into effect. When he returned to New York he knew he had made an impression and informed the board: "I get better hearings now than I have been able to get in the last two years. My shortest conference with anyone was at least two hours and some lasted as long as three and four hours." His two articles in the *Nation* and the one in *Harper's* attracted a lot of attention. He also pushed himself to the limit with 125 new pages of damning analysis to be added to the third edition of *Insecurity*, to be issued in 1936.

Offers to lecture poured in. People were confused about the new law and wanted to hear him speak. He toured the Midwest and East in the spring and fall of 1936, and at first, because he was not sure how the public would react, his lectures were calm and measured. For example, in Grand Rapids, Michigan, on February 11 he suggested that "the national security act violates the most fundamental principles of social security." Nothing harsh there. But he sensed audiences were with him, and two weeks later in Providence, Rhode Island, he was scoffing. "If the Social Security Act had any good at all to it, I'd embrace it, but there aren't in the whole country a thousand people who know what this law is all about and I doubt if more than six of them are in Congress." The reaction was positive, and suddenly he felt on a roll. He picked up the pace. On October 5 in Washington he proclaimed, "The Act's major features are neither social nor conducive to security," and later that same month in Cleveland he called it the "most absurd and cockeyed piece of social legislation ever passed . . . probably the most antisocial measure ever enacted." Audiences laughed and applauded. They loved his biting wit and acid comments. All at once he was receiving more recognition as a critic than he ever had as an advocate. Taking on the administration in a public challenge was working. To one of his Washington supporters he wrote, "I have been jockeyed into a position which, in all my life, I had never dreamt I would find myself in . . ." But there was more than a hint of delight in his words.

––––––––––

To face Roosevelt in the 1936 election the Republicans had chosen the genial governor of Kansas, Alf Landon, a stolid and unimaginative businessman who had actually been an early admirer of FDR and his ideas. But for the most part he was a traditional conservative with solid approval from the party rank-and-file. The press and the business community with its advertising money were behind him, just about all he needed to oust Roosevelt. It helped that he was also the only Republican governor re-elected in the 1934 Democratic sweep. He was a true midwesterner with a noticeable flat twang in his voice, and he was never a match for Roosevelt when speaking in public.

The Republicans took note of Abe's fiery denunciations of the Social Security Act, and he received a letter asking him if he would be interested in having a talk with Landon. Abe looked on it as an opportunity. The thought in his mind was that if the Republicans publicly supported him, perhaps they would then give him a chance to actually rewrite social security. Abe always made it clear that he didn't care where the support came from as long as he got it. He had worked with both Republicans and Democrats, and it didn't matter to him. He took the train to Landon's headquarters in Topeka and for a few hours told the candidate what was wrong with FDR's Social Security Act. That first step led to an offer to speak live on the radio before the Young Businessmen's League for Social Security, a Republican crowd, of course. They liked his words about the payroll tax—"a system of compulsory payments by the poor for the impoverished"—but as Republicans they misrepresented his thinking by ignoring the rest of the sentence: "that conveniently relieved the well-to-do from their share of the social burden." Still, Abe had offered the Republicans some convincing ammunition with which to vilify the Democrats, and they made attacking the payroll tax one of the main points of their campaign. Nasty leaflets were printed that looked like they had come from the Social Security Board showing workers how much money was being taken out of their salaries. Many companies, including Ford and General Motors, would slip them into the pay envelopes. Another widely distributed leaflet showed a man with a dog tag around his neck. "Snooping and tagging," it said—everyone who wanted social security would have a number, it implied, just like a convict.

Abe's jollying up to the Republicans was an extremely risky move. His anger toward the New Deal blinded him to the fact that it looked to others like he was being used. Public attacks on what many felt was FDR's greatest legislative achievement did not go over well with his traditional allies and made him sound like a sore loser. Some were convinced that he had been recruited by the Republican Party. His talk on radio before the young businessmen had been noted, and many of his friends were upset. When Abe was told this by Paul Douglas, he reacted fiercely. "The law is unsound. I know when to compromise. I've compromised through political necessity all my life. But this isn't a compromise—it's a complete sell out . . . it violates every sound principle of social security. I can't be silent . . . I've got to fight!" The only way to change bad legislation was to speak out publicly, make it over, and it didn't matter where the support came from. As always with Abe the operative word was "fight."

---

Landon's campaign only energized the dispirited Republicans when he attacked social security as "a cruel hoax" on September 26 in Milwaukee and proposed that the despised payroll tax be dropped. But in a very odd twist that only a few took note of, he also "advocated the substitution of a uniform benefit with all costs paid out of general revenues." In other words, let the government foot the bill, not the individual. This idea had actually been offered to FDR's Committee on Economic Security by Abe and Rubinow as a way to fund the bill. The cautious committee turned them down. The government should stay out of it. Unfair to the rich, FDR had been advised—the man who made more should get more. But the two men's idea was a pointed one: why should the employee be the one to contribute almost all the money for his own retirement? That's what government taxes were for, they made the rich pay a greater share of the burden. In fact, in Britain a tax on inheritances funded unemployment insurance. That the principle of government funding should come out of a Republican mouth was symptomatic of the confusion over social security. No one understood how it was meant to work or where the money was to come from. And unfortunately for Abe, when Landon was crushed by Roosevelt in the election, government funding was discredited forever. But what really sent Abe into fits of despair were those who were convinced he was on the side of the Republicans. In their view the GOP was trying to abolish social security and Abe was helping them. He was accused of taking money from the GOP, being paid off because he was bitter at being ignored by Roosevelt. Abe was deeply hurt by the charge, because it had no basis in fact. He never received a nickel of support. In fact the association was taking in less and less every year.

The personal attacks got to Abe. The neglect and defeat he had already suffered haunted him. He was exhausted from his speaking tours, during which he sometimes gave two or three talks a day. What Henriette noticed was that he was up at dawn to take a train to the next lecture, having been unable to get much sleep the night before. He took his meals on the run, and even when back in New York rarely came home before eleven or twelve at night, having skipped dinner. For years he had been told to get more rest, but he paid no attention. His pace grew more frenzied. Damn the Republicans. Damn Roosevelt. He had to win. But with Rubinow's death he had lost the elder man's calming hand, and now when Abe spoke out he was more truculent, no longer the smooth campaigner who could find allies everywhere. Some of his oldest companions were so disturbed by his behavior that they quit the association. Even the newspapers, which had almost always been on his side, now became critical. The *Cleveland Plain Dealer* editorialized that he was "being a perfectionist, always dissatisfied with anything less than 100 per cent attainment of their objective."

Abe's replies to his adversaries were like Timon of Athens from his hermit's cave, a curse on the world and its corruption. At the start of a course he taught at New York University in September 1937 on the theory and principles of social insurance, he was singled out for attack. Someone from the office of the regional director of social security had called NYU to complain that "Mr. Epstein does not represent the official point of view," then added, "we would like to offer some other person to supplement the course." A man less on the edge than Abe might have laughed it off as a silly, but he was instantly enraged. He called an urgent meeting of his board, and when they had gathered in his tiny office he burst out in his high-pitched voice, "This is an attempt to throttle free speech!" The board, some of whom were seriously worried about Abe's health, went along, passing a resolution of protest, and a letter was sent to the American Association of University Professors asking for an investigation. And as always Abe went out and talked to the press. The *New York Times*, Associated Press, *Washington Post, Detroit Free Press,* and other news organizations around the United States ran the story. The editorial in the *Detroit Free Press* was typical: "a rather crude attempt to encroach on academic freedom . . . For when government begins trying to impose its official views on students in American universities as part of their education, a decidedly vicious effort to regiment thought will be in progress."

Abe also sent a letter to Arthur Altmeyer, the chairman of the Social Security Board, which read in part, "Unlike in Germany, Italy, and Russia we have so far not become familiar with what are official and non-official points of view . . . I consider this an unwarranted attempt to curtail my constitutional liberty of speech . . . a serious encroachment on academic freedom . . . I do not want to be forced to take public steps to protect myself against continuous hounding for convictions which I have held steadfastly for over twenty years." Altmeyer, who had been assistant secretary of labor under Perkins, was a tough and stubborn character. He and Abe were guarded friends—the social security community of experts was a small one, and everyone knew everyone else—but he didn't appreciate being baited by Abe. As far as he was concerned, "if such a suggestion was made—having more than one person lecture on social insurance—I do not know why you should object . . . the problems arising are complex enough to warrant consideration by different points of view." Anna Rosenberg, the regional director for social security, insisted that all they had in mind was another course on administrative problems. But she hadn't done her homework because the university was already offering three other courses on that same subject at the same time that Abe was teaching theory. The conflict was about to get out of hand. Abe was threatening a lawsuit. The American Association of University Professors was about to move on an investigation into academic freedom, when one day the phone rang in Abe's office. Henriette picked it up.

"Hello, this is Anna Rosenberg from social security."

"Yes?"

"I would like to talk with Mr. Epstein."

"He's not in right now."

"I see . . ."

Henriette was afraid that some further trouble might be brewing.

"Would you tell Mr. Epstein to call. And tell him that I regret the problems that have arisen between him and the regional office."

Rosenberg explained that she had not authorized her employee to do what she had done, and then stunned Henriette with a sudden turnaround.

"We would like to have Mr. Epstein come and talk to us in the New York office so that we can have a grasp of what he believes social security is all about . . . We believe it will help us in administering the law. I hope he will be interested so please have him call."

Henriette felt a great sense of relief. Until that moment she was afraid Abe was only making himself more enemies. She thought the issue had been blown out of proportion, particularly by the newspapers, and was afraid that Abe would soon blow his top about something else. But she was afraid of tackling Abe on his emotional reactions, so when Rosenberg called the burden was lifted from her shoulders and all she worried about was whether Abe would be calm enough to accept the offer. She needn't have worried, because he was always eager to educate people. There was at least someone in the administration showing interest in his ideas. He went and spent an afternoon with Rosenberg and her staff and in the years to come Anna Rosenberg, who subsequently had a distinguished career in American government, became one of Abe's staunchest supporters. So much so that when Abe had his fiftieth birthday testimonial dinner she sent him a telegram: "I would like to pay my respects to the lasting contributions you have made to the cause of social security . . . a field which owes so much to your perseverance, cooperation and devotion."

Again Abe had made news. And been victorious. When people paid attention to his words he usually won—but never with the administration in Washington. They kept him at a distance. He was too outspoken, too well-known, too confrontational, and in their view, too unreliable. Whatever he did—and it didn't matter whether he did or didn't approve of the government's work—he was kept farther and farther from any center of power on what mattered to him the most. He knew that he was making progress, he was having an effect, but it wasn't fast enough. And he was still battling resistance from all sides, Left, Right, Republicans, Democrats, Communists, crackpot old-age groups. The ignorance and stupidity of the opposition drove him to fits of despair, draining his shrinking strength. The pace of his work grew frenzied and desperate. For those around him he became more difficult, unpredictable, and even irrational.

2

To hell with the Washington bureaucracy, Abe decided. Let's toot our own horn and tell the American public who did all the hard work. "A Decade Which Changed the Face of America" proclaimed the boldface headline announcing a historic conference for April 1937 to celebrate ten years of accomplishment starting on the day the American Association for Old Age Security first opened its one-room office in 1927. Below that heading in the newsletter Abe dramatized the story with two maps of the United States. On the left was the nation in 1927: states that offered any sort of old-age pension were marked in white, and there were only two, Montana and Wisconsin. Together they paid a minuscule pension to slightly more than one thousand people. The other states were colored black. On the right was the United States in 1937: every state, except Virginia, was in white with a pension law on the books. Not only that, but forty-three states had unemployment laws. Even the federal government had moved into the white when it passed the 1935 act. Abe was fiercely proud of what had been done in those ten years—it was time to rejoice and not be shy. The now enlarged four-room office on Seventeenth Street went into overdrive, pouring out leaflets, press releases, invitations, and requests for sponsoring letters to governors, senators, and clergymen. Henriette was in the thick of the excitement, organizing the dinner, the registration, and the fund-raising letters. At times she would look down from her thirteenth-floor office on the hurrying crowds in Union Square and her thoughts would drift back to the 1927 trek with Abe, just the two of them bumping along by car through the empty West. She remembered her first glimpse of a solitary Indian on horseback, the time when the car overturned in the Rockies, also her amazement when the obstreperous Abe burst in on the county commissioners in Montana demanding to be heard, and the look of awe on the faces of the impoverished aged in California listening to her husband like he was the messiah. Finally, she would see again the grandeur and colors of the Grand Canyon at dawn. And now they were celebrating. Ten years had gone by, and Abe had brought it off. And without her, she asked herself, could he have done it?

The conference on April 9–10 told the whole story, year by year, even month by month, of the tough but triumphant struggle leading to old-age insurance in America. But looking back was only a prologue, and Abe made sure the principal discussion panel would be about "The Next Decade in Social Security." For that he invited a notable group that included Congressman Jerry Voorhis from California, Senator James Pinckney Pope from Idaho, Murray Latimer of the Social Security Board, and two union presidents, Charles Howard of the Typographers and William Green of the AFL. The remarks of Green and Pope went out live on CBS Radio. Also featured were letters of congratulation from governors, senators, congressmen, a host of legislators, religious leaders, writers, seven union heads, and numerous professors including the celebrated historian

Charles A. Beard. The six discussion sessions and dinner were packed with supporters, more than twelve hundred of them, and the papers covered it in depth; to Abe it looked like the world was solidly on his side. In September he was teaching at NYU and was also appointed one of three members of a legislative committee to study how to improve the New York unemployment law. Following that, he went on an extensive lecture tour that took him as far as California—thirty-eight talks in twenty-four cities, before crowds of anywhere from five hundred to a thousand—nearly a reenactment of the pioneering tour of 1927. Abe was Johnny Appleseed once more, only this time he was being paid for his lectures, and planting seeds was not the problem. People were eager to hear everything he had to say. They wanted to understand how the law might help them, because the depressing truth was that it had done little to influence unemployment and poverty. And the state pensions varied enormously. California had the highest pensions, an average of $31.36 per month. Mississippi came in at the bottom at $3.92. The federal social security payments were five years away.

On the lecture circuit Abe hammered his audiences on the failure of the act. But he also brought up its widening corruption by state officials. They were milking the federal funds, and scandals were being revealed everywhere. In Oklahoma a federal auditor uncovered a series of outrageous abuses—pensions that were mailed to dead people or to many who had made no application of any sort. Records had been criminally altered to include numerous people who were not yet sixty-five years old, the true age of many had not been determined, and in one notorious unemployment case "the investigator was received at the door by the pensioner's butler." There were similar problems in Missouri and Illinois. In Ohio the governor blatantly used patronage in hiring the pension staff, insisting they campaign for his reelection if they wanted to keep their jobs. From office heads to clerks they were told to solicit votes for the governor from the applicants and pressured to sell subscriptions to magazines that supported him. Administering the law was turning into a financial windfall. Abe angered many public officials by denouncing their corrupt behavior, but his real point was that the states by themselves could never handle it. Local officials were too narrow-minded and venal. Only Washington was capable of running social security fairly and seeing that the money went directly to those who needed it.

He was also desperate to stem a frenzied wave of lunatic old-age pension ideas that was sweeping the nation once again. They included a new version of the Townsend Plan giving two hundred dollars every month to everyone over the age of fifty as long as they spent it that month, and there were similar unsound propositions being campaigned for in Oregon, Arkansas, Florida, North Dakota, and Colorado. Loony schemes to help the old and unemployed were popping up everywhere. "Give me your money now and you'll get a pension later" was the huckster cry from all sorts of insurance scams. And legislators were listening to the public's disgruntlement, going along, hoping for votes when election time rolled around. In his speeches, articles, and lectures Abe retorted that "elimination of basic defects must precede broadening the scope of the Social Security Act. Congress must not try to outbid the panacea peddlers since nothing would so quickly and definitely launch us upon a policy of national suicide." The *New York Herald Tribune* picked up the warning and wrote that "strong language against appeasement of crackpots comes from an organization devoted to the social security cause [it was Abe, of course] . . . what the cause has to fear most are its purely political allies, the gentlemen who would trade it in for votes." The press always seemed to understand what Abe was talking about.

---

While this free-for-all was getting louder, the U.S. Supreme Court suddenly ended the debate with a historical decision, never challenged since, to uphold in its entirety the Social Security Act of 1935 as constitutionally valid. Until then it had been touch-and-go as to whether it would all be thrown out, forcing the Congress to start all over again. The court at that time was conservative, and the five in the majority were known as the "battalion of death." States' rights were primary and the federal government secondary, and on that basis the majority had already overturned a number of New Deal programs. To overcome this problem FDR had tried to pack the court with fifteen justices instead of the current nine. The justices fought back, but pressure was still being applied on the "nine gray men," another notable nickname, and they could not escape the inevitable. Somewhere along the line several justices realized something in the temper of the people had changed, so when the issue of constitutionality finally reached the court, two justices underwent a conversion. Seven different appeals from lower court decisions were pending, five for and two against the act. And though the press thought for the most part that FDR would be handed a loss or at best a qualified victory, unexpectedly, on May 24, 1937, the unemployment statute was upheld by a slim 5–4 majority, but more importantly, on that same day old-age insurance, the core of social security, was broadly accepted in a 7–2 decision. In spite of the power of the states to run their own affairs, the Supreme Court had decided that social security was a matter that concerned the general welfare of all the people.

Wilbur Cohen, an original staffer at the commission that wrote the act of 1935 and later secretary of the Department of Health, Education, and Welfare under Lyndon Johnson, vividly recalled the excitement of that day. As an employee of the Social Security Board he was friendly with Abe because he attended all the association's conferences, and he had followed the case closely and even gone to the Supreme Court to hear the oral argument. When decision day arrived he made sure to get a seat and listened with wonder as Chief Justice Charles Evans Hughes, with his nineteenth-century beard of near biblical proportions, turned to the justice who had written the decision and asked him to read it aloud. Justice Benjamin Cardozo, in contrast to Hughes, was an intensely private New York Jew, and what he read was remarkably radical for its time: "Needs that were narrow or parochial a century ago may be interwoven in our day with the well-being of the Nation," Cardozo spoke. "What is critical or urgent changes with the times . . . the award of old age benefits would be conducive to the general welfare . . . The number of persons in the United States 65 years of age and over is increasing proportionately as well as absolutely. What is even more important, the number of such persons unable to take care of themselves is growing at a threatening pace . . . the problem is plainly national in area and dimensions." The opinion read as if it had sprung verbatim from the mind of Abe Epstein, and for Wilbur Cohen, an idealistic young man starting on what would become a long, distinguished career in government service, Cardozo's words "were like poetry." He ran down the steps in a "glow of ecstasy" and later that day sent off telegrams of celebration to anyone in government he could think of. Thomas Eliot, who had drafted the law and was now working for the attorney general, was there as well, and when he saw Hughes turn to Cardozo, one of the progressive judges, he said to himself: "Victory!" When he had fully digested the impact of what had happened he dashed off with his wife to see Secretary of Labor Perkins and with several colleagues imbibed a bottle of champagne. "It was fitting," he wrote, "we should drink domestic champagne for a major moment in American history." A major law had been decided on the basis that the welfare of all was more important than the rights of the states. For the few who understood its import it was a stunning victory, establishing forever the role of the federal government in the welfare of the people as a whole.

Abe himself had mixed feelings about the court's decision. At one point he had vehemently hoped it would all be thrown out. Start from scratch was what he wanted, but when the ruling came down he was ready to accept it with his own principled caveats. "Nothing would be more detrimental than accepting the Court's affirmation as blanket approval of the defects embodied in the Act. As Cardozo stated, the Court's concern was with the power of the Congress to enact such legislation, not with the righteousness or correctness of the methods adopted." In other words, the path was now open to reform and it was time to stop dawdling. In this he was not alone. Among his supporters was perhaps America's most influential journalist, Dorothy Thompson, the wife of Sinclair Lewis. In several significant articles she quoted extensively from a report Abe had written for the League for Industrial Democracy and called him "our outstanding expert." She listed every one of his criticisms and concluded "that there is really no excuse for not reforming it." But in 1937 the country was still mired in recession. The payroll tax was draining money from purchasing power, and pensions and unemployment benefits were inadequate and doing very little to turn things around. For Abe, court or no court, it was still an unjust mess.

---

Another man who was cheered by Cardozo's decisive ruling was Princeton professor J. Douglas Brown. Of Scots descent, his rimless glasses gave him a precise scholarly look that did not quite fit with his remarkable public career. At Princeton he rose from director of Industrial Relations Studies to dean of the faculty to the top academic post, provost, in addition to his almost continuous service to the government as adviser on old-age insurance. It was in that latter capacity that he came into Abe's orbit and influence as a member of the old-age security section of the committee that wrote the 1935 act. Later he was proud to have supplied Charles Wysinski, the government's attorney, with facts and theories for his winning argument in the Supreme Court. When Cardozo let it be known that old-age insurance was constitutionally secure, Brown wrote in his understated way that "Cardozo did demonstrate that American constitutional law is a living science."

Brown first met with the intense Abe when the old-age section held a secret meeting with him and Rubinow, after Roosevelt had opined, "I don't know if this is the time for any federal legislation on old-age security." During those desperate and mostly surreptitious meetings on how to save old-age security from FDR's ax—Brown was aware that Perkins and Witte were furious at his "freewheeling tactics"—Abe and Brown be-

came close allies. Then, when both men pushed the newspapers into condemning Roosevelt for abandoning old-age insurance—Brown appears
to have been the one who leaked FDR's negative words to the press—they
realized they had one common goal—old-age insurance must be part of
the legislation. By their efforts, as well as through editorial and public
clamor, the Roosevelt administration was forced to include it in the act,
despite FDR's inclination to forget it. Thereafter, Brown became a regular
panelist at Abe's annual conferences, supporting the association's positions on all the work that still needed to be done.

It was a part of Abe's talent that when he uncovered a supporter he often made a friend as well—when it came to those he wanted on his side,
he would use his considerable charm to put the relationship on a personal basis. His exuberance, his raft of stories, his extravagant praise of those
who worked for the cause, easily endeared him to his allies. This was the
case with Rubinow, Jim Maurer, Paul Douglas, Wilbur Cohen, and many
others. If you were on his side you were also his friend. If you were not
then watch out. So, with Douglas Brown, weekend visits to Princeton came
along frequently. Brown lived in a traditional campus mansion painted a
shining white with black trim and with a porch on three sides as befitted
his position as dean of the faculty. He would sit with Abe on that porch,
rocking away, discussing how to improve the world and social security in
particular. Henriette would stroll the campus with Mrs. Brown, enamored
of the tranquil beauty of traditional academia, so different from her tem-
pestuous life in Manhattan. She would have loved to move her hectic life
into that almost bucolic setting. I myself was struck by the beauty of
Brown's thirteen-year-old daughter, a bouncy adolescent with flaming red
locks down her back. Bubbly in bobby sox and floral print dresses, she
would be assigned to take me on walks as well, but usually I would linger
on the sidelines as she ran into one or another of her gabby friends. I was
nine or ten at the time, and back in New York I would dream over her ex-
otic presence long after the weekend visit. I got to see the glamorous red-
head one last time when Brown's entire family came to New York to con-
sole Henriette when Abe died. He remained a lifelong friend and in 1972
sent her a copy of his memoir with an inscription, "To Henriette, the story
of the continuing battle for social security in which Abe was the great pioneer and inspired leader." Abe had that kind of effect on people.

Brown entered Abe's life just when Abe needed him the most. When the
Supreme Court sustained that pioneering step in American governance,
an inventive idea that had nothing to do with pensions or benefits sprang
to life as well: the Advisory Council on Social Security. Some of the sena-

tors who approved the bill knew that in the few intense months of its creation, from committee to law, there would be mistakes, there would be need for revisions, there would be need for the instrument of social security to grow and change as the needs of the people would grow and change. It was decided that an ongoing means of revision should be put in place, like a British Royal Commission, that would take testimony and recommend improvements. And there Abe was truly in luck for the first time. J. Douglas Brown was appointed chairman of the first advisory council.

In Abe's ardent mind there was now not a moment to waste. The council had been formed in May, but as late as November no meetings had taken place. Abe was furious at the delay, finally could take it no longer, and issued a satiric statement to the press: "Lost Somewhere: An Advisory Committee appointed last May by the Senate and the Social Security Board to study a means of revising old age insurance. Finders please send them to Washington." He kept up the sniping with a notice in his monthly bulletin: "The existence of the Council was finally revealed in an announcement that the first meeting had been called for Nov. 5 and 6, seven months after its creation." When he wanted results Abe was always ready to tweak someone's nose, and by the time the council finally "stirred up," as Abe put it, he took off for Washington to be sure he would be in the starting lineup for testimony.

He was known to most of the panelists and they had already heard most of his arguments, but a photo of his bespectacled face, hand raised theatrically as he faced the microphone, appeared in many newspapers. His colorful, passionate presentations got him more attention than most witnesses. And luckily Secretary of Labor Frances Perkins was not available to offer any kind of aggravating resistance. Some conservative members of Congress were determined to force her out for her role in the West Coast dock strike and she was close to impeachment for being a Communist stooge. With lawyers constantly at her side, she went through hell for months to ensure survival in office. FDR himself ignored the advisory council—arch politician that he was, his mind was focused on winning the 1938 congressional elections. And in that campaign the "panacea peddlers," as Abe called them, were out in force with numerous pie-in-the-sky old-age pension schemes. It was uncertain whether Congress would vote for genuine reform or cave in to suspect solutions. But during the council's eighteen-month period of research and testimony some remarkably important other officials had an almost revolutionary change of heart on old-age insurance.

Henry Morgenthau, treasury secretary and the most influential mem-

16 (Above) A joint committee of the Senate and the House of Representatives meets to consider a proposed amendment to the Social Security Act. (Right) The late Abraham Epstein, one of the nation's foremost authorities on social insurance, as he testified in 1939 before the House Ways and Means Committee regarding the need for amendments to the Social Security Act. Testimony of Epstein and other experts convinced Congress that families of workers also should receive protection, especially in the event of a worker's death. Epstein was the author of several books on social security.

WIDE WORLD PHOTOS

173

Abraham Epstein testifying before Congress in 1939. From *Building America* (Philadelphia: Association for Supervision and Curriculum Development, 1946).

ber of the cabinet, stunned everyone when he told the council that the payroll tax was bad for the economy, that it would be better to have a pay-as-you-go plan, that the huge reserve wasn't really so necessary. Then the stolid Arthur Altmeyer, the current chairman of the Social Security Board, also acknowledged the act needed reform. He came around cautiously, having resisted the creation of the advisory council as undercutting his authority, but he decided to support an idea Abe had always championed: that the government should be the one to fund old-age insurance, as well as the employee and the employer. Gone as well were the secret proceedings of 1935. All was out in the open and the newspapers could report it. It seemed clear that revisions would finally be enacted.

When the advisory council issued its final report in December 1938, most of what Abe wanted was in it. To publicize his success he used one of his favorite journalistic tricks—the art of the parallel columns. The January 1939 issue of *Social Security* had a two-page spread headlined, "The Parallel That Needs No Comment." On the left side of each page were statements from the council's recommendations, and on the right side were similar statements from Abe's book, *Insecurity*, and issues of the bulletin. Abe was never bashful about taking credit. His excuse: it helped to raise money.

But the New Deal administration could not be counted on to do the right thing. For when the president made his recommendations to Congress, he completely ignored the advisory council report. Instead, he urged passage of recommendations from another report put together by the Social Security Board itself. Although the Democrats had prevailed easily in the 1938 congressional elections, Roosevelt was content with the status quo—the present system was perfectly sound and should not be altered except for a little bit more coverage. Abe, as might be expected, was outraged, seeing his passionate pleas go down the drain. "What is the use," he exclaimed in the bulletin, "one may humbly ask, of creating . . . the Advisory Council to devote months of study . . . only to have its report thrown into the White House waste basket?" And he quoted from an editorial in the *St. Louis Globe-Democrat* that supported him totally. The Senate Finance Committee, however, was on Abe's side, ignored FDR, and accepted the report of its own creation, the advisory council. Abe testified before them on February 27, 1939, spending hours analyzing the defects of the present system and emphasizing that above all the aged needed to have a living stipend, not one based solely on the size of one's contribution. Abe brought in a number of lawmakers and officials to speak on the need for reform at the April 1939 annual conference, including the now very influential J. Douglas Brown. He did everything possible to keep the pressure on Congress. Finally the House voted for its version of reform on June 10, but the Senate dithered and only a month later, on July 13, voted its own version. Time was growing short because Congress was set to adjourn by August 6 and no one knew whether the joint committee to work out a compromise would do so in time. There was constant wrangling between House and Senate on such minor issues as whether employers should give employees a monthly statement of payroll deductions. It was touch-and-go as always. The bill was on the verge of dying when two days before adjournment the administration let it be known that social security had overwhelming popular support and Congress had better listen. An agreement was quickly reached, the bill was passed the next day, and Congress went home for the summer. Roosevelt signed the law revising the 1935 act on August 10, though it was obvious his eyes were looking elsewhere, mostly at the war clouds that three weeks later were to crack open over Europe.

Abe's little publicity machine immediately went into operation. It was his greatest triumph, the bulletin said, "a successful culmination of the Association's bitterest battle of the last four years." Now finally the retirement system would provide adequate income based on the needs of the individual and his family. Coverage was extended to those who had been left out in 1935—widows, orphans, farmers, and others. Stricter administrative control was put in place to prevent political manipulation and corruption. And all the crackpot schemes up for approval, including the ever-present Townsend Plan, meant to "solve all the ills of the universe," had been defeated. In addition, old-age insurance payments were moved up two years to 1940, and the amount taken out of payroll checks would be stabilized to avoid enlarging a reserve fund that would sit there doing nothing. Of course, the unemployment insurance system was barely touched—it was still a jumble of fifty-one different plans—and health insurance had been ignored again. As always there was more to be done.

---

Abe finally began to receive the official recognition he had long deserved. Brown wrote him a public letter in his official capacity as chairman of the advisory council to thank him: "No agency, outside of the government itself, deserves more credit than the American Association for Social Security. Your Association faces an ever larger challenge and responsibility in the development of real security." Then in September, Arthur Altmeyer, long a stubborn adversary, issued a public letter praising Abe for his "complete analysis of the Social Security Act and the necessary amendments you have presented." He also asked Abe to serve as a consulting economist, yet one more task to be added to an exhausting round of work that now included running down to Washington on a monthly basis and pressing for more progress on unemployment and medical care, never letting up. Yet, beginning with Frances Perkins's devious and dismissive treatment in 1934, through the New Deal administration's exclusionary resistance to Abe's firebrand demands, through demeaning and bitter times, Abe had finally become the person he had desperately wanted to become, the man whose knowledge the government needed and wanted.

Six months later, on February 1, 1940, the very first old-age checks were mailed to waiting retirees throughout the United States. Real social security had arrived, beginning a series of payments that have never missed a month to this day. "At last!" Abe exclaimed in the bulletin,

the Day towards which we have labored and looked forward to for decades has actually arrived. The new Federal system becomes trans-

lated into reality: cash for food, rent and the other necessities of life . . .
We are grateful beyond all words for having been permitted to see this
day, which is bringing new life, independence and self-respect to hundreds of thousands who for years had despaired of such a turn in their
lives.

It seemed that Abe's long battle that had begun in Harrisburg in 1918 was
finally over.
Or was it?

3

Morris Fishbein was a short, dark-haired man with a bulbous nose and
the unsavory look of a tough little street fighter from the wrong side of the
tracks. It fit his job as editor of a publication he had transformed into a
bludgeon defending a doctor's right to practice in total freedom: the *Journal of the American Medical Association* (JAMA). No socialized medicine, no
government regulation, the journal warned, or anyone who tried to pass
a law to that effect would regret it. As a medical practitioner Fishbein himself was a bust. He barely made it through medical school, and his only
work consisted of five months as an intern. His real talent was unleashed
when he was hired by the American Medical Association in 1924. There
he discovered what could be done with money and publicity. The scheme
was simple. He went to America's biggest companies and told them that
if they advertised in *JAMA* they would be guaranteed a captive, affluent
audience. In return *JAMA* would endorse their products. Fishbein's first
big catch was Philip Morris. The company paid for ads in *JAMA,* and in
return they were rewarded with an article on the beneficial effects of tobacco. Soon the drug companies saw the results of Fishbein's clever tactic
and joined up. For those who didn't, their products might as well have
never existed, at least as far as the AMA was concerned. The scheme
worked so well that by 1940 the organization had an income of more than
two million a year and assets of more than five million. These huge sums
flowed into publicity campaigns to portray doctors as saintly, altruistic,
freedom-loving Americans. Start regulating them and the wonders of
American medicine would be ruined—any form of health insurance that
involved rules, whether federal or state, was un-American. Fishbein was
a truculent fighter who kept the members of the AMA under tight control,
a powerful and ruthless opponent to anyone interested in any form of

medical insurance. Doctors who thought differently were ostracized by their local AMA affiliates. Legislators and congressmen knew that Fishbein had plenty of money to go after them if they sponsored any "socialistic" plans. Under his guidance the AMA became one of the most powerful lobbies in the nation.

Down at 389 Bleecker Street the words "Morris Fishbein" morphed into another scornful epithet like the earlier "Merit Rating" and "Wisconsin Plan." His name came so close to that of "fishwife," it seemed to smell when it was spoken (always with a sneer). Once, after hearing it said repeatedly in disgust by Abe and his friends, I went into the bathroom, looked in the mirror, and practiced saying "Morris Fishbein" with a vicious downward curl of the lips. It was easy for me. But for Abe and his associates it wasn't, because the AMA, in the opinion of many reformers, had the New Deal in its pocket. Thomas Eliot, drafter of the Social Security Act, remembers telling Frances Perkins that he was worried about "the impact of any health insurance in the bill. My advice wasn't needed—she and her colleagues had reached the same conclusion . . . inclusion would have aroused such vehement opposition, sparked by the American Medical Association, that the whole bill . . . would have gone down the drain." Even Roosevelt knew better than to risk challenging the AMA. When laying the cornerstone of a new medical center in New Jersey, he promised that "The medical profession can rest assured that the federal administration contemplates no action detrimental to their interests." And so it went for the entire New Deal administration. Health insurance stayed in the dead letter office.

Of course FDR had made health insurance a part of his proposal when he called for "security for all Americans" back in June 1934, well before social security had been passed in 1935. Health insurance had always been part of Abe's grand vision as well, but he knew that it had the least chance of becoming law. As soon as Roosevelt spoke, Fishbein and the AMA were quick to warn the New Deal to scuttle any possible plans. Abe, who was never one to shy away from a powerful opponent, decided to confront the doctors by any possible means. If they were not blasted publicly they might bury the issue before it ever came up. It was not a wise move, adding one more job to the many he was trying to handle. If only for his own health and energy, he should have stayed focused on old-age security and unemployment. But he tackled the AMA, published a number of articles singling them out for "refusing to face facts" and not giving voice to their many members who believed in the need for health insurance. He brought the issue to the forefront with a special conference in October

1934 to write a model health bill, and in several speeches compared America's nonexistent health plan with Britain's comprehensive coverage. But his timing was off because the conference was scheduled for the same time he was fighting his nastiest battles with Perkins and the New Deal administration over the rest of social security. By the end of 1934 Abe was stretched as thin as could be and soon tumbled into the complete exhaustion that led to his two nervous breakdowns, the first one at the end of 1934.

Despite these difficulties and with as much publicity as the association could muster, Abe published the full text of his model bill in the January 1935 issue of *Social Security*. It was the first national health plan placed before the public since the Progressive era during the early years of the twentieth century. Twelve thousand copies were mailed to legislators, governors, Congress, newspapers, and anyone else of influence. It was a brief twelve pages, written in legalese, so that it could be quickly introduced before legislatures and Congress. Only the facts, clearly stated, with no twisting of the truth was how Abe liked his ideas to go before the public. Still, an explanation was needed, and in a side letter Abe did just that: he laid out a basic plan meant to cover only those who earned less than three thousand dollars a year or sixty dollars a week, compulsory, funded by employee, employer, and government, intended to cover that "47 percent in the lowest income group who have no medical, dental or optical care whatsoever." It would also help thousands of doctors who during the depression "either sit idly by waiting for patients or are working night and day for a bare living, while the mass of our population goes without adequate care." And there was one innovative idea—cash benefits were to be paid to those unable to gain an income because of illness, a form of medical disability.

The bill was introduced by friendly legislators in Massachusetts, Pennsylvania, Wisconsin, Connecticut, Oregon, Washington, Rhode Island, and New York. The AMA did not wait very long to make a rebuttal, condemning "the Epstein bill as vicious, deceptive, dangerous and demoralizing." The AMA did not speak for the medical profession, Abe responded—California, Michigan, and Washington had local medical associations ready to sponsor health insurance. He put forth a series of quotes from doctors that reflected his satirical scorn. "Blindly following our medical confreres into mudholes of stall, stand pat and muddle, our national officials give no evidence of leadership," said one. "When AMA officials pull the strings . . . mannikins stick out their tongues and shake their fists," said another. Abe also let go with a few of his own. "Faced with the only practical proposal on health insurance in twenty years . . . the AMA has sought refuge in vile language . . . based on selfishness and prejudice." Finally, as 1935 ended, Arthur Capper of Kansas, one of Abe's best allies in the Senate, introduced the association's model bill. Abe was ready to go after another part of his dream.

---

The best way to expose Fishbein, Abe realized, would be in a person-to-person confrontation. It would provoke needed newspaper coverage, and Fishbein could be seen for the nasty little gutter fighter that he was. So whenever Abe scheduled a public health insurance debate he extended an invitation to Fishbein. Come and represent the views of the AMA, Fishbein was told, you will be treated with respect and listened to. Fishbein would not fall for it. He was better known than Abe, and his organization was more powerful. He saw no reason to give any helpful publicity to his enemies. But by 1939 health insurance had advanced on several fronts and there were two major health bills before the Congress, the one sponsored by Senator Capper and another by Robert Wagner of New York. Fishbein now realized he had to deal publicly with Abe and those wanting health care. So in 1939 he accepted an invitation to debate Abe at the annual conference of the American Association for Social Security. The grand ballroom of the famed Astor Hotel in Times Square was the arena. The date was Saturday, April 15. The hated enemy had accepted the challenge in Abe's own ring. He was expecting a bruising bout.

The debate began at ten in the morning. The room was full of Abe's supporters and everyone was aware that a major confrontation was at hand, not quite like Lincoln-Douglas, but still an encounter of opposites. Abe made a smart tactical move and appointed himself chairman of the session. That way it would appear that he was just there to guide the debate, maybe get in a jab from time to time, but mostly to look like he was above the fray. Others would do the job of taking on the AMA spokesman. When Fishbein arrived he was offered the place of honor, a seat at the center of the dais in the ornate ballroom. Abe had a chair far away at the end of the table. Fishbein had been told he could speak first, but he didn't fall for Abe's tactic. He knew where his adversary was, and he quickly rocked the meeting with a fast sucker punch at Abe the person. Abe was inflexible, Fishbein exclaimed, because he had only one "solution to the problem of medical care . . . without change." He, Fishbein, was just the opposite, a man open to other ideas. Playing the part of the beleaguered public servant, he went on, "I shift . . . because I have to go where I am told." Besides, the AMA was a democracy, but "according to Mr. Epstein, the American Association for Social Security is not a democracy." After those jabs he turned to the core of the AMA position. All forms of government-run health insurance were totalitarian because they were about bureaucracy and not medical care. In a state-run plan the doctor-patient relationship would be destroyed. The indigent only lacked medical care, he asserted, because those social work groups in charge of helping the poor did nothing to get them to doctors who were just waiting to be of assistance. His opponents were running a vast propaganda machine, Fishbein continued, "turned on the medical profession with the hope of obtaining a concession toward a vast spending program for the expansion of preventive medicine and the administration of medical service." America had the best medical care in the world, there was no emergency, and the right way to solve problems in a democracy was to experiment. He doubted any members of the American Association for Social Security would agree with him, "which is one hundred percent in accord with Mr. Epstein's idea." But he could not finish without another gutter gibe. "It is astounding that some of those who came in search of what America could give should be willing to sacrifice what has been given for some vague hope of complete security against all the hazards of life." The parting shot was not lost on Abe, the immigrant who had benefited from American freedom.

Three medical experts on the podium were the first to reply, all carefully chosen by Abe: Helen Hall was a well-known social worker and former member of the Advisory Council on Social Security, Hugh Cabot was a doctor at the Mayo Clinic, and George Jones was the former president of the New Mexico Medical Society. They were all authorities, not hotheads, and accordingly their responses to Fishbein were polite and nonconfrontational. They stressed the fact that too many Americans had no care when they were sick and suggested the country needed some form of government-run health plan. For a moment it looked like the head-on meeting with Fishbein would wind down with just a few mild statements. But questions were called for, and two others rose from the audience to challenge the accuracy of Fishbein's words. Why did he always refer to health insurance as "socialized medicine," one asked, when it was not. Why was the AMA getting enormous sums from drug manufacturers and then hiding the fact that the money was being used to engage famous public relations people such as Edward Bernays to fight health insurance plans? A second questioner, James Rorty, a writer and close friend of Abe's, went for the jugular, demanding to know what Fishbein did with the four hundred thousand dollars in yearly contributions from Hoffman-LaRoche, a pharmaceutical company. Was it just to fight compulsory health insurance? Or did it go somewhere else? Abe's former professor at Pitt, Frank Tyson, an elderly, mild-spoken academic who had often counseled Abe against his uncontrolled vituperative outbursts, was incensed at Fishbein's attack. He rose and accused him of using "stereotyped shibboleths when he referred to Mr. Epstein as an autocrat and to himself as a democrat." He wanted to say more, but Fishbein interrupted and took on his questioners with sarcastic venom. Rorty had tried to libel him before, he said. "I could have sued, according to a great many lawyers but I have never wished to because that would have circulated his books beyond the very small circulation they have now. Rorty," he went on, "is constantly smelling for dirt . . . an unsuccessful bloodhound sniffing for scavenge and unable to find it." He rejected all the money-raising and secret contribution charges. Any propaganda against health insurance had nothing to do with him, he said; local groups could say what they wanted. Why did the AMA only offer *anti*-health insurance information to its members, someone asked? Fishbein angrily denied it. The information they supplied was disinterested, he said, and then fired off one last dig at Abe: "and the list circulated includes Mr. Epstein's pamphlets." It was a mean-spirited slur on a man who had written four major books on social insurance. But Fishbein had had it and rose from his place and stalked out, not bothering to stay for lunch.

Abe and his friends never really laid a glove on the AMA spokesman. Fishbein had answered a few questions, insulted a few people, and fled. The newspapers were not much help either. Health insurance just could not generate the coverage that old-age and unemployment insurance did. The important news was elsewhere—the buildup to the German attack on Poland and the reaction of England and France to the threat dominated the papers. Accordingly, little progress was made in advancing health insurance throughout all of 1939. In fact the AMA was still controlling the debate and succeeded in getting the Senate Committee on Education and Labor to postpone any consideration of the pending bills. FDR was unwilling to support health insurance and the Senate went along with him. The campaign came to a grinding halt.

Abe's tenacity was by now legendary, and he went back and mapped another plan to keep medical insurance in the news. He announced a conference to showcase an improved model bill—it "would start the health system with the group in greatest need," those making less than two thousand dollars a year, and included better coverage for dependents, a ma-

ternity benefit, and smaller payments from those covered. In the course
of a year Abe had picked up strong endorsements from people such as
Arthur Altmeyer, the chairman of the Social Security Board, and Herbert
Lehman, the influential governor of New York and close friend to FDR.
Things were moving, and perhaps this time Fishbein could be cornered
and exposed, but the wily AMA spokesman declined to show up for a re-
match at the 1940 conference. He had no wish to give Abe and the association any more publicity. So Abe went right on hounding the AMA in articles, in particular one in which he cited a survey of more than twenty
thousand doctors by the magazine *Modern Medicine* that showed 88 percent of those questioned favored government funding for medical care
compared to 31 percent the year before. But people were not interested.
The public was looking across the Atlantic at the war in Europe, where
France had stunned the western democracies by surrendering to Germany in June and Great Britain was under ferocious assault by the Luft-
waffe. America was now close to panic, looking at how to defend itself in
case of war, which in fact was not very far off. Industry was converting to
a wartime footing, producing more tanks, guns, and planes than ever before, and thousands of young men were being plucked from their homes
and jobs and drafted into the army.

Health insurance seemed to be totally irrelevant to the concerns facing
the nation, but Abe noticed a series of statistics relating to the young men
being drafted and in an odd twist tried to turn them to his advantage. The
director of the draft had told FDR that he had a crisis on his hands—
380,000 out of 1 million of those called up had to be rejected because they
couldn't pass the physical, a shocking percentage. Those who failed the
physical were underweight, undernourished, had bad teeth, bad eyes, in
short were sorry specimens of American manhood. They would have
been no match defending freedom against the Nazi blitzkrieg. Paul Mc-
Nutt, the federal security administrator—precursor to today's secretary
of health and human services—jumped on those numbers and warned
that the bottleneck in protecting American democracy "is not strikes, but
human health." Abe loved it, and whenever he could told the public and
the press that good health insurance would have gone a long way in helping America to defend itself. But after Pearl Harbor he knew that any hope
for his health plan was dead for a long time to come. It was another one
of Abe's great social insurance ideas that never came to fruition during his
lifetime. Despite all the health bills introduced in Congress and the states
since the turn of the century by Abe and others, not one ever came close
to being enacted. It took Harry Truman in 1948 to restore it to political life.

By then Morris Fishbein was a spent force with little influence, although he still served as editor of *JAMA*. And Abe was long dead.

4

In Katonah, New York, fifty miles from Manhattan, up a long winding dirt road there was a great columned mansion facing a sweeping grass lawn. Below, in the dense birch woods, were several cottages and even a swimming pool created from a dammed-up stream. In 1921 this secluded country estate had been acquired by Brookwood, a unique school where for the first time a union worker could receive a college education and later return to work. Brookwood had been an outgrowth of the Workers Education Bureau, also started in 1921, where Abe had served as the first secretary-treasurer under his old Pennsylvania colleague, Jim Maurer. Now Maurer was the president of Brookwood and Abe, who believed passionately in Labor's Own School, as it was called, would come up to lecture. He never taught on any regular basis, but almost all of the teachers were his friends, and they shared his vision of the educated progressive worker who could change the world. "Action based on knowledge is power," was the often-repeated slogan.

In this former capitalist paradise with its fields, lawns, great oak and pine woods, and gurgling stream, workers who had never left city sidewalks could now experience the transformation of the seasons and the mind. They did outdoor chores and performed all of the maintenance. Among the many photographs that document the history of Brookwood is one of a group of students digging out the drive after a blizzard. They are spread out along the winding uphill road, bundled against the cold, shovels and plows in their hands, grinning, having fun, like children playing in snow for the first time. All this was in addition to their classes in history, English, and science. And of course, this being the era of progressive education, there was drama, there was art, and there was Marxism. For many it was not easy to adjust. "Brookwood lies upon a hill," one teacher wrote, "and the climb up towards those buildings is a tough job, especially for those who come weakened by hunger, bad labor conditions, strikes, or a few months in jail . . . it is hard after many years absence from school . . . sitting in class . . . reading books and magazines which are so new to most of the students." And it wasn't always a school of placid uplift and idealism. "Stormy was the life of Brookwood," wrote Fania Cohn, the famed labor leader from the International Ladies Garment Workers

Brookwood Labor College. Students working on a road.

Union. "Misunderstanding was rampant. Some accused it of excessive radicalism and others that it was not radical enough. Being caught in the midst of a whirlwind, even its best friends doubted whether Brookwood would survive." Communists, Socialists, Trotskyites, progressives, anarchists, all fought over the right path. But Brookwood did survive and by 1936 had more than four hundred graduates who had gone out from the mansion on the hill to strengthen the march of the American labor movement.

---

In early June 1935, Abe drove Henriette and me up Brookwood's curving, dusty road to spend the summer out of New York. Abe had been given the use of one of the cottages for a nominal rent: the Stone House, a two-story gabled lodge built entirely from the local fieldstone with a slate roof sloping down from the attic, pierced by oddly angled windows with pointed arches. There were three brick-and-stone fireplaces, a vast yard around the house, and beyond that a grove of birches on the high ground above the road that led up the hill. It had the air of a small castle built as a private lair for a son or daughter of the privileged owner's family. Abe was rarely there, mostly traveling by train back and forth to Washington, frantically trying to convince Congress to rewrite FDR's Social Security Act before it became law. Henriette was afraid that he was running himself into another nervous collapse, and she was always examining him for any signs of another breakdown. For her it was an uneasy summer with an uncertain outcome.

One incident at the swimming pool scared her to death. Abe had been assigned to watch me, but I was fooling around too close to the edge, abruptly tumbled into the water, and quickly went under. An alert worker-turned-student, lying by the pool and enjoying perhaps for the first time the comforts of the capitalist life, quickly jumped in and pulled me out. But it had been Abe's job to watch me, and his distraction and neglect told a lot about how much his fragile mental state was near to breaking apart.

But otherwise for me Brookwood was ideal. I roamed the grounds and found playmates. On one outing I found the estate's former garage in the woods, six doors that opened into another fieldstone building. There I came upon a group of several students trying to bring back to life a large square-bodied bus that had obviously seen better days. They were all over it, fixing the roof, checking the tires, repairing the rear door. Over the summer I became friendly with one of them, and I would trail after him while he fixed cars, cut wood, and repaired buildings. His name was Paul Niepold, and he was a young Socialist from Germany who had emigrated to the United States in 1927. Frustrated with working-class jobs in New York, he came to Brookwood as a student. His attachment to the school and its ideals was so strong that after a stint in New York working for a Socialist newspaper, he returned to take on the job of superintendent of grounds. Paul was a handsome man with a receding forehead and a well-pompadoured shock of blond hair. His eyes were sunk in their sockets, deep and brooding. His wife was the drama teacher at Brookwood. When I attached myself to him, he was twenty-nine.

On one of my frequent trips to the garage to find Paul, I saw a car I hadn't seen for a while. It was a convertible roadster with the top down, and it had a rumble seat. Rumble seats are long gone, but they folded out from the rear of the car where the trunk was supposed to be. They could hold two additional passengers and were fun to ride in. As I was admiring this sleek beauty, Paul came by.

"Have you ever seen this car before?" he asked.

"Yes," I said. "It belongs to Mr. Saposs. I've seen him drive it."

Dave Saposs was one of Abe's oldest friends from his earliest days in New York. He was currently teaching labor history at Brookwood and I had frequently seen him in laced-up jodhpurs and battered felt hat—a kind of driving look of the 1930s—start the car and drive off down the road.

"Want a ride?" Paul asked. "I'm fixing the car for Dave and have to take it to the garage."

Paul opened the rumble seat with a twist of its gleaming chrome handle. It sat there like the lid of a popped-up candy box.

"Hop in."

I didn't wait a second. I placed my feet on the rubber steps, Paul gave me a lift, and I slid into the seat. The car started up and we went bouncing down the hill, Paul in front with his hand on the wheel, I upright in the rumble seat with the wind flowing through my hair.

Paul was one of the many students who came to see Abe when he made it up from New York. A group of young men and women would arrive at the Stone House to spend the evening in his presence. If the night was chilly, one of them would get a fire going in the hearth, and the men in their unironed work clothes and the women in rough wool pants would sit on the floor surrounding Abe. He would have discarded his three-piece city suit and tie and put on casual pants and shirt, though by no stretch of the imagination could it be said that he looked as working-class as the students. Abe's appeal to others, that magnetic pull he had with people that had dazzled Henriette on their 1927 cross-country trip, what Paul Douglas tried to explain when he wrote, "Tough politicians . . . were always captivated by him," that is what sent the students trooping down the hill to see him. For the young he seemed to have a certain star quality. They knew he had written books and articles, that he was an authority, that he was out in the world, influencing legislation, making reform happen, and they could see he respected their desire to learn. The young men and women of Brookwood were passionate and earnest about the world they were trying to change, and Abe would be peppered with questions about the New Deal and its policies, about social security and what it was for, a subject so new that most people did not even know what the words meant. And always he would try to probe the thoughts of those he thought leaned toward the Communists. He questioned their reasoning, asking tough questions such as, "What kind of a country would America be if it were governed by the Communists?" or "If you follow the dictatorship of the proletariat to its conclusion what would happen to someone who likes to speak out all the time? Would he have free speech?"

Abe was fearful of the growing influence of the Communist Party. He had seen what they had done in Russia to brutalize the people. In America they had tried to infiltrate and wreck his own movement. And for his work on social security they called him a "capitalist stooge." But with the students he was never hostile, never angry. He stayed calm even when a young man or woman resisted his argument. His method was Socratic, meant to instruct, using questions to lead them on with probing dialogue until the young man or woman had little left to say. They were students and needed to be guided—they were not like the politicians and "experts" he had to confront all the time. He was a natural teacher, and in that role he may have been at his happiest. Over the years as he taught more and more, at Brooklyn College, NYU, and Brookwood, his courses developed into full investigations of all parts of social security. He spent hours constructing a step-by-step syllabus that included extensive reading. As with most teachers, the students had to read his own books—where else would they find social security fully explained?—but many others as well, including sections of the Elizabethan Poor Law. His many pupils over the years were increasingly devoted to him, creating their own club which they called "The Abraham Epstein Alumni Association." A gathering would take place from time to time at Giusti's Spaghetti Inn on Sixteenth Street where a "one-half broiled chicken dinner plus the works" would cost one dollar. And on occasion Abe would show up to speak.

Paul Niepold, with his German Socialist background and his anti-Fascist politics, was a young man Abe could relate to. In December 1936, Brookwood sent out a letter about Paul, who had decided to go to Spain and enlist in the Republican forces fighting the Fascists. "With a background of loyal activity in the movement in Germany before coming to America, Paul is determined to return and do his bit," it read. Abe told me that on our next trip to Brookwood, Paul would not be there.

"Why?" I asked.

"He's going to Spain."

At the age of six and a half, I already knew a lot about the Spanish Civil War. Everyone around Abe and Henriette talked about it. "What is he going to do there?"

"Fight for the cause of the Republic against Franco."

"Will he be gone long?"

"I'm sure he will be back soon." Abe left it at that.

Paul sailed for Spain on January 16, 1937. He joined the International Brigade, fighting for the Loyalist side. He was sent to the front lines outside of Madrid. One day while on duty he crawled out from his post to rescue a wounded comrade. What happened next was described in a *New York Times* report from Spain: "Mr. Niepold climbed from a trench in sight of machine gunners of both sides. He had almost reached the wounded soldier when an Insurgent marksman picked him off." Less than three months after he left Brookwood, on April 8, 1937, Paul was killed. He was thirty-one.

When the news about Paul's death came, Abe did not tell me right away. He may have been too affected himself. But there was a part of Abe that always wanted to treat his son like an adult. He never spent time with me playing childhood games—what mattered was to learn to read and write. His youth had been joyless, filled mostly with cold and hunger, and the ferocity with which he had reached for learning is what had saved him, he believed, from the brutality and ignorance of Russian and Jewish life. His gifts to me at Christmas or for my birthday were always books, rarely a toy or game. Life was a struggle for learning, and with that in mind Abe may have felt I should always be told the truth. "Paul has died," he said one day. I must have looked confused because he went on. "He was killed by the Fascists in the war."

"In Spain?"

"Yes. Everyone is very sad."

"Why did he die?" I asked.

"He was a hero," Abe responded.

"A hero?"

"He was trying to rescue a man who had been wounded. Only a brave man does that. Paul was a brave man."

I could not understand. And I repeated my question. "Why did he die?"

For the first time I could remember Abe was at a loss for words. "Why did he die?"

Abe shrugged and said nothing. But I persisted and for days afterward I kept asking him about Paul. I could not understand how I would never again see a man I had seen only a few months before. In most cases Abe would have been irritated by my pestering, but this time he tried to help. He was relieved perhaps that I shared his suffering, because one day he told me that he was writing to Martha, Paul's widow, and he would tell her how I felt. Later he called me over, sat me down on the couch next to him, and read me the letter: "It was generous and heroic of Paul to go to Spain . . . to die while trying to save a comrade . . . only great men are privileged to die in such a manner. In this tragic moment Pierre joins us in sending condolences. He has been heartbroken since he heard the tragic news. He has talked about nothing else since."

———————

A year later, Abe's state of mind had improved enough for us to return to Toulouse and our vacation days at La Tour de Carol, the small mountain village in the Pyrenees that had been the scene of much of Henriette's joyful childhood. The border with Spain was nearby and visible, marked by little stone columns dotted in the middle of wheat fields, along the roadside, on the other side of the railroad tracks. The border was officially closed, but an air of menace seemed to hang in the hot air of summer. French soldiers were stationed at intervals near the stone markers, guarding the frontier. The sun flashed off their rifles and their bayonets were fixed as if ready for hand-to-hand combat. Marching back and forth in their woolen overcoats in the summer heat, wearing their out-of-date First World War helmets, they appeared like pop-up figures in a shooting gallery. From time to time one of them would stop a car and ask to see everyone's papers. Up close they looked young and uncomfortable, not so terrifying as at a distance, and when Henriette would talk with one they seemed not to know why they were there. But there was a real war going on beyond those stone markers, and the sounds of heavy artillery could be heard day and night. Franco's troops were getting closer, warplanes flew overhead, and their loud, droning motors forced everyone to look up into the clear blue August sky of Catalonia to see whether they were French or Spanish. One day the mayor's car was riddled by Spanish bullets as he drove along a border road. At night refugees snuck into the village, avoiding the police, asking to be sheltered in barns to avoid being sent to internment camps by the French government. The villagers, most of whom were Catalan and had lived easily on both sides of the border all their lives, talked of their fear of the mass exodus that would take place when Franco's ferocious African troops came up to the frontier with France. Mountain walks along the wildflower-strewn paths that were so dear to Henriette were now dangerous excursions. Spanish civil guards on horseback in their three-corner hats, rifles slung over their shoulders, would suddenly pop up on hilltops where the border ran. They seemed to look down on France with contempt.

Back in the United States Henriette told Abe of what she had seen. They both knew then that their European playground was about to come apart. In America few paid attention to the cruelties of the Spanish Civil War.

In the Pyrenees, 1936. Henriette, Abe, the author, and Henriette's mother, Elisa.

The public believed neutrality was the best course. America should stay out. Besides, if you wanted to help the Spanish Republic against the Fascists you were probably a Communist. But for Henriette there was a world of horrors on the other side of those little stone markers, pushing to cross into her beloved France. The fight for the doomed Spanish Republic had become closer and more personal. She tried to find words to explain her mounting sense of despair. "All the memories of my childhood were mixed in this." There was much worse to come in Spain and throughout Europe, and she knew that we would not escape it.

5

The sphinx of Egypt are an awesome sight. What is even more awesome to me is the photo of Abe and Henriette sitting primly on the paws of one at Memphis, near Cairo. It is Egypt in summer, and the sphinx looks more bored than mysterious while the travelers pose awkwardly on his ancient clawed feet. Abe is dressed in his customary three-piece suit with tie, holds his hat in one hand, and cradles a cane in the other. Henriette looks

Abe and Henriette in Egypt, 1937.

smart in a cool summer dress with starched white collar, her purse de-
murely in her lap, and she is hatless, rare for her. Although they are
dressed in what must be considered the traveling clothes of the day, they
have the imperial look of a British Lord and Lady. Against the background
of two frail, collapsing palm trees that provide a spot of shade, a small boy
in robe and cap is off to one side looking as disinterested as the sphinx.
On the back of the photo the date is scrawled: July 1937, hardly the coolest
time of the year along the venerable Nile.

Another photo is inspired by Henriette's idea that it would be "fun" to
send a picture back to France of herself on a camel, proof to everyone she
had been to Egypt. Abe preferred not to risk the stunt, so in the snapshot
taken for the stay-at-homes Henriette is perched perilously high on the
beast, clutching her hat against the desert wind, her dress daringly hiked-
up well past her knees, her other hand grabbing the saddle for dear life.
In the background there is a crumbling pyramid lending authenticity. In
the foreground are Abe and the camel keeper, who stands serenely in long
white robe and muslim cap while Abe, by contrast, looks like he has just
dashed from the doors of his office in New York and by some strange twist
been whisked to the sands of Egypt wearing a black hat and suit. This time

his cane is at the ready, planted firmly in his left hand and angled toward the camel, prepared for a quick swipe.

It's a strange and unexpected set of pictures—Abe and Henriette seemingly having a gay old time touring the wonders of ancient Egypt, only a year after Hitler defied the European nations by occupying the Rhineland and with the Spanish Civil War at its climax. It came about when Henriette opened the office mail one day and found a small envelope with a letter folded around a check for a thousand dollars. She was astounded to discover that the check was made out to Abe himself and not the association. It was a gift from a woman of wealth who had been sending contributions to Abe's work since 1929, when she had been introduced to him at a conference by Norman Thomas, the leader of American socialism.

Ethel Clyde was one of several wealthy women who saw in Abe the chance to put their money where it would do the most good for social justice. In 1929 and 1930 she had given one thousand dollars, in 1931 she raised it to fifteen hundred, and in 1932 made total contributions spread out over the year of forty-seven hundred dollars. In 1933 it was two thousand dollars, and in 1934 it was more than two thousand. This is only a partial list from inadequate records, but the sums she gave were enormous for that era and bailed out the association on more than one occasion. When Abe met someone like Ethel Clyde, he turned on the charm. His enthusiasm when he discovered someone who cared about what he cared about was infectious. His unaffected ardor would sweep them into his crusade, as his thank-you letters show: "We are deeply indebted to you for your very gracious and timely help . . . without your wonderful cooperation and most generous assistance, however, none of our accomplishments would have been possible . . . I can find no fitting words to tell you what your check for $2000 means to all of us . . . With friends like yourself the fight for social justice is a genuine pleasure and thrill." Abe was lavish in praise of what Ethel Clyde had done to help his work and encouraged her to participate more fully by joining the board of directors in 1931. She was delighted, immediately accepted, and soon became a close friend as well, coming to dinner, attending the conferences, and writing letters to influential people on behalf of the association. She was one of several wealthy women whom Abe became close to; others included Margaret Gage from Boston and Ethel Katz from New York. But by 1939 Ethel Clyde's financial situation had worsened, as had that of the association. Abe grumbled about how the average contribution had gone down from $8 to $2.50 and he didn't know what to do about it. In 1939 she could only send him $300. By 1940 she was down to $75. And in 1941, the year of her last contribution, it was $25. Abe stayed in touch with her nonetheless, though by 1939 she had left his board, moved out of New York, and was in very reduced circumstances. The depression was still in effect and the money many of his benefactors had once possessed had slowly dwindled. Abe strained to finds ways to raise the needed funds, but people like Ethel Clyde were hard to find. He continued to correspond with all those who had contributed, hoping that something might break open with one of them. To Ethel Clyde he wrote, "I have always hoped we would break all precedents by not perpetuating the Association once its tasks were completed. As you well know mere job holding was never one of my sins . . . In the short span of its fifteen years the Association has indeed accomplished wonders . . . Our very name, "Social Security," has become deeply rooted in American life . . . Even more important are our unfinished positive tasks . . . the perennial struggle to raise our small budget of $19,000 has become almost impossible . . . I can no longer assume such burdens with less and less money. By this Spring, I shall pass the half-century mark and my health, the past few years, has not been all it should be . . . As one who is so much responsible for the success of the Association's work, we must turn to you again . . . " There just wasn't much that Ethel Clyde could do any more.

---

But in 1937 she still had money, and when Henriette saw the size of the check she had given Abe, she could not hold back her excitement and rushed into his office.

"Look at this!" she exclaimed.

Abe broke into a smile. "Well, this is going to be a tremendous help to the association," he said. He started to put the check into the drawer of his desk but Henriette tried to stop him.

"Not so fast," she said. "This is a gift to you personally. Read the letter carefully."

Ethel Clyde had addressed him as "Dear Ep," and her words showed her concern for him personally, not just for his work as a social pioneer: "Please accept this tribute . . . as my friend, my admiration for your splendid work, and my gratitude for all that you have taught me." The next sentence made clear why she had sent it. "I suggest that the check be used for vacation purposes." Ethel Clyde had seen clearly that Abe was running himself into the ground.

"Take a holiday just like Ethel Clyde said," Henriette pleaded. "You need to take a rest. You cannot keep up the pace . . ."

Abe shushed her and was noncommittal. But during the next few weeks Henriette kept up the pressure. At various times she told him, "Look, this is the first time anyone has ever been generous to you personally." Or, "It is a present to you. You must look on it as a gift, paying you back for all your wonderful work." Abe did not react. The truth was that he was numbed by her gesture. And for once Henriette decided she was not going to argue back. She dropped the subject because she sensed that the unsolicited money had made Abe think over a lot of things, not the least of which was his being so moved by what Ethel Clyde had done. No one had ever treated him that way.

The first order of business was to find a way to express to Ethel Clyde what such a gesture meant. "I have never experienced anything like this before. My first reaction was natural bewilderment since I have become so habituated to little else but brickbats and criticism. I need not say that your affectionate tribute is worth more than twenty years of bitter struggle and disillusionment. I shall treasure your friendship to the end of my days as one of the happiest assets a man can possess." Two days after his reply he called Henriette into the office, took the check from his desk drawer, and said, "I would like to visit the Middle East and Palestine, see the officials in charge of social security. I could get all the necessary letters of introduction."

"Could we go by way of Egypt and see the Pyramids?" Henriette chirped.

"I suppose."

And because of those grudging words, Abe and Henriette found themselves sitting on the rough, sandy paws of a sphinx during the summer of 1937.

Three events in the first half of 1937 had contributed to Abe's willingness to leave New York for an extended period. The association had celebrated its tenth anniversary in April with a spirited and celebratory convention, the Supreme Court had declared the Social Security Act to be constitutionally valid, and an advisory council to improve the 1935 law had been appointed.

It was a time for optimism, and time for a trip.

———————

Henriette and I arrived in Paris for a reunion with her parents before the start of her Middle East excursion, another trip made possible by her

On board ship to Alexandria,
1937. Abe is only forty-five
at this time, yet he looks
years older.

marriage—for better or worse—to the venturesome Abe. He came over
later, always hesitating to leave until the last minute because of some
brewing crisis. In Paris we were greeted by the last blast of merriment that
was to take place in 1930s Europe, the Exposition Internationale of 1937.
Grouped along the curve of the Seine near the Eiffel Tower, the national
pavilions and exhibition halls of many nations lined the promenades on
both sides of the river. The tower itself blazed incandescently in the night
sky, illuminated by a new system of "eclairage." Papa and Maman Castex, Henriette, and I reveled in the festival atmosphere created by the exposition. All Paris seemed like an outdoor party in the soft June air. We
strolled from exhibit to exhibit, soared to the top of the Eiffel Tower for
dinner in one of the new restaurants, gazed down on the meandering

crowd below. On one night we boarded a barge and floated down the river, looking up at the nightly fireworks bursting over the city and its many monuments, officially called "Visions of Fairyland on the Seine," while all the fountains gushed forth in luminous colored water. It was meant to be the great festival of modern science and art deco at the same time. The wonders of French civilization, its ancient crafts, wine, cheese, foods, region by region, were on display everywhere, offered up by guides clothed in the old costumes of rural France. The major French fashion designers held exclusive exhibits, showing off their swirling ball gowns and new hats—at that time an accessory for all women. The most striking building—it still remains as the exposition's unique legacy—was the newly built Museum of Modern Art. The old Trocadero was torn apart and the Art Deco museum building was put up in its place, fronted by steps of fountains pointed across the Seine at the Eiffel Tower. It put on display all the great modern paintings and sculpture belonging to the French nation. French technology was also vivid in two of the most popular pavilions, the Palais de l'Air and the Railway Pavilion. My favorite was the one with the trains. With Papa Castex making sure my hand was held tightly in his, we roamed there together, gazing in wonder at the life-size cutaway model of the newest locomotive where flashing lights radiantly told how power was generated and transmitted. The highlight of the exposition for many was a special animated model of the Golden Arrow train (La Flèche d'Or) as it traveled at night from Paris to London. It was an enormous and intricately detailed model—running the length of one side of the hall—that had the miniature train pull out slowly from the Gare du Nord as night fell on Paris, lights twinkling, picking up speed as it moved through the French capital "with much of the city, including Montmartre, rendered with almost photographic accuracy," as one writer put it, past sleeping French villages, disappearing through tunnels, past lit-up train stations, arriving in Dunkirk where a boat was waiting, the train on board crossing the English Channel to reemerge at Dover, and as the light of day began to break over England—and the exhibit—the train, its night's work done, pulled into Victoria Station. It was every child's vision of what his train set could turn into. Grandfather Castex and I remained transfixed before the dramatic re-creation at least three times. I clamored to be taken to it again and again. Traveling from Paris to London—how exciting and simple it all seemed.

Yet the wonder and novelty of the 1937 Exposition Internationale was taking place against a background of unease and strife. The French Pavilion had not been finished in time for the opening because of numerous strikes. Left-wing unions battled business and the government in a never-ending confrontation over wages, working hours, and vacations by staging sit-down strikes, a uniquely French invention. In contrast, the first pavilions to be finished on time were those of the totalitarian nations, Nazi Germany and Communist Russia, set across from each other in a striking architectural confrontation under the shadows cast by the Eiffel Tower. The Russians had placed on the top of their pavilion an enormous marching statue of a Russian workingman and woman clasping hammer and sickle. On the other side of the divide, Hitler's architect, the devilish Albert Speer, had by chance seen a sketch of the Russian Pavilion and decided to make a direct statement to the future enemy. A Nazi Eagle, its claws clutching a wreath containing a huge swastika, fanned his wings militantly at the idealized Communist workers. At ground level, one writer wrote, Speer erected "a massive naked Teutonic couple staring at the Russian monument with grim determination." It was obvious to many in France that the stage was being set for war. But in a brave gesture of hope the authorities had put up a "Peace Column" near the new art museum, luminescent every night, but lost in the background, the view of it obliterated by the massive abutting buildings of Germany and Russia. In less than three years Hitler would be strutting triumphantly on the same esplanade where the new Museum of Modern Art and its accompanying "Peace Column" had been erected. Only one nation had warned of the coming horrors, Spain, where the centerpiece of the embattled Republic's pavilion was Picasso's surreal painting of the horrors of the bombing of Guernica by German planes supplied to Franco. It made no difference.

---

Abe sailed for France on June 12, filled with anxiety himself about the future of Europe. Several friends asked him to send back letters explaining where things were going: "tell us how you feel France will turn," was how one friend expressed his worries. He skipped the wonders of the exposition, went directly to Toulouse, picked up Henriette, said good-bye, and headed for Marseille and the ship to Alexandria. I paid almost no attention when they left. I had brought my cowboy clothes with me, chaps, shirt, hat, pistol, and badge, and was busy chasing the cats through the high foliage of the garden like they were mounted Indians. My summer fun was already staked out.

Abe's main object in taking the trip was to visit Palestine to see how the Jewish settlers might survive in such a harsh environment. It seemed a precarious situation to him. But Egypt and its ancient wonders was the first stop, and the grand tour almost reversed course when Abe had his wallet stolen as he and Henriette were wandering through the old markets of Alexandria. In the 1930s, before the advent of credit cards, travelers were given letters of credit to different banks along the way. Abe had just cashed one and now ominously found he was cleaned out. Telegrams flew back and forth to Toulouse, and in a few days Henriette's parents had provided money through American Express. But for a brief moment it looked like the trip would end before it began. Egypt suddenly seemed a daunting enterprise; nonetheless, Henriette was determined to see the pyramids and hired prominent guide Abdul Kader Abdul Salam, "English Dragoman and Guide," to take them into the desert to see the Grand Sphinx, pyramids, and tombs. He seems to have been a man well acquainted with the needs of the tourist aristocracy, judging by his very elaborate bills and letterheads informing clients he was a "Contractor for 1st. Class Dahabias on the Nile, Camping on the Desert, Shooting Party Terms Moderate. Everything will be O.K." But Henriette's needs were more modest: she wanted photographs of her and Abe among sphinx, camels, and pyramids. Abe dutifully took in the sights with her, but it was clear that ancient Egypt was only a stop on the road to visit the Jewish pioneers.

They finally arrived in Palestine in July, with Abe brandishing half a dozen letters of introduction from the Amalgamated Clothing Workers Union to leading members of the Jewish labor federation, the Histadruth, in Haifa and Tel Aviv. Another even more important introduction came from Rabbi Stephen Wise to Moshe Shertok, the head of the Jewish Agency for Palestine. Shertok later changed his name to Moshe Sharett. It became policy at David Ben-Gurion's insistence that those in government should use Hebrew names instead of their Russian ones because Hebrew would be the language of the future Jewish state. Sharett rose in political life and became Israel's second prime minister after Ben-Gurion.

At the time of Abe's visit Palestine was a vast territory taken from the Ottoman Turks and given to the British as a prize from World War I. The British were supposed to convert it into a self-governing state, but the mandate, as it was called, was an unsettling mixture of Arabs, Jews, and Christians and proved to be almost impossible for the British to keep peaceful. In fact, the year before Abe's tour the Arabs had rioted against the British and attacked the Jewish settlers. The Foreign Office in London was shocked by the intensity and fury of the Arab revolt, and a British official named Robert Peel was sent out to investigate. By July 1937—just when Abe arrived—Peel reported back that there was no hope of settling the conflict—it would be best instead to partition the country between Jews and Arabs, an opinion which delighted the Jewish settlers—a Jewish homeland at last—and infuriated the Arabs who were to be transferred out of the proposed Jewish lands. The demonstrations and assassinations became more violent all through 1937, and by September the British had resorted to martial law. It was a very dangerous time for anyone to be visiting the troubled land of the Bible, but you would not be able to detect any concern on the part of Abe and Henriette in posed photographs outside the gates of the New Hebrew University in Jerusalem. Palestine was as hot as Egypt and Abe soon changed from his natty travel clothes into something more casual, short-sleeve shirts and loose, flapping pants. Henriette remained in cotton dresses but donned sandals and firmly grasped her broad-brimmed hat against the fierce desert winds.

Abe's interest in the Jewish presence in Palestine had nothing to do with his work in social legislation. What he wanted to know was why the Jews wanted to be there; gnawing at him was the violence of the struggle to survive in a hostile land. Was it really worth it? Would the Jews be better off living in other lands as they always had? Abe did not think that retaliation against the British and the Arabs would help one bit. The Jews were bound to suffer for it. Another question that troubled him was what future would the immigrant Jews have living in a land with an economy based on agriculture? Abe viewed the problem through the prism of his miserable youth in rural Russia and did not think the Jews had any future as farmers. In truth, many educated immigrants were unable to adapt to such a life in Palestine, gave it up, and returned to Russia, Poland, or Germany.

But Abe needed to see for himself. A member of the Histadruth arranged to take him on a trip to one of the new Jewish settlements that were hastily thrown up under the cover of darkness on barren land in the desert. They drove out from Tel Aviv on rocky dirt roads, no other vehicle to be seen, passing the scattered camels and donkeys driven by Arab Bedouins who repeatedly whipped the beasts with sticks. On arrival, they saw a village of tents and a few wooden shacks encircled by a flimsy wooden wall. The sole prominent structure was a two-story tower in a corner of the settlement. They spent the day with the young Jewish "kubutzniks," tanned, muscular young men in shorts and undershirts, handkerchiefs tied around their heads against the sweat from their labors. Abe was introduced to them as an important social reformer in America, prominent in Jewish circles in New York. He talked with them in English, Russian, Yiddish, and that old language with which the immigrants were trying to recreate their biblical past, Hebrew. He had listened to his religious father praying in that ancient tongue and had learned it during his studies at the yeshiva in Slutsk. He wanted to know what they hoped for, and the sweltering pioneers replied that with their hard work in the desert they were building a new land for the Jewish people. Abe took in the harsh landscape of where they were standing and the thin wall that enclosed the young men, but kept his thoughts to himself. Henriette nervously gazed up at the tower. Why was it there, she wondered? In photographs taken with the determined young Jewish settlers, the group stands facing the photographer, shielding their eyes from the desert glare, against a background of sand, tents, walls, and the tower ever present in a corner of the photograph. Everyone seems blotted together in tight camaraderie, and Abe appears to fit right in, at one with the settlers in their struggle. But the sun was fierce and Abe looked worn-out despite his short-sleeve shirt and black hat. Henriette still managed to be chic in a light summer dress, sandals, and scarf. When the first pictures were finished, she broached the subject of the tower and asked what could be seen from the top.

"It's a watchtower," one young man said. "Come along. I'll take you up and show you."

Abe and Henriette climbed the rickety ladder to the second story and looked out over the wall. From the top Abe snapped a picture that showed a trackless rocky wasteland, some faraway hills, some scrub vegetation, and in the near distance a small building shaped like a ziggurat.

"What is that?" Henriette asked.

"An old Arab tomb," their guide replied. "The Bedouin who built it are gone."

Henriette looked out at the daunting emptiness, at the forgotten Arab presence, and still did not understand what the watchtower was for.

As the harsh sun began to descend and the desert began to cool off they returned to Tel Aviv and the next morning went off to Jerusalem, where Henriette was fascinated by the Old Quarter and its mixture of Jews, Arabs, and Christians crowding the streets together, so different from the harsh isolation of the desert settlement they had visited the day before. In Jerusalem Abe went to see Moshe Shertok, hoping to get the newest thinking on the Jewish presence in Palestine from a top political official. They met in Shertok's simple office in old Jerusalem and Abe was told that any friend of Rabbi Wise, particularly a man of Abe's accomplishments, would be given any assistance he needed on his tour. Wise, in his letter to Shertok, had laid it on rather thick, particularly when he wrote, "Dr. Epstein's name will probably be familiar to you . . . whatever we have in the

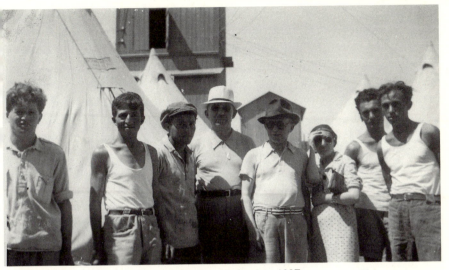

Abe and Henriette visiting Jewish settlers, Palestine, 1937.
The watchtower is in the background.

field of old age insurance is very, very largely his achievement." Shertok
was a small, solid figure, with a full black mustache, prominent nose, a
thick head of dark hair, and a no-nonsense manner. At the time he was the
liaison for the Jewish community with the British mandate authority. His
goal was to get better treatment for the Jews from the British, and he told
Abe that he was organizing a Jewish Auxiliary Police to work with them
to ward off Arab attacks.

Abe was blunt and asked Shertok, "Do you think the Jews can survive
here when the Arabs hate us so much?"

"Of course—and we will do very well. This is our home," he replied
like the tough militant he was. "Of course this land is not for everyone.
My father found it too difficult, could not adapt to agricultural labor, and
went back to Russia."

This only served to confirm Abe's theory about Jews and farming.

Shertok went on and told him the rest of his own story, including that
fact that he had served in the Turkish Army during World War I and at
one point believed that Jews should accept Turkish citizenship so that
they would not be thrown out of Palestine if the politics of the area
changed. But now, he made it clear to Abe, he believed the Jews would
have a state of their own and, with the help of the worldwide Jewish community, be able to survive and prosper.

Abe took in all that Shertok told him and replied that he also wanted the Jews to survive in a world that was trying to see them disappear, particularly in Germany and Russia. Shertok agreed but pointed out that Palestine was the place for those who were persecuted in those totalitarian states. It was their natural refuge and home. The men parted with handshakes and Shertok told Abe to "come back again to see how we are progressing."

A few days later Abe and Henriette left Palestine by car for Damascus in Syria, once again passing bedraggled Bedouins with camels and donkeys. She was relieved to get back to tourism and visits to the tombs and cities of that ancient desert world. Abe was silent for a large part of the car trip, staring out at the passing emptiness. Something was on his mind. Seeing Abe so preoccupied, Henriette tried to tell him of her unease when they had visited the Jewish settlement.

"Why was that watchtower there?"

"Arabs," Abe answered. "They might want to attack the settlement."

"Why? They are in the middle of the desert. There is no one around for miles."

"It's their land," Abe replied.

He paused for a time and finally gave voice to the thoughts that had been churning in his brain. "You need to understand. An all Jewish country in the middle of all those impoverished Arabs—it might never survive."

The Middle East tour continued for a week more. In Turkey they took in Istanbul and its Grand Mosque. In Greece it was Athens and the Acropolis. They were back in France at the beginning of August, where Abe felt that he needed to write to Ethel Clyde about the experience her money had provided. It was the most educational trip he had ever taken, he wrote her. But the poverty and ignorance had surprised and appalled him. "I had no idea the Moslem church [sic] had such a stranglehold over the masses, and progress seems centuries away . . . they live in conditions not very much different from those that prevailed in the days of the Pharaohs . . . we actually encountered strata of the upper classes who were so far away from the people as to be unable to speak the native language and who speak French as their native tongue." Palestine shocked him even more. "The contrast between the Arabs and the Jews is beyond all description. There seems a difference of at least 2000 years between them. On the one hand the most primitive conditions and ignorance and on the other hand blooming gardens and the most heroic idealism. But the great sacrifice seems all so wasteful and futile. We found cultured, even professional Jews cultivating the meager soil happily . . . but it seems to me that all that can be achieved by all these efforts . . . is the lowest peasantry subsistence."

By the beginning of September everyone was back in New York, where life resumed its nerve-racking pace with Abe on the lecture circuit, teaching, and trying to raise money, Henriette back at her desk sending out mailings and organizing the next annual conference, and I back in school. On the surface everyone seemed the same. But for Abe there was now one more fear to add to his anxiety-laden brain besides money for his work, the rise of fascism, a war in Europe, and American neutrality—there was also the uncertain fate of his fellow Jews.

6

On May 23, 1938, it was raining heavily in New York—it had been for the last two days—when Henriette and I set out for the French Line pier and one more summer in Toulouse. Abe did not come to see us off, and as the *Paris* slipped away from its mooring and moved out into the Hudson River the rain was still cascading in sheets down its iron sides and onto its broad wooden decks. The dock was barren of well-wishers to gather in the streamers usually thrown by the departing passengers. No one ventured out on deck to wave good-bye to New York. The skyline slid by masked in the gloom of rain. The ship was half empty, the purser had informed Henriette—two hundred passengers had canceled their bookings at the last moment. Few people wanted to go to Europe. Too dangerous.

Earlier that year Adolf Hitler's Germany had annexed Austria into its thousand-year Reich. In Spain, Germany's tanks and planes were supplying Franco's Falange with the tools of inevitable victory over the Spanish Republic. What else might Hitler want? Czechoslovakia? He had threatened to invade unless it gave a large piece of its territory, known as the Sudetenland, to Germany. Henriette had been warned by many people not to go back to France. "Be cautious," her friends advised. "If war breaks out, you will be stuck, you won't be able to come back to America and safety." But after the bitter cold of another winter in New York and the strain of life with Abe, she could only think of being with her parents in Toulouse, the maids, the food, the warmth. She wanted to sit in the garden and dream of the wonders of the City of Light, glowing and glamorous during the previous year's World's Fair. She couldn't wait to take the train from Paris to the south, to watch the "poppies on the side of the highways and traintracks like streaks of blood in the grass." She made notes about a recurrent fantasy that the train would stop and she would alight at some small village station to wander in the nearby fields, all the while picking armfuls of wildflowers. She wanted to go back to what she loved the most, "the cats, the chickens, the flowers, the garden, the gossip."

But the ambiance surrounding her voyage felt ominous and she was overwhelmed by a feeling of impending disaster, particularly when she was offhandedly informed by a ship's officer, as she walked up the stairs to the lounge to write letters, that the *Paris* was not fireproof. More unsettling had been her transfer from another ship, the *Lafayette*, to this one because the *Lafayette*—named as a symbol of the ancient ties binding France and America—had burned in the harbor in France. The rumor was that German spies had done it. Her favorite ship, the *Champlain*, named for another man whose life was connected to America—the one she always loved to sail on, where she had become friends with many members of the crew, and knew the stories of their families and their children—had broken a propeller and was under repair. Was German sabotage behind all the problems? And then there had also been a terrible fight with Abe the evening before because his sister had wanted to spend the night and Henriette did not want her getting in the way of her packing. Anxious and exhausted at preparing for her departure, she was irate at the imposition. But after a week at sea, crossing the Atlantic, she began to relax as she always did on her maritime journeys. She was excited to see the coast of France come into view when all of a sudden the calm she was beginning to experience was abruptly shattered. The first sight for all the passengers lining the decks as the *Paris* slowly moved into the harbor at Le Havre was the burned, capsized hull of the *Lafayette*, like a rusting island in the gray water. Everyone on board was shocked at the vision. On land she felt right away that people had changed. The country had been besieged with dozens of workers' strikes that year; the most sensational, and the one everyone still talked about, had been an angry sit-down strike at the Renault automobile factory. The taxi drivers and porters had become surly and unhelpful. "Where do you think you are?" one barked at her. "Don't you know we have the forty-hour week now?" Old-fashioned politeness had vanished. Talk of the coming war was on everyone's lips. When would it start, who would fight, would America stay neutral? She tried to account for her fears with a phrase in her notebook—"the simple fact that this is my last crossing and I can't understand why it should be so."

She tried to bring back the good times by returning with her parents to vacation at La Tour de Carol, the small village on the Spanish border where her mother and father had ritually returned every summer to see old friends and eat fresh trout from the mountain streams, accompanied by enormous plates of fresh-picked mushrooms fried in olive oil, followed by raspberries gathered the same day. But instead she found the villagers anxious like everyone else, always asking what she thought would happen after Franco won in Spain. Before, she had loved to go on hillside rambles, gathering bouquets of flowers, casually crossing the frontier to buy olives and oranges in a small Spanish village. Now that was too dangerous. The border, as it ran over the hills and through the fields, was even more heavily patrolled than before. *No passeran.* Franco's troops were getting closer and the menacing sounds of his approaching artillery, pounding towns near the frontier, gave the local people the jitters. Refugees had appeared on the hills with increasing frequency, dashing dangerously down the rocky slopes to get away from the mounted Spanish police, visible from the French side as they rode along the crests. In the tiny village square one day everyone stopped what they were doing to look up into the clear blue Catalan sky as the drone of airplanes was heard. Three black planes with no markings—everyone said they must be German—made a run over the French frontier. They seemed to be heading straight for the village. Suddenly hidden French antiaircraft guns fired warning shots, violating the peace of the sky with loud booms. The three planes wheeled, turned and glided back over the frontier. The mayor told Henriette he was already making preparations for the coming refugee crisis, that the international train station built by her father which had made crossing from France to Spain so easy had been closed. "We will make use of it now, maybe this winter. Its empty halls will serve for the evacuation," he said. At the annual village festival in August when everyone was dancing in the square to the shrill, jumping music of a Catalan orchestra, a bewildered Spanish boy, wearing a beret and carrying a blanket over his shoulder, suddenly appeared. The dancing stopped and people gathered around him. He had traveled over the mountains for three days without food. He looked like a child, although he said he was sixteen and a coal miner. Offered food, he was too scared to eat. When told he was now safe in France, he didn't understand. "Isn't this Spain?" he asked in Catalan, a language that would soon be banned by Franco. The French police came to get him and interrogate him, then took him away to the local jail. Henriette watched the scene along with other villagers and wrote down in her notebook, "Where will he go? What will be his fate?"

Back in Toulouse everyone was surprised to see huge mounds of sand piled in front of every house. There were posters plastered on the walls of buildings, notices in the papers, ordering the residents to store it inside in case incendiary bombs rained down on the city. But it had poured for several days and the sand was caked and heavy, nearly unmovable. A hired laborer struggled for a day carrying it through the house to dump it into the garden. Friends spoke to her of rumors that the Germans had 360 planes parked on the Spanish border ready to drop bombs on the cities of southern France and that Toulouse was on the flight plan.

When the summer ended we traveled to Paris for the return sailing. As the train clattered through the night, Henriette slept fitfully. She took in the darkened towns and passing trains, she noted in her journal, and, half awake, had a vision of herself as a terrified adolescent in 1914. Then the passing trains were full of soldiers off to war, and for a moment she saw her father just as she had remembered seeing him in the window of one of them, in his captain's uniform, staring ahead, vanishing quickly for the four and a half years of World War I. The dread of those days was returning to haunt her.

That winter, when the snows of March were still on the ground, covering the hills and fields, masses of desperate, terrified refugees and defeated soldiers of all nationalities swarmed into France from Spain, tumbling down those rocky slopes on the frontier, hungry, threadbare, and frozen. The Spanish Civil War was drawing to a close with a crushing defeat of the Republic by Franco's Falange. But instead of the expected twenty-five thousand refugees there were half a million, a tidal flood engulfing the ancient tiny villages of southern France. La Tour de Carol was overwhelmed by the human exodus. When Henriette, safe in Greenwich Village, heard the story from her friends and visualized the mad scramble of those begging France to save them from the horrors of war, she wrote a few succinct words: "1938. A particularly tragic year." It was too much for her to describe further.

For Abe in New York, the fear of war was uppermost in his thoughts. Hitler's annexation of Austria added to his distress. He signed his name to a mass telegram and newspaper advertisement by well-known public figures such as Albert Einstein that was sent to President Roosevelt and Congress urging "Non-recognition of the annexation of Austria by Germany." It seemed a hopeless gesture to Abe. Letters poured in to him from friends all over Europe, describing their increasingly desperate situation. From Czechoslovakia one wrote about the betrayal of his country at Munich, the depressed state of the people, how the banks were closing, and how the Germans had taken control of the roads and railroad lines out of the country, making it nearly impossible for people to escape. Yet, "the beer is still overflowing in the steins and the sausages are as good as ever," the man wrote, and almost as an afterthought he added, "So far the Jews are safe." Soon, other more alarming letters arrived, frantic letters with requests for help—friends or relatives trapped in Europe with no visas with which to get out. Emergency visas would only be given by the United States in cases where someone had obvious proof that they were in danger of being killed by the Nazis. But for this to happen, immigrants first had to be approved by the Justice Department and then by the State Department. They were then eligible for a visa from the nearest American consul if they could get to him and if he decided to give one out. Many consuls did not because of their own anti-immigrant views, and the State Department itself was playing a double game of offering visas but telling the consuls in Europe to look for clearer proof of the applicant's fears.

Abe was increasingly involved in finding a way to get around these obstructionist tactics. Social security seemed to take a back seat to his newest concerns—how to save Jews, family, and refugees from the Nazis. The wife of a cousin on his mother's side, living safely in the United States, called Abe and asked for help for her husband who was trapped in Lithuania. Could he do anything with the State Department to get him out? He wrote the Immigration Bureau to find out what had happened to the application for entry of his cousin, Chaim Lwowicz, expecting to get some information quickly, but the bureau did not respond for more than a month. Abe decided to be more forceful and wrote directly to the commissioner of immigration in Washington, reminding him that they had met several times at the home of a mutual friend. Two months went by and there was still no response. Finally, he made a direct appeal to a congressman with the unlikely name of Rockefeller who gave Abe's request directly to the State Department. Abe continued to write and call for a response, but nothing came. Finally, after a five-month delay, the acting chief of the visa division wrote to inform him his cousin would be given preference for a visa. But, the official warned, Lithuania had now been overrun by the Russians and the State Department would not be allowed to issue visas to anyone presently in the Soviet Union. His cousin would have to apply in some other nearby country. Poland was suggested. This might take some time, the acting chief went on, because Warsaw had been recently bombed by the Germans and there had been damage to records at the Consulate, so "Lwowicz must expect some delay will ensue in connection with the examination of the dossiers of visa applicants." It was a maze of Kafkaesque complications, but Abe kept right on pushing for results and agreed to sign a letter guaranteeing financial support for Chaim, which he was told could only be sent directly to the American Legation in Lithuania. The U.S. mails were no longer going to that country, but as a special courtesy to Abe the State Department would send it in the diplomatic pouch. "And by the way," the man at State continued, "your cousin's wife must also send as many letters of support as she can generate. The more the better." Eventually, a ticket for boat passage was bought for Chaim Lwowicz to sail from Kobe, Japan, on September 12, 1940. But the question remained: how was Chaim Lwowicz to get from Lithuania to Japan and pick up a visa on time, a visa that would have to be transferred from Warsaw to the Consulate in Kobe while he struggled to get to Japan? It seemed impossible.

Two weeks later, Abe decided he had to confront the Department of State in person. He was granted a meeting with the acting head of the visa division, Eliot Coulter, who told him that at that time the embassy in Tokyo had no record of Chaim Lwowicz. But he assured Abe that as soon as his cousin showed up he would be "accorded every possible consideration," a vague encouragement. Eventually—Abe never knew how he did it—Chaim Lwowicz appeared in Kobe. He had managed to leave Lithuania, cross all of Russia, pass through China to Shanghai, then cross to Japan, travel to Kobe, and claim his visa and his ticket. He eventually set sail for the United States, where he landed in Seattle in November 1940. Abe felt momentarily uplifted and effusively wrote to Coulter, "Please accept our heartiest gratitude for all your fine help bringing to a success the union of two broken-hearted persons." It had taken a year and a half for Chaim and his wife to be reunited. His saga, it turned out, was not that unusual, but rather was typical of the hardships and panicky journeys suffered by the thousands desperate to flee Hitler, Stalin, and all the lesser Fascist dictators. Chaim's migration to America was only one of many Abe was involved in bringing about. He did everything he could, using his personal contacts, begging for interviews with influential people, writing passionate letters, and signing petitions to help those close to being caught in the Nazi dragnet, people of all nationalities and religions, Austrians, Germans, French, Poles, Lithuanians, the list went on. And as the situation in Europe grew worse, the house in Greenwich Village began to overflow with strange-sounding English spoken by the many refugees grateful beyond all words for being in America. They came to tell their stories of escape and to share the platters of America's abundant ood that Henriette had prepared for them, and they tried to answer Abe's questions as best they could about conditions in Germany, Czechoslovakia, Austria, or wherever they had come from, and also to help him determine the location of others in need of help.

---

In spite of small victories the times seemed more and more desperate, and Abe's pessimism deepened. On March 15, 1939, Hitler abrogated the pact he had signed at Munich and overran Czechoslovakia. Several weeks later Roosevelt tried to forestall the oncoming tide of Nazi conquest in a speech where he asked Hitler and Mussolini to guarantee that they would not attack any other nation for at least ten years. He named thirty-one countries on his list of those to be left alone. The Nazis ignored FDR for a number of weeks, then suddenly informed him that there would be no exchange of diplomatic notes but that instead Hitler would make a reply over the radio in his speech to the Reichstag on April 28. Since his words would be live, he had insultingly and deliberately chosen an hour when most of America would be asleep, including its president.

Abe, however, still knew the German language he had grown up with, in part from all the Marx and Engels he had read, and made up his mind that if Roosevelt would not hear the speech live when it was given, then he would. For him the fate of the world would hang on Hitler's reply—would he back down to FDR, or would he go ahead? On April 28, in the dark before dawn, in the black of a night symbolic of all his worst fears, Abe rose and padded downstairs in bathrobe and slippers and turned on the table-top Pilot radio. Slowly, its eerie green-glowing warm-up light grew brighter and its emerald color filled the room. In moments Hitler's screaming bellicosity spewed forth, heaping contempt on Roosevelt. Those violent sounds sent me scurrying down the stairs and I huddled next to Abe while he sat rigidly attentive on the couch taking in the babble that sounded so strange to my ears. Hitler's harsh, strident German rose and fell in cataclysmic waves. "Who wrecked the League of Nations?" he ranted. "America!" How had the United States come to dominate North America? Look at the history of the Sioux tribes, he screamed convulsively. "Mr. Roosevelt! I took over a state faced with complete ruin . . . I have conquered chaos, reestablished order, increased production . . . I have succeeded in finding useful work for the whole of the seven million unemployed. You, Mr. Roosevelt, have a much easier task. From the very outset you stepped to the head of one of the largest and wealthiest states in the world. My world, Mr. Roosevelt . . . is unfortunately much smaller." Raucous laughter from the Reichstag deputies flew from the radio and echoed in our house. When Hitler's cunning, belligerent tirade was finally over and the harsh and scary German words had vanished, I turned to look over at Abe. His body was slumped down on the sofa, and his face had gone all white.

---

Later in 1939 Abe made it clear to Henriette that he would not let her go back to France for the summer. "War will break out, and you will not be safe," he told her. Henriette protested, but her mother and father soon wrote to tell her to follow Eppie's advice. They had hesitated to suggest it; they had wanted her to come, but now they were afraid. Everyone in Toulouse was on edge, they reported, and the sons of their friends were being mobilized and sent off in the middle of the night to unknown military destinations. Air raid sirens were being put up on lampposts and buildings. There were daily tests and every time one went off people in the street scattered, racing into the cafés to what they thought was safety. The 1914 war would be nothing in comparison to what is coming, Henriette's mother wrote. But if it starts they will have made plans to take care of themselves—leave Toulouse and live in the country with their friends and relatives. Cash had been put aside in a safe place, food could be gotten from the land they rented to farmers, and their old furniture could be used to stay in one house or another. They would survive. Another piece of news stunned Henriette into realizing the peril she would be under if she decided on another Atlantic crossing. After the destruction of the *Lafayette* the previous year, she was shocked by the news that the *Paris* had suffered the same fate, burned in port, turned over on its side, its blackened, rusting hulk lying in the water. She had a vivid recollection of the officer on board the year before telling her that the ship was not fireproof. Rumors of German sabotage abounded. Everyone suspected that the *Normandie*, France's newest, most elegant, and fastest ocean liner, was the target. The World's Fair was to start in New York and a great quantity of precious French art was to be transported there on the *Normandie*. Instead, it was the *Paris* that succumbed while the *Normandie* had raced at top speed safely across the Atlantic.

In May a strange period of diplomatic calm took over, the rush to war seemed to slow, and there was even talk of peace. Hitler's statements were less bellicose and the French and English governments began to believe a European war might be avoided. Henriette's parents changed their minds and told her it was safe to come. In fact, they were excited at the prospect and had bought two new chairs for the garden and a ham weighing more than thirty pounds to prepare for another joyous summer. But Abe absolutely refused to let her leave and instead drove us all up to look at a small house he had rented at West Stockbridge in the Berkshire hills of Massachusetts, surrounded by dairy farms and chicken farmers. It was as far as he could get from the anxieties of war and still be near New York.

That summer the look of rural peace that surrounded us was deceptive; we could not escape from the newspapers and the radio that daily brought the news of the approaching war. Henriette was increasingly in a state of nervous exhaustion, worried about her parents, her homeland, all her friends, and one day, August 23, she made a note of how weary she was of the sounds of the "cursed radio, news, forecasts, last hopes, impending crashes, advertisements and commentators, Paris, London, Berlin, but now no one will turn it off because the nightmare that has turned into cold reality has happened." What she meant was that Stalin had signed a nonaggression pact with Hitler and the way was free for the German dictator to do what he wanted anywhere in Europe. When the news came, I was in Pittsfield with Abe. We had gone to pick up the newspapers and he had promised to buy me an ice cream cone as well. The warm August sun poured down on the peaceful streets of that classic New England town, and I waited while Abe scanned the front page. Suddenly from his outstretched hands the newspaper came loose and fluttered silently to the sidewalk. I watched it fall and looked up. Abe's face was awash in tears.

---

For everyone in Abe and Henriette's circle of friends, the world was done for. In the Pyrenees where Henriette's parents had gone for so many summers, the news of the Russo-German pact had sent all the vacationers scurrying home, and the hotels and restaurants were emptied. A week later, on September 1, Hitler marched into Poland, France and England declared war on Germany, and World War II started, a bare twenty-one years after the end of the first one. Henriette's mother, Elisa, described it the best anyone could when she wrote to her daughter in West Stockbridge, "The irreparable has happened. It is 1914 all over again. Stay calm."

For the first time in a long time Abe and Henriette were united emotionally. Abe seemed strangely relieved that the war had finally arrived.

As they sat at breakfast one morning in the house on Bleecker Street before Abe went off to his office, he said, "I think I'll go down to my local draft board and try to sign up."

Abe, Henriette, and the
author. West Stockbridge,
Massachusetts, 1940.

"They'll never take you. You're too old and too sick."

"I know, but I feel I should offer America my services."

"Why?"

"When the war lights in the West we shall be in it within a month. Everyone will be needed."

Henriette was not as hopeful. "Too many Americans want to stay neutral."

"At most six months, most probably after January, in 1940," Abe asserted. "Or perhaps they will wait until Parliament and Westminster Abbey are bombed."

"But the reason?"

"It will be found."

Henriette was not convinced. France would be alone against a more powerful Germany. Even together France and England could never match Hitler. She foresaw only disaster.

"No," Abe replied, "the old tricks will not work. Some new ones will have to be thought of. All the Jews will help the Allies and enlist in their armies, of course quietly."

Henriette said nothing.

"Want to make a bet?" Abe said.

Henriette nodded her head. They shook hands. The war bet was on.

# The Blue Vase

*The most flamboyant and entertaining of all the refugees who frequented the house on Bleecker Street was the Russian conductor and composer Igor Bouryanine. Each time he arrived there was an elegantly dressed woman on his arm—never the same one twice. Invariably, one of the guests would call out, "Ah, Igor. You must tell the story of the Blue Vase."*

*Igor, in his heavy Russian-accented English, would reply, "Everyone has heard it already. It is silly to repeat it once again. And besides. I would prefer to play the piano and offer everyone some music."*

*"But there are people here who have never heard you tell it. Gustave over there, he's just come from England."*

*"Ah well," Igor would answer with a heavy sigh.*

*"Quiet, everyone," a guest would call out. People would put down their plates and glasses, stop what they were doing, and prepare to listen to a story that most of them had heard many times over but one that always seemed to captivate them. They had endured similar experiences fleeing the Nazis, yet were unable to talk about them with the humor and dramatic flair of Igor.*

---

*Igor would always appear well dressed in tailored double-breasted suits, as if the misery of the war was incapable of disturbing his innate elegance. His manners were filled with the charm of Old World Russia and he courteously kissed the hands of all the women when presented to them. He was lavishly emotional about what he cared about, of his mother, whom he revered, and of his privileged youth in the Caucasian part of Russia. He had encountered Abe and Henriette one summer while having lunch at the newly opened Grand Hôtel built high on the forested slopes of a small town in the Pyrenees to take advantage of the clear,* crisp air and abundant sunshine. Speaking in Russian, Abe and Igor hit it off right away, and Igor immediately entranced Henriette with the picaresque tale of his escape from Russian communism to Paris, where he had established himself as an orchestra conductor and cellist. Igor had no children of his own and soon became a special friend to me. He showered me with toys, the best a child could dream of having. Once he gave me a big blue box that contained a miniature blue Renault convertible that could be steered by hand. He always addressed me formally as "Monsieur Pierre," or in Russian as "Piotr Veliky," and when we stopped to see him in Paris he always took me shopping for some expensive gift to take home to New York. His apartment, on the suitably named Rue Beethoven, was like a magic castle. There was an immense grand piano in the center of the room beneath a loft balcony under a vast skylight, and I would run up and down the stairs with abandon. At the top I would pose fiercely and cry down like a knight at the top of the battlements, threatening the guests below with all sorts of maledictions that I had picked up in books.

When France was invaded in 1940 and Paris fell to the Germans, we lost track of Igor. Letters to him at the Rue Beethoven were returned marked "undeliverable." Abe and Henriette worried that he might be another of their friends who had vanished into the abyss of a German concentration camp. Or that he might even be dead. But in August that year a letter arrived with a Lisbon return address. It was Igor, writing in his oversized, curving, dramatic orthography—he always used artist pens with flowing nibs—pleading for help to get to America. He had narrowly escaped from Paris, one step ahead of the Nazis, reached the Spanish border at Perpignan, and finally struggled to make his way to Portugal, where he was broke and unable to pay his rent and the landlord was threatening to throw him out on the street. The letter finished with a plea so powerful, it seemed a scream capable of sailing across the ocean to America by itself. In capital letters he howled: "AIDEZ MOI!"

Abe immediately set about finding a way for Igor to get to America. He arranged for emergency help from one of the relief groups, had his rent paid by money order, and after the now habitual complications, including letters of support; transit, exit, and entry visas; ship's tickets; and appeals to refugee groups, Igor sailed from Lisbon and arrived at Ellis Island. But he was obliged to immediately leave the next morning on another ship bound for Colombia, where he had an entry visa. Eventually he entered Canada on another visa, and after another wait and a letter of support from Abe he received a third visa to enter the United States. He took the train to New York and the house on Bleecker Street and arrived for the Christmas holiday of 1940. The turkey was on the table, the guests were already gathered, and a bottle of wine had been opened when Igor rang the bell and climbed the stairs, looking dapper in a clean white shirt, elegant tie, and *freshly pressed suit despite all that had happened to him. At once he fell into the arms of all his friends, overjoyed at his being saved. There were kisses, there were hugs, there was applause. And when the dinner was nearing its end one of the guests exclaimed, "How did you escape? Tell us what happened." It was then that Igor told the tale of the Blue Vase for the first time, an amazing chapter in the saga of his fleeing from the Nazis across the length and breadth of Europe.*

*"I was driving south from Paris by car to escape the Germans with my friend Franck, a pilot who had been wounded, his wife, and his mother," he would be-gin.*

*They had been on the road for three days criss-crossing France on little rural lanes to avoid the major highways where the Nazis were chasing after the fleeing French. Somewhere in the center of France, not far from Poitiers, they had stopped for the night. They had not had a full meal in those three days, and Franck and Igor left the car to go to a nearby farmhouse to buy something from the local farmer. They were greeted by a surly woman dressed in the usual peasant black who refused to offer them anything. Igor told the woman he would pay for what-ever she could spare. But the woman said she had nothing, that the larder was bare. Igor knew this wasn't true. So he tried making his plea more emotional. He pointed to his friend, Franck, and said, "Madame, you see before you a pilot who has been wounded fighting to save France from the Germans." Then he became more dramatic: "Franck, show her your bandaged leg." Franck rolled up his pants to show his wounds. The woman didn't even look.*

*"It's because of cowards like you that France has lost the war. I have no food."*

*"But Madame, take pity, this man nearly gave his life to save France."*

*"I don't believe you. If he was such a hero he should have died instead of try-ing to run away. I have no food, I tell you."*

*Igor felt anger getting the better him. He moved toward the woman. But Franck pulled him away and they went back to the car.*

*Igor shook his head and said, "I was a failure."*

*"It's no use," Franck told him. "Let's just go to sleep. We'll try again tomor-row morning."*

*"I will not accept defeat," Igor said. He refused to believe any French farm woman would be so hard-hearted. There must be a way to reach her. Without an idea in mind, he went back to the farmhouse and pleaded with the woman. He told her of his life in Paris, that he was a musician, that he was from Russia, anything to see what might spark her sympathy. But all she would say was, "It's because of foreigners like you that France lost the war. I tell you I have no food."*

*"I was desperate," Igor continued, "saying whatever I could think of, that*

France was a wonderful country, her people the best in the world, her farmers grew the world's best food, they were the salt of the earth. I kept on and on, from time to time looking to see if I was having any success. Then I noticed out of the corner of my eye that a little boy had crept into the room and was standing near a table with a vase on it." Igor kept on trying to find a way into the woman's heart, but he could not keep his eyes off the little boy who stared at him with a look of fear and suspicion on his face. "The more I noticed the boy, the more nervous he became, and he began to tug at the cloth covering the table on which the vase sat. Suddenly the vase was pulled by the cloth and began to topple off the table. I sprang up." Igor lunged dramatically. "The boy sprang back, terrified by the sudden movement. I jumped toward the table, reached out and grabbed the vase just as it was about to fall to the ground."

The woman cried out, "Ah, my beautiful blue vase!"

"Your vase?"

"Yes, my blue vase, my beautiful blue vase, that I bought at the fair at Argenton."

"I was suddenly inspired. That vase," I said, "that magnificent blue vase. You bought this work of art at a country fair. It's not possible. It's too beautiful."

"You saved my vase. How can I thank you? My beautiful blue vase."

Igor wanted to say, "Give me food and that will be thanks enough." But instead he went on, "I love this vase. I am glad I could save it for you. Let me say to you, Madame, that you could prowl all the antique shops of Paris and you would never find a vase as beautiful with such a magnificent tone of blue. Where did you say you bought it?"

"Argenton. At the fair. You really think it's beautiful?"

"Magnificent is the only word I would use. Allow me, Madame," and Igor rose from the floor and with an ornate bow gave the woman her blue vase. Again he acted the scene, including a flourishing attempt to kiss the woman's hand.

"Monsieur, you have done a wonderful service. Finally, someone who appreciates my blue vase. Wait here. Don't move." The woman turned to the door leading to the next room and yelled, "Françoise, Antoine, come here at once. Come and see what this stranger has told me about my beautiful blue vase that you think is worthless."

The door opened and a man and woman entered. He was in farm clothes and had a droopy, sad look and a heavy mustache, while she was wiping her hands on her apron. Obviously they were the son and daughter-in-law of the woman. "She was picking her teeth with her tongue, and I was certain they had just eaten," said Igor. "Tell them, Monsieur, tell them, what you think of this blue vase, my blue vase that I bought at the fair at Argenton and which they think is ugly. Tell them."

"This vase," Igor began, "is no ordinary object, it is extraordinary. I have been in the business of antiques for many years and know everyone in Paris and I can assure you that this vase, this blue vase, its shape, its color, is a work of art. Your mother is a lucky woman to have spotted it at the fair and realized its beauty and what it is worth."

"You hear, Antoine. Now who's right. The vase is a work of art. I always told you so. This man is from Paris where they know about such things."

Igor was afraid that he might start a family quarrel over the object, so he slowly moved to leave.

"Wait," the woman said. "Stay where you are. I am going to see if we might have any food to offer to people fleeing les sales boches. Go back to your car, Monsieur, and bring your friends here. Antoine, Françoise, go down to the cellar and see what you can find. Perhaps we can spare something. Now!"

"When I returned with my companions the table was set with a magnificent feast, country ham, chicken, bread, tomatoes, wine, cider, cheese. And while the four of us poor refugees stuffed ourselves with the good country food, you know me, I could not remain silent. I kept talking about the blue vase, its beauty, its color, how few people could appreciate such art, even in Paris only a few had the eye to spot such objects. I kept up this conversation until all four of us had finished the food and my friends began to yawn with fatigue. They extended their hands to the woman and thanked her for her kindness. We rose to leave, but I whispered to my three friends that they must say something complimentary about the blue vase.

"Beautiful color," Franck said.

"An amazing find," said his wife.

"A lovely shape," mumbled Franck's mother.

The farm woman said, "No need to leave. You must be very tired. You will sleep here tonight. How can I turn such cultured people out of my home? And you, Monsieur, will have a special room," she said to me. "The bed where I slept when I first became a bride."

---

"And," Igor concluded his story to the enthralled guests, gathered in the house that represented their American safety, "That night I slept the sleep of the most worthy of men. The sheets were of the softest of linen, the bed had been perfumed, and I knew that I would one day make it to America, to this house, to this room, to be with you."

At first there was silence, then there was laughter, and finally applause, which Igor interrupted. "And now I would like to play what I came here to do." He went to the piano and began Beethoven's "Moonlight Sonata," playing it in a way that

*Henriette loved. The slow, rolling chords of the opening bars filled the room. Hen-
riette swayed slowly to the rhythm and Abe sat quietly, a happy smile on his face,
his despair momentarily lifted. Everyone seemed suddenly at peace, able to believe
that there were better things in the world than having to escape from the Nazis.*

7

"I have something to show you," Abe said to me.

We were seated together at the diminutive Cherry Lane Theater located on a twisted street in Greenwich Village. It was March 1942, and what
he took out of the pocket of his winter overcoat was a cream-colored,
three-fold brochure printed in brown ink. My voice boomed out in the tiny
space as I painstakingly read out the words.

"He has been called a radical, a Socialist, a liberal, a reactionary, a Republican and a reformer. He is . . ."

"Not so loud," Abe leaned over and interrupted. "You wouldn't want
everyone to know I've been called those kinds of names, would you?"

I stopped. I had no idea what all those words meant but I had thought
they were compliments. I felt embarrassed. But when Abe leaned over to
me I noticed a little smile on his face. That smile said the brochure was
only for the two of us, no one else. We were sharing a secret. I looked up
at Abe and began again in a whisper.

"He is none of these—yet he is all of them. In twenty-five years he has
fought with or against them whenever and wherever sound social security is at issue."

I knew that Abe would insist I read every word, and I was determined
to do it. But I was a slow reader and struggled to reach the end, nervous
about how he might react if I didn't finish. I lived in fear of his anger, and
I could not forget how he had raged at me when I failed at reading *David
Copperfield*. So I slowly and quietly read on until the lights began to dim
and the first chords of the overture rumbled over the audience. The last
words I read were, "If to be great 'a man must be the servant of a cause
greater than himself,' Abraham Epstein is great."

On that winter day I was eleven and America had been at war against
Germany and Japan for less than six months. The news was bleak, and the
United States was reeling from defeat after defeat. Abe needed some distraction, so together we went to see Gilbert and Sullivan's *Ruddigore*. He
loved the wit and theatricality of their comic operas, and I loved the silly
characters and the patter songs sung by the leading comics. I had memo-

rized nearly all of them and at any and all times would sing them out until I was told firmly to stop. For me *Ruddigore* was the perfect treat. Besides, it wasn't often I had the chance to spend time with Abe alone, doing something we both liked. I was impatient for the first act to end because the second was the scariest part, when the eight malevolent but dead lords of Ruddigore, who up until that moment had only been scenery, paintings on the stone walls of a very gloomy castle, suddenly revolved and came to life. They would lurch down from their frames and sing a grand and grisly song that would send shivers down my spine: "When the Night Wind Howls." The Cherry Lane was once a stable and the stage was tiny, which meant there was room, and that barely, for only two ghosts to step down and sing. The shortage of ghosts probably was also due to a shortage of actors, most of whom were undoubtedly off fighting in Europe or Asia. Nonetheless, when the lights dimmed and the lone piano banged away, the stage was immediately bathed in a scary blue, a spectral glow in which the picture frames revolved to allow those two apparitions to come to life. I was thrilled and grabbed Abe's arm in excitement, oblivious to everything but the duo of ghastly singing and dancing specters. I was alone with my father, joined together in our love for the play, and for once I was not worrying about his anger at some shortcoming in me such as not reading, not easily learning to ride a bike, or being afraid of the water when learning to swim.

---

That spring of 1942 was a time of impending disaster for Abe. The American Association for Social Security was running out of money. At its peak in 1934 the group had raised more than thirty-four thousand dollars. Not a great deal, but still enough to make the association's voice heard. By the end of 1940, fund-raising was down by half. By February 1941, the financial situation seemed hopeless. "Unless increased help is forthcoming at once, the Association will be forced to suspend its activities before long," the bulletin pleaded. The budget was down to nineteen thousand dollars a year, "less than 50 per cent of the expenditures of a few years ago. The situation is desperate . . . please act at once!" During the course of 1941 only small donations dribbled in. Ethel Clyde, who had once been Abe's strongest backer, had little money and was reduced to the occasional twenty-five-dollar contribution. The war was at all times on everyone's mind, including Abe's staunchest supporters. Even Henriette had given in to her fears and become an American citizen on March 16, 1942. Reform in America—especially in social security—was on hold.

Abe decided on a desperate measure. It is doubtful he would have done it if he had not been so worried about the future. He agreed to have a testimonial dinner in his honor to follow the national conference in 1942. The sole purpose, in his view, was to raise money for the association. But when the big day rolled around Abe was more and more depressed, not only by the lack of progress in social security but also by his own physical problems—diabetes, high blood pressure, and continual exhaustion. The Allies' never-ending military defeats, which included the fall of the Philippines, the surrender of Singapore, and Hitler's devastating blitzkrieg into Stalin's Russia, only added to his deep despair.

But there was one wonderful event that lifted his spirits. On August 21, 1941, a little more than three months before the attack on Pearl Harbor, Churchill risked the German submarine dragnet in the Atlantic and sailed from Britain to the icy waters of Placentia Bay, a deserted mining camp on the Newfoundland coast. There, in the fog-shrouded waters, FDR was waiting. (The press had been fooled into thinking he was off on a cruise, and in fact when the presidential yacht was sent as a decoy through the Cape Cod Canal, someone had gone on deck to pose as the president, complete with cigarette holder, pince-nez, and wheelchair.) When Churchill's battleship, the *Prince of Wales,* finally pierced the mist to settle alongside Roosevelt's *Augusta,* a cheer went up from the sailors on board the American cruiser. Churchill was piped on board where Roosevelt stood on his weakened legs to greet the British prime minister. For three days the two leaders held secret meetings far away from anyone's knowledge, and when they finally spoke out, seated side by side and looking frozen on the deck of the *Augusta,* they offered the world a pact that came to be known as the Atlantic Charter. In it they spelled out eight "common principles" for the democratic nations of the world. In the fifth they spoke of the desire "to bring about the fullest collaboration between all nations . . . with the object of securing, for all, improved labor standards, economic advancement and *social security.*" (emphasis added)

When he heard the news, Abe was jubilant and wrote in the bulletin, "As the creator of the term 'social security' and as the organization that has devoted itself to the task of bringing it to the American people, The American Association for Social Security hails the inclusion of this objective in the war aims of the two freest nations on earth . . . The Association dedicates itself to furthering this noble task!" But his announcement lacked its usual feisty confidence. The statement was not a banner headline on the front page, as in the days of the great legislative victories; instead it was buried inside on the bottom of page two. Even more disappointing was that the significance of the Atlantic Charter was lost on the American public. The war news, the air assault on Britain, Japan's victories in China, and when America might enter the conflict, those were the topics that grabbed the headlines. Abe's desire to be included in the significant declaration meant a lot to him—after all he had dreamed up the words and ideas used by Roosevelt and Churchill—but his voice resonated faintly like that of a solitary man crying in the wind of a world about to blow apart.

The three-fold brochure that I read so painstakingly at the Cherry Lane described the program of a testimonial meant to salute the fifteenth anniversary of the American Association for Social Security, to honor as well Abe's twenty-five years of service to the cause, and finally to celebrate his looming fiftieth birthday. On the front in block letters the brochure read, SOCIAL SECURITY AND THE MAN, and on the back in equally large letters, 100 NATIONAL LEADERS PAY TRIBUTE TO THE MAN AND HIS WORK.

The event had been planned for months, its real purpose to raise money—social security must not be forgotten in an America at war. And as the big day drew closer, I was in a fever of excitement. After school I went to the office to help take letters to the post office and pester the secretaries—at home I learned the words and sang the songs that would accompany the festivities. Finally, on the great day, in the afternoon before the testimonial dinner, I was asked to hang around the reception desk at the fifteenth annual conference and run errands. My overwrought energy was relieved a bit when I overheard someone ask for the missing Nelson Rockefeller who was due to deliver a speech. No one had seen him in the building.

"I'll find him," I yelled and darted off before anyone could stop me, weaving and dodging my way through the milling hotel crowd, and just as I arrived at the entrance, I spotted Nelson Rockefeller circling through the revolving doors. I jumped in the air, made an immediate u-turn, and scooted rapidly back through the teeming lobby to the reception desk where I cried out, "He's here! He's coming in! I just saw him!"

Once more the role of Phidippedes, the messenger, seemed right up my alley.

The conference that afternoon was an extraordinary success, later described in a news report as "a thought provoking series of discussions by world famous thinkers and doers . . . a rostrum for national and international leaders to assess the numerous economic, political, military and social factors which will determine the role of social security during the war and in the post war period." There had been a notable list of speakers who spoke on how essential social security was to the war effort. They included Noel Hall, chief counselor of the British Embassy, Paul McNutt, the federal security administrator, William Green, president of the AFL, Senator Wagner from New York, Walter Fuller, the former head of the National Association of Manufacturers, Nelson Rockefeller (who had just begun his political career), reporting on Latin America, and two former cabinet ministers from France and Spain as well. From Abe's viewpoint the most important participant had been Arthur Altmeyer. Altmeyer was then head of the Social Security Board, had been Frances Perkins's right-hand man, and had resolutely backed the Wisconsin Plan, whose concepts Abe abhorred. Now here he was giving a speech that told how he had changed his mind and supported the ideas Abe was fighting for. Things were looking up; there was a positive ring to the chances for real reform. Abe's own deeply felt speech likened social security to "guns, tanks and airplanes" for a nation at war, laws that were not newfangled inventions but "stem from the same flesh and blood reflexes which are responsible for the primitive instinct of self-preservation." This basic instinct was like that of the ancients who "built walls and moats and bulwarks against marauders, so modern societies build walls of social security against the greatest enemy within—insecurity." America was living in dangerous times and solving insecurity was essential. But he warned that the pace of progress has "definitely slackened as vested interests sink their roots deeper into the existing plans." Beneath his words was a feeling that what he had wanted to achieve for America would never happen during his lifetime.

---

That evening at 7:30, April 11, guests gathered in the grand ballroom of the now vanished Murray Hill Hotel in New York. The festivities began when the audience of more than two hundred rose and together sang the "Star Spangled Banner." America was at war, people were fearful, and it was important to show one's patriotism. The music continued with Renee Treer of the Chicago Lyric Opera singing several arias by Verdi and Rossini. Then the toastmaster, Abe's old friend the lawyer Walter Frank, set the tone for the evening when he got up, pointed at Abe, and said, "The program is carefully calculated to bring you to bed in time to have a nice night's sleep, and then to get up early and start drawing up new social legislation." There was laughter and applause. "It is to be hoped that it is a bill to prohibit more than forty hours a week for social reformers," Frank continued, and there was more laughter and applause. Then another speaker got up and said, "somehow he had the feeling that when Abe got to his office the first thing in the morning he called in his secretary and said, 'Take a law.'" Again laughter. A clergyman compared him to the Apostle Paul. A congressman declared that while he did not wholly agree with Abe's philosophy, "it is with a considerable degree of temerity that I interrogate him." Abe's professor and mentor from the University of Pittsburgh, Frank Tyson, told the crowd that he was going to make sure that the university gave Abe "the doctorate he so richly deserves." Messages of congratulations were read from three governors, four senators, and six congressmen. The legendary mayor of New York, Fiorello LaGuardia, was particularly extolling. William Green, head of the AFL, and George Meany, head of the CIO, were on the testimonial committee, as well as historian Charles Beard and writer Fannie Hurst. People had fun, and the dinner was more in the nature of a "roast" as various spoken profiles testified. It was a lighthearted evening, interspersed with popular songs such as "Pop Goes the Weasel," only with verses written for the occasion:

> Our Abe is a remarkable man
>    He grew by easy stages,
> Nobody can as well as he can
>    Write brilliant pages.
> Can master all as far as it goes
>    Or anything you mention,
> When Abe gets in his telling blows
>    SOUND is your pension!

Another, sung to the tune of "Frankie and Johnnie," made fun of Abe's contrarian rages.

> Abe is a man of refinement,
>    Able to come into his own
> Handling all sorts of obstructions
>    In the cutest, sweetest tone.
> He's done his best,
>    But he's done it wrong.

At the end there was a satirical version of "God Bless America," which made fun of Abe's battle with the Social Security Board:

> They get retorts
> To their reports

They just didn't go far enough.
God help the S.S. Board
When Abe gets rough.

One of Abe's associates, Professor Eveline Burns, another authority in social security, did the final honors in a speech where she called Abe "a bully, bossy, brutal and bumptious." She went on and said "that one of the worst cases of poetic license I ever heard" was in a song they had all just sung that referred to Abe's "handling all sorts of obstructions in the cutest, sweetest tone." There was laughter, which Abe interrupted by yelling out, "I didn't write that, you know." This got another laugh. Eveline Burns continued to lambaste Abe to everyone's delight and finished by quoting a high Washington official who had told her that "the one trouble with Abe is that he is too damned honest." Wouldn't that be "a fine thing," she ended, "if after twenty-five years in the field of social security somebody would say about us that the only trouble with us was that we were too damned honest." Henriette also came in for a share of the cheers when one speaker turned to her and said, "what do you think of Mrs. Epstein?" The audience rose and applauded.

On the surface the evening was a triumph, an outpouring of love from the people Abe cherished. But underneath there was desperation lurking. It came out in Abe's speech, the one he gave to show his gratitude. The entire evening "left him in a state of mixed emotions," he began, "because one cannot express with any degree of coherence the gratitude and happiness that such an occasion brings." The future was on his mind. "There is only one thing left and that is I hope I will have a few more years to carry on. Even though my doctor says I cannot do it . . . I should like to continue doing the work of Social Security. During the last few years every time I have gone to see my doctor, he did not believe I would live to see an anniversary celebration of this sort. I did suspect that, perhaps, at my funeral some of you might say a kind word about me, and while I knew that was going to come it was not so much a terribly kind thought. Therefore, for me to really have lived to witness this is something." Mortality, perhaps premonition, led him to think of all those who had gone before and served the cause, particularly I. M. Rubinow. Then, without warning, his thoughts veered, and he turned toward Henriette and said she was "a very obstreperous person. She will never agree with me. I think this week was the first time she said my speech was all right." The audience laughed and he went on, "I told her I had never received such a compliment from her before. But I will say this: she stood by me during those bitter fights, which took away my sleep, my desire for food, and some of the most productive years of my life, because it is not easy to be fighting with my own friends, and nobody cherishes being called a sellout—but she agreed with me on every one of those fights and said never one word against my course of conduct. This is an intellectual accomplishment for which she deserves great tribute." Henriette tried to hide her emotions, but some thought her close to tears. It was an extraordinary moment for her, one that she never expected, and one that, uncharacteristically, she remained silent about for the rest of her life.

A student of Abe's had written a short biography to be given out at the testimonial dinner and in it he quoted Abe's repeated use of the phrase, "Cut out the bouquets!" Abe was blunt and would almost never let anyone compliment him about an article or some legislative accomplishment. It was always "cut out the bouquets," and on to the next job as far as he was concerned. Earlier that day, at the lunch for the fifteenth annual conference, Wilbur Cohen, who had been involved with social security from the very beginning, told Abe, "Well, we did it, didn't we?" referring to the various improvements in social security that had taken place. Abe's reply isn't recorded but his speech that night may have been his answer.

It is going to be a terrific job to think of myself as just sitting down, satisfied with the way everything in social security is going . . . so on the one hand I am worried as to how I am going to carry on and in another way I am worried as to what I am going to carry on. (Laughter) How am I going to carry on the Association without a fight? (Laughter) After all I have only one interest—and I am very narrow minded in that—and that is to be able to carry on in terms of social security. The work is not done and if you believe the Association is really performing a job which is worth while . . . delegate yourself, each one of you, to see that our financial condition is improved . . . our total budget is only about $18,000 a year. It is not much for the work we are doing. I think we deserve it, for the country needs us more than ever.

When the evening was over Abe had been lionized. And he had pleaded—perhaps begged would be a better word—for money. But a sense of weariness seemed to lie under Abe's final words. It sounded as if he was ready to call it quits. His high-pitched Russian accent had sounded weak, more strident than before, as he tried to overcome his feelings. In appearance he looked like a shell of the once-energetic militant who had brought the words "social security" to the American people. The few wisps of hair on his head were pure white. His face looked drained of energy, he had gained weight, and he no longer sat bolt upright and attentive, but instead slumped, leaning to one side as if his body could not hold him together. In photographs taken at the dinner he seemed at times to stare into space, his expression empty. He looked like an old man, yet he was not yet fifty.

Underneath the laughter there was a depressing secret about all the recent fund-raising. Abe had been hoping for fifteen or twenty thousand dollars. But the net result after all the publicity was a check presented to the association for only $2,290. Two speakers at the dinner pledged another $1,100. It was never going to be enough.

# A Photograph

*Something has always bothered me about that testimonial dinner. I have many memories of that time. Among them are the afternoon trips to the office to help the secretaries,* Ruddigore *at the Cherry Lane, the three-fold brochure announcing the dinner, Abe's words to me, the scary ghosts, learning the songs to be sung at the dinner, the mad dash to find the elusive Rockefeller; all that has remained vivid. But I have no memory of being there. I was not allowed to go and for years I wondered why Abe and Henriette had kept me at home. All I had in my hands was a transcript of words that I had never heard spoken.*

*One day, when I was prowling through the grubby back room after Henriette's death, I spotted a cracked picture frame among several stacked against a wall. It was a long, horizontal photograph of one of the conferences, of which I had seen many others. The glass was broken, the frame was detached, and I pulled it out carefully. There was a date written on the bottom, "April 11, 1942," and at first I thought it must be the official photograph of the annual conference that afternoon. But beneath I saw more writing: "Abraham Epstein Testimonial Party." Rapidly I scanned the picture of all the people seated at the tables in the ballroom. I located Abe at the center of the dais, flanked by his friend Walter Frank at his left, and next to Frank I found Henriette. Far down the table on the right was Dave Saposs, perhaps Abe's oldest friend, who had also come to America to get an education. Down front, at the dinner tables closest to the photographer, were many faces I recognized: Wilbur Cohen and his wife, J. Douglas Brown and his wife, Lionel Naftalason and his wife, Walter Plaut, Florence Bass, Ruth Bernstein, Sol Bloom, Konrad Bercovici and his wife, Naomi, on and on it went, people I recalled looking just as they had when I was eleven. I also found Abe's two sisters, Gertrude and Esther, seated just under the dais and not far from their brother. But the one person I really wanted to see I could not find.*

The testimonial dinner for Abraham Epstein, April 11, 1942.

*I removed the broken glass and frame, tossed them into the garbage, and put the picture aside. It rolled itself up like an ancient piece of papyrus. I unrolled it, tried to flatten it, and began scanning it with the aid of a magnifying glass, giving myself one more chance. My eyes moved slowly from table to table, like a surveyor marking a quadrant, remembering more names, asking myself who some of the others might be. I moved slowly up the photograph, again table by table, and near the top, off to the side, I spotted some of my favorite people from that time. The first were two of Abe's secretaries, the DiDonna sisters, Phyllis and Mary, who had been there since the office opened in 1927. They were like family, gave me Christmas presents, came to visit in the country, sat me at their desks and let me fold envelopes. Next to them was one of my favorite "uncles," Harry Elias, the publicity man who had told Abe he needed to use photographs to dramatize the plight of the aged poor. And finally I spotted Igor, my great friend Igor, looking dapper as ever, he of the wonderful presents, who had nicknamed me "Pytor Veliky." Between Harry and Igor was a smaller face peering out from between the two men.*

*My God, I thought, is that me? Yes, there I was, dressed for the occasion in jacket and tie, at the back of the room, a big mop of unruly hair prominently visible, being shepherded by my two favorite "uncles," Harry and Igor.*

*Abe and Henriette had wanted me there all along, they had wanted me to share in that remarkable moment in the life of my father—only three weeks before it ended. But I have only that picture to remind me of what my presence meant to them.*

8

The long hours of work preparing for the fifteenth annual conference and the testimonial dinner had been exhausting and emotional, so Abe and Henriette decided to take a few days off. They drove up to the Berkshires to see the leaves come back and the flowers begin to bloom. But when they returned on Sunday night, Abe was not well. He went to bed immediately, hoping to shake it off, but when morning came he felt no better. He was unusually tired and his face pale. Henriette told him not to go to the office. Abe would not listen and tried to get up, but had almost no energy. He lay back down, exhausted, and stayed at home for the rest of the day. Henriette called the doctor, who told her to tell Abe to stay in bed until he could get there to examine him. He promised to be there early that evening. Henriette begged her husband to remain under the covers, but he ignored her and kept slowly getting out of bed to make telephone calls. She became more and more distraught. Abe would not listen to her begging him to rest, even though he felt worn out each time he got up to use the phone. The doctor arrived late that night, and when he came up the stairs he found Abe sitting in an armchair in pajamas and dressing gown reading one of the five newspapers he read on a daily basis. The doctor was firm.

"Get back in bed, Abe," he said.

Abe went back under the covers, and the doctor listened to his heart and took his pulse.

"Abe," he said. "It's your heart again. It's very serious this time."

Over the last several years Abe's heart had become weaker. He had been told again and again to slow down, not to work such long hours, not to travel so frequently, advice he had for the most part ignored. The diabetes that developed in 1939 had become more severe and every two or three days, with Henriette standing by, he plunged a large metal needle laden with insulin into his arm. Beginning with his student days in Pittsburgh he always seemed to have a cigarette in his hand, judging by the photo record. At one point he had indulged in long Turkish and Russian ones with their pouch of powerful tobacco fixed at the end of a paper tube. But a few months before he been told to stop altogether. Now the doctor emphatically told him he must remain in bed. There was no other choice. No work of any kind, he admonished. No other exertion. His heart must rest. "But he won't listen," Henriette interrupted, frantic. "He only wants to go to the office. No matter what you say it will have no effect."

The doctor, who knew Abe well, said he would arrange for nurses to come the next day to see that he followed orders. He told Henriette he would be by as well to see how the patient was doing. Henriette asked the doctor for some pill to quiet her husband. She knew she could not control his overactivity, but the doctor had nothing to offer.

I was already asleep when the doctor came that night, but the next morning I was told that I could not go in and see Abe because he was sick and needed rest. When I came out of school that afternoon, I found the mother of one of my school mates waiting. She took me to her house, where I had dinner. Later, when I returned home I was asked to go directly to my room and to be careful not to make any noise. Abe needed sleep. My bedroom was right next to that of my parents; only a doorway separated us, which I often banged through. But now the door was locked. By the middle of the week I was staying overnight with my best playmate from across the garden, Mickey Rosenau. We were always outside together, throwing balls, bicycling, inventing games; his nickname for me was "Goofy," and mine for him was "Dopey." We were often uncontrollable and our parents frequently had to separate us. But now we were free to fool around together at all hours. I did not go home for the rest of the week, nor did I see Abe.

He was not supposed to have visitors, but Henriette could not keep them away. Some came from work, others were friends who wanted to see how he was doing. He would not stay in bed; instead, in pajamas and robe, he was up and down, talking, making phone calls, dictating letters to one of his secretaries at the office. Although there were nurses present on a twenty-four-hour basis, they made little headway against their obstinate patient. On Saturday there was no school but I still did not return home; instead I rushed off with Mickey and his mother to see Charlie Chaplin in The Gold Rush, which had just opened. I laughed hysterically at Charlie in his little wooden cabin teetering on the edge of the cliff, and at his wonderful hands doing the "bun dance" while he waited for the girl who never showed up. That afternoon the two of us giggled and horsed around trying to imitate Charlie, and that night I was still staying at Mickey's. On Sunday morning the two of us were whisked off by car to Bear Mountain where we raced around in the warm spring weather flying balsa wood airplanes that we had made from kits. Finally, at the end of the day I was taken home for the first time in a week. When I reached my room on the fourth floor everything seemed very hushed and empty. My mother greeted me at the door to my parents' bedroom. Their bed was made up. There was no one in it.

"They've taken Dad to the hospital," she said.

I nodded, as if I understood. But I had been gone all week and I was not sure what had happened.

"It will help him to get better. Tomorrow after school we will go there and see him."

The word "hospital" suddenly made me nervous. I knew about the nurses. There had been whispered phone calls about me to Mickey's mother, but I did not want to know what was going on. I had driven away my fear by playing with my mates, going to the movies, giggling at the dinner table with Mickey. Now I was back home where everything seemed to have changed. My father was gone, he was in a hospital, and such places were full of sick people. I was suddenly gripped by fear. I was terrified of what Abe might look like if I went to see him. I looked up at Henriette and tried to say, "No."

---

Only a week earlier there had been the optimism of the fifteenth annual conference and in the evening the gaiety of the testimonial party. Despite the gloom of war, the crowd seated at tables for ten among the fluted Grecian columns of the formal banquet hall of the Murray Hill Hotel had reveled in songs and jokes at Abe's expense. But it was obvious to many that he had not seemed like the terrier of old. The speech he gave to close out the evening reflected his countenance, a disturbing look of pessimism and exhaustion.

There were serious frictions at work that Abe had been unable to clear up. For one, the board was divided over his continuous attacks on the New Deal. A number of them felt that his outspoken public criticism was causing membership to drop and revenue to disappear. And they were split over what to do about his poor health that had put much of the association's business on hold. The issue needed to be faced. But no one dared confront Abe. Others, who had only known him by his reputation for action, were shocked by his wan, exhausted look when they came to see him.

Milton Konvitz, then a young law professor at New York University, was one. He had asked if he could see Abe about starting a branch of the association in New Jersey. He admired Abe's cause and wanted to be part of it. But when he came for the meeting he was "startled to find him lying on the couch in his small office . . . a rather depressing scene of an ailing man in a darkened room. He was very courteous and apologetic. I called on him several times, sat beside the couch and we talked, mostly about the political situation of the time." Abe was not able to do much to help him, and Konvitz never succeeded in getting a branch started, but the casual relations he developed with Abe during his trips to the office left him with "memories of a fleeting friendship with a remarkable person." But his main memory was that the man he had wanted to meet was a very sick one.

Into the bargain, Abe was teaching at both Brooklyn College and NYU, which included inviting many of his students over to the house, where late in the evening I would hear his piping voice animating the discussions. This was Abe at his best, always the educator, carefully steering his students toward his beliefs. Even in summer, at the house he rented in the Berkshires during the war, despite orders to take it easy by "lying on his back and doing nothing," he would seek out college students serving as camp counselors. They would come over and be served lemonade, and Abe would slyly probe their political awareness. The one who made the greatest impression on me was Seymour, dark, handsome, and very muscular. Abe had engaged him to teach me how to swim at the camp across the road. I was scared of the water, but Seymour was a reassuring physical presence and eventually taught me how to put my head under and not be afraid. He was a student at City College where the Communist Party had made serious inroads, and when Abe found out, he invited Seymour over to check on his political leanings. It did not take him long to realize that the Communists were trying to snare another naive college student, and that Seymour was close to actually joining the party. Abe had to act, so he invited Seymour over to spend the evenings at the house whenever he was off. There, on the back porch, Abe worked his magic. The porch was away from the road, small and intimate with room for only two chairs, and in the shadows of night looked out on the leafy trees of an old, badly maintained apple orchard. I would hear Abe's voice in the darkness rise and fall as I lay above in my bed reading before falling asleep. Seymour rarely said a word; instead he seemed awed at all the attention he was getting from a man like Abe, and over the course of a week it was obvious that the Communists would never get their hooks into Seymour. He became a regular dinner guest, my swimming improved, Seymour gained a sound understanding of social security, and Abe seemed less grouchy. Consciously or not, Abe was determined to leave a legacy among the youth he taught.

Abe's failing health was also the cause of a power struggle over who would control the association should he die. Herman Gray, a member of the board, began to maneuver for a takeover. By promising her the future job of executive secretary, Gray enlisted the aid of Abe's assistant, Adele Bloom, believed by many to be a card-carrying Communist. She had access to all the files and finances. The board itself was in the dark about what Gray was up to. He had only approached those he thought could be relied on to support his moves, directors who were not happy with Abe's confrontational policies. Henriette had little knowledge of the extent of the schemes to replace her husband. She was not a member of the board and was unaware of what went on at meetings. Her contributions had always been in the area of fund-raising and publicity, never policy. But rumors began to reach her. Mary and Phyllis DiDonna, Abe's loyal secretaries, warned her that Adele Bloom was up to something. While Abe lay sick at home, she had been spending time in his office with the door shut. From time to time she would come out with files under her arm. Bloom tried to avoid the two women; she knew how loyal they were to Abe. But they disliked Bloom and thought her dismissive and ambitious. They passed their suspicions on to Henriette, who despite her worries about Abe's heart condition decided to take steps to counter Gray and Bloom. She came up with the idea of a letter for Abe to sign:

Should anything happen to me suddenly during this illness, it is my last wish that my dear wife: Henriette Marie Louise Castex Epstein, cofounder with me and life member of the American Association for Social Security should succeed me. She should have all my papers, writings and worldly goods and use as she thinks best . . . for Social Security. I want it to be remembered that without her there would have been no Association. We both coined the word Social Security, she and she alone will one day be able to tell the story of a great movement from its humble beginnings to its tremendous developments. I, who have done all in my power to bring about security to the widows and orphans and aged . . . want to be sure everything will be done to help my wife and my son Pierre, both of whom I love more than I can express. Indeed I cannot make this plea strong enough with all the life that is left in me, to my friends, my associates and the members of the Social Security Board. May they do all in their power to help her carry on the tasks I am leaving in her hands.

The document was witnessed by two people, one of whom was the ever-faithful Igor Bouryanine. Abe's signature is a nearly illegible scrawl;

his hand so lacked strength that he was barely able to handle the pen. The very next day—the Sunday I was flying planes at Bear Mountain—Abe left the house for the last time in an ambulance. The letter had been drafted and signed at home the day before.

Henriette's greatest fear was not that Abe might die. It was that if he did she would probably be shut out of the work to which she had devoted her life. Her parents would be unable to help her. France had been occupied by the Germans for two years, and communicating with them was difficult. If anything should happen to Abe, she would be alone with a twelve-year-old boy on her hands. And nowhere to turn.

Henriette picked me up after school that Monday and we went up to the Polyclinic Hospital, a square, ordinary building, its outside made of sickly green bricks. Inside, the walls were tiled with the same green color, a cold industrial look. As we moved down the corridor with its many doors open to the rooms of the sick, I grew anxious. From time to time I glimpsed a hospital bed with someone under white sheets lying in it. When we arrived at Abe's room I was totally unprepared for what confronted me. From the door I took in a large, semitransparent dome. Inside it, far away, lay the pale figure of my father. His bald head, the chalk sheets, the total lack of color, made him look less than human. I stayed by the door, afraid of going closer. He waved to me and seemed to say a few words, but the pulsing hiss of the oxygen being fed into the tent made it difficult to hear him. Even when Henriette approached and tried to talk it was still not clear that she could understand him. Abe waved me in and I moved warily toward the bed. He said something. I tried to understand, but I could not.

"How are you, Dad?" was all I could think of to say.

I waved to him and moved back to the door. Henriette tried talking to him again and shortly after that failed conversation, we left. I felt huge relief to be outside of that green building. But two days later we returned, and again I was scared when I entered the room. I did not want to look at my father, at the ghostly presence under the oxygen tent. I stayed as far away as I could. All I wanted was to get out of there, to go back to the garden to play with my friends and forget about what I was seeing. On Friday Henriette wanted to take me on a third visit. I begged not to go. I was terrified of being in the same room as the white figure under the gauze tent, a man I could not recognize but whose look frightened me. She didn't insist. She went and I stayed home. I went down into the garden and wiped away my fears with a snappy game of catch, an effort at masking my guilt about not going to the hospital.

During the day Henriette was desperate to be with Abe, to see him, to talk with him, despite his weak voice and the hissing oxygen tent that made hearing so difficult. But at night, in the lonely quiet of the house, she wrote letters, covering sheets of paper with her neat French schoolgirl handwriting, asking Abe's friends to write him some cheering words. She begged Frank Tyson, Abe's devoted mentor at the University of Pittsburgh, to send good news about his promised fund-raising: "It's the only thing that will pull him out of his present condition . . . do all you can to spare him worries and anguish." She wanted someone to tell him, other than herself, that things were looking up, that he should have faith in the future. Wilbur Cohen and Arthur Altmeyer, both with the Social Security Board in Washington, promptly responded with uplifting letters. Henriette read them out loudly and slowly to Abe under his tent. He looked up and smiled, and she thought that his spirits had been lifted. "The next day he asked me to read them again," she told both men in her reply. "He was so happy, remembering Arthur's speech of approval at the annual conference even as he was then in an oxygen tent fighting his last battle." That battle was ending. She knew she would soon lose the only man she had ever cared for.

---

Years later a cousin of Abe's, training to be a nurse at that same time in that same hospital, gave me her impressions. She had stopped by to see him each day at the end of her shift and tried having a little light conversation with him through the barrier of the tent.

"After all," she told me, "he was my famous cousin and it was the very least I could do." But he didn't have much to say despite her best attempts. Finally, when I asked her to remember what he might have looked like, she replied, "He looked like he had lost the will to live."

---

Early in the morning on Saturday, May 2, the day after I had begged not to go to the hospital, I was seated in the dining room with Henriette having breakfast. The phone rang and she answered. A doctor from the hospital was on the line, one she did not know. Abe had suddenly taken a bad turn. There was a blood clot in his veins that they could do nothing to dissolve—this was before anticoagulants—and it was in danger of traveling to his heart. She should come to the hospital right away. She put down the phone and instantly let out an unearthly scream, like that of an animal that had been mortally gored. I was frozen in fear by a sound that still lives in me. There was a moment of unnerving stillness, then Henriette fled into the bedroom where Abe had lain less than a week earlier. I could see her through the door from the dining room, where I was afraid to move. She flung herself at his bed, crossing her hands in prayer; enormous sobs over-whelmed her and through anguished sounds I could hear her howl, "Please God, don't let him die! Don't let him die!" I didn't move, my eyes were fixed on my mother, pounding on the bed covers like a wild, fright-ened animal, pleading for mercy from the abandoned God of her Catholic girlhood. She kept on wailing, again and again, chanting, "Don't let him die! don't let him die!" Then the phone rang again. I watched her run back into the kitchen and pick up the instrument. Another doctor was on the line. His only words were: "Mr. Epstein is dead."

Henriette immediately left for the hospital, hoping for her last glimpse of Abe before they took him away. But she was startled when she came to his room. Two people were just leaving, Herman Gray and Adele Bloom. They were holding papers in their hands, and she was certain they had tried to get Abe to sign something. But what? And who had told them he was dying and why had they gotten there before her?

Henriette was so stunned that she could only stammer, "What are you doing here?"

The bald-headed Gray, always immaculately dressed in a stylish busi-ness suit, was a smooth talker and apologized for the intrusion. "I'm so sorry, Henriette, so sorry," he said. Bloom stood to one side, slightly be-hind, as if she wanted to disappear from Henriette's view, and said nothing. Together, they scampered down the corridor, with their papers grasped in front, hidden from Henriette's view.

What arrangements had they made? was the thought that came to Hen-riette's mind.

The days that followed were intense and my memory of them is hazy. The house was full of many people I had never seen before. The air was frenzied and the rooms crowded—a man I did not know was talking on the telephone about the funeral—several others were making lists of those who should be told—another was suggesting the names of speakers for the service. Everyone seemed to be talking at once. Henriette was on the couch, her arms held firmly by two women who were trying their best to restrain her agitation. She would fling them aside at times and wander around the room, huge wrenching sobs pouring forth, while people tried to get her seated again. Her hysteria dominated the frantic atmosphere.

No one paid much attention to me, and I moved to a corner of the room, next to the solid safety of a prized Louis XV cabinet with a marble top where I hoped I might remain invisible. A large vase of flowers stood there, giving forth a pungent, wild odor that made me feel protected, like a smoke screen. I stayed there for a long time, doing my best to hide. The scent that surrounded me at that moment has lingered with me for many years, and from time to time when I find myself in a similar room, with any sort of flowers, seeping a vaguely similar odor, that frenzied after-noon comes surging back to me, the babble of voices, my mother's hyste-ria, and in particular my own frightened, wide-eyed bewilderment.

Matters moved very quickly after that because Jews are supposed to be buried within twenty-four hours. On May 3 Abe's obituary was printed in the New York Times, the Herald Tribune, and later that week in Time mag-azine. The Times, whose editors had always been great backers of Abe and his work, devoted two columns and a photograph to the story of his life:

> Abraham Epstein, American's leading advocate of sound social secu-rity for the last quarter century and outspoken critic of crackpot schemes, whose book, Insecurity—A Challenge to America, is regarded by experts as a primary source book . . . died yesterday. Until his death he fought for reform in the unemployment insurance system and for the enact-ment of health insurance . . . he was also actively engaged in drafting plans for a post-war program of social security. These activities were characteristic of his entire career, spent fighting for social reforms, re-gardless of his personal welfare. For many years his frail, five-foot fig-ure, his bald head and his high pitched voice were familiar attributes of Congressional and legislative hearings. He dared the power of the Roo-sevelt Administration, he also crossed swords with Labor . . . his views were first ignored, then hotly contested, but finally accepted in the main when the act was modified in 1939.

The funeral was held on May 4 at Riverside Chapel in New York, a large, somber establishment where many prominent Jews have had their farewell ceremony. More than two thousand people crowded into the chapel. The principal eulogy was delivered by Bishop McConnell, the president of the association, who had held the post since Abe had opened his office in New York. Another was given by Steven Wise, by then the best-known rabbi in America, an old personal friend and a member of Abe's board from the very first days. I came with Henriette before the hall had filled, accompanied by an entourage of friends and relatives of Abe's. Many in the seated crowd tried to talk to her and touch her as we went down the aisle. I was swept along with them. Someone tried to steer me to a seat, but the throng was such that I was forced to move with it. Whoever was meant to watch over me soon lost track. I was enveloped by people who were unaware of my presence and swept along with the group into a side chapel where Abe's body lay in his coffin, open to anyone who wished to view him. I had no idea of what I was supposed to do. The group of friends with Henriette quickly left, and there I was alone staring at my father in his casket. I could barely see him, it was only a moment and I did not have time to become scared, because someone suddenly grabbed me by the arm and yanked me out, muttering as they steered me to the door, "That child should not be alone in here." I was then brought to the front row and seated next to my father's brothers and sisters. Someone held my arm again to make sure I stayed there. I stared straight ahead at an enormous bank of flowers just below the speaker's chair. Suddenly the rustling stopped, there was a hush, and the coffin was wheeled in from the side room. It came to a rest right in front of me and there was my father's face inside, now transformed into a fearsome image. He had been livened up with color, but he looked like no one I had ever seen; instead he had turned into a terrifying waxed mask. I was afraid to move. Who was that man? How could he be my father? I stared petrified at that gruesome facsimile for the entire service. I was afraid it might rise and look straight at me.

The burial took place at a cemetery on Long Island. A large mound of earth was piled up next to a hole in the ground. The casket was lowered. I was told to pick up some dirt and throw it down into the pit, and when I did the scattering crackle of the pebbles against the wood startled me. We did not leave the cemetery until Abe's grave had been completely filled in and a mound of earth piled on top. As we started to walk away I looked back and noticed that next to the fresh grave there was a stone with lettering on it—that of his mother whom he had brought to America twenty years earlier. She had never wanted to leave her impoverished Russian village and the grave of her husband, but Abe's will had been the stronger. Now despite the never-settled conflict between the two of them, they would face eternity side by side. She had died only seven months before.

The next day Henriette went back to the office at 22 East Seventeenth Street, the small set of rooms overlooking Union Square where Abe had spent the last fifteen years. The house on Bleecker Street seemed empty of life. The crowds and relatives who had overflowed the rooms in the last two days had gone, returning to the routines of their lives. Henriette was determined to do the same, and the day after Abe was put into the ground she went to work to send out renewals and brochures, and to prepare the transcript of the fifteenth and last conference for publication, doing what she always did. She was determined to carry on—she had promised Abe in the hospital—it was her duty. But once seated at her desk she felt nervous. The office was quiet, and without Abe nearby in his accustomed place as protection she was unsure of who would be running things. She kept on working, diligently sorting out the papers she had not tended to in the last few weeks. But she not could help being drawn to the closed door of Abe's office. Finally, she couldn't stand it any longer and got up to see where Abe had always sat, opened the door, and was frightened to see someone sitting at his desk going through his papers. It was Adele Bloom, Abe's assistant, whom she had found in Abe's hospital room clutching papers. Henriette paused at the door, not knowing what to do. Suddenly she burst out. "All those papers are private. That desk belonged to Mr. Epstein. How dare you touch those papers."

Bloom looked up, stared at Henriette as if she had never seen her before, and cooly replied, "You have nothing to do with this. Mr. Epstein was secretary of an association. And you have nothing to do with it. Now please leave."

Henriette was numb. She had not been aware of how fast things had been moving behind her back. She turned and went back to her desk, but her heart was pounding. She was angry, could not work, and returned home.

Henriette continued going to the office every day for a few hours and sent out the monthly renewal letters for membership and subscriptions to the bulletin. She kept to her desk and avoided any contact with Adele Bloom. But when the board convened for its initial meeting after Abe's death, the first one to arrive was Mary K. Simkovitch, a tall, imposing, outspoken woman, the founder of Greenwich House and a well-known leader in the settlement house movement. She noticed Henriette and in her commanding manner said, "The board meeting is about to begin and you are not a member. You will have to leave."

Henriette felt she was being treated like a disobedient student by an overbearing headmistress. She glared at Simkovitch and said, "Mrs. Simkovitch, I do not intend to leave. I have important work to do." There was a moment of silent confrontation, and finally Simkovitch went into Abe's office, where the meeting was to be held, and shut the door. Henriette had no idea what might be taking place inside but kept to her desk, out of the way, doing whatever work she could. She was anxious, but was now determined to remain a presence in the office and would not let herself be taken for granted. She knew she had allies among some of Abe's major associates who wanted the association continued and also wanted her to be involved with it. She had intended to call them, but the conspiracy against her had evolved very rapidly. She waited at her desk, and an hour later the door to Abe's office opened and Adele Bloom came out. She closed the door behind her and walked straight to Henriette, who did not look up. Suddenly Bloom thrust out her hand and grabbed a paper that Henriette was holding.

"What is this?" she said. "What are you doing? From now on you are going to take orders from me. I am appointed."

"Appointed what?" Henriette asked.

"Acting secretary," Bloom retorted.

"Why? Who told you so?"

"The board of directors."

Henriette noticed the triumphant look on Bloom's face. She was shattered. No one had said a word to her in advance about this possible change. Even more surprising, she found out later, no one had even informed those board members who disagreed with Gray that a special meeting had been called to find Abe's replacement. Gray had been trying to move policies in a direction he favored: more state involvement in unemployment insurance and less emphasis on national plans for it and health insurance. This made sense to him since he was an important figure on the New York State Unemployment Board, but not very well known on the national level. Abe's vision had always been a larger one and most members of the board favored it. That is why they served—they believed in Abe. But Gray saw his chance and had moved fast. He kept opposition board members ignorant about plans to decide the future, and had cajoled Mrs. Simkovitch and the aging president of the board, Bishop McConnell, into supporting his moves by installing his proxy, Adele Bloom, as acting secretary. It had all happened before Henriette knew it was even a possibility, like a coup d'état.

As Henriette sat at her desk, absorbing the unsettling news, Mrs. Simkovitch came out of the office, walked straight over and told her that she would no longer be needed at the office. She knew that Simkovitch did not approve of the association spending so much money on the monthly bulletin and on publications explaining social security. She had wanted to cut down the overhead and had had a running battle with Abe on the issue. He, of course, had always believed strongly in the educational mission of the group, but now that he was dead, she would be able to get her way and cut expenses.

"We will not be publishing any more," the ramrod-straight Simkovitch told her. "That includes future issues of the bulletin and the proceedings of the last national conference. So you can go home now. Your job is no longer needed."

Henriette walked out of 22 East Seventeenth Street that day facing, as she later put it, "a future without money, little insurance from Abe, and a heavily mortgaged house." Worse, she knew that no one involved with the association would help her get a job anywhere else. She had devoted her entire life to the work and Abe had wanted her to do all she could to continue it. She had promised. She had always been in the office and had done all sorts of tasks, always alongside Abe; her life had been devotion to the association. "But it was not to be," she wrote down. "I just simply went home from that office, with nothing but a handful of rain which slipped through my fingers."

What was most upsetting to Henriette, aside from despair at her abandonment, was the fact that the proceedings of the fifteenth and last annual convention would not be printed. The wonderful speeches from the British minister, and the federal security administrator, Paul McNutt, and in particular the words of the chairman of the Social Security Board, Arthur Altmeyer, praising Abe and his ideas, would never be available to newspapers, libraries, and the general public. And Abe's powerful words about social security being like tanks, guns, and airplanes for a nation at war would be forever lost.

Henriette got in touch with the members of the board who had been ignored by Gray, such as Douglas Brown and Steven Wise, and they were furious with the elderly Bishop McConnell for allowing the secretive coup by Herman Gray and Adele Bloom. They insisted in letters and subsequent meetings that Henriette be consulted on the future of the association. A tentative compromise was reached when she was asked to write Abe's biography for the bulletin. She worked on it over the summer with the help of one of Abe's students, Fred Preu, who had written the biographical handout at Abe's testimonial. Several board members tried to tell Bishop McConnell that Adele Bloom was a Communist, but he really didn't feel it was his job to hire and fire. Still, other employees, who had been working for Abe since he first opened his doors, could not stand working for Bloom. They included Abe's personal secretary, Belle Frendel, and the DiDonna sisters. They quit even though it was still hard to find jobs during the aftermath of the depression. All through 1942 and 1943 the American Association for Social Security drifted, published nothing, held no conferences, seemed to exist only as a memorial to Abraham

Abe's loyal staff. From left to
right: Belle Frendel, his secretary,
and Phyllis and Mary DiDonna,
office secretaries. They started
working for Abe at his office in
1929 and never left until he died.
They were like family and always
came to Brookwood and West
Stockbridge to visit.

Epstein. It was obvious that Adele Bloom could do little to keep it going;
it was beyond her abilities. She collapsed with nervous exhaustion and
was hospitalized. The board replaced her with a neutral figure from outside who had never been involved in the politics of the struggle to control
the association. Henriette's devotion was finally recognized, not with a
job, but with a salary of twenty-five dollars a week for one year starting
on October 1, 1942. She also was made an honorary vice-president. But
without Abe around no one was interested, very little money was raised,
and his former backers found other organizations to become involved
with. Finally, in May 1944, two years after Abe had died, just as the Allied
armies were rolling to victory over Germany, President McConnell sent a
letter to everyone on the mailing list.

Never has the need been greater for an organization such as ours—independent, objective, prepared selflessly to battle for principles which
it has accepted as right. Unfortunately, the Association has been under

a severe handicap since Abraham Epstein died . . . the kind of leadership he furnished cannot be replaced . . . our financial support has weakened. The Association has made a contribution which will be lasting. It is in the same tradition that the Association must continue, if it is to continue at all. At the moment we do not have the resources equal to the task. We have therefore decided it is best to suspend for the present. We will close our office at the end of this month. With this letter go the deep appreciation of the officers and directors . . . and our thanks for the loyal help which you gave Abraham Epstein . . . we hope that all of you will continue the work of building a broad and sound system of social security for America.

The American Association for Social Security went out of business; its papers were scattered to various library archives and its creator and passionate driving force left behind only his name on the many books and articles he had written to try to change the face of America by giving a modicum of "security" to the many people left out of the American dream. On May 29, 1942, the Social Security Board granted Henriette $21.20 a month in dependent's benefits for me until the age of eighteen. It was a revision of benefits that Abe had insisted on when the act was amended in 1939. He had won that battle, his last one, despite the resistance of the administration and the Congress.

I was one of the first to benefit from that modicum of "security."

9

In March 1941, more than a year before Abe's death, Arthur Altmeyer asked Wilbur Cohen to get in touch with Abe. Altmeyer was then chairman of the Social Security Board, and he wanted to know what Abe had in mind by choosing the term "social security" when he changed the name of the association back in 1933. Wilbur Cohen was then a technical adviser to the board, and both men wanted to know why the government had not chosen the title "Social Insurance Board" or "Economic Security Board" but used Abe's words instead. Cohen also told Abe about a curious inscription over a gateway in the Department of Justice building which read, "Justice is the great interest of man on earth. Wherever her temple stands there is a foundation for social security, general happiness, and the improvement and progress of our race." Cohen added that it appeared to be "an early use of the term but not exactly in the same sense as we are using it now. I thought you would like to know about it."

Abe was "grateful for the letter and had long been expecting it," he wrote back, because, he explained, "I was sure that fifty years after my death some historian would ask that question, but I wasn't sure he would get the right answer . . . The change early in 1933 to The American Association for Social Security was entirely my own idea and I had definite reasons for using the words, 'social security' rather than 'economic security' or 'social insurance.' Indeed, Dr. I. M. Rubinow definitely opposed the new name as being all too-encompassing and some time later criticized me for this in a speech or article." Abe could not resist bringing up one of his old battles with Rubinow despite the fact his cherished companion-in-arms had been dead for nearly five years.

Abe then went on to give the clearest description possible of the true meaning of social security. "I insisted on the term 'social security' because by that time I had a clear conception of the differences between social insurance . . . and social protection. I definitely did not want 'social insurance' because this would give it the German twist of actuarial insurance—as worked out by Bismarck—in terms of compulsory savings which did not justify governmental contributions. I did not want 'economic security' because what I hoped for was not only a form of security for the workers as such but that type of security which would, at the same time, promote the welfare of society as a whole . . . no improvement in the condition of labor can come except as the security of the people as a whole is advanced. In other words 'social security' meant to me a clear distinction from the German concept of actuarial insurance. My aim was in the direction of . . . the English system of social protection wherein governmental contributions become part and parcel of the program."

But Abe could not get away from the personal in explaining his ideas, nor resist reliving his old struggles: "This, perhaps, may help to explain why I was burning up in 1935 when our program [the Social Security Act] reversed the concepts which were precious to me. I am convinced that the naming of the Perkins committee 'economic security' was a deliberate attempt to get away from our name . . . Naturally, I was quite happy that Congress restored our name . . . and I am particularly glad to see that even in Europe today the term 'social security' is very commonly used."

But he also turned on the charm with Wilbur, perhaps still hoping for more influence over the government's social security program: "Can we lunch together Thursday?"

---

At Abe's death a fundamental principle was still missing: social protection. Payments for the aged, the unemployed, and the sick and disabled were still not adequate for their needs and the needs of those who depended on them. Abe had wanted payments to be weighted in favor of the poorer classes, instead of being a reward for those whose payroll tax contributions were higher because of their income. Unemployment insurance needed to be adequate to cover both the worker and his dependents. These were always the battles that were hardest to win. The American public still believed in the virtues of individual effort: "What I put in to the social security fund is what I should get out of it. It's my money. I can do what I want with it. Never mind what others have put in." These ideas have not gone away. They can be seen even today in all the proposals to privatize social security or to create individual medical accounts. This archaic nineteenth-century American credo maddened Abe. He battled to show why such thinking was totally misguided in a modern industrial economy. As he explained in *Harper's* in 1940: "Only gradually did it dawn on Washington that social insurance cannot operate like private insurance because the principle here is not individual protection but the insuring of the economy as a whole." Eventually protection was extended in 1939 to the aged widows of the insured, to those with surviving minor children, to orphans, and, in some cases, even to their dependent parents. But it still left a lot of gaps. Many sections of the population were still uncovered, including domestic workers and agricultural labor. Social protection was still a distant prospect. And of course with the refusal to enact any laws on health insurance, there existed a huge hole in the principle of social protection.

"Insuring the economy as a whole" was a difficult concept for the public to grasp. The idea was too big and imaginative, too broad for a nation that still believed, despite the catastrophic depression, that all should take care of themselves. Abe did his best to counter that thinking when he wrote:

> Three reasons make social security legislation imperative today. One is the civilized desire to feed and shelter the helpless and destitute in the least degrading manner. Another is the sound political instinct that, unless a minimum of economic protection is established, the suffering masses may become politically dangerous. The third reason is that social security is regarded as the best medium for underpinning the purchasing power of the masses which is essential to the maintenance of production and the stability of the national economy.

In short, *Social Security* is good for the American people.
Sadly, at the end of his career, few in public office were listening to what

Abe had to say. And he had been powerless to get their attention because of lack of funds. He may have sensed that his time had passed, that soon the world would continue without him, that he would leave it with his goals unfulfilled. Certainly his weary, exhausted look at the testimonial party made it look that way. Yet he pressed forward, pushing himself to accomplish whatever reforms he could. His last major effort came in early 1942 when he gathered together a committee of sixty-eight prominent economists and writers to publish a pamphlet that argued for the importance of social security: *Can We Stop a Post-War Depression Now?* It was meant to get people to start thinking ahead to the kind of problems America would face after the war.

The wartime economy was booming and the mass unemployment of the depression years had ended. Anyone who wanted a job could get one. But what about after the war? It would take time for the wartime industries to convert to peacetime products. And while that was taking place, many would lose their jobs. And this would happen just as the soldiers were returning home and looking for work.

Abe did not put his name on the publication as its author, preferring to have the committee of sixty-eight take the credit, but he wrote all of it and it fully expressed his thinking. His favorite aggressive noun was laced throughout, as in the title of the opening section, "Facing the Challenge." And because it was wartime, the tone of the writing was suffused with military metaphors, as in, "The Committee is convinced that the attack must be made on a wide front with offensive and defensive weapons in the economic as well as the social security fields." His basic concern was the potential disaster of mass unemployment, and to meet this a new nationwide program should be put in place. Unemployment insurance would be guaranteed for six months with adequate benefits to maintain the worker and his family. If a worker was still unemployed after that, then an emergency benefit of another six months would be available, again socially adequate, with the only difference that it was conditioned on a postwar depression lasting for a longer period. Finally, if this did not work, the government should offer employment itself or at a minimum some form of general assistance.

Those were Abe's very last words on the subject.

Two years later, in 1944, Roosevelt sent his next-to-last State of the Union message to Congress. World War II was coming to its end, but his message was not a posturing torrent of bravado over the defeat of the Axis powers. Rather FDR was worried about what to do about the postwar period just as Abe had been. America should not be "content with mere survival," the president told the legislators. "The one supreme objective for the future . . . for all the United Nations, can be summed up in one word: Security." The term meant "not only physical security which provides safety from attacks by aggressors" but also "economic security, social security, moral security." Then he made an extraordinary proposal. He asked for a second bill of rights, an economic one, to be placed alongside the first ten amendments. America, he said, could not be "content, no matter how high the general standard of living may be, if some fraction of our people—whether it be one third, one fifth, or one tenth—is ill-fed, ill-clothed, ill-housed and insecure."

It's impossible to know if Abe's constant use of the word "insecure" may have influenced FDR. Certainly, *Insecurity* was the title Abe chose for his major book: to him "insecurity" was the defining disaster of the American economic system. Roosevelt had used the word himself when he accepted the Democratic Party nomination for the presidency in 1932. But now the word was as significant to Roosevelt as it had been to Abe. To cure it, Roosevelt proposed eight different rights every American was entitled to:

1) The right to a job.
2) The right to earn enough to provide food, clothing and recreation.
3) The right of every farmer to a decent living.
4) The right of every businessman, large and small, to trade in freedom from unfair competition and domination by monopolies.
5) The right to a decent home.
6) The right to adequate medical care.
7) The right to protection from old age, sickness, accident and unemployment.
8) The right to education.

As the president put it in his speech, "those rights spelled Security." He grounded that belief in a quaint formal phrase that he used on more than one occasion, as well as in his message to Congress: "Necessitous men are not free men."

---

Both Abe Epstein and Franklin Roosevelt had a transforming, visceral response to the plight of the poor. Abe had experienced it when he stood alone on the Brooklyn Bridge staring down at the swirling water below, watching all those with jobs hurrying home over the bridge after a day at work. No one wanted him for anything; he was useless. Why not just jump into the depths of the East River? Who would care? That incident of despair remained with him all his life and informed all his work on *Social Security*. To be poor, to not have a job, sucked the dignity out of a human being.

In 1932, when he was running for president, FDR had recalled an incident that had deeply disturbed him. Farm neighbors, three brothers and a sister, had grown too old to manage, and during the winter the men had been taken out of their homes against their will and placed in the county poorhouse, while the sister had been taken to the local insane asylum. When Roosevelt returned to Hyde Park he was shocked at the callous consequences of their poverty. He decided then and there and publicly declared that if elected president he would do all he could to keep poor old people together in their own homes.

Both men had tried to keep their promise to the poor.

---

"Social security" is a phrase we use every day, a nearly universal term. From the wintry banks of the Susquehanna River in 1927 when Emil Frankel ran into Abe Epstein and they first spoke of it, "social security" has been used to describe old age, unemployment, and medical insurance in most of the countries of the world: Great Britain, France, Germany, most of the Spanish-speaking countries, and many others in Africa and Asia. But Henriette's description may have been the most vivid when she said it was "like little snowballs that turn into a great avalanche . . . words that have brought hope, cheer, and happiness to millions in the United States and other countries."

When Abe died in 1942 he left behind a lot of unfinished work to complete his vision. Consciously or not, Franklin Roosevelt, a year before his death, seems to have absorbed them into his vision of America as well.

"Social security"—those two words and all they embody are Abe's enduring bequest.

10

Life without Abe—that was the existence Henriette was facing. But it wasn't until the doors were shut on the American Association for Social Security that she became aware of what that truly meant. For two years she had tried to find ways to keep Abe's spirit alive. But now the little office at 22 East Seventeenth Street was no more and the association had become a part of the dust of history, with nothing left but books and papers from filing cabinets and office shelves.

But in Henriette there was a stubborn streak, a survivor's sense of mission. They could kick her out, they could close the office, but they could never prevent her from trying to keep Abe's ideas alive. In the 1970s when she was interviewed, she recalled her feelings: "My main aim in life was to continue, because he had said time and again that he wanted me to do all I could to continue his work."

In fact, before the association was closed, she took her first independent steps in the summer of 1942. In the unaccustomed quiet of 389 Bleecker, she sat down at Abe's still-cluttered claw-foot desk and pecked away slowly at the ungainly black upright. The result was a letter to an important senator, Arthur Vandenberg of Michigan, a Republican friend of Abe's. The social security payroll taxes should not be raised, she told him, and listed all the arguments against it. Later, she acknowledged, that to be "quite safe and sure" she had lifted them word for word from Abe's earlier testimony before Vandenberg's committee. She was carrying on, doing exactly what Abe would have done if he were still at his desk dictating letters and keeping up the pressure. She also sent a copy to the *New York Times*, again something Abe would have done. Next she called Abe's old ally at the paper, A. H. Raskin. When he came on the line she told him about the letter. "I'll see that it gets published," he replied. Henriette was thrilled by what she had accomplished so easily—but instantly there was trouble. The letter appeared in the paper and the very next day there was a reply to her from Bishop McConnell, president of the association. She was "not to express an opinion on the payroll tax, only the Association would determine what positions to take." In effect he told her to keep her mouth shut. She was shocked at first that the mild-mannered, elderly McConnell would treat her so rudely, and then she got angry and wrote back, somewhat melodramatically, that "From now on I will not be silenced." Her inward feeling that others always refused to listen to her, that to them she was an inferior being, inflamed her. She realized that McConnell would most likely be irked by her reply, but she really didn't care what anyone thought. She was seething. How dare they try to shut her up? Frank Tyson, Abe's mentor at the University of Pittsburgh and a member of the board, came all the way from Pittsburgh to search for a way to calm things down. He met with McConnell at the office and was astonished to hear that he was dead set against Henriette having anything to do with the association. She was out and others were in, and that was it.

Tyson felt as strongly as Henriette about Abe's legacy. He was proud of the achievements of his former student, but he was a much older man now. Like Rubinow, it seems he had been an early father figure to the youthful Abe, who over the years always sought his advice. When Abe had suddenly died Tyson was hard at work trying to get him an honorary doctoral degree at Pitt.

Tyson came down to see Henriette after the meeting with McConnell and told her he was unprepared for what he had heard.

"Did you do anything to antagonize anyone?" he asked.

"No," she replied, then acknowledged, "it's true my husband's secretary left because she felt that she couldn't get along with Bloom in the office. And my own secretary left for the same reason."

Tyson shook his head. He didn't know what to make of it. Henriette eventually conceded that "maybe I said something that upset the good lady and Herman Gray . . . but I don't think that should come into consideration."

Now she was an outcast and didn't know where to turn. All she could think of was escape, to flee New York, to return to France. In her journal she wrote, "I don't want to have anything to do anymore with a country that has such ingratitude towards people." But the war was raging, her parents were unavailable, and she had almost no money. Stranded, she felt her only salvation was to remain involved in Abe's crusade.

She wrote letters to anyone she could think of, asking for work. She started with the big names, such as Arthur Altmeyer, the chairman of the Social Security Board, but he told her that if she would not leave New York then she should try Anna Rosenberg who ran the local office—the interview turned up nothing. Subsequently she was in touch with her husband's favorite associates—Douglas Brown at Princeton and E. Wight Bakke at Yale. But whatever suggestions they came up with led nowhere. She was bewildered by the way the wife of Abraham Epstein could be treated with such indifference. There was a conspiracy against her, she soon believed, and it was Abe's fault. He had made no provision for her. The life insurance she received was minimal. And for all the work she had done he had never given her what she deserved. He had never put her name on the letterhead. He had never given her a title. He had never asked her to sit on the board. He should have told them before he died to install her. He should have insisted. The letter he had signed just before he was taken off to the hospital was just ignored. He had abandoned her and left her alone.

She became more irascible, given to sudden outbursts of hysterical anger. I once heard loud thumping noises in the kitchen and went upstairs to see what was wrong. Clumsily, she was attempting to take the top off a can of food with an opener she could not make work. Instead of asking for help she grew more frustrated and began banging the counter in anger, screaming at her dead husband.

"Damn you, Abe! Look what you've done to me. Left me with nothing. All you ever cared about were poor people. You never cared about me. Just your intellectual cronies."

She threw the can down on the floor, where it rolled noisily for a moment, and stormed out in pain and anger. From the closed door of her room I could hear sobbing and then cursing at Abe. I ran down the stairs and into the garden, picked up a ball, and began throwing it back and forth against the brick wall of one of the buildings. Such episodes were to became more frequent. She would angrily blame Abe for all that was wrong and more and more I tried to be somewhere else when I imagined the outbursts might come on. I would remain late at school or go to a friend's house to do homework for as long as possible. If asked to stay on for dinner, I felt relieved that I didn't have to go home and face Henriette in the kitchen damning Abe as she struggled to cook.

That is how it went for several years.

---

There was an underside to her anger that she could never face directly. It sprang from her sense of inferiority in relation to Abe. She read his impatience, his driving energy, his scholarly achievements as a way of dismissing her importance in his life. He had laid on the charm that evening in Harrisburg long ago when he put a book in her lap and told her he had written it. He had made her head swim. In the small towns of southern France where she came from no one knew anyone who had actually written a book. But perhaps she should have paid more attention to the conversation that preceded the gift. Abe and his friends had been passionately talking about old-age pension laws, which Henriette knew nothing about. Instead of listening she had started dancing by herself in the middle of the room. It had certainly entranced Abe, but in so doing she had missed understanding what Abe was all about. And over the years that missed understanding turned into a sense of inferiority over Abe's accomplishments. She knew she had not studied the way he had, read as widely as he had, nor done any serious research, but she felt it did not matter. If you were marching alongside a dynamic husband and devoting yourself to creating publicity for the movement, then what difference did it make if you were an intellectual or not? She refused to believe she needed to learn more about the complicated ideas that motivated the politics of social security. She preferred the emotional side to the story—the photos of the bedraggled poor that were released for publicity, the tales of the one hundred neediest cases of suffering and illness. Her role had always been that of a social organizer, for the conferences, the meetings, the parties, and she was good at it. But when pushed to talk about social security she always relied on Abe and his words, quoting from books, articles, and speeches. In the long oral interviews she gave, which she brazenly called "my biography," she reeled off page after page directly from Abe's writings and speeches.

She was proud of her place in his career. She had not missed a moment of the great advances in social security. But as people they were from two different worlds. Abe's entire life had been a struggle to get somewhere. Henriette, on the other hand, had grown up in ease and comfort and had had all her wishes granted. But it was those very differences in background and education that meant she was not qualified for the jobs she thought she had a right to. And so when rejected, instead of looking at herself, she blamed Abe. Now that he was dead he could not answer back or, as he had usually done, ignore her. So the mess she was in was all his fault. She was never truly aware that others might have a reason for thinking that she was not up to the task.

The future of Abe's papers became a terrible obsession to her. Now that she was excluded from the association, she wanted them given to her. She went there late one afternoon and took home what she could: "it was my duty," she explained. But Adele Bloom found out and refused to let her in again to take anything more. Herman Gray accused her of stealing. "Everything in the office is the property of the association," he wrote her. But friends on the board, Walter Frank and Nicholas Kelley, intervened to try and reach a compromise. Herman Gray wouldn't budge. For several months nasty letters flew back and forth until eventually the two board members forced Gray to back down. An agreement was made whereby Abe's more personal papers were given to Henriette, trucked down to 389 Bleecker Street and put in the basement. But obviously someone was needed to organize them. And eventually when the historian Allan Nevins realized their importance, he arranged to have them given to Columbia University, where they were preserved and catalogued in the Special Collections Library. Columbia became the first of three universities to house Abe's lifetime of work. The others were Cornell and Wisconsin. But the fight over Abe's papers made Henriette increasingly hysterical. Her letters to Bloom and Gray were shrill and angry, and though she eventually won control, those who didn't want her around disliked her even more. When the association began to drift toward its eventual demise and Herman Gray and Adele Bloom had left, having failed in their attempts to capitalize on Abe's work for their own purposes, Henriette tried to return and help the new executive director, Harvey Lebrun, a friend from the old days of the pension battle in New York State.

"He tried to do whatever he could," Henriette wrote, "and he was very friendly to me . . . the Association finally collapsed of its own weight, because there was no money. There was no activity. There were no conferences. There was nothing. It just carried on, running on its own momentum, on the good name of Abraham Epstein, which was always used to try and raise money, over my protest, because I felt that if you just don't want to have anything to do with anyone by the name of Epstein, then why do you just use his name for raising money?"

With no job, the need for money became an increasing worry. But despite her anger at Abe for not providing for her future, there was one asset she could count on—the old brick house at 389 Bleecker Street. Real-estate brokers and others who knew she was facing hard times implored her to sell. But despite her increasing debts, she refused. It was wartime and she knew they wouldn't give her anything, and besides she loved the house, had wanted it from the moment she saw it despite its lack of plumbing and trash-filled backyard brimming with laundry lines and outhouses. She had bought it over everyone's advice using her parents' money, tied Abe down with a mortgage, and bit by bit had transformed it into a center for political agitation during the reform era of the 1930s. Every corner swelled with memories, and Greenwich Village was where she lived—all her friends were there. Nobody was going to move her out. They could take away everything else—the office, Abe's papers, her work at the association—but they would not get her home. She had the French bourgeoisie's feeling for property. Real estate meant security and once acquired was meant to remain in the family.

A friend surprised her one day and told her that because of the war New York was crowded with people desperate for a place to live. Had she thought of renting?"

It was true. Housing in New York was at a premium. Sailors, soldiers, and wartime officials crowded the city, and all needed places to stay. The hotels were packed, the college dorms were filled, and so the solution that appeared from almost nowhere was to rent some parts of 389 Bleecker, rooms that she could live without. Bit by bit the living space grew smaller as the house began to fill with roomers, returning to the state it had been in when Henriette had first spotted it in 1929. There were still many doors from the old rooming-house days, and they sprang into use again, sealing off the rooms into separate apartments.

A fighter pilot back from the fog-shrouded Aleutian Islands needed a place to stay and took over the top floor where Henriette and Abe had once had their bedroom. He was on some sort of psychological rehabilitation due to his many months of living in the cold and mist of Alaska. He wasn't very talkative and didn't stay very long, but when he moved on he tossed his fur-lined leather flight jacket into my surprised hands, pointed to his fur-lined boots as well, souvenirs of a place where he hoped never to return, and said, "Take 'em. They're yours." Neither fit me, but I put them in the closet and waited until I was big enough to wear those relics of World War II. He was followed by a naval officer from Memphis, an Annapolis graduate by the name of Harry Gunther, on temporary assignment in New York. He arrived, accompanied by his petite blonde Southern belle of a new wife named Peggy. They stayed for several years, filling the house with Southern charm, the smell of Southern cooking, and the drawl of Southern speech. I was dazzled by all the gold on Lieutenant Gunther's uniform and proudly exaggerated his presence, telling my friends I was sure we had an admiral living in the house. When they went home to Tennessee, the war was ending and the city was even more full-up with people looking for places to live. For the most part the newcomers were returning military personnel hungry for schooling and with some money that was guaranteed to them by the G.I. bill. So when the Tennessee Southerners left, another set of Southerners moved in, Harold and Minnie Lou Bell from Fort Worth, Texas. He took business courses at Pace College and she worked as a librarian in the city system. When he graduated he became a salesman for Coca-Cola. They gave him a car that was stuffed with bottles of Coke and huge signs that said, "Drink Coca-Cola." He took me on his rounds and saw to it that I had summer jobs in the soft-drink stands he serviced. Minnie Lou counseled me on what clothes to wear to school dances and always checked my shoes before I left to see that they were properly shined. I still hear her slow, commanding tone with its Texas sound, "Now Pierre, you aren't gonna leave this house looking like that? Harold get me that shoe shine kit."

On the third floor there was a turnover of many tenants who lived in Abe's former office. One was a literary critic who lived upstate and needed an in-town study. He saw that I was reading Dumas's *Three Musketeers* for days on end—all the way through its two sequels where all the musketeers die off, one by one. He asked me what I thought of the books and when I told him how sad I was at the death of D'Artagnan and Athos and Porthos and Aramis, he became interested in my literary opinions. My thoughts on the book found themselves onto a radio program called *Invitation to Learning*, on which the critic was a frequent guest. He told me to listen to the program, and I was stunned to hear my words quoted by someone on the radio. The house at 389 Bleecker was crawling with interesting and entertaining people, coming and going, but with so many tenants our living quarters were reduced to a fourth-floor hall bedroom that belonged to me and another bedroom on the third floor where Henriette lived. We shared the kitchen and one of the bathrooms.

Restricting as it all was, Henriette slowly came to terms with the fact that her life had been changed permanently. Her tenants were not New Yorkers and they might never have come to the great American metropolis if not for the war. They were more small-town yet open in spirit, dazzled by the city, and grateful for a place to live. Greenwich Village entranced them with its twisting streets, its neighborhood feel, its little stores and restaurants. They had sacrificed for their country in the war and they were ready to embrace all that was now open to them. And they found Henriette fascinating. They listened to her stories, heard the names of the important figures she had known, learned about a world unknown to them. They connected her to possible jobs, looked for people who wanted French lessons, shared meals with her, took her out to meet their own friends or to parties. She began to have fun again. It was an amazing turnabout for a woman who had once lived in the exciting world of political reform where her acquaintances had always been writers, intellectuals, and well-known political figures. She adjusted, and her sense of frolic, her stories of people she had known, and her French accent and background charmed her tenants and their guests. She had always been entertaining and flirtatious, but now she capitalized on it. She transformed herself. She discovered a new network of friends, with whom she visited and corresponded. She went by train to Memphis to visit the Gunthers, became friends with their children, and showed them around New York when they came to visit, even taking in one of the daughters when she came to take ballet classes for a few weeks. The Bells, back in Texas, kept in touch as well, and when their son wanted to study in New York she took him in as another boarder, repeating the entire experience for the next generation. She became a frequent visitor to the Bells' large Fort Worth house, which required her first airplane flight at the age of seventy. I thought it might turn into a traumatic experience—after all she had always traveled long distances safely by train or by ship. So I accompanied her to the airport just to be on the safe side, constantly reminding her that she should not be afraid, the airplanes were safe and she would be fine. The hostess let me accompany her to her seat.

"The Bells will be at the other end to meet you. So don't worry," I told her. "You will be in safe hands all the way."

Her reply was not addressed to me but to the hostess.

"When do we eat?"

She had figured out how to survive. And although it wasn't the life she had lived before, it was one she didn't mind having.

Through it all she never gave up on social security and her obligation to fulfill Abe's legacy. She was an inveterate letter writer, pecking away with one finger on the heavy black office typewriter, more often though filling the backs of envelopes with her clear French penmanship and then getting someone else to type it for her. She kept up a lively correspondence with many of Abe's former associates. But there was one in particular from the old days who resolutely kept up the relationship: Wilbur Cohen.

He had first come to Washington to work for the Committee on Economic Security that wrote the Social Security Act of 1935 and slowly rose through the ranks of the social security administration to become assistant director. He then transferred to the Department of Health, Education and Welfare as undersecretary. He finished his governmental career as a member of President Lyndon Johnson's cabinet when he was named secretary of the Department of Health, Education, and Welfare.

As major figures in the movement had returned to follow other pursuits after the 1939 amendments, like Paul Douglas who went into politics and Edwin Witte who returned to academia, Wilbur Cohen became much closer to Abe. He turned to him frequently as the senior figure he would consult for his government work. He attended all the conferences that Abe sponsored, was a frequent speaker, and made sure that he and his wife would be present at Abe's testimonial in 1942. There, down front in the photograph of the gathering, sits Wilbur with a look of delight on his face. It is clear that he would not have missed the event for all the world.

After Abe's death, Wilbur replied to everything Henriette wrote him, and he fulfilled all her requests for reports, publications, and congressional testimonies. His conscientious correspondence helped to give Henriette hope that at least one person of importance was not dismissive of her. In 1948 he began to put together a book that was eventually called *Readings in Social Security*, and he asked her for the rights to reprint several chapters from *Insecurity*. The chapter that he really wanted was titled, "The Catastrophe That Is Unemployment," perhaps the most emotional one in the book. She was thrilled; she had always wanted the book to be reprinted and gave him her approval. As icing on the cake Wilbur told her that he was also going to refer to a letter Abe had sent him "telling me how he originated the term social security. I think it would be a nice idea, don't you . . . to give him credit for the idea."

Eventually, Wilbur Cohen saw to it that Henriette was invited to various conferences such as the National Health Assembly in 1948. Then in 1950, when revisions to the Social Security Act were proposed by the Truman administration, he asked if she might be interested in testifying before Congress. She could represent the American Association for Social Security—although it was defunct—as its vice-president. "I was very scared, because I had never spoken at one of those hearings. I had stage fright. I worked very hard on that testimony . . . that it should be worthy of a poor little woman like me."

She wrote up a statement, checked and rechecked all her references, and went down to Washington the night before she was to appear before a Senate committee. On arrival she immediately called Wilbur, who reassured her and told her how wonderful it was of her to come and do it. Nevertheless, she could barely sleep the night before. For the first time she realized how Abe must have felt when he went through the ordeal at his first hearing, how hard it had been for him, and what courage he must have had to do it again and again, particularly when he was becoming sicker. But she told herself if he could do it, then so could she. Once in the hearing room that morning she calmed down, spread her written speech in front of her, and spoke, she felt, for a long time—in fact she thought the session would never end. Finally when she had finished she was asked to answer several questions. The formidable Robert Taft, a powerful Republican, was particularly interested in what she had to say. Then it was over, she was thanked and excused, and she walked back to her hotel room in a fog, lay down on the bed, and fell asleep for five hours. But when she awoke she knew that something great had happened to her. She was back on the field of battle.

She repeated the experience several times, always at the request of Wilbur Cohen. He got her listed as a witness, arranged for a hotel room, and always thanked her profusely for the help. It was as if Wilbur had found a way to invoke the spirit of Abe through Henriette, a way of honoring a man he always admired.

Henriette's final testimony in her series of appearances before Congress came on April 15, 1959, when she went before the House Ways and Means Committee, chaired by the influential and acerbic Wilbur Mills. By then Cohen was temporarily out of government and teaching at Michigan, but she didn't need his support any more. Her fears had subsided and she knew she could handle the subject of the committee's work, which was unemployment insurance. She identified herself as representing the American Association for Social Security, spoke of her support for the expansion of benefits that was under study, and made sure to add a quote from Wilbur Cohen in her testimony. When it was over, she rose to leave, but Representative Thomas Curtis of Missouri stopped her. Would she answer a few more questions about the organization she represented? She told him that it was an independent group, but Curtis persisted.

Curtis: Are there chapters throughout the country?

Henriette: We have no chapters.

Curtis: Your only chapter is in New York City?

Henriette: We used to be called the American Association for Old Age Security before the Social Security Act. We changed the name then.

Curtis: I did not happen to be familiar with the organization and wanted the information for the record.

Henriette: We have done a lot of work. Mr. Epstein has published a good many books on this subject. Of course, for a long time we did publish a magazine which lack of funds did not permit us to continue.

Curtis: What is your membership now? Have you any idea?

Henriette: I do not know exactly.

Curtis: Would it be 4,000?

Henriette: Perhaps less than that. It is the quality that counts.

Curtis: Thank you.

Henriette's testimony was part of a series of hearings that were spread out over eight days. When printed it took up four pages in a record that came to more than eleven hundred pages.

The idea that someone in Congress did not know about the American Association for Social Security, or even who Abraham Epstein was, must have been momentarily depressing. The names of the old social security groups and their warriors were unknown to the current generation. Even the name Abraham Epstein had passed into history. But if it bothered her, she said nothing about it. She accepted it. After all, what mattered was that social security was still important and she was fulfilling Abe's mission.

11

In the 1970s oral biography became a new research tool, a way of preserving memory without the writing of books. Many universities, making use of newly portable tape recorders, created archives using this method. The Wisconsin Historical Society was amassing a large amount of material on social security and sent Janice O'Connell, one of their researchers, off to New York to talk to Henriette. She was thrilled.

She began her spoken memoir with a flourish. "I would like to preface my remarks about the life of Abraham Epstein with a little quotation from a French poet, Jacques Brel. It seems to me to express what I always thought about the man's character and about his accomplishments. This little poem is simply about a girl dancing in the square in the noonday sun, and people refusing to listen and closing their windows . . . like a door between the dead and the living."

She then launched into the story of Abe's early days in Russia and the United States, and kept on talking for two days. Thus began for Henriette a new stage of her American life. She became an authority, a historical asset, practically a consultant, on the story of social security in America. She repeated the experience several times with other oral projects. Soon writers began to contact her, and she was happy to supply them with photographs, copies of letters, and the right to quote from Abe's writings. Always her name was mentioned and she was thanked. True, she was no longer active in pushing legislation, but she was becoming recognized as one who had worked in the early days of the movement and was treated with respect by those who sought her help. The attention increased her belief in her own significance and soon she took to calling the oral memoirs "my biography."

A number of other events took place to enhance her newfound sense of importance. *Insecurity* was reissued in a new edition in 1968 with the addition of a glowing preface by Abe's old companion, Paul Douglas, then a senator from Illinois:

> Abraham Epstein did more in my judgment to initiate social security than any other man of my generation . . . He was slight of build and cross-eyed. His eyes shifted constantly under his glasses. He had a squeaky voice which frequently rose to shouts when, as often happened, he was moved to anger. He was by birth a Russian Jew and had an accent one could cut with a knife. But I have often thought that though he died relatively poor he was the most truly successful man I have ever known . . . The early heroes who, beset by poverty and indifference, nevertheless persist in advancing a good cause are generally shunted aside when reform comes about . . . Recorded history is frequently very negligent in these matters.

Henriette was thrilled by those words. At last the world was hearing the truth about her husband and his work. The reissuing of *Insecurity* had come about through the efforts of my brother in law, a publisher who knew little about Abe and his work, but saw the value of the book. He was part of a new generation that Henriette had no hesitation in embracing. In fact she was indefatigable in talking about all the work she had done with Abe and the famous people she had met, for the most part known to others only as names in history books.

I would watch her body language during those discourses. She would lower her head, shake it a bit from side to side, as if helpless to prevent herself from bringing up the past. But she would keep on talking to a person who might at first be baffled by her references to old laws and obscure names. Still, she was listened to, and if her conversationalist didn't totally get it, she nevertheless left them with a clear feeling of the significance of what she had been part of. At times when I met one of her new friends, he or she would tell me with an amused look, "Pierre, your mother is such a fascinating person."

Her focus on herself and life with Abe was dogged. It paid off when another of Abe's books, his first one, *Facing Old Age*, was republished in 1972, with another extolling preface, this time by the faithful Wilbur Cohen. In it he wrote, "Abraham Epstein was one of the most extraordinary men I ever met. He was a rare combination of the Jewish scholar, the Madison Avenue publicist, the Broadway showman, the missionary social reformer, and the determined, persevering lobbyist." Abe's second book, the one dedicated to FDR, *The Challenge of the Aged*, was reprinted in 1976, with a preface by another one of his faithful friends, A. H. Raskin of the *New York Times*. "If America were as disposed to build monuments to its social heroes as it is to its generals," he wrote, "every city would have an imposing statue of Abraham Epstein. He was a tiny man but a giant in ideas—his body all head, his head all brains."

And finally there was a biography—of sorts. For years Henriette had been trying to get someone interested in the story of Abe's life. One of his students had written a biography years earlier for Abe's testimonial, but it was only twenty pages and meant specifically for publicity. After Abe's death Henriette wrote a series of letters to university professors, friends of his, including the notable historian Allan Nevins, searching for someone who might want to write a biography. Nothing developed for a long time, but then one day she was approached by a doctoral candidate from the political science department at Columbia University. Louis Leotta was blind and relied on his wife to transcribe everything for him, and he wanted to do his thesis on Abe and needed her help. She was elated by his proposal and Leotta spent days coming up the stairs at 389 Bleecker, sitting with Henriette, asking questions and being handed papers and letters which his wife read to him. Henriette looked on it all as a collaboration, a way to get her version of the events of the past into print. But what emerged was not exactly what she had in mind. Leotta's dissertation was of necessity a piece of matter-of-fact research, not the exciting and glamorous story Henriette was hoping to see published. Its title, *Abraham Epstein and the Movement for Social Security: 1920–1939*, underscored its academic outlook. Henriette pored over the manuscript and made many notes in the margins for Leotta to liven up the dry factual tone of his writing, but the work was carefully constructed to fit the doctoral program. She found much to irritate her. For one, Leotta used a quote from Roosevelt to open the book, and she wondered why he hadn't used one from Abe. She relived in vivid detail the bitter experience of Frances Perkins insulting Abe publicly and wrote firmly that Leotta should make more of it. When Leotta wrote, "Epstein was so absorbed in criticizing the Social Security Act," she immediately penciled in the margin—with a big exclamation point—"To Improve It!" And when Leotta in his conclusion barely mentioned Abe's crowning achievement, the 1939 amendments to social security, she wrote in capital letters on the final page, "WHAT ABOUT THE 1939 AMENDMENTS?" She had wanted more, a true biography, but although disappointed, she still made efforts to find a publisher for the dissertation. It never was published.

Finally, in 1992—still recovering from her double knee-replacement surgery—in her final burst of energy she had made certain that the one hundredth anniversary of Abe's birth was noted publicly by members of Congress and the newspapers. Time had transformed Henriette once again. And Abe as well—from the difficult man with whom she was often furious into an iconic figure for the advances of the twentieth century. Through her persistence, he lived on—and through him she lived on as well.

Of more particular concern to me, as Henriette recovered from her double knee operations, were the stairs at 389 Bleecker Street. She had lived with them all her life. They were what she had chosen from the very beginning when she bought the house in 1929. The downstairs would be rented—we would live upstairs. But as she grew older I would watch her nervously as she started to go up those stairs.

"You really must be more careful when you climb up and down," I would say in my most commanding tone.

She would turn to face me, flash her usual formal grin, and reply, "You see how careful I am?"

And then resolutely, hand firmly gripped to the bannister, cane at the

ready, she would start her ascent. She seemed a master of the entire operation. Every one of those steps, every creak, was known to her. When she
was past ninety and her knees and other joints crippled her, watching her
was like observing a small child. I would follow carefully to see that she
did not trip and fall. She never faltered, although of course there might be
the occasional wobble. After all, those stairs represented more than sixty
years of her life. People came up to visit, arrived for parties or refugee
gatherings, and came with papers for political meetings, while others
would shout up their presence. She knew every sound that came from below. It was out of the question that she would ever move to the downstairs
apartment. She had always lived upstairs, and there was absolutely no
reason to change. No, she would rather labor, a methodical step at a time,
until she reached her floor than move from her familiar surroundings.
Stubborn and determined, not about to change her ways, she chugged
slowly up like the little engine that could. But conscious of my wary gaze
she would inform me, "Look, how well I do it."

On March 13, 1993, Henriette was climbing the stairs from the third
floor to the fourth-floor kitchen to make her nightly "cuppa" when she
lost her footing and fell back down. She cried out, tumbled backwards,
and hit her head. When she landed on the third floor she was dead—three
months short of ninety-three.

I was in Los Angeles when I was given the news. "Of course," I said to
myself, and then out loud, "I knew it would happen that way." Her
beloved stairs had gotten her. Yet she died where she had always wanted
to die, in the house on Bleecker Street, where she had spent almost all of
her American life, and where she had been transformed from a daughter
of the French bourgeoisie into one of America's progressive citizens.

# Conclusion

Henriette was laid to rest in the Castex family vault in the tiny and ancient farming village of Longages near Toulouse in France's southwest. It was far from the bustle and noise of New York, but it was where she had been born, and where she wanted to be. It seemed the right place.

The day after the funeral I returned to the sleepy calm of the village. I was meeting the local mason to order a plaque to be attached to the side of the mausoleum to join those of the five other occupants: Henriette's mother, father, grandparents, and aunt. It was a glorious day, sunny, and the air held a gentle glaze of springtime green. I decided I would first walk to the cemetery for a last look. I made an effort to rearrange the flowers left at the funeral—to create a floral display that might survive my absence. A droning bee, more at home among the dead than I was, seemed to eye me. He wouldn't leave, darting toward me, then moving away, then nosing around again. What did he want? With all the flowers scattered about at other tombs why was he hanging around me? In a receptive state I wondered—did he want to communicate with me? Absurd, I thought, and left to see the mason, a mustached, sturdy man in French "bleu" working clothes, obviously more at home building houses than carving funeral plaques. I told him what I wanted: "Henriette Castex Epstein— Longages, 1900—New York, 1993." He assured me he would have it done and put up in a few weeks. I left the mason to his cinder blocks and cement and walked slowly back to the train station, following the road I had taken so frequently during my French childhood, savoring the new furrows in the lush land that had been turned every spring for so many centuries. Looking down at the earth I spotted them, the famous "violettes de Toulouse"—from which perfume and soap are made—little thrusts of purple among the matted grasses at the side of the road, the first true signs of spring. Kneeling, with the sun warming my back, I picked a cluster, inhaled their intense odor—overwhelming for such a little fragile flower. I held them up against the intensely blue sky that hovered over the cemetery outlined by its row of dusty cypress. The violets, the quiet little village basking in the sun, the inquisitive bee who wanted to talk—my mind was stirred. What had made my mother leave this old rural world for the intense life of a twentieth-century New Yorker? Longages, 1900—New York, 1993. Why had she done it?

An answer surfaced back in New York, but not the expected one, when I first noticed a fortune cookie on a table in my mother's bedroom. When opened it read, "A new voyage will fill your life with untold memories." Again, like the buzzing bee, I wondered if I was the subject of other-worldly communication. It was ridiculous and yet, after many months of poring through my mother's papers, the prophetic cookie seemed to have a point. Henriette had held onto nearly everything, and as I turned pages and pages and opened hundreds of envelopes—many with the same two words scribbled on the outside, "Please Keep"—the "new voyage" I began to go on was a totally unanticipated one. It was the story of Abe. I began for the first time to know him in ways I never had when I was young, when he was mostly an unpredictable and forbidding presence.

Then, my father was mostly an enigma to me. I was never sure of who he was or what the rage that had so burdened me was all about. As the years passed, Henriette continued to revere him but also remained very angry at him. As a result his accomplishments seemed far away, part of a distant time. But in the process of discovery I began to see why Paul Douglas, Wilbur Cohen, A. H. Raskin, and so many others, even some of his enemies, were captivated by his oversize personality and had written such extolling words about him. I also began to see why I had been so mad at being kept away from his testimonial, as I then believed. Commonplace it may be, but I had always wanted his approval, wanted to be part of his life, wanted him to tell me that I mattered. But as I explored more deeply, read the testimonial transcript, read what others wrote, reviewed what he had accomplished, I could see that he was being consumed by something I had not understood at the time: a monstrous sense of failure.

When he reached the age of fifty he was a very sick man. He would have had to slow down, do less—and therefore accomplish less. Would he have been able to develop the patience necessary to calm his overworked heart?

I don't think so. I believe that for him no life at all was better than a diminished life, one of restrained behavior and reduced output. The life of a professor, a guru, a man who was listened to and respected, was not one he would have ever wanted for himself. As a sideline, yes, perhaps. No doubt he would have been very good at it—he taught in two places and had many adoring students—but he had worn out his mental and physical abilities for another reason.

I was at first very resentful that he wanted to give up, that he was not willing to accept an honorable retirement from the field of battle. Why, even if things had not turned out the way he wanted, had he abandoned me? Why leave me out of his thinking? I should be angry at him—but strangely I am not.

Among the artifacts discovered among my mother's papers there is a postcard of a lake in Maine. It was sent in 1939 when the war had already started in Europe. It is from me to Abe and Henriette: "I won the bet with Dad. I improved my swimming." Then, more significantly: "I saw news about Dad in the paper." Two things seem clear to me. First, there is the anxiety about swimming, and Abe's angry insistence that I learn. But more importantly there is my desire to stay involved with what he was doing. His name was in the paper, and I was proud of it—just as I was proud to be part of the conference and the testimonial dinner preparations, of going to the office and licking envelopes, of parading around the living room and making him laugh. I wanted to be part of what he did. His absence after his death hurt me and puzzled me for many years.

I think I now know what I had not understood when I was young. Abe's life is indeed the story of the poor immigrant who comes to the land of opportunity, but instead of becoming rich and famous, in a revealing twist to the traditional story he makes sure that the United States is a better place to live in than when he arrived. He once quoted Carlyle in a book: "It is not to die or even die of hunger, that makes a man wretched; all men must die. But it is to live miserably, we know not why; to work sore yet gain nothing; to be heart-worn, weary, yet isolated, unrelated, girt in with a cold, universal laissez-faire."

What Carlyle's words meant to Abe he explained just below the quote: No social order can for long remain indifferent toward the problems and difficulties confronting some of its members, without directly or indirectly paying the price of its unconcern.

That feeling that he first experienced in Pittsburgh when studying the misery of the black migrant population, he developed into a coherent philosophy that was best expressed in his view of the need for social security. That unique contribution helped to change the course of America. And if there are those who would undo it now, I do not think they will succeed without a fight. That is Abe's legacy. If you believe in something, then don't give up, go down fighting if you must. Every town should have a statue to him, as A. H. Raskin put it—for he was a man who wanted to bring out the best in a country he believed was the best in the world.

I forgive him his neglect of me, for he left me with a gift that I can only now appreciate. I am happy to be his son.

## Afterword

This book would not have been written without the answers that emerged after Henriette's death from inside a tiny, almost impenetrable back room of a four-story house in New York's Greenwich Village. Piled to the ceiling with boxes on top of suitcases on top of bureaus, mixed in among old check stubs and dry-cleaning bills, I uncovered photographs, yellowing periodicals, torn French newspapers from the early 1900s, old passports, Russian visas, diaries, an ancient radio, and boxes of letters in English, French, Russian, and Yiddish, many more than one hundred years old. Completing the treasure were three memorable oral biographies that my mother had recorded beginning in 1979.

The most exciting moment was when I came upon a torn envelope with a scribbled note on the back: "From Abraham Epstein for Christmas 1924, to Henriette in Philadelphia—after going to the theatre. Please Keep!" Inside, like an archeological find, I came upon a delicate beaded purse glinting with encrusted tiny red and blue stones, a delicate treasure I had never seen before. An immigrant Russian Jew by the name of Abraham Epstein had given it to Henriette not long after he first set eyes on her.

I never knew that such a love had existed between those two opposites.

# Acknowledgments

There are many people who have contributed to the shape and message of this book. Among them are a number of fellow writers who have wrestled with work of their own and who took the time to look over this book. They are Ralph Klein, Denise Reed, Jeff Garigliano, Peter Szabo, Anya Grottel, and Peter Bricklebank, who guided a number of meetings we held to discuss the progress of our different books. I owe a debt to all of them. Lydia Fakudinny, Senior Lecturer at Cornell, was among the very first to tell me that what I was working on had possibilities. And one writer in particular stands out for the intelligent guidance she offered: Bettina Drew. She has a special gift. There are also those who willingly responded to my requests for information: Milton Konvitz, Harold Kaspar, Bernard Crystal, Curator of Manuscripts at Columbia, and Olga Rubinow, I. M Rubinow's daughter, among many others. My two children, Marc and Suzanne, along with their mother, Doree Lanouette Epstein, kept up a subterranean drumbeat of encouragement. Then there are friends I have known from my early childhood such as Peter Reich and Harley Frank. They knew my mother and father and kept prodding me along, always asking, "How's it going, Eppie?" Yes, I have inherited my father's nickname. Not least among those friends is Anne Codding Tonachel, who watched me suffer through this work; a very special person I have known for over sixty-five years. The folks at the University of Missouri Press have diligently worked to make this book possible and for that I thank them. They include Sara Davis, Beth Chandler, and John Brenner. Gary Kass, in particular, the editor I have never set eyes on, looked over this book, decided it needed to be published, and guided it through the acceptance process with patience and grace; my grateful thanks. I must thank the printer Robert Warhover whose electronic wizardry made the manuscript look acceptable. And much appreciation goes to the publisher, Burton Lasky, who took the risk of publishing a new edition of Abraham Epstein's great book, *Insecurity*, keeping it alive for future generations. His act more than likely led to the republication of Abe's other books. Little did he know that without his willingness to take that risk, this book might never have taken root. Finally, to Henriette, who kept it all hidden somewhere until I was grown up enough to look it over. She always wanted someone to write about Abe. And now someone has.

# Notes

Prologue
The article "Is American Capital Intelligent?" appeared in H. L. Mencken's *American Mercury* 51 (January 1929). The words on Adam and Eve are from Abraham Epstein's *Insecurity: A Challenge to America*, 3. Moynihan's words appeared in the *Congressional Record*, vol. 138, pt. 54 (April 10, 1992). Jean Bandler's letter appeared in the *New York Times* on April 29, 1992.

Part One
The Socialist Johnny Appleseed
1. Most of this section is taken from Mrs. Abraham Epstein's oral interviews for the State Historical Society of Wisconsin conducted in April and May 1973.
2. Again, much of this section is taken from Mrs. Abraham Epstein's oral interviews. The story of the departure from Russia was taken from "Abraham Epstein," a short biography written by Fred L. Preu for the 1942 Abraham Epstein Testimonial dinner. Preu was a student of Abraham Epstein and interviewed him for the biography. The story of Abe and the big Russian peasant can be found on page 1. The biography was mimeographed at the time but never published.
3. The story of Abe and Mr. Armstrong can be found in Preu, "Abraham Epstein," 9–10. The first use of the nickname "Eppy" and the information about Abe's student days are taken from the *East Liberty Academy Echo*, the commencement number dated June 1914, on pp. 8, 12 (personal property of the author). The quote from Philip Roth can be can be found in *The Anatomy Lesson*, 78. The two quotes from Abe's first book are from *The Negro Migrant in Pittsburgh*, 66, 28.
4. The statistical information gathered by Abe comes from the Report of the Pennsylvania Commission on Old Age Pensions, March 1919. There is more on the Pennsylvania Report in "Abraham Epstein and the Movement for Social Security," Louis Leotta's dissertation at Columbia University. The story of the radical duo setting off for Europe is from Mrs. Abraham Epstein's oral interviews. The words of Paul Douglas are from his Introduction to *Insecurity: A Challenge to America*. The story of the Worker's Education Bureau and the "little dictator and know it all" quote, from a letter by Fania Cohn on June 9, 1920, can be found in Leotta's dissertation on p. 41. The Cohn letter can also be found in the Epstein papers at Columbia in the Rare Book Col-

lection. The words about James Maurer, "you could say he was Maurer's political son," are from Mrs. Abraham Epstein's oral interviews.

5. The source for most of this chapter is Mrs. Abraham Epstein's oral interviews.

6. The Abraham Epstein quotes are from *Facing Old Age: A Study of Old Age Dependency in the United States and Old Age Pensions*. Frank Hering's words are quoted from "Awakening Interest in Old Age Pensions," *American Labor Legislation Review* (June 1923): 143. For Abe's job fiasco with the Eagles see also Leotta, "Abraham Epstein and the Movement for Social Security," 54–55. For Roth's words see *The Anatomy Lesson*, 75.

7. Most of this chapter is taken from the personal correspondence between Abraham Epstein and Henriette Castex in 1924–1925. Another source is Abraham Epstein's pocket diary (personal property of the author).

8. The dialogue in this chapter is taken from Mrs. Abraham Epstein's oral interviews.

An Affair with the Atlantic

The background on the vessels of the French Line is drawn in large part from Christian Clères, *Le Havre-New York* (Paris: Editions Hazan, 1997): 26–33, translated by David Britt.

9. The story about the man in Cincinnati who was "more than likely a con man" is from Leotta, "Abraham Epstein and the Movement for Social Security," 89.

10. The legendary stroll along the banks of the Susquehanna River and the first use of the word "security" can be found in a letter from Emil Frankel to Wilbur Cohen dated October 9, 1949. There is also a letter from Abraham Epstein to Wilbur Cohen dated March 4, 1941. (Both letters are personal property of the author.) More detail can be found in the *Social Security Bulletin* 55, no. 1 (Spring 1992): 63. The story of John Andrews and his disagreement with Abraham Epstein is detailed in Mrs. Abraham Epstein's oral interviews. The story about Andrews and his attempts to sink the fledgling American Association for Old Age Security are described in Henry J. Pratt, *The Gray Lobby*, 20. There is also a letter from John Andrews to Paul Douglas dated February 15, 1927, that is cited in Leotta, "Abraham Epstein and the Movement for Social Security," 96. Paul Douglas's description of the battle between Andrews and Epstein can be found in his Foreword to *Insecurity: A Challenge to America*, x.

11. Details of the trip across the United States in Abe's car nicknamed "Madame Nash" are described in the personal diary of Mrs. Abraham Epstein. It is written in pencil on two small pads and the original is quite delicate (personal property of the author). "Lights Out," the story that Zona Gale wrote for Abe and his work, was reprinted by the American Association for Old Age Security as a fund-raising pamphlet in 1928 (personal property of the author). The trip across the United States is told in more detail in Mrs. Abraham Epstein's oral interviews. "The number of those over 65 . . ." is a statistic found in David Hackett Fischer, *Growing Old in America*, 177.

Part Two

The Blooming

1. The quotes on Calvin Coolidge and "the Lorelei of possibility" are from T. H. Watkins, *The Great Depression*, 26. The words about retirement are from David Kennedy, *Freedom from Fear: The American People in Depression and War, 1929–1945*, 23. "Abe's most brilliant move . . ." is from Leotta, "Abraham Epstein and the Movement for Social Security," 117. The quotes about the conservative opposition, the call for an immediate study, and from the *New York Times* review are also from Leotta's disserta-

tion, 127, 122, 115. Abe's words to the first national conference and the quotes from Assemblyman Miller are from Social Security in the United States, 3, 23. Roosevelt's words about the election can be found in Kenneth Davis, *FDR: The New York Years*, 45. Roosevelt's words about the letters he was receiving come from the *New York Times*, January 21, 1929. The dedication to Roosevelt is in Abraham Epstein, *The Challenge of the Aged*, dedication page. Roosevelt's reactions to Abe's book are in Davis, *FDR: The New Deal Years*, 444 and *FDR: Into the Storm*, 8.

2. The material from Abe's writings is from *The Challenge of the Aged*, 113–48. On the illiteracy of poorhouse directors, 130. Hoover's secretary of labor, 123. The Blackwell's Island information can be found in Roy Lubove, *The Struggle for Social Security, 1900–1935*, 133. The description of the Information Bureau is available in the *Old Age Security Herald* (September 1930). Also see the photograph in the *New York Herald Tribune*, September 1, 1930.

3. The material on Rubinow is in large part taken from J. Lee Kreader, *Social Science Review* (September 1976): 402–25. On Douglas and FDR see Davis, *FDR: The New York Years*, 223. The story of Perkins is available in Martin, *Madam Secretary*. FDR's deviousness can be found in Davis, *FDR: the New Deal Years*, 452; the analysis of the president's speech is on pp. 164–66. The story by Paul Douglas is in his Foreword to *Insecurity*, x.

4. The depression-era violence in the United States is in Watkins, *The Great Depression*, 81. Roy Lubove's words can be found in *The Struggle for Social Security*, 176. Frances Perkins's Introduction is in *Insecurity: A Challenge to America*, xi. The review of Abe's book is from the *New York Times Book Review* (June 25, 1933.)

The New Element
The article from the *New York Times* appeared in the real-estate section, February 25, 1929.

5. The quotes on Abe's contributions to old-age security are from Lubove, *The Struggle for Social Security*, 143 and also Davis, *FDR: The New Deal Years*, 443. Abe's opening lines on Adam and Eve are in his *Insecurity: A Challenge to America*, 3. Abe's final speech is available in his Address to the Fifteenth Anniversary Conference of the American Association for Social Security (April 10, 1942), 5.

6. The description of Abe as a writer is from Arthur M. Schlesinger, Jr., *The Coming of the New Deal*, 302. Sam Tannenhaus's words are from "Un-American Activities" in the *New York Review of Books*, November 30, 2000. Eliot's words are from *Recollections of the New Deal: When the People Mattered*, 73. The writer who remarked on Abe's colorful side is Pratt, *The Gray Lobby*, 5. The praises of Arthur Capper and Walter George and many others are from Testimonial Dinner for Abraham Epstein (April 11, 1942). This is a stenographic transcript of the dinner (personal property of the author). The snide article by Abe appeared in the *American Mercury* (January 1, 1931): 94–103.

7. The description of FDR's inaugural in 1932 is from Davis, *FDR: The New Deal Years*, 28. Abe's letter to Senator Dill is dated January 13, 1932 (personal property of the author). The words about all the schemes for old-age pensions are in Davis, *FDR: The New Deal Years*, 403–5. Abe's letter to Frances Perkins urging her to support Dill-Connery is dated May 9, 1934 (personal property of the author). There is more on this in Schlesinger, *The Coming of the New Deal*, 303. The letter to Rubinow about FDR being an enigma is in the Rubinow archive, Catherwood Library, ILR School, Cornell University. It is dated February 21, 1934, and can be found in the box containing the Rubinow-Epstein correspondence.

The various quotes from those who tried to understand why FDR delayed on Social Security are from Theron Schlabach, *Edwin Witte, Cautious Reformer*, 95; Davis, *FDR: The New Deal Years*, 448; Schlesinger, *The Coming of the New Deal*, 303. Walter Lippmann's caustic view of FDR is in Davis, *FDR: The New York Years*, 252. The idea that if FDR had encouraged Dill-Connery it might have passed is in Schlabach, *Edwin Witte, Cautious Reformer*, 93. The letter from Perkins was received by Louis Leotta and can be found in Leotta, "Abraham Epstein and the Movement for Social Security," 243. Finally, Thomas Eliot's story of social security is in Eliot, *Recollections of the New Deal*, 83.

8. The article "Social Security—Fiction or Fact" appeared in the *American Mercury* (October 1934): 129–38. The letter from Rubinow to Abe is dated July 11, 1934, and can be found in the Rubinow archive in the box containing the Rubinow-Epstein correspondence. Witte's words are from his 1962 memoir, Edwin E. Witte, *The Development of the Social Security Act*, 19. The story about Tommy the Cork and his negative opinion of Abe is in Davis, *FDR: The New Deal Years*, 449.

9. The story about Frances Perkins and the various conferences to which Abe was not invited is in Mrs. Abraham Epstein's oral interviews, 150–51. Much of this chapter is sourced from those interviews. Louis Stark's support of Abe and the various telegrams that were sent can be found in the Rubinow archive. The one from Stark is dated February 14, 1934. There are telegrams from others as well. Abe's four-page memorandum contained in a letter to Ernest Angell et al. is in that same archive and is dated February 17, 1934. Paul Douglas's description of the various sections and Kenneth Davis's words about Abe's belief in a national system of social security are in Davis, *FDR: The New Deal Years*, 450.

10. The various letters from Belle Frendel (October 13, 1934), Abe (October 16, 1934), and Henriette (October 15, 1934) are all in the Rubinow archive in the Rubinow-Epstein correspondence. "Witte later offered the excuse . . ." is derived from Witte's book, *The Development of the Social Security Act*, 43. Louis Stark's support can be found in his November 1, 1934, telegram and Abe's letter of October 30, 1934, all of which is in the Rubinow archive. Witte's analysis of the failure of the conference is in Witte, *The Development of the Social Security Act*, 45. Barbara Armstrong's now legendary crying out can be found in Davis, *FDR: The New Deal Years*, 454. Schlesinger also offers a good description of the November 14, 1934, conference in *The Coming of the New Deal*, 306. Abe's letter about Perkins and Witte burning their fingers (November 30, 1934) is in the Rubinow archive. Davis's analysis of the "disastrous conference" is in *FDR: The New Deal Years*, 455. Rubinow's letter to Abe about "Madam Secretary" (December 3, 1934) is in the Rubinow archive.

11. Belle Frendel's letter of December 22, 1934, can be found in the Rubinow archive. The letters from Henriette's mother and father are the personal property of the author.

12. Perkins's letter to Abe dated December 28, 1934, is in the Rubinow archive. Eliot's analysis of the badly drafted bill is in *Recollections of the New Deal*, 105. Eliot's story about Morgenthau raging about the bill is in the same book, 102–3. The story of the reporter blurting to Roosevelt about the government making contributions can be found in Fred L. Preu, "Abraham Epstein," biography prepared for the testimonial dinner in 1942, 24. Rubinow's letter about his frustration was written to Abe on February 15, 1935, and is in the Rubinow archive. Abe's attempt to get Black to change the bill is in a letter from Abe to Black dated February 25, 1935. It is in the Rubinow archive. Abe's reply to Rubinow's frustration is in a letter to Rubinow dated February 18, 1935, and is also in the Rubinow archive.

Sinclair Lewis, Dickens, and Me

Henriette's reply to Abe's encouraging her to read Sinclair Lewis is in a letter dated June 25, 1925 (personal property of the author).

13. The words about searching the archives are from Mary Gordon, *The Shadow Man: A Daughter's Search for Her Father*, 164. For the rest of this chapter see the Rubinow archive, the box containing the Rubinow-Epstein correspondence. The letters start on March 26, 1924, and continue until June 10, 1936. Rubinow died on September 1, 1936. Specific parts of the chapter are as follows: "Rubinow intrigued by Abe's brash behavior . . ." Rubinow to Epstein, April 14, 1924. "Abe should calm his temper . . ." Rubinow to Epstein, October 22, 1924, Epstein to Rubinow, October 23, 1924. "Of course it was just a line of caution . . ." Rubinow to Epstein, January 16, 1927, Epstein to Rubinow, January 19, 1927. "A book is not a speech . . . " Rubinow to Epstein, October 28, October 31, 1927. "The Soullessness of Present Day Social Work," Rubinow to Epstein, June 15, 1928, Epstein to Rubinow, July 7, 1928, Rubinow to Epstein, July 18, 1928. "Your name should really not be Abraham but David . . ." Rubinow to Epstein, September 30, 1930. "I have no intentions of preaching any sermons to you . . ." Rubinow to Epstein, January 21, 1931. "But on the issues of the Nazis Abe was outspoken . . ." Epstein to Rubinow, May 15, 1933, Rubinow to Epstein, May 16, 1933. Abe's review of Rubinow's book, *The Quest for Security*, is in a typescript, date unknown (personal property of the author). There is also a letter from Epstein to Rubinow about the book dated May 10, 1934, in the Rubinow archive.

14. Witte's mistrust of Abe is in Witte, *The Development of the Social Security Act*, 139. The story about Senator Wagner's confusion is in a letter from Epstein to Rubinow, March 15, 1935, in the Rubinow archive. Rubinow's "Mickey Mouse" letter to Epstein, March 11, 1935, and Epstein to Rubinow, August 14, 1935, about the signing ceremony are both in the Rubinow archive. The quote from William Leuchtenberg about the inept Social Security Act is in Davis, *FDR: The New Deal Years*, 523. Henriette's confidential letter to Rubinow about Abe's "undignified statements" is an undated, handwritten note in the Rubinow archive. The article "Our Social Insecurity Act" appeared in *Harper's* (December 1935): 55–66. There was a free-for-all discussion on changing the name of the act, and some of it comes from Eliot, *Recollections of the New Deal*, 110. There are several versions about how the name of the bill was changed, including one by Edwin Witte. There is also an interview with Wilbur Cohen in 1995 that can be found on the Social Security Administration Web site. There is confusion on what took place. It appears that the House Committee on Ways and Means wanted to assert its independence from FDR, some have said. Personally, I am inclined to believe the version where Congressman Roy Woodruff suggested the name change. Woodruff was a close ally of Abraham Epstein and spoke at several of the national conferences. Witte seems to agree that it was Woodruff. There is also more from Wilbur Cohen on the story in Cohen, *Social Security—The First Thirty-five Years*, 10.

15. For Perkins's words about Abe see the *New York Herald Tribune*, December 11, 1935. For the profound disagreement between Abe and Rubinow see the letters in the Rubinow archive dated from October 1 to October 22, 1935. Shaw's letter concerning Abe's health is dated April 13, 1935 (personal property of the author). On Abe and Rubinow's final meeting in New York see the letters in the Rubinow archive dated from January 15 to June 10, 1936. Ida Rubinow's letter to Abe is dated October 28, 1936 (personal property of the author).

Part Three
Abe's Bitter Harvest

1. The newspaper articles are from the *Grand Rapids Herald*, February 11, 1936; *Providence Journal*, February 15, 1936; *Washington Post*, October 5, 1936; and *Cleveland Press*, January 9, 1937. The description of the nasty leaflets can be found in Cohen, *Social Security—The First Thirty-five Years*, 15. The quote from Abe about the the Social Security Act being "unsound" is in Preu, "Abraham Epstein." Landon's proposal for government funding can be found in Cohen, *Social Security—The First Thirty-five Years*, 16. The editorial in the *Cleveland Plain Dealer* appeared on January 11, 1937. The most complete version of the incident concerning NYU and Anna Rosenberg is available in Mrs. Abraham Epstein's oral interviews, 156–57. See also *Social Security* (November 1937) about academic freedom.

2. Details of the 1937 national conference can be found in the American Association for Social Security, report of the national conference, 1937. There is also an article in *Social Security* (April 1937). Wilbur Cohen's story of the Supreme Court decision is in *Social Security—The First Thirty-five Years*, 14. Eliot's story is in his *Recollections of the New Deal*, 143. Dorothy Thompson's article appeared in the *New York Herald Tribune*, May 31, 1937. Douglas Brown's words about the Supreme Court decision are in *An American Philosophy of Social Security: Evolution and Issues*, 13–14. Much of the story about the advisory council is from Leotta, "Abraham Epstein and the Movement for Social Security," 282–85. The article about Abe's greatest triumph appeared in *Social Security* (September–October 1939). Brown's letter to Abraham Epstein is dated September 5, 1939 (personal property of the author). Arthur Altmeyer's letter is dated September 15, 1939 (personal property of the author).

3. The photograph of Morris Fishbein can be found on the Web site kclibrary.org/sc/zelden. Eliot's conversation with Perkins is in Eliot, *Recollections of the New Deal*, 111. The debate with Fishbein is from the American Association for Social Security, record of the 1939 national conference (April 14–15, 1939), 166–200.

4. The description of Brookwood Labor College is from *Brookwood: Labor's Own School* (personal property of the author). Paul Niepold's death was reported in the *New York Times* on April 9, 1937. Abe's letter to Martha Niepold was dated April 13, 1937 (personal property of the author).

5. Abe's relationship with Ethel Clyde is documented in correspondence between the two beginning March 31, 1931, and continuing until October 17, 1941 (personal property of the author). The information on the Exposition Internationale in 1937 is from: *Exposition International des Arts et Techniques dans la vie Moderne 1937*. Photographs from this article can be seen on the Web site Users.globalnet.co.uk/. Also see Arthur Chandler, "Confrontation: Exposition Internationale des Arts et Techniques dans la Vie Moderne" (*World's Fair Magazine* 8, no. 1 [1988]). The introduction to Shertok is in a letter from Stephen Wise dated June 10, 1937. Much of this chapter is also taken from Mrs. Abraham Epstein's oral interviews.

6. The story of the return to France in 1938 is in Mrs. Abraham Epstein's personal notebook (personal property of the author). On the mass telegram see Abraham Epstein to Raymond M. Schwartz, letter of March 21, 1938 (personal property of the author). The background on Abe's efforts to help refugees get to America is revealed in letters to Congressman Lewis K. Rockefeller, James L. Houghtailing (the American Legation, Kaunas, Lithuania), Mrs. Dora Lwowicz, Eliot B. Coulter, acting chief of the Visa Division, and others. These letters are dated from April 20, 1939, to November

1940 (personal property of the author). Hitler's reply to FDR is described in Davis, *FDR: Into the Storm*, 437–40. The house in West Stockbridge and the events of 1939 are in Mrs. Abraham Epstein's personal notebook.

The Blue Vase

Most of this chapter is from an original draft copy of the story, "The Blue Vase," taken down from the words of Igor Bouryanine sometime in the early 1940s. I believe an attempt at publication was made, but it did not work out. There are also numerous documents and letters from the personal files belonging to the author. These are separate from the other letters that I have called "personal property of the author." The letters from Lisbon by Igor Bouryanine are also part of my personal files.

7. The three-fold brochure printed in brown ink is the personal property of the author. The story of the Atlantic Charter is from Davis, *FDR: The War President*, 252–72. Abe's reaction is in *Social Security* (September–October 1941): 2. The report of the national conference is detailed in *Social Security* (April–May 1942). The transcript of the testimonial dinner for Abraham Epstein is available at the Butler Library, Rare Book Division, Columbia University, Abraham Epstein archive. There are also several copies held by the author.

A Photograph

The photograph of the testimonial dinner is the personal property of the author.

8. Milton Konvitz's view of Abe is from the correspondence between Konvitz and the author dated from July 22, 1997, to August 14, 1997. The document written for Abe to sign about what should happen if he should die is dated Saturday afternoon, April 25, 1942 (personal property of the author). Cohen's and Altmeyer's letters to Abe are discussed in Henriette C. Epstein, letter to Wilbur Cohen, May 22, 1942 (personal property of the author). Bishop McConnell's letter to the members of the association is dated May 1944 (personal property of the author). Other material is taken from Mrs. Abraham Epstein's oral interviews.

9. The information concerning Abe's use of the words "social security" can be found in letters from Wilbur Cohen to Abraham Epstein, March 3, 1941, and Abraham Epstein's reply, March 4, 1941. There are more details on this in the *Social Security Bulletin* 55, no. 1 (Spring 1992): 63–64. There is also a statement from Emil Frankel dated October 1949 and that is in the files of the Social Security Administration. *Can We Stop a Post-War Depression Now?* is a pamphlet published by the American Association for Social Security, 1942 (personal property of the author). Material on FDR's State of the Union speech comes from Cass R. Sunstein, *The Second Bill of Rights*, 11.

10. Most of the material in this chapter is derived from personal correspondence with Mrs. Abraham Epstein (personal property of the author). Wilbur Cohen's role in encouraging Henriette can be found in her correspondence with him (personal property of the author). The testimony before Congress can be found in U.S. House of Representatives, Hearings before the Committee on Ways and Means, April 15, 1959, 1022–26.

11. The description of Henriette's memoir is derived from Mrs. Abraham Epstein's oral interviews.

Conclusion. The quotes from Abraham Epstein are from *Facing Old Age*, 46.

# Bibliography

## Books

Altmeyer, Arthur J. *The Formative Years of Social Security.* Madison: University of Wisconsin Press, 1968.

Baker, Dean, and Mark Weisbrot. *Social Security: The Phony Crisis.* Chicago: University of Chicago Press, 1999.

Brown, J. Douglas. *An American Philosophy of Social Security: Evolution and Issues.* Princeton, N.J.: Princeton University Press, 1972.

Burns, Eveline M. *Towards Social Security.* New York: Whittesley House, McGraw-Hill Books, 1936.

Cahan, Abraham. *The Rise of David Levinsky.* New York: Grosset and Dunlap, 1917.

Davis, Kenneth S. *FDR: The Beckoning of Destiny, 1882–1928.* New York: G. P. Putnam's Sons, 1971.

———. *FDR: The New York Years, 1928–1933.* New York: Random House, 1994.

———. *FDR: The New Deal Years, 1933–1937.* New York: Random House, 1986.

———. *FDR: Into The Storm, 1937–1940.* New York: Random House, 1993.

———. *FDR: The War President, 1940–1943.* New York: Random House, 2000.

Douglas, Paul. *Social Security in the United States: An Analysis and Appraisal of the Federal Social Security Act.* New York: Whittesley House, McGraw-Hill Books, 1936.

Eliot, Thomas H. *Recollections of the New Deal: When the People Mattered.* Boston: Northeastern University Press, 1992.

Epstein, Abraham. *The Challenge of the Aged*. New York: Macy-Masius and Vanguard Press, 1928. Reprt., New York: Arno Press, 1972.

———. *Facing Old Age: A Study of Old Age Dependency in the United States and Old Age Pensions*. New York: Alfred A. Knopf Inc., 1922. Reprt., New York: Arno Press, 1972.

———. *Insecurity: A Challenge to America*. New York: Harrison Smith and Robert Haas, 1933. 2nd rev. ed., New York: Random House, 1936, 1938. Reprt., New York: Agathon Press, 1968.

———. *The Negro Migrant in Pittsburgh: A Study in Social Economics*. Pittsburgh: Published under the supervision of the School of Economics, University of Pittsburgh, 1918.

Fischer, David Hackett. *Growing Old in America*. New York: Oxford University Press, 1978.

Gordon, Mary. *The Shadow Man: A Daughter's Search for Her Father*. New York: Random House, 1996.

Howe, Irving. *World of Our Fathers*. New York: Simon and Schuster, 1976.

Kennedy, David M. *Freedom From Fear: The American People in Depression and War, 1929–1945*. New York: Oxford University Press, 1999.

Konvitz, Milton R. *A Guide to the Papers of Milton R. Konvitz*. Ithaca, N.Y.: School of Industrial and Labor Relations, Cornell University, 1994, Box 88, Folder 25.

Lubove, Roy. *The Struggle for Social Security, 1900–1935*. Pittsburgh: University of Pittsburgh Press, 1986.

Martin, George. *Madam Secretary, Frances Perkins: A Biography of America's First Woman Cabinet Member*. New York: Houghton Mifflin, 1976.

Maurer, James Hudson. *It Can Be Done: The Autobiography of James Hudson Maurer*. New York: Rand School Press, 1938.

Perkins, Frances. *The Roosevelt I Knew*. New York: Viking Press, 1946.

Pratt, Henry J. *The Gray Lobby*. Chicago: University of Chicago Press, 1976.

Raushenbush, Paul, and Elizabeth Brandeis Raushenbush. *Our "U. C." Story. 1930–1967*. Madison, Wisc.: Privately printed, 1979.

Roth, Philip. *The Anatomy Lesson*. New York: Vintage, Random House, 1996.

———. *Patrimony*. New York: Touchstone, Simon and Schuster, 1979.

Rubinow, I. M. *The Quest for Security*. New York: Henry Holt, 1934.

Saposs, David J. *Left Wing Unionism: A Study of Radical Politics and Tactics*. New York: International Publishers, 1926.

Schieber, Sylvester J., and John B. Shoven. *The Real Deal: The History and Future of Social Security*. New Haven, Conn.: Yale University Press, 1999.

Schlabach, Theron F. *Edwin Witte: Cautious Reformer*. Madison: State Historical Society of Wisconsin, 1969.

Schlesinger, Arthur M., Jr. *The Coming of the New Deal.* Cambridge, Mass.: Riverside Press, 1959. Also New York: Houghton Mifflin.

Sherwood, Robert E. *Roosevelt and Hopkins: An Intimate History.* New York: Enigma Books, 2001.

Skidmore, Max J. *Social Security and Its Enemies: The Case for America's Most Effective Insurance Program.* Boulder, Colo.: Westview Press, Perseus Books, 1999.

Sunstein, Cass R. *The Second Bill of Rights: FDR's Unfinished Revolution and Why We Need It More than Ever.* New York: Basic Books, 2004.

Watkins, T. H. *The Great Depression.* Boston: Back Bay Books, Little, Brown, 1993.

Witte, Edwin E. *The Development of the Social Security Act.* Madison: University of Wisconsin Press, 1963.

## Other Sources

American Association for Social Security. Social Security in the United States. A Record of the National Conferences of the American Association for Old Age Security and the American Association for Social Security, 1928–1942. New York: American Association for Social Security.

———. *Old Age Security Herald.* Monthly bulletin sent to subscribers, 1927–1932.

———. *Social Security.* Monthly bulletin sent to subscribers, 1933–1943.

*Brookwood: Labor's Own School.* Fifteenth Anniversary Review. Academy Press, 1936.

Cohen, Wilbur J. *Social Security—The First Thirty-five Years.* Papers from the Twenty-third Annual Conference on Aging, 1970. Institute of Gerontology. Ann Arbor: University of Michigan–Wayne State University, 1970.

Epstein, Abraham. *The Almshouse Child. Care of Dependent Children in Twenty-Eight Counties as Administered by Poor Law Authorities. A Study Made by Abraham Epstein.* Pamphlet. Harrisburg: Published by the Child Welfare Division, Public Charities Association of Pennsylvania, January 1924.

———. *The Case for Health Insurance: The Debate Handbook, 1935–1936.* New York: Reprinted by the American Association for Social Security and the Julius Rosenwald Fund.

———. "Social Security." *New Frontiers* 5, no. 3 (March 1937). New York: League for Industrial Democracy.

―――. *Social Security in Wartime and After: Statements and Recommendations by Sixty-Eight of the Nation's Leading Experts and Students of the Problem.* New York: American Association for Social Security, 1942.

Kreader, J. Lee. "Isaac Max Rubinow: Pioneering Specialist in Social Insurance." *Social Service Review* (September 1976). University of Chicago.

Leotta, Louis. "Abraham Epstein and the Movement for Social Security, 1920–1939." Ph.D. diss., Columbia University, 1978.

―――. "Abraham Epstein and the Movement for Old Age Security." *Labor History* 16, no. 3 (Summer 1973).

National Conference on Social Welfare. *The Report of the Committee on Economic Security of 1935.* Fiftieth Anniversary Edition. Washington, D.C.: National Conference on Social Welfare, 1985.

Preu, Fred L. "Abraham Epstein." Biography prepared for Abraham Epstein testimonial dinner, April 1942.

U.S. House of Representatives. Hearings before the Committee on Ways and Means on H.R. 4120, January 21 to February 12, 1935.

―――. Hearings before the Committee on Ways and Means. On Proposed Amendments to the Federal Laws on Unemployment Compensation, April 15, 1959.

U.S. Senate. Hearings before the Committee on Finance on Senate Bill 1130, January 22 to February 20, 1935.

## Collections

Abraham Epstein archive. Rare Book Collection, Butler Library, Columbia University.

Abraham Epstein archive. ILR School, Catherwood Library, Cornell University.

I. M. Rubinow archive. ILR School, Catherwood Library, Cornell University.

## Oral Histories

State Historical Society of Wisconsin. Interviews with Mrs. Abraham Epstein, 1973.

Columbia University Oral History Project. Interviews with Mrs. Abraham Epstein, 1975.

Women's City Club of New York. Interviews with Mrs. Abraham Epstein, 1976.

# Index

Page numbers in italics refer to photographs.